VICTORIA
& VANCOUVER ISLAND

*A Personal Tour of
an Almost Perfect Eden*

Help Us Keep This Guide Up to Date

Every effort has been made by the authors and editors to make this guide as accurate and useful as possible. However, many things can change after a guide is published—establishments close, phone numbers change, facilities come under new management, etc.

We would love to hear from you concerning your experiences with this guide and how you feel it could be improved and kept up to date. While we may not be able to respond to all comments and suggestions, we'll take them to heart and we'll also make certain to share them with the authors. Please send your comments and suggestions to the following address:

The Globe Pequot Press
Reader Response/Editorial Department
P.O. Box 480
Guilford, CT 06437

Or you may e-mail us at:

editorial@globe-pequot.com

Thanks for your input, and happy travels!

HILL GUIDES™ SERIES

VICTORIA
& VANCOUVER ISLAND

*A Personal Tour of
an Almost Perfect Eden*

THIRD EDITION

*by Kathleen Thompson Hill
&
Gerald Hill*

The
Globe
Pequot
Press

Guilford, Connecticut

Maps: Clover Point Cartographics, Victoria, B.C.
Cover and text design: Lana Mullen
Illustrations by Mauro Magellan
Cover painting entitled *Butchart Gardens, Victoria, Canada* by Judy Theo Lerner, M.F.A.
Studio address: 134 Church Street, Sonoma, CA 95476. (707) 996–5111.
Medium: monotype.
Photos by Kathleen Hill and Gerald Hill, except for Victoria 1997 snow by Earl Schmidt, Hornby Island by Megan Hill, Port Hardy by Bob Carver, Chesterman Beach by Wickaninnish Inn, and Aerie courtesy of Aerie Resort. In chapter 8, "History of Victoria and Vancouver Island," all illustrations are photo-copied archival photographs from B.C. Archives & Records, Province of B.C., Canada, except as noted.

Library of Congress Cataloging-in-Publication Data

Hill, Kathleen, 1941–
     Victoria & Vancouver Island : a personal tour of an almost perfect
     Eden / Kathleen Thompson Hill & Gerald Hill.– 3rd ed.
          p. cm.– (Hill guides series)
     Includes index.
     ISBN 0-7627-0822-0
     1. Victoria (B.C.)–Guidebooks. 2. Vancouver Island (B.C.)-Guidebooks.
I. Title: Victoria & Vancouver Island. II. Hill, Gerald N. IIII. Title.
F1089.5.V6H55 2000
917.11'28044--dc21   00-057666
                                                              CIP

Manufactured in the United States of America
Third Edition/First Printing

For

**Erin and Mack,
again,**

Still hoping that they will
eventually love
British Columbia
as we do

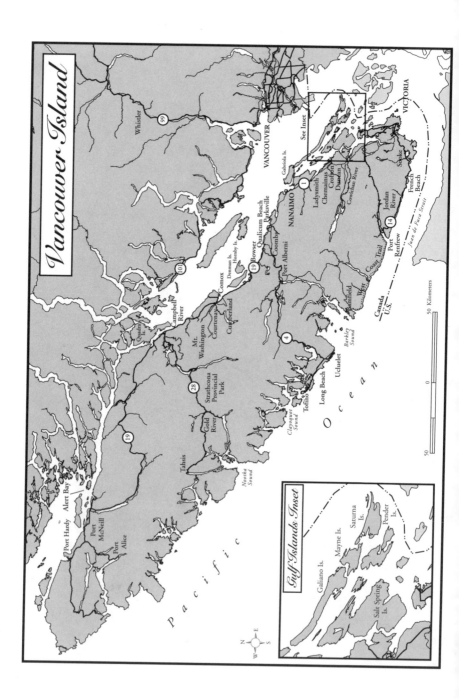

Vancouver Island

Whistler

99

VANCOUVER

See Inset

Gabriola Is.

NANAIMO

Ladysmith
Chemainus
Crofton
Duncan
Cowichan River

VICTORIA

Jordan
River
Port
Renfrew
Sooke
French
Beach

14

Juan de Fuca Strait

Canada
U.S.

50 Kilometers

0

50

West
Coast Trail

Bamfield

Barkley
Sound

1

Qualicum Beach
Parksville
Coombs

Bowser

19

Port Alberni

4

Denman Is.
Hornby Is.

Comox
Courtenay
Cumberland

Mt.
Washington

Campbell
River

Quadra
Is.

10

Ucluelet

Long Beach

Tofino

Clayoquot
Sound

Strathcona
Provincial
Park

28

Gold
River

Nootka
Sound

Tahsis

19

Port
Alice

Port
McNeill

Port Hardy Alert Bay

Pacific

O c e a n

Gulf Islands Inset

Galiano Is.

Mayne Is.

Saturna
Is.

Pender
Is.

Salt Spring
Is.

N
W   E
S

CONTENTS

The prices and rates listed in this guidebook are in Canadian dollars and were confirmed at press time. We recommend, however, that you call establishments before traveling to obtain current information.

PREFACE

We firmly believe that we need to live in a place for a while in order to write about it clearly and accurately enough to give our readers the best possible mental and emotional picture of it before they visit. That way we can save you time and grief and provide you with sufficient information to make good choices, still find adventure, and maximize your enjoyment.

Jerry's older adult children, Megan and David, have lived in British Columbia since high school, and both graduated from the University of Victoria. Megan administers the Biology Department there now and lives in Victoria with her husband, Sean, and son, Sam; David and his wife, Deidre Matheson, live and work in Victoria with their new son, Thomas. All four of them have deep knowledge and opinions that are fairly representative of the twenty- and thirtysomething crowds.

It is because of them that we first came to Victoria and fell in love with the city. Now we live here as much as we can.

We do not presume to judge which of anything is the best. We simply tell you which places are our favorites, because you might have different tastes. When we say "one of our favorites," it means all four of us love it. When a place is tagged as one of Kathleen's, Jerry's, Megan's, or David's favorites, it will give you a hint of to whom it appeals, and perhaps a generational difference of opinion. But then Kathleen and Jerry have their favorite toy stores, too.

Instead of categorizing places as inexpensive to expensive, we simply tell you what things cost so that you can make your own judgment based on your budget.

Where else in the world can you enjoy Canadian urbanity with fine wines and restaurants, shops, museums, and theater, and in five minutes be at the beach or in thirty minutes be deep in the rain forest? Still wondering? Turn the pages and explore Victoria and Vancouver Island with us.

—Kathleen Hill
—Gerald Hill

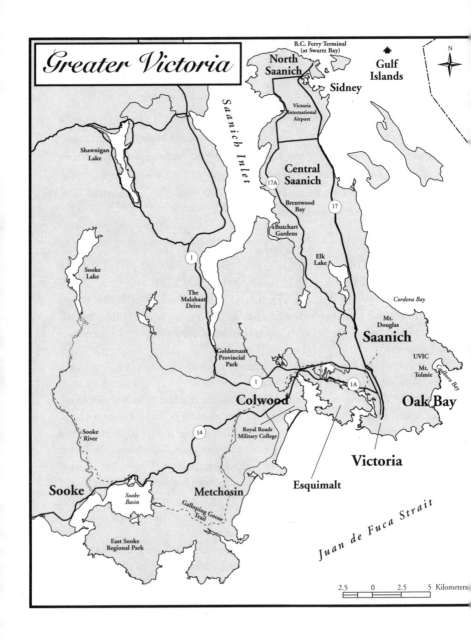

Greater Victoria

B.C. Ferry Terminal
(at Swartz Bay)

North
Saanich

Gulf
Islands

Sidney

Saanich Inlet

Victoria
International
Airport

Shawnigan
Lake

Central
Saanich

17A

Brentwood
Bay

17

Butchart
Gardens

Sooke
Lake

Elk
Lake

1

Cordova Bay

The
Malahaat
Drive

Mt.
Douglas

Saanich

UVIC

Mt.
Tolmie

Goldstream
Provincial
Park

1

1A

Colwood

Oak Bay

Sooke
River

14

Royal Roads
Military College

Victoria

Esquimalt

Sooke

Sooke
Basin

Metchosin

Galloping Goose
Trail

Juan de Fuca Strait

East Sooke
Regional Park

N

2.5   0   2.5   5 Kilometers

CHAPTER 1

HOW TO USE YOUR HILL GUIDE

Read this Hill Guide to Victoria and Vancouver Island as you ride or walk along, following the natural walking patterns we've discovered for you. Since we have visited every place, shop, gallery, and restaurant we tell you about, you'll have the latest information available at press time, even including the shopkeepers, maître d's, and winemakers you encounter. In every case, we guide you to the best values for your money and pleasure.

Do read the sections in this chapter called "Basic Facts" and "How to Be a Visitor and Not a Tourist in Victoria," including the "Terms of Endearment" glossary of Canadian terms. Hopefully these will help you to better understand Victoria, Vancouver Island, and Canadians.

"Basic Facts" gives you vital information—about medical insurance and emergencies; driving in British Columbia; weather and how to dress; wheelchair accessibility; gay and lesbian friendliness; money exchanges and taxes; and business hours.

"Getting Here and Getting Around" tells you about the most picturesque, efficient, and convenient ways to get to Victoria and Vancouver Island from Seattle and Vancouver, B.C., as well as the best values in transportation by airplane and the best ways to combine airplane, bus, and ferry travel to the island. Have a yacht or sailboat? Find out where to dock.

Then, for once you're here, it tells you about car rentals; bus routes for tourist attractions and destinations; public buses and bus tours; parking; getting around by carriage or pedicab; sight-seeing ferries; scooters; bicycle shops and rentals; and, of course, how to get there by foot or wheelchair.

"Neighborhoods of Greater Victoria" takes you door-by-door through downtown Victoria and also visits James Bay, Cook Street Village, Fairfield, Fernwood, and Oak Bay. We guide you up one side of the street and down the other in a logical walking or wheeling pattern. Look for a special section on Antique Row.

"Significant Others" points out restaurants and destination inns out of the normal touring routes that you'll enjoy, and "Don't Miss These" helps you zero in on valuable places to visit if your time is limited or if you want to be sure to experience local history, culture, and fun.

"Outdoor Things to Do" gives you all the vital information you need to partake of the outdoor activities you love or might want to try, from biking, diving, fishing, and boating to whale watching and golf. "Annual Events and Festivals" lists interesting local events to enhance your visit or plan your trip around.

"Exploring Outside Victoria" takes you out the Saanich Peninsula to Sid-

TWO CULTURES MEET AT THE INNER HARBOUR

ney and then along the western side of Vancouver Island.

"Up Island" guides you through the wineries and farm shops of Cobble Hill, the maritime exhibits and restaurants at Cowichan Bay, the city of Duncan, the muraled city of Chemainus, and to and through Nanaimo. From Nanaimo, we go north to Parksville, Qualicum Beach, and Courtenay, and on to Port Hardy, where some people catch ferries to the mainland and their Alaskan cruise ships.

We take you to the upper western side of Vancouver Island, via Nanaimo to Port Alberni and over the hills to Ucluelet, Pacific Rim National Park, and Tofino.

We suggest accommodations in all price ranges.

Our "History of Victoria and Vancouver Island" traces the lively story of the island, Victoria, and its people from their earliest days.

Some of our fondest memories of places we have visited include wonderful regional food experiences, with recipes that will help you re-create your own memories.

"List of Lists" includes antiques shops; new, used, and antiquarian bookstores; laundromats; nightclubs; pharmacies; public and quasi-public rest rooms; and is followed by a detailed calendar of events and festivals.

We hope that all of this eclectic information will come in handy whether you are visiting Vancouver Island for the first time or have lived here all your life. Welcome!

BASIC FACTS

One fact that most Americans and other non-Canadians find nearly impossible to comprehend is that Victorians are the most considerate and pleasant people you may ever encounter. This calls for a cultural adjustment, so be forewarned.

Remember to check your guns at the border. Canadians don't allow them or any other weapons in—including pepper spray.

We are happy to report that smoking is no longer allowed in public buildings, including restaurants and bars. A few restaurants with patios or sidewalk tables allow smoking.

Basic medical insurance costs each adult Canadian about $36 for singles to $72 for a family of three or more per month, with no deductibles and no "preexisting conditions."

Community is important here. The government actually subsidizes artists and writers, poets and publishers, although federal and provincial governments are cutting back on those grants.

Local drivers are courteous and generous with their time. They actually stop to let you merge into their lanes and stop for pedestrians approaching the curb to cross the street.

If you have out-of-province license plates and your parking meter expires, you are likely to get a welcome to Victoria message instead of a ticket, for the first offense anyway.

Most speed limits and distances in Canada are posted in kilometers, with a few around Victoria in miles also. A kilometer is .6 of a mile. Remember: 50 gets you 30, 80 gets you 50, 100 gets you 60, and 120 gets you a $100 fine. It's OK to turn right on a red light after stopping. If you drive without insurance and get caught, you're off to jail.

If you don't like the weather, wait twenty minutes. The weather in Victoria is the best in Canada, which is why Canadians known as snowbirds come here in the winter. It rarely snows in Victoria—about as often as it does in San Francisco. (And then there was the winter of 1996–97.)

Temperatures in Canada are given in Celsius, which, by whatever formula you think you remember, never seems to translate correctly to Fahrenheit. For a rough approximation, double the figure for Celsius, subtract a few degrees (the greater the temperature, the more you subtract), and add the result to 32°F. For accuracy, multiply Celsius by nine, divide by five, and add 32. Thus 10°C is 50°F; 20°C is 68°F; 25°C is 77°F, and so on.

Victoria's worst weather month is January, when the temperature averages 38°F or 3°C with sixteen rainy days. It gradually warms each month. While the averages are only 62°F and 17°C in July and slightly lower in August, there are many days in both months that are warm and even hot by California standards.

It rains only about 29 inches annually in Victoria, less than half what Vancouver city gets. The storms roll in from the Pacific, blow right by Victoria, up against the mountains around Vancouver, and dump there. For weather updates call (250) 656–3978; for marine weather, (250) 656–7515.

Victorians dress less formally than eastern Canadians and regard the slightest glimmer of sun-generated warmth as permission to break out in Bermuda shorts and tennies. Subtle natural colors dominate, and Victorians spot Americans partly by their loud colors and voices.

Homelessness and panhandling are low here, although increasing. You see more of both in the summer months when the weather is pleasant and people in need are out in the open more.

Locals often drink bottled or filtered water, although we have drunk tap water throughout the island with no uncomfortable results.

Victoria has quickly become much more conscious of the needs of persons in wheelchairs and is moving rapidly to make things accessible. We will tell you which facilities are accessible. More than half of Victoria buses are accessible. Call B.C. Transit (250–382–6161) to check on which buses are and when they come.

Generally Victoria is a tolerant city. We find nearly all businesses in Victoria are gay friendly; a few are gay owned.

Differences and diversities are encouraged, because Canada lives by the *mosaic principle,* in which all kinds of people are expected to live and work together with pride, instead of the U.S. melting pot, into which everyone is supposed to dive and come out as alike as possible.

Here is a rundown of other basic facts that you should find useful:

Money. Banks and ATMs are the best places to exchange currency, because you get the best exchange rate and rarely are charged a fee. The exchange rate varies, but you will get approximately $1.44 Canadian for $1.00 U.S. Many businesses on Vancouver Island take American dollars but give you change in Canadian currency, including a slight charge for doing you the favor. *All prices quoted in this book are in Canadian dollars and are subject to change.* Money exchange shops have the poorest exchange.

Shopping. Business hours vary in Victoria by season. Shops along Government Street and the rest of the downtown area generally open at 10:00 A.M. and close at 6:00 P.M. during summer season, while some shops selling T-shirts and other souvenirs stay open later. In fall and winter, most shops close at 5:00 P.M.

Emergencies. Call 911.

Eyeglass repair. There are loads of eyeglass places on Douglas Street between Broughton and Fisgard, as well as in the Eaton Centre mall and on Fort Street.

Medical care. You can walk into any doctor's office labeled as a clinic or walk-in clinic or a hospital emergency room and get treatment. Non-Canadians usually have to pay for the doctor's services and then recover the amount from their insurance company.

Hospitals. Royal Jubilee Hospital, 1800 Fort Street, (250) 370–8000, emergencies, (250) 370–8212; Victoria General Hospital, 35 Helmcken Road, (250) 727–4212, emergencies, (250) 727–4181.

Hot lines. Emotional crises center: (250) 386–6323; help line for children: 0 and ask for Zenith 1234; poison control center: (250) 595–9211; sexual assault center: (250) 838–3232; British Columbia road conditions: (250) 380–4997; SPCA (animals): (250) 385–6521.

Library. Greater Victoria Public Library (250–382–7241) has its main entrance on Blanshard Street, but the library extends through the block to Broughton, where there is a parking garage right next door to the entrance. This is one of the busiest and most exciting libraries we have ever seen. Children and teen sections are on the first floor, and there is a great espresso cart in the courtyard as you enter.

Liquor stores. Hard liquor is sold primarily at government liquor stores or at stores adjacent to or within hotels. Hours vary by location. Most open at 10:00 or 11:00 A.M. and close between 6:00 and 11:00 P.M. On Friday nights many stay open late. All liquor stores are closed on Sunday (the government is reexamining the law by popular demand). Taxes keep prices high. Legal drinking age is nineteen. Driving drunk sends you to jail. Period. Three drunk driving offenses and Canadians have their licenses withdrawn for life; foreigners are kicked out of the country.

Newspapers. Victoria's local daily, the *Times-Colonist,* comes out every morning; the weekly television schedule is in the Friday edition. The what's-happening newspaper is *Monday Magazine,* which comes out on Thursday, of course. There are several alternative and neighborhood papers, which are great sources for up-to-date local information. The national *Globe and Mail* is the Canadian equivalent of the *New York Times*. Its Saturday edition is big, and it also puts out a weekly export edition that we find extremely informative.

Pharmaceuticals. You can get anything here that you can get in the United States and more. Most over-the-counter medications made in the U.S. are also made in Canada. Aspirin, its substitutes, and even toothpaste seem to cost less than in the U.S. (see List of Lists for pharmacies).

Taxes. Oh yes. Everyone pays 7 percent provincial sales tax (PST) and another 7 percent goods and services federal tax (GST). GST and PST taxes do not apply to groceries or essential cosmetics such as soap, toothpaste, and shampoo. Clothing (even backpacks) for children younger than sixteen is PST exempt. Visitors from outside Canada can get the GST part refunded by filling out a form available at most stores.

HOW TO BE A VISITOR AND NOT A TOURIST IN VICTORIA

Residents of Victoria and Vancouver Island are remarkably nice to visitors and tourists. They know and respect the fact that tourists bring a large portion of Victorians' income with them, and they want to make parting with money as enjoyable and as painless for visitors as possible. Try to make payment in Canadian currency by exchanging at banks before venturing out. Use a nonbank commercial currency exchange only if you are desperate.

Modulate your voices, wait your turn, and tone down the clothes. Generally everyone strolling up and down Government Street in shorts is a tourist. If you want to fit in, dress as if you are going to work in informal clothes. If you don't care—don't.

Wearing Victoria T-shirts may give you away as a tourist, although you will see many residents of Victoria and Vancouver Island wearing shirts and caps supporting the Vancouver Grizzlies basketball team, the Vancouver Cannucks ice hockey team, or the University of Victoria (UVic) Vikes. It's best to buy your shirts on the island and then wear them back home.

Canadians do not throw paper, garbage, or drink containers in the street or on public property. We once watched a street clown admonish an American boy who had tossed a candy bar wrapper on the sidewalk on Government Street. The clown suggested so politely to the young man that he pick it up and dispose of it properly that the kid didn't get it. After five or six tries, the clown finally convinced the boy that he should put the paper in the can next to him. His parents were, fortunately, sensitive enough to be embarrassed.

Terms of Endearment—A Glossary

aboriginals: natives who inhabited North America before white people arrived; Indians

B.C.: British Columbia

bill: the charges presented to you at a restaurant

brown bread: wheat bread

bum: one's bottom or rear end

buns: rolls, as in breakfast rolls or rolls on which sandwiches are served

busker: a person who performs independently outdoors to entertain the public

cheque: a check, such as a bank check or paycheck

chips: french fries

cutlery: silverware; forks, knives, and spoons; utensils

elastics: rubber bands

esthetician: beautician

European: white people, presumed by natives to be of European descent

family name: maiden name

First Peoples: original inhabitants of North America before white people arrived; Indians

First Nations: same as First Peoples, more politically correct in the late nineties

flat bread: from First Peoples' tradition, similar to pizza

fuel: gasoline

fully licensed: licensed to serve hard liquor, beer, and wine

heritage: historic; e.g., a heritage house

continued on next page

interior: the part of British Columbia east of the Coast Mountains; e.g., east of Vancouver city

interpretive center, tour, etc.: spoken guide or explanation

licensed premises: bar or restaurant that serves beer and wine (see *fully licensed*)

lineup: a waiting line or queue

lounge: bar where alcohol is served

Lower Mainland: all the population centers within 100 miles of the Canada-U.S. border; in British Columbia, specifically from the Canada-U.S. border to Whistler Resort

mum: mom, mother

parkade: parking garage

pension: pay one receives from a former employer; the government check seniors receive, like U.S. Social Security

poutine: a Quebec-origin concoction of french fries, white cheese curds, and gravy

return: round-trip

serviettes: table napkins

suite: apartment, condominium, or office space

sweets: desserts and pastries

till: cash register

UBC: University of British Columbia (Vancouver)

UVic: University of Victoria (Victoria)

upisland: any part of Vancouver Island north of Greater Victoria

Van Isle: Vancouver Island

washroom: bathroom or rest room

wharfinger: the person who manages a marine wharf or marina

wicket: bank teller's window; upright sticks behind a batter in cricket that the batter has to keep the ball from hitting

CHAPTER 2

GETTING HERE AND GETTING AROUND

T̄t's easy to get to Victoria and Vancouver Island by air or ferry. Lots of airlines fly to Seattle and Vancouver, and then you can fly or take a ferry to Victoria.

By Air

You have three choices: fly to Vancouver and transfer to a bus and ferry; fly to Vancouver and transfer to another plane; or fly to Seattle and transfer to another plane or take a ferry. Be sure to compare ticket prices to Seattle and Vancouver, because at certain times of the year airlines' competitive rates may influence your decision.

Fly to Vancouver and take the bus and ferry to Victoria. If the airfares of the moment allow you to do so, we recommend you fly to Vancouver and then connect by bus to B.C. Ferries to Victoria, or simply fly connecting flights all the way to Victoria.

Our favorite airline to Vancouver is Air Canada, which has just acquired Canadian Airlines. Both are excellent. The staff treats passengers gently and with good humor, and the food is far superior to other airlines' offerings. Compare Air Canada's mid-afternoon snack served between San Francisco and Victoria—rolled lean turkey, roast beef, mortadella, and salami with gouda cheese, a fresh roll, Dijon mustard, black bean/brown rice salad, and three-chocolate brownie—to United Airlines's offering—a small, not-yet-thawed, fatty ham sandwich, package of potato chips, and a Tobler chocolate bar.

Pacific Coach Lines runs three buses daily directly from the Vancouver airport onto the B.C. ferry and into downtown Victoria. Generally they leave the airport at 11:50 A.M. and 1:50 and 3:50 P.M., but it is best to call them directly in Vancouver at (604) 662–8074 or in Victoria at (250) 385–4411 for information and en route pickup reservations.

The PCL buses drive right onto the front of the ferry, you get off and go upstairs for a meal if you wish, and then you get back on the same bus and complete the trip into Victoria. You can also get off at Swartz Bay (where the ferries dock on Vancouver Island) and connect to ferries to other islands. All this costs about $26, but the price fluctuates slightly with B.C. Ferries's charges.

If your airport arrival does not coincide with these bus departures, walk outside the terminal to the second lane of traffic and catch the van/bus to the Delta Pacific Hotel ($2.00 for hotel guests, $4.00 for others). At the hotel, go in the front door and turn immediately left to the PCL ticket desk, where you can leave your baggage until your bus arrives. The Delta Pacific has an espresso cart in the lobby, a lounge and restaurant, a more formal dining room, and the Suehiro Restaurant. Oh yes, and a 200-foot water slide for the kids.

B.C. Ferries sails its pleasant car ferries hourly both ways between Vancouver (Tsawwassen) and Victoria (Swartz Bay) from 7:00 A.M. to 10:00 P.M. from late June until early September, and on uneven hours in winter. The trip takes one hour and thirty-five minutes, and slightly longer during fuel price crises. You can also board as a walk-on passenger, or with a bike or motorcycle. Fares vary by season, size of vehicle, and number of passengers. Every trip we make we marvel at how those ferries float with loaded lumber trucks, new-car transport trucks, and several tourist buses on board.

We recommend the Pacific Island Buffet, if your ferry has one, as transition sustenance, especially if you are extremely hungry. Buffet staff will answer all questions on food ingredients. Meals range from about $10 to $15 depending on time of day.

The large ferries have snack bars with hot and cold foods, as well as cafeterias catered by White Spot restaurants, Canadian hamburger legends.
➹✿ *B.C. Ferries: 1112 Fort Street, Victoria V8V 4V2, (250) 386–3431 or (888) 223–3779; Fax: (250) 381–5452; Web: www.bcferries.com.*

Fly to Vancouver, and then fly to Victoria. You have several options for flying on to Victoria from Vancouver:

Helijet Airways (in Victoria: 250–382–5222; in Vancouver: 604–273–1414; Web: www.helijet.com) flies helicopters from a floating pad off the Pan Pacific Hotel in Vancouver and from the Vancouver International Airport for $95 on up. In Victoria Helijet flights land at and leave from 79 Dallas Road (Ogden Point) near where cruise ships and the Royal Victorian (Victoria Line) ferry from Seattle dock. Helijet makes the thirty-five-minute flights more than twenty times daily, with four round-trips on weekends.

Harbour Air Shuttle (in Victoria: 250–384–2215; in Vancouver: 604–688–1277; Web: www.harbour-air.com) flies Twin Otter sixteen-seat seaplanes between Vancouver and Victoria harbours (ten round-trips weekdays and four on weekends). The thirty-five-minute flights cost $89 one-way plus tax on every flight. In Vancouver, Harbour uses the floating pad near the Pan Pacific Hotel, and in Victoria it lands off Wharf Street in the Inner Harbour between Bastion Square and Yates Street.

West Coast Air (in Vancouver: 604–688–9115; in Victoria: 250–388–4521 or 800–347–2222; Web: www.westcoastair.com) flies eighteen-seat deHavilland Twin Otter float planes and a Vistaliner. You may also charter the Vistaliner for flights around B.C's south coast and Gulf Islands. There are six thirty-five-minute flights each way weekdays on the hour (except 11:00 A.M. and 1:00 P.M.) with added flights at 9:00 A.M. and 4:00 P.M. from Vancouver to Victoria Harbour and at 11:00 A.M. and 5:10 P.M. on weekends. West Coast lands in the Inner Harbour between Broughton and Courtney Streets, about 2 blocks from The Empress hotel.

AirBC (604–273–2464 or 250–360–9074) is the Air Canada connector for major airlines that fly direct into Vancouver from San Francisco, Los Angeles, Chicago, New York, Ottawa, Toronto, and Montreal. It makes eight flights daily from Vancouver to Victoria on Dash 100 or Dash 300 planes carrying thirty-seven or forty-eight passengers and landing at Victoria International Airport. (See the following section on transportation from the airport.)

Fly to Seattle and fly to Victoria. You have several options for continuing your trip by air if you choose to land at Seattle/Tacoma Airport (SeaTac):

Horizon Air (800–547–9308) flies from Seattle to Victoria International Airport and back six times daily, with direct flights to Victoria taking about thirty-five minutes. From Victoria to Seattle, Horizon stops in Port Angeles or Bellingham, Washington, for U.S. Customs, making these trips about one hour and fifteen minutes.

Kenmore Air (800–543–9595, U.S. and Canada; 206–486–1257, Seattle) makes three seaplane flights daily from Seattle to Victoria. In the summer Kenmore provides scheduled shuttle vans from Seattle/Tacoma Airport to its departure point, Seattle's downtown Lake Union (950 Westlake Avenue North). If you plan to take Kenmore from Seattle to Victoria outside of May–Labor Day (early September), you can either call a shuttle (about $20) on arrival at the baggage claim area at SeaTac or take a cab (about $30).

Kenmore's flight from Lake Union to Victoria takes about fifty-five minutes and deposits you in the Inner Harbour at 1000 Wharf Street between Broughton and Courtney Streets, about 1 block from The Empress hotel. The schedule varies wildly by season, but basically there are flights every day both ways.

Transportation from Victoria International Airport. Once at Victoria airport, excellent airporter service is available to get you downtown and to your hotel. AKAL Airport Shuttle Bus provides daily service every half hour from

4:30 P.M. to 1:00 A.M. to and from Victoria International Airport and all hotels, motels, and downtown. After 8:00 P.M., call for a pickup reservation. The trip from Victoria International Airport takes about one hour.

✿☞ *AKAL Airport Shuttle Bus (250–386–2525 or 877–386–2525 toll free; Fax: 250–386–2526; Web: www.akalairporter.travel.bc.ca). Fares (one-way): adults $13.00 children younger than five free, seniors and students $11.70, airport or airline employees $11.70 including taxes.*

If you're part of a group of three or more, you might want to consider a taxi. Taxi fares from the airport, which is near Sidney, to downtown Victoria are about $40. Your options: Victoria Taxi, (250) 383–7111; Empress Taxi, (250) 381–5577; and Blue Bird Cabs, (250) 384–1155.

By Water—Ferries from Washington and Vancouver, B.C.

Victoria Clipper's high-speed catamarans are the quickest and most efficient ferries to Victoria, making the trip in about three hours. Now Victoria Clipper has outdone itself with the new turbojet that skims the water between Seattle and Victoria in one and three-quarters hours. No automobiles on board. Meals may be ordered at your seat. Both catamarans and turbojets leave Seattle's Pier 69 at 7:30 or 8:30 A.M. daily, with additional turbojet sailings in the summertime. Some early sailings follow a scenic route through the San Juan Islands, including a stop in Friday Harbor.

✿☞ *Victoria Clipper (800) 888–2535; (206) 448–5000 (U.S.); (250) 382–8100 (Canada). Fares one-way/round-trip in U.S. funds: vary by season and average $54–$89 and $75–$89. Group, senior, and children's discounts are available. The Victoria Clipper's schedule is confusing because at some times of the year it changes every two weeks and varies according to turbo vs. nonturbo hydroplanes. Be sure to call their 800 number for current departure times and fares.*

Black Ball Transport runs the *Coho* ferry between Port Angeles, Washington, and Victoria, B.C., several times daily. Since increased security at the border check at the Peace Arch south of Vancouver, we highly recommend traveling on the *Coho*. Traveling to or from Port Angeles, you wind along the lovely Olympic Peninsula from either near Olympia or Tacoma, hence avoiding the traffic jams possible through Seattle.

Check in at the tiny Port Angeles–Victoria Tourist Bureau (360–452–1223) right beside the ferry dock for loads of excellent advice on where to have lunch, where to stay, and even how to make reservations for accommodations in Victoria. Be sure to browse in the pier shops, and don't miss the Hegg & Hegg canned–in–Port Angeles fish stand.

The number of trips the *Coho* makes practically varies by month, so be sure to call or check its Web site for the latest details. Fares are around $30.00 for a car, van, camper, or motor home with driver, plus $7.00 for each additional passenger. Motorcycles are $17.00 (helmets required in B.C.), and bikes are $3.25 (helmets required also).

✦ *Black Ball Transport Inc.* Coho *ferry: Port Angeles, Washington: 101 East Railroad Avenue, Port Angeles 98362, (360) 457–4491, Fax: (250) 457–4493; Victoria: 430 Belleville Street (near Parliament Building), Victoria V8V 1W9, (250) 386–2202, Fax: (250) 386–2207; Web: www.northolympic.com/coho.*

By Train

Leaving from the United States, Amtrak, the national railroad system, runs its Coast Starlight from Los Angeles up the West Coast; the Empire Builder from Chicago across the top of the U.S.; and Pioneer from Chicago through Utah to Portland, Oregon. They all get you to Seattle, from which a new high-speed train wisks you to Vancouver in about four hours. From there you can take a B.C. ferry, or fly, to Victoria.

✦ *Amtrak (800) USA–RAIL. All Amtrak trains are wheelchair accessible. The train from Seattle to Vancouver leaves at 7:45 A.M. and arrives at 11:40 A.M. Fare: $28.*

From train to ferry. Pacific Coach Lines (604–662–8074 in Vancouver; 250–385–4411 in Victoria) will take you from Vancouver's Civic Central Station

---

CHARCOAL-GRILLED SEAFOOD STEAKS

Hegg & Hegg fish cannery, Port Angeles, Washington. Courtesy of National (U.S.) Federation of Fishermen/Washington Sea Grant

Ingredients

2 lb. fish steaks, fresh or frozen
½ cup oil
¼ cup lemon juice
2 tsp. salt
¼ tsp. white pepper
dash liquid hot-pepper sauce
paprika
citrus sections or cut fruit pieces

Preparation

Thaw frozen fish steaks, cut to serving size, and place on greased grill. Combine remaining ingredients, except paprika. Baste fish with sauce and sprinkle with paprika. Cook about 4 inches from moderately hot coals for eight minutes. Baste again and sprinkle with paprika, turn over, and cook for seven to ten minutes longer or until fish flakes easily when tested with a fork. Serves six.

to B.C. Ferries for $23 right onto the ferry and into Victoria. Coaches leave every two hours from 5:45 A.M. to 7:45 P.M.

If you'd like to depart from Canada, VIA Rail Canada comes straight (well, not exactly) across Canada, and at Jasper, Alberta, you can go southwest to Vancouver and make connections to Victoria. The train arrives in Vancouver at 8:30 A.M. Friday, Sunday, and Tuesday. Pacific Coach Lines buses will again transport you from the train station onto the B.C. ferry and into downtown Victoria.

❧ *VIA Rail suggests travelers in the United States call a travel agent. In Canada VIA Rail has separate phone numbers for each province and some cities, so look it up or call information for the number. In Canada VIA Rail has a TDD line for the hearing impaired: (800) 268–9503 everywhere except in the Toronto area, where it is (800) 368–6406.*

By Water—Boat

Yacht enthusiasts can dock at many harbors on Vancouver Island. Since Victoria's Inner Harbour has a three-day maximum stay in front of. The Empress hotel, many people dock at marinas on the eastern side of the island, such as Oak Bay Marina and Sidney.

Port Sidney Marina offers all services and the proximity of a resort town with fine shops and restaurants as well as a complimentary shuttle bus during the summer to Victoria and the Butchart Gardens. Port Sidney Marina features twenty-four-hour customs check-in, concierge services, transient berths to 140 feet length, dockominium sales, annual moorage, laundry, garbage, pump-out, boat repairs, parking, ice, power, water, cable, washrooms and showers, carts, affordable fishing charters, whale watching, a well-stocked marine supply store, and Sidney Harbour Shuttles for waterfront and pub tours and shopping.

Local bus No. 70 (Pat Bay Highway) goes to downtown Victoria, and bus No. 75 goes to the Butchart Gardens and then on to Victoria. You can catch both at the corner of Beacon Avenue and Fifth Street in Sidney.

❧ *Port Sidney Marina, 9835 Seaport Place, Sidney, BC V8L 4X3; (250) 655–3711; Fax: (250) 655–3771; VHF channel 68. Rates vary by season and boat length. Register with dock attendant for day moorage. Monthly rates off season only.*

Oak Bay Marina is an elegant full-service marina barely on the eastern side of Vancouver Island and therefore protected from some weather, with magnificent views of the Haro Strait and Mount Baker. Showers and laundry facilities are available.

Oak Bay Marina also offers boat rentals and sailing charters, nature cruises and fishing charters.

❧❧ *Oak Bay Marina, 1327 Beach Drive, Victoria V0S 2N4; (250) 598–3366 or (250) 598–3369; Fax: (250) 598–1361; VHF channel 68. Bus 2. Hours: 6:00 A.M. to 10:00 P.M. daily in summer. Rates: overnight, 85 cents per foot; annual, $4.85 per foot.*

Victoria Inner Harbour Marina, call (250) 363–3760 for wharfinger (manager), in front of The Empress hotel, or check boating radio at frequency VHF channel 73.

GETTING AROUND ONCE YOU'RE HERE

Once you're here, you have several options for getting around Victoria and the surrounding area. The cheapest and best means of transport are your feet. If you are capable, the city is small enough that all you need are good walking shoes to see the real Victoria.

Buses

Of course, you probably won't want to walk to all the sites all the time. B.C. Transit's Victoria Regional Transit System is the best we've ever been on. Buses are clean and graffiti-free. The front seats are reserved for seniors or people with disabilities. Nearly half of Victoria's buses are wheelchair accessible. Nearly all evening and weekend bus service is accessible; at rush hour, about half the buses are accessible.

Bus drivers graciously answer your questions without making you feel like an idiot and help you with the correct change if you get confused. Generally, young people give up their seats for seniors. What's more, the buses are on time and comfortable!

❧❧ *Victoria Regional Transit System (250–382–6161, twenty-four hour information line; Web: www.transitbc.com). Fares: $1.75 for one zone, $2.50 for two zones, $5.50 for a DayPass. Discount fares for seniors sixty-five and older with ID, children five to fourteen, and students fifteen to twenty with GoCard: $1.00 one zone, $1.50 two zones, and $4.00 DayPass. Pick up the bus schedule known as the Rider's Guide for a full and easily understandable schedule, including accessibility information. See the list of buses for popular destinations in chapter 9.*

Other buses. Several other companies also provide bus transportation in Victoria and on Vancouver Island. For information on all buses, in Victoria call (250) 385–4411; in Vancouver call (604) 662–8074. Also call these numbers for pickup at certain locations. Here is some information on the specific companies:

Pacific Coach Lines (700 Douglas Street, 250–385–4411) is the easiest way to get from Victoria to Vancouver (on the Lower Mainland) by public transportation. Its buses take you from the depot at Douglas and Belleville or pick you up at many other spots. Buses run every two hours in winter and every hour in summer, as do the ferries.

Laidlaw (700 Douglas Street, 250–388–5248) delivers people and packages all over Vancouver Island. Laidlaw buses are your best bet for getting to the far reaches of the island without a car. They provide carefree passage through some of the most beautiful and dramatic scenery in North America, including examples of ancient forests and blatant clear-cutting.

Maverick Coach Lines Ltd. (250–380–1611) takes you by bus and ferry from Vancouver to Nanaimo every two hours from 6:00 A.M. through 8:00 P.M. The trip from Nanaimo to Vancouver through the Gulf Islands leaves Nanaimo every two hours, starting at 6:15 A.M. through 8:30 P.M.

Bus Tours

Bus tours are often the best way to get a good overall look at a city. If you only have a few days in Victoria, a bus tour is an excellent way to get an overview and see what you want to explore further.

Gray Line of Victoria starts tours in front of The Empress hotel and will pick you up at your hotel at no added charge if you call. Grand City and Craigdarroch Castle Tour (adults $26.50, children $14.00, $69.00 family), one of its most popular tours, takes in the best of Victoria's lovely homes and gardens, points of historic interest, the city center, Chinatown, Antique Row, the exclusive Uplands and Oak Bay residential areas with their luxurious gardens, Victoria Golf Club, Beacon Hill Park, spectacular views of Washington's Olympic Mountains and the Strait of Juan de Fuca. It also includes a stop at Oak Bay Marina to view wild seals, visit the gift shop, or enjoy a snack or beverage. The Grand City Drive tour is also offered in combination with other destinations.

Other representative Gray Line tours include Butchart Gardens and Butterfly Gardens (adults $47.25, juniors $38.50, and children $18.50); and a Marine Wildlife and Whale Watching (adults $79, children $49), which is not recommended for pregnant women or people with neck and spinal problems. Garden lovers will enjoy the Great Gardens of Victoria Tour (adults $97.50, children $79.00, family $299.00).

✣✤ *Gray Line of Victoria, 700 Douglas Street, (250) 388–5248. Gray Line tours run from April or May 1 through mid-September or November, depending on the tour.*

Oak Bay Explorer transports guests from the *Coho* ferry on Belleville Street and many hotels and The Empress to art galleries, historic sites, and to Oak Bay. The tour is excellent, only $2.00, and you can get on and off. Available Monday–Saturday.

Taxis

Taxis in Victoria are all reliable and clean. Most do personalized sight-seeing tours, many for a fixed, agreed-in-advance fee. Major companies include the following:

Victoria Taxi: (250) 383–7111 downtown; (250) 383–1515 Oak Bay; (250) 381–2030 Gordon Head.

Empress Taxi: (250) 381–2222; (250) 381–2242.

Blue Bird Cabs, Ltd.: (250) 384–1155; (800) 665–7055.

AllStar Taxi: (250) 475–2511.

Empire Taxi: (250) 383–8888 downtown; (250) 384–2511 Gordon Head; (250) 381–1121 Oak Bay.

Automobiles

With Victoria's excellent public transportation system, and if you are able to walk freely, you rarely need a car except to go out of town. Driving a car in Victoria is a refreshing experience, since Victorians are polite in everything, including driving.

Lots of locals ride bikes around town and want to share Victoria's narrow streets. Please use extra caution when passing cyclists, turning, opening your car door, or pulling away from the curb.

Whenever a person appears to be approaching a curb to cross the street, *stop* and let him or her cross, whether a crosswalk is there or not.

Watch the one-way street signs—those in Victoria don't make much sense. Several in a row go the same direction down to Wharf Street. It's hard to learn to get around by car—another reason we encourage walking if you are capable.

Oh yes, Victorians will stop dead to let you enter their lane of traffic, on a city street or on a highway. In order to preserve their dignity and sanity, please go when they motion you to.

Car rental agencies. Victoria and Victoria International Airport have the major automobile-rental agencies as well as some minor and innovative ones.

Many used-car companies and automobile dealerships rent the cars on their lots, so inquire at those located on outer Government and Douglas Streets. Reservations are suggested for cars in Victoria.

Avis Rent-A-Car, 2507 Government, (250) 386–8468; at the airport, (250) 656–6033.

Budget Rent-A-Car, 727 Courtney (downtown), (250) 388–7874; at the airport, (250) 656–3731.

Enterprise Rent-A-Car, Oak Bay, (250) 480–1766; at the airport, (250) 656–4808 or (800) 325–8007.

Hertz Rent-A-Car, downtown, (250) 360–2822; at the airport, (250) 656–2312.

Tilden (National), 767 Douglas, (250) 386–1213 or (250) 381–1115; at the airport, (250) 656–2541.

Parking. While some people lament parking difficulties in downtown Victoria, we have never found a problem. Certain shopping times make things more complicated, like Saturday and Sunday, of course. The city of Victoria runs several parking garages (parkades); a few are privately run. Many downtown businesses will provide one-hour, free-parking validation stickers for city-operated parkades. Just ask the staff in any shop you're in.

Downtown Parkades

Broughton Street between Broad and Douglas.

Broughton between Douglas and Blanshard (near the library).

Fort Street, 1 short block off Wharf on Langley.

View Street has three: between Government and Douglas, between Douglas and Blanshard, and between Blanshard and Quadra.

Johnson Street has three: across from Market Square below Government Street, between Douglas and Blanchard, and between Blanshard and Quadra.

Chinatown Parkades

Pandora, between Store Street and just up from Market Square below Government Street and on.

On Fisgard Street at Store Street, up Fisgard toward Government, or on Fisgard behind City Hall near Douglas Street.

Carriages and Pedal Cabs

Picturesque horses pulling picturesque carriages are used for touring rather than for transportation from one place to another. While some people object strongly to the inhumanity of driving the horses to work this hard, others delight in the experience. We have seen only one horse bolt from sudden fear, break free of its harness, and gallop down the street into oncoming traffic. The carriages gather at the horses' feed and watering spot in the street just west of the Parliament buildings and south of the Royal Victoria Wax Museum. The carriages and drivers range from casual and smallish to big and formal—something for everyone.

Kabuki Kabs (250–385–4243) are pedicabs that will pick you up anywhere downtown and take you anywhere downtown. Their healthy-looking drivers are always fun to talk or listen to. Pedicabs usually board passengers at the Inner Harbour on the water side of Government Street across from The Empress hotel.

Kabuki Kabs offers a wide range of tours based on $1.00/minute for one to two people and $1.50/minute for three to four people, with tours of the Inner Harbour ranging from fifteen to thirty minutes. Some operators have developed specialized tours such as cyclist Freddie Kruger's (yes!), a $300 tour from The Empress hotel to Butchart Gardens, special architecture or church tours, and heritage home tours.

Heritage Tours and Daimler Limousine Service (713 Bexhill Road; 250–474–4332) takes you on a luxurious tour of the city in a British Daimler limousine. For only $62 per hour per carload, up to six passengers can see Victoria, the Butchart Gardens, and Craigdarroch Castle or just about anything else. What a way to go!

Tallyho Tours (180 Goward Street, 250–383–5067) takes you on horse-drawn carriage tours of the Inner Harbour, Government Street, Beacon Hill Park, James Bay, Dallas Road and the beach, Thunderbird Park, and heritage homes, including Emily Carr's residences. Tallyho operates from March to September and begins its tours from Belleville and Menzies Streets or from the front of The Empress hotel. Traditional Tallyho wagons accommodate up to

KABUKI KAB

twenty adults, while private Central Park–style carriages seat up to ten. Informed guides accompany the tours. Fares: adults $11.00, students $7.00, children $5.00. Central Park–style carriages: Waterfront/thirty minutes, $50; City Park/forty-five minutes, $75; Grand Tour/one hour, $90.

Black Beauty Carriages (180 Goward Street, 250–361–1220) conducts private, single horse-drawn carriage tours of Victoria. Call for reservations for a routine tour or one designed for your interests.

Sight-Seeing Ferries

The little green and yellow ferries of **Victoria Harbour Ferries,** which bills itself as "the tour you can get off of," will take you on "hops" between various points in the harbor; full tours of the Gorge and Inner Harbour, or a romantic thirty-minute moonlight cruise ($8.00). In summer, a couple can rent the ultimate ferry as a bed-and-breakfast overnight cruise. Wow!

✈✿ *Victoria Harbour Ferries, (250) 708–0201. Inner Harbour ferries depart every twelve minutes, and the Gorge tours leave every 30 minutes from 11:00 A.M. to 4:00 P.M. Fares: $2.50 per hop, $12.00 adults and $6.00 children for the Inner Harbour tour, and $14.00 adults, $12.00 seniors and $7.00 children for the Gorge tour. Harbour Ferries sail beginning mid-March, with the full schedule afloat May 1.*

Sight-Seeing by Train

The **E&N** (Esquimalt & Nanaimo) runs its lovingly restored two-car Malahat back and forth between Victoria (east end of the blue bridge at 450

SIGHT-SEEING FERRIES

Pandora and Wharf Streets, 250–383–4324) and Nanaimo and Courtney, with as many stops along the way as passengers call out. The yellow train's red leather seats let you bask and take in the sights with plenty of leg room. No food or beverages are served on the two-and-a-half-hour trip, so bring yours along.

Running along the same tracks is the new Pacific Wilderness Railway (250–381–8600), the personal project of New Jersey entrepreneur Ross Rowland. His environmentally sound tourist train will make a two-hour-and-fifteen-minute trip up to the Malahat summit with a picnic option. Eventually Rowland hopes to run excursion trains from Victoria to Courtney and Port Alberni, luxury excursions to the island's west coast, and $100 dinner trains to Niagara Canyon, as well as a commuter train between Duncan and Victoria (a great idea!).

Scooters and Bicycles

Scooters are popular with visitors for venturing to beaches and the outer reaches of town, but operate them cautiously.

Bicycles are an even more popular mode of transportation in Victoria and on Vancouver Island. Island highways often have bike lanes, but the roads to Tofino and Port Renfrew are a little hairy where the edges have fallen down the cliffs into the water. Plan for climbs on many routes. You can easily ride around Victoria with only slight inclines if you plan well. Helmets are now required by British Columbia law for your protection.

You can **rent scooters or bicycles** at the following spots:

Budget (727 Courtney Street, 250–388–7874) rents little red Yamaha scooters, helmets included, for $10/hour or $35/day "with a little instruction included also if you need it." These are ideal for scooting around Victoria and have wire baskets to carry backpacks, picnics, and water bottles. Budget also rents mountain bikes, with helmets, for $6/hour and $18/day year-round.

Cycle Victoria (327 Belleville, 250–385–2453) rents scooters, motorcycles, bikes, and in-line skates in the summer season only.

Harbour Rentals (811 Wharf Street, 250–995–1661; Fax: 250–386–3370) rents Rocky Mountain bikes, kids' bikes, tandems, trailers, and in-line skates during the summer season only.

Sports Rent (611 Discovery, 250–385–7368) rents bikes and equipment for roads and trails including hybrid, moderate terrain, technical, and advanced mountain bikes in a variety of frame sizes year-round. It offers higher-end popular in-line skates with full protection padding, group and private lessons, canoes, kayaks, water skis, surfing gear, mountain climbing and camping equipment, plus winter skis and snowboards. Reservations suggested. *Rates:* differ depending on length of rental, ranging from $20 to $100.

CHAPTER 3

NEIGHBORHOODS OF GREATER VICTORIA

In a society where community is extremely important, neighborhoods form and are formed by the focus of community identity. Some neighborhoods attract people of like backgrounds or ethnic and national origins. Others attract people of common interests and attitudes, or people who just like the view.

Most visitors see only downtown Victoria, including the Inner Harbour, Old Town, Chinatown, and maybe James Bay. Other neighborhoods well worth seeing are Fairfield, Oak Bay Village, Cook Street Village, Fernwood, Rockland, and Fisherman's Wharf.

Then there are all those other places many tourists never reach but should if there's time: Sidney, twenty minutes northeast of Victoria; Sooke, forty minutes west of Victoria, Port Renfrew, another ninety minutes west; and the up-island communities of Duncan, Chemainus, Nanaimo, Quallicum Beach, Courtenay, Campbell River, Port Hardy, Port Alberni, Port Renfrew, Ucluelet, and Tofino. These are all small to medium towns with distinct characters, some stemming from the original countries of their founding parents.

Some neighborhoods and settlements are more British than others, some more earthy than others, and some more interesting.

We will now take you on a tour of Victoria and Vancouver Island, neighborhood by neighborhood, so that you can discover it yourself and maximize your enjoyment.

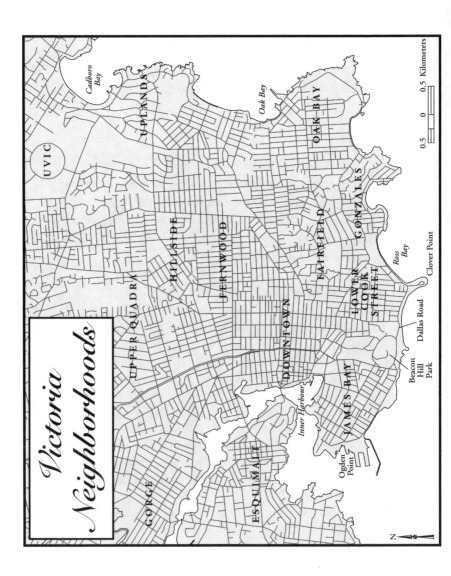

Victoria Neighborhoods

Cadboro Bay

UVIC

UPLANDS

Oak Bay

OAK BAY

GONZALES

HILLSIDE

FERNWOOD

FAIRFIELD

Ross Bay

Clover Point

UPPER QUADRA

LOWER COOK STREET

DOWNTOWN

Dallas Road

Beacon Hill Park

Inner Harbour

JAMES BAY

Ogden Point

GORGE

ESQUIMALT

N

0.5   0   0.5 Kilometers

Downtown Victoria

N

Cook Street

Pandora St
Johnson St
Yates St
View St
Fort St (Antique Row)

Vancouver Street

Quadra

Pioneer Square

Blanshard

Royal Theatre

McPherson Theatre

Victoria Conference Centre

Douglas

Tourism Victoria Info Centre

City Hall

Eaton Centre

Chinatown

Herald St

Government

Market Square

Wharf

Empress Hotel

Library

Royal B.C. Museum

Beacon Hill Park

Emily Carr House

E & N Railway Terminal

Maritime Museum

Bastion Sq.

Victoria Clipper

Royal London Wax Museum

Black Ball Ferries

Provincial Legislature

Menzies Street

Belleville

Quebec

Kingston

Superior

Oswego

Johnson Street Bridge

SONGHEES

Inner Harbour

Laurel Point Park

JAMES BAY

Fisherman's Wharf

Ogden Point Breakwater

0   100   200 Meters

DOWNTOWN VICTORIA

Begin at the Inner Harbour, at or near The Empress hotel or the many near-by hotels and motels. By nature, we would start somewhere else just because *everyone* starts here, but we're going to conform this once just to help you out. (You're welcome.)

Baskets of gorgeous, cheerful, tasteful flowers hang from all the light posts downtown in the spring and summertime. They are everywhere. No one we know has ever seen anyone water them or trim the flowers. If you do, let us know. In the winter, the flowers are replaced with attractive pine arrangements, pleasing everyone and offending no one. Every spring the chamber of commerce sponsors a flower count, and each year Victorians try to produce more blossoms than the year before. The count is currently in the billions. All for your pleasure and theirs, of course.

Do go right over to the TOURISM VICTORIA CENTRE (812 Wharf Street at Government, 250–382–2127), a short tower overlooking the inner harbour. This art deco tower was built in 1931 for an anticipated seaplane base in the inner harbour. When the base wasn't developed, the building was used for years as an automobile service station.

Tourism Victoria's endearing staff will answer almost any question you can imagine, make reservations for you, find you a place to stay or dine, sell you tickets for performances or native salmon barbecues, and let you take hundreds of brochures on almost any interest you might want to explore on Vancouver Island.

Before you get distracted by the commanding edifices of the Parliament buildings and The Empress hotel, take a deep breath and look around at what's here: the INNER HARBOUR itself.

This is the *new* Inner Harbour created in 1905. Originally a bridge was built in 1859 to link Parliament to downtown. Then a causeway was constructed to keep the water away so that fill could be dumped to create a site for the Canadian Pacific Railway to build its luxury Empress hotel. The hotel, built on 2,680 gumwood pilings sunk into goo and bedrock, constantly sinks into the silt ever so slightly, causing the Canadian Pacific to shore it up and redecorate.

The cement railing along the sidewalk above the three-sided causeway holds up people as well as plaques memorializing ships' captains and war heroes. At the top of the southern stairway down to the causeway you will usually find a bagpiper playing for a living next to a totem pole, fodder for a photo epitomizing two of the tiles in Canada's great cultural mosaic.

The causeway below is not easily wheelchair accessible. At the far northern end, past Milestones restaurant and cafe, is a steep slope driveway from Wharf Street. A wheelchair can be brought down in a car to the causeway level, and there is a slightly steep ramp behind the Royal London Wax Museum on Belleville Street.

There are rewards at the bottom. A young local sells espresso drinks from a cart at the southern end. In the middle of the causeway you can walk right down the gangplank and up to visiting yachts, often having fun conversations with their passengers. Artists and other hopefuls sell their art,

CAPT. JAMES COOK PRESIDES OVER
VICTORIA'S INNER HARBOUR

while musicians of many proficiencies play guitars, saxophones, and banjos for whatever your generosity will allow you to contribute.

Enjoy a stroll and a beverage, and bask in this rarefied atmosphere reminiscent of the banks of Paris's Seine, but with clean air.

A visit to the causeway at night is a must for cheap fun and entertainment. Mostly talented buskers entertain nightly in the summer, with juggling comedians (or comedic jugglers) stealing most of the attention. These entertainers must obtain approval and licenses from the city of Victoria. Please do make a donation into their passed hats in return for enjoying their talents.

This is where you board VICTORIA HARBOUR FERRIES, "the tours you can get off." We usually shun touristy experiences and try to live as locals in the places we visit or stay in, but we finally took a Harbour Ferry this summer to satisfy some guests from California. It was terrific!

We selected the GORGE TOUR (adults $14.00, seniors $12.00, children $7.00), a fifty-minute tour of the more relaxed side of the Harbour, including

Victoria's last remaining industrial harbor and shipyard, Banfield and Gorge Parks, and POINT ELLICE HOUSE, an Italianate villa featuring an unusually interesting collection of Victoriana, high tea (reservations a must), and light lunches. This is easily the prettiest way to reach the house, the other being from Bay Street and north on Pleasant Street, .5 block through industrial Victoria.

Many locals believe this is the best tea in Victoria, along with that at the James Bay Tea Room, and it's far less expensive than the one at The Empress hotel. Breads for all three are baked by Rising Star Bakery on Broad Street. There's a little chill in the garden after three, so plan to go for tea earlier. The breeze comes off the water, and large arbutus trees shade the garden, which, of course, is actually an asset on hot days.

Point Ellice House was built in time for the Peter O'Reilly family to buy it and give birth to second daughter Kathleen there on New Year's Eve, 1867. The O'Reillys added on to both their seven-room cottage and to their family, resulting in a rambling 4,000-square-foot house and four children. Kathleen lived there all her life and died there in 1945. Many locals believe her ghost is still there and appears frequently.

The O'Reillys did much of the gardening at Point Ellice House themselves, and fortunately they catalogued and wrote about many of the plantings and flowers. But by the early 1900s the gardens had become an overgrown mess. In the mid-1960s, their grandson, John, and his wife, Inez, began the restoration and replanting that is still going on today. They lived in the house until 1975.

Among the interesting stuff you can see here: "Kings Border" pattern Minton china from England, porcelain place cards, chairs with removable wicker backs to keep the heat off the backs of people seated near the fire, a large Albion Iron Works range dated 1889, a rare 1897 copper water heater, Victorian cooking implements such as jelly bags to strain cows and calves foot jelly, butter molds, and assorted food grinders.

❧ *Point Ellice House, 2616 Pleasant Street, (250) 380–6506 or (250) 387–4697. Admission to house: adults $5.00, seniors/students $4.00, children six to twelve $3.00; afternoon tea and house tour $16.95. Hours: early May–mid-September, daily noon–5:00 P.M., last house tour at 4:30 P.M. If you go by car rather than ferry, head north on Government, west on Bay, then right on Pleasant. By bus: Bus 14 Craigflower.*

Harbour Ferries's Harbour Tour (adults $12.00, children younger than twelve with adult $6.00, babies younger than one free) takes you on a forty-five-minute tour of the Inner and Outer Harbours, including small marinas, floatplane moorings, the Canadian Coast Guard Station, views of the Olympic Mountains in neighboring Washington state, and lots of seabirds and occasional seals and otters.

TEA, PLEASE

Victoria is the ideal place to sample your first English tea or enjoy your customary indulgence, depending upon your background and experience. With few exceptions, tea is not a snooty ritual here. Rather, it is a friendly, celebratory break in your day.

"Afternoon tea" or "light tea" are nearly the same thing, meant to be an interlude between meals. "High tea" or "full tea" might replace your evening meal.

The lighter, less expensive tea often includes small sandwiches, scones, clotted cream, jams, berries, and coffee or tea. The heavier high tea includes more varieties of the above, plus English trifles. A more expensive tea does not necessarily mean a better tea.

For an authentic English experience, try any of the following places. Beginning in the Inner Harbour area, these tearooms then fan outward geographically. Reservations are recommended.

The Empress (721 Government Street, 250–389–2727) offers Victoria's most famous tea experience. In the summer, book reservations three days ahead. If you don't want to indulge here, at least walk through the hotel in the afternoon to catch a glimpse. A strict dress code is enforced in the Tea Lobby: no jeans, sports clothes, or sport shoes. Considering ambience, decorum, and service, this is the ultimate tea in Victoria, for a mere $25–$32 per person, depending on the season.

Murchie's (1110 Government Street, 250–383–3112) is officially a "cappuccino and dessert bar" but sells most of the components of a good tea at its counter. You can easily have a scone with preserves and clotted cream with coffee or tea for less than $5.00 and sit indoors or outdoors at green tables along the sidewalk.

The James Bay Tearoom & Restaurant (322 Menzies Street, 250–382–8282) is just a block beyond the southwestern back corner of the Parliament buildings. A favorite of locals and visitors alike for value and friendliness; afternoon tea served daily for only $7.00, and high tea on Sunday afternoons is $10.00.

The Blethering Place Tea Room & Restaurant, 2250 Oak Bay; 250–598–1413) is a cozy comfortable tearoom in Oak Bay Village frequented by locals. Teas are served from 11:00 A.M. to 7:00 P.M., or any other time if you ask. Light tea, $12.95, full tea, $14.95, or you can assemble your own for less than $6.00. Bus 1 Willows or 2 Oak Bay.

continued on next page

Enjoy another friendly, welcoming tea experience at the Oak Bay Tea Room & Restaurant (2241 Oak Bay, 250–370–1005), which serves finger sandwiches, raisin scones, clotted cream, and the works for $22.95 for two. Bus 1 Willows or 2 Oak Bay.

The Oak Bay Beach Hotel (1175 Beach Drive, 250–598–4556) is a historic hotel and room with a pleasant informal English ambience and incomparable views of the Oak Bay Marina. Afternoon tea in the summer is $19.95. Bus 2 Oak Bay.

At Point Ellice House (2616 Pleasant Street, 250–387–4697), a heritage (historic) home, teas are served outside on the lawn, where one sits in white wicker furniture while overlooking the Gorge. It's one of the best teas in Victoria, with afternoon tea and house tour at $16.95. Bus 14 Craigflower or Harbour Ferries' Gorge Tour.

Four Mile Roadhouse (199 Island Highway, View Royal, 250–479–2514) is a pleasant old home where you can sample teas at $8.95.

Adrienne's Tea Garden (5325 Cordova Bay Road, Saanich, 250–658–1535), in the Mattick's Farm complex, offers tea for $10.95 during the summer.

Butchart Gardens (800 Benvenuto Avenue, Central Saanich, 250–652–4422) serves tea in the Dining Room for $18.95 for afternoon tea and $24.95 for high tea, or you can assemble parts of tea at its other facilities. Bus 75.

Point-No-Point Resort (1808 West Coast Road, River Jordan, 250–646–2020) is well worth the beautiful trip by car out to this cozy home-turned-fine-restaurant-and-resort, nestled in tall trees and overlooking the water for afternoon tea at $9.95, or for lunch or dinner.

White Heather Tea Room (1885 Oak Bay, 250–595–8020) is Agnes Campbell's lovely new Scottish tearoom with made-from-scratch soups, tea sandwiches, delicate shortbreads, scones, and miniature tarts. At once elegant and casual. Set teas from The Wee Tea ($6.95) to the Big Muckle Giant Tea ($27.95 for two people) are offered, or put together your own combination. Hours: 8:30 A.M.–5:00 P.M. Monday–Saturday, 10:00 A.M.–5:00 P.M. Sunday.

Windsor House Tea Room and Restaurant (2540 Windsor Street at Newport, 250–595–3135) is in a tudor-style building facing Windsor Park, with set teas ranging from $6.95 to $25.95. You can also enjoy Welsh rarebit and deep-dish chicken potpies ($7.95). Hours: 11:00 A.M.–5:00 P.M. Monday–Saturday.

The Harbour Tour stops at Ocean Pointe Resort, Songhees Park near popular Spinnakers Brew Pub (great local beers, housemade breads, seafood, Caesar salads, and views back at Victoria), Coast Harbourside Hotel, Fisherman's Wharf (and Barb's Place—a local hangout for fish and chips), and West Bay Marina with its RV park, floathomes, and a coffee shop with outdoor tables and views.

You can get off these tours anywhere they stop and get back on after enjoying the local sites at no additional charge. Occasionally you will have to wait for a few ferries to come by before there's space, particularly at Point Ellice House.

You can also just take the Harbour Ferries's hops from one stop to another for $2.50, $1.25, or free, depending on distance. What a refreshing way to commute!

Sunday mornings at 9:45, Harbour Ferries do a "ballet" to the "Blue Danube" waltz right in front of The Empress hotel from mid-June to mid-September.

Harbour Ferries's Brass Bell Bed & Breakfast offers a unique experience of staying on the water on a very private boat, for just $185 per night, including breakfast at a nearby restaurant. Can you stand it? (See "Where to Stay.")

The majestic English lady facing the inner harbour looking ever so slightly imposing is THE EMPRESS hotel. With its hat and veil straightened for the foreseeable future, its sensible shoes and straight legs shored up again, it is now, thank heavens, sinking more slowly toward China. Do not try to enter through the front door; i.e., up the obvious front stairs entrance, which used to serve as just that. Go to the left and enter where you see cars dropping off people and doormen opening the door to the reception lobby. You can also enter from Douglas Street through the Victoria Conference Centre or at the hotel's south end across from the Royal British Columbia Museum.

Owned by the Canadian Pacific, The Empress is currently managed by the excellent Fairmount Hotel group. The original lobby, where tea is served, is up the circular stairway. The Garden Cafe is downstairs, as is Kipling's, which serves an excellent buffet at breakfast, lunch, and dinner, as well as Sunday brunch.

Francis Rattenbury designed the original center block of The Empress, which opened in 1908. More wings were added in 1910, 1913, and 1929 (a good year!), doubling the size of the hotel. When the Canadian Pacific shored up the old lady and put on her face in 1989, a recreation center, swimming pool, and the reception lobby, where you should start, were added.

It is the restored old center of the hotel that you must see to appreciate Victoria's heritage. On your way to the tea lobby you will see the warmly elegant oak-paneled dining room and the lobby lounge. Once you get to the tea lobby, notice the inlaid hardwood floors, for decades protected by a thick covering of carpet, which muffled sounds as if in a living room. The decor is elegant English staid.

Jeans, shorts, sweats, and T-shirts are not allowed at tea.

The Empress serves afternoon tea in the lobby to nearly 80,000 people a year, so reservations are a must. High tea is a meal. Afternoon tea, which is served here, is meant as a snack to tide you over until dinner, although it certainly could serve as a meal. Each offering is served to be tasted and digested, not to be chowed down.

Afternoon tea at The Empress usually includes crumpets with honey; scones with Devonshire cream and strawberry preserves; berries with Chantilly cream; cucumber, watercress, and egg salad sandwiches (our favorite); salmon and cream cheese pinwheels; lemon rolls; black currant tartlets; and The Empress's own tea blend served in a silver teapot.

Be sure to check out the stained-glass dome of the Palm Court, just before the Crystal Ballroom with its ten huge crystal chandeliers reflecting on the mirrored ceiling.

Beyond and east of the tea lobby and toward Douglas Street, you will find the famous Bengal Lounge, originally the hotel's library, built in 1912. It is worth walking into the Bengal Lounge just to experience the deep warmth of the decor and atmosphere, the Indian-style ceiling fans, the tiger-skin wall hanging, and an exotic or customary beverage. You may also stay for curry or other Indian dishes, fish and chips, or other interesting light fare.

Past the Bengal Lounge toward Douglas Street you will find the conservatory and its tropical plants (are they producing enough oxygen for the whole building?) and one entrance to the Victoria Conference Centre. You can also exit through the courtyard to the south and walk to the bus station, Royal British Columbia Museum, and Crystal Garden. If you do leave The Empress via the Victoria Convention Centre on Douglas Street, you will find loads of imported clothing boutiques on this side of Douglas.

❧ *The Empress, 721 Government Street, (250) 389–2727. Reservations for afternoon tea should be made three or four days in advance.*

Across the street, at 713 Douglas, you can visit the CRYSTAL GARDEN. But before you do, you may notice along the east side of Douglas Street what looks like a collection of ultimate tourist-trap shops. While they do offer T-shirts and teaspoons, they also sell English sweets, British Columbia native artifacts and crafts, Murchie's tea and coffee, the Not-Yet-Famous Tilley hats, and even film.

The Crystal Garden, another fabulous building designed by Francis Rattenbury and Percy James and built by the Canadian Pacific Railway, opened in 1925 with the largest saltwater swimming pool in the British Empire, ballrooms, tearooms, and a promenade conservatory. Generations of "everyone"

THE EMPRESS HOTEL AND THE ACTIVE INNER HARBOUR
IN SUMMER

hung out here in the thirties, swimming in the daytime, dancing at night. The salt water eventually affected the iron roof supports, weakening them and strengthening a move to tear down the whole place. Substitution of freshwater stalled both until 1971, and then locals raised money to save and restore the building. Thank heavens! The waterfall is at the old pool's deep end.

The Crystal Garden is a conservatory of animals either now or soon to be on the International Endangered Species List and operated by the Provincial Capital Commission. Its major focus is the preservation and conservation of endangered species of tropical birds and animals, with the goal of returning some endangered species to their natural habitats.

So take advantage of this one. Take the indoor strolling safari and get up close and personal with the world's smallest monkeys (only 4 inches fully grown), Indian fruit bats (flying foxes), more than sixty-five species of endangered birds and animals, and free-flying butterflies. Wander among the hundreds of tropical plants and gorgeous blossoms and check out the flamingos and macaws. Cameras encouraged.

❧ *Crystal Garden, 713 Douglas Street, (250) 381–1213 or (250) 381–1277; Web: www.bcpcc.com/crystal/. Wheelchair accessible. Hours: Summer 9:00 A.M.– 6:00 P.M. daily, winter 10:00 A.M.–4:30 P.M. Admission: adults $7.50, children five to sixteen $4.00, under six free, seniors $6.50, family day pass $20.00.*

The OLD SPAGHETTI FACTORY, at 703 Douglas Street, is a great casual restaurant for lunch or dinner for the whole family. Lunch and children's menu items are all less than $8.00, and you can also enjoy a wide range of pastas and steaks. All entrees include soup or salad, garlic bread, coffee or tea, and spumoni ice cream.

ᴥ The Old Spaghetti Factory, 703 Douglas Street, (250) 381–8444. Hours: 11:30 A.M.–10:00 P.M. daily. Fully licensed. Mostly wheelchair accessible. Credit cards: Visa, MasterCard, American Express.

As you come out of the Crystal Garden or the Old Spaghetti Factory, look across the intersection of Douglas and Belleville and you will see a huge native carving facing northeast on the Mungo Martin House, a tribute to the internationally renowned aboriginal artist (1881–1962). Mungo Martin House serves as a training center for young aboriginal artists, who learn their traditional craft with mentors such as Martin's grandson, famed artist Tony Hunt.

HELMCKEN HOUSE, at Douglas and Belleville Streets, is Victoria's oldest home, built in 1852. Dr. John Sebastian Helmcken had it built for his bride, Cecilia, daughter of Governor James Douglas, on an acre given to the newlyweds by Douglas.

MUNGO MARTIN HOUSE

The stereo-taped tour (included in admission price) allows you to hear "the good doctor" describe what Victoria was like in the good old days; Cecilia recounts her life as a pioneer mother; and Aunt Dolly reveals why she left her father's room untouched as a shrine to his memory after he died in 1920. Upstairs you can see Dr. Helmcken's famous medical collection.

In December, Helmcken House puts on its Christmas programs, first for schoolchildren, and then from December 21–31 for the rest of the world. Experience the spirit of giving by walking into a play of characters dressed and acting the parts of an 1899 family Christmas.

Helmcken House, Douglas and Belleville Streets, (250) 361–0021 or (250) 387–4697. Hours: May 1–September 30, 11:00 A.M.–5:00 P.M.; February 1–April 30 and October 1–November 15, noon–4:00 P.M. Admission: adults $5.00, students/seniors $4.00, children $3.00, family of four $12.00. Tape use included. Wheelchair accessible first floor only. Ramp is at the east end of Royal British Columbia Museum. Admission is half price for those unable to go to the second floor.

While in this neighborhood, you must visit the ROYAL BRITISH COLUMBIA MUSEUM, without a doubt the most people-friendly state or provincial museum we have seen. It is in the late stages of remodeling, so some of our detailed description locators may be out of date when you read this.

Before you even get inside the museum's doors you can buy great coffee and snacks from outdoor vendors to sustain you inside. Or you can visit the Museum Cafe, which, lucky us, is now run by Murchie's Tea and Coffee on Government Street. At the cafeteria-style cafe you can select hot lunches or sandwiches and pastries, as well as excellent teas and coffees and sit inside or out. If you can, avoid normal noonish lunchtime, because it gets very crowded. The cafe is 100 percent nonsmoking.

In the main floor lobby you buy your tickets, get information, and find washrooms, including a special accessible washroom. The other great temptation is the expanded Royal Museum Shop, which is loaded with books on every British Columbia subject imaginable, from cookbooks and history to First Peoples studies and fish, as well as fabulous native jewelry and other artifacts.

Elevators and escalators are toward the rear of the building.

On the second floor you find a variety of permanent exhibits—*Open Ocean, Living Land, Living Sea, Mammoths,* and *Coastal Forest* among them— as well as temporary galleries of special exhibits. Handicapped washrooms are also on this floor.

The third floor has must-sees for all ages. There are galleries on recent histories, and an Old Town with so much atmosphere and societal relics that you might want to live in those "good old days," whenever they were. You can sit

THUNDERBIRD PARK, DOWNTOWN VICTORIA

down and watch old Charlie Chaplin movies and wait in an old train station replica for the train to come by. The Chinatown exhibit is hauntingly accurate with little peekaboo alleys. The galleries devoted to the First Peoples are an enlightening experience, and the Totem Gallery is breathtaking. The third floor mezzanine (which is not wheelchair accessible) has more recent history and First Peoples galleries, as well as special exhibits.

Each year the Royal British Columbia Museum also hosts special landmark exhibits, which often go on to major cities throughout the world. One such recent exhibit was *Leonardo da Vinci—Scientist, Inventor, Artist. Circus Magicus,* featuring an entertaining array of circus artifacts and history, runs through May 2001. National Geographic's IMAX Theater opened in July 1998 and is an absolute must-see for families.

As you leave the museum, check out the replica of a ceremonial longhouse in Thunderbird Park next to the museum entrance—a great learning and sensitivity experience. Take a walk around this forest of totem poles.

🌺 *Royal British Columbia Museum, 675 Belleville Street, (250) 356–RBCM (7226), (800) 661–5411, or (888) 447–7977; Fax: (250) 387–5674; Web: www.royalmuseum.bc.ca. Hours: July 1–September 8, 9:30 A.M.–7:00 P.M.; September 9–June 30, 9:00 A.M.–5:00 P.M. daily except Christmas and New Year's Day. Admission: adults $9.65, seniors sixty-five and older $6.65, children six to eighteen $2.14, family $23.35. Public and accessible rest rooms on the first three floors.*

One of the most stately of Canada's edifices, the **PARLIAMENT** building, at 501 Belleville Street, has become a world-famous symbol of Victoria, the capital of British Columbia. How many provinces or states can you think of that have their capitals offshore? Perhaps this is just symbolic of British Columbia's and Victoria's different-from-the-rest-of-Canada nature.

Parliament is the building with 3,330 light bulbs burning around its exterior to create one of the most beautiful nighttime sights anywhere.

The provincial legislature actually meets here in the second-floor chamber designed by Francis Rattenbury to resemble the British Parliament; it was completed in 1897 to commemorate Queen Victoria's diamond jubilee. The legislative chamber aisle is just wide enough to make it impossible for two swords to reach across from opposing sides. Handy! Notice the throne slightly above the other leaders' seats kept properly just in case the Queen shows up. This is an important place because the legislature makes decisions that guide the provincial government, which is the largest employer in Victoria.

For the easiest entry, go to the east end of the main building, where there are just three or four stairs, compared to the imposing staircase at the front. The hallways are lined with fascinating historic photos and Rattenbury's architectural drawings. Attentive guards and other staff are extremely helpful in answering questions and directing you to the next free tour. You are also encouraged to join tours already in progress.

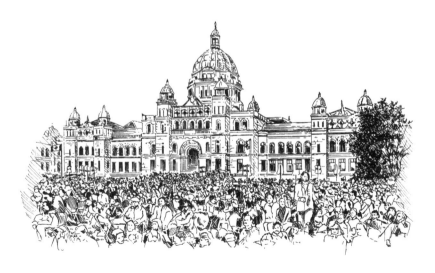

BRITISH COLUMBIA'S PARLIAMENT BUILDING DURING THE
SYMPHONY SPLASH

On the second floor you can see the legislative chamber, worth the trip even if parliament is not in session. You will see photos of all B.C. premiers and notable Canadian women; the famous stained-glass window ("The Jubilee Window") depicting the original B.C. coat of arms (before Queen Victoria's foreign office insisted it be changed so it wouldn't look as if the sun were setting on the British Empire); and photos and memorabilia of British royal visits.

You can watch the seventy-five members in action from public galleries when they are in session, but that is somewhat hard to predict. Normally they meet from sometime in early spring to sometime in early summer, and sometimes they don't. If they are meeting, catch the action between 2:00 and 2:30 P.M. when they indulge in the British traditional question period during which members can ask the premier or cabinet members questions directly. Americans might find this a refreshing approach.

✤ *Parliament, 501 Belleville Street, (250) 387–3046 for private or group tour arrangements. Hours: 8:30 A.M.–5:00 P.M. daily except statutory holidays. Admission: free. Rest rooms, which are a half floor above and below the first floor, are not wheelchair accessible, though the building is. The wheelchair entrance is from Government Street; take ramp to basement and follow signs to elevator.*

THE JUBILEE WINDOW IN THE BRITISH COLUMBIA PARLIAMENT BUILDING

Across Belleville Street is the ROYAL LONDON WAX MUSEUM. Originally the Canadian Pacific Railway's marine terminal building, it was Vancouver Island's equivalent of Ellis Island and most visitors' entrance to Victoria until 1965. One of the last of Francis Rattenbury's and P. L. James's collaborations, this 1924 neoclassic structure with Ionic columns was the first Victoria building to employ precast concrete.

The museum houses 250 wax figures depicting the famous and infamous from history and show business (some looking like death not yet warmed over). The royal family forms an interesting group, while Princess Diana has been moved around to the royals' back side so that you see her at the end of your main-floor tour. Try the Chamber of Horrors downstairs, which you "enter at your own risk!" Young children and the faint-hearted may pass right by to Storybook Land, the Garden of Literature featuring Charles Dickens, Rudyard Kipling, Mark Twain, and many other literary guests, before they move on to Frozen in Time, in which the challenge of finding the Northwest Passage is told in a multimedia theater format. In the Galaxy of Stars you will meet Charlie Chaplin, John Wayne, Marilyn Monroe (with that famous white dress blowing up), Clint Eastwood, Goldie Hawn, Christopher Reeve, and many others. Don't miss the Crown Jewels' Treasury.

Royal London Wax Museum, 470 Belleville Street, (250) 388–4461; Web: www.waxworld.com. Hours: 9:00 A.M.–5:00 P.M. October 1–mid-May; 9:00 A.M. to 9:00 P.M. mid-May–August 31; 9:00 A.M.–7:00 P.M. September. Admission: adults $8.00, military $6.50, seniors $7.00, students thirteen to nineteen or with university ID $6.50, children $3.50, disabled $3.00 with no charge for attendant, family package $23.00, special group rates. Museum and rest rooms wheelchair accessible.

The UNDERSEA GARDENS, at 490 Belleville, offers a wonderfully real and fantasy experience for all ages, featuring at least 5,000 kinds of marine life from salmon to ferocious-looking wolf-eels, prehistoric sturgeon, brilliant red snapper, white and crimson anemones, and the world's largest octopus. There are continuous shows with scuba divers feeding fish and entertaining people. This exhibit actually floats and you can't miss it in the water opposite the Parliament buildings, or from anywhere in the Inner Harbour for that matter.

Undersea Gardens, 490 Belleville Street, (250) 382–5717. Hours: winter 10:00 A.M.–5:00 P.M.; summer hours vary but generally 10:00 A.M.–10:00 P.M. Admission: adults $7.00, seniors $6.25, juniors twelve to seventeen $5.00, children five to eleven $3.50. Not wheelchair accessible. No rest rooms, but we suggest public washrooms in Coho Ferry Terminal west of the Royal London Wax Museum.

MINIATURE WORLD (649 Humboldt) is located at the north end of The Empress hotel. Billed as the "The Greatest Little Show on Earth" and "Little People's Wonderful World of Smallness," this is a terrific show for collectors and children of all ages. While the exhibit emphasizes historic war scenes, there is lots more to see.

Inside you can see "the world's smallest operational sawmill," which took eleven years to build; the "world's largest doll house," circa 1880, with fifty rooms furnished in unusually exquisite detail; and the great Canadian railway model as part of one of the world's largest model railways, which winds its way through replicas of Canada's ten provinces. Take in the Wonderful World of the Circus, including the Grand City Parade, Big Top, Wild Beasts, and "death-defying high wire acts." Guaranteed educational and fun entertainment.

❧ *Miniature World, 649 Humboldt Street, (250) 385–9731; Fax: (250) 385–2835; Web: www.miniatureworld.com. Hours: summer daily 8:30 A.M.– 9:00 P.M., winter 10:00 A.M.–5:00 P.M. Admission: adults $8.00, youths $7.00, children $6.00, families with three or more and seniors get 10 percent discount. Building, but not rest rooms, wheelchair accessible. Credit cards: Visa, MasterCard, American Express.*

If you're in the mood for shopping while in the area, you'll find several boutiques in the street level of The Empress, with their entrances on Humboldt Street. COLLECTIONS BY FIFTH AVENUE (II) is an elegant boutique that features the finest classic and up-to-date designs of Chanel, Bally, Valentino, Versace, Dunhill, Givenchy, and Longines.

❧ *Collections by Fifth Avenue (II), 651 Humboldt Street, (250) 382–3166. Hours: 9:00 A.M.–6:00 P.M. daily. Wheelchair accessible. Credit cards: MasterCard, Visa, enRoute, American Express, JCB.*

Fine points: There's a Currency Exchange nearby at 637 Humboldt Street.

At 633 Humboldt you'll find the classic CHARLES DICKENS PUB. This elegant English-style pub with cheerful dark decor features Canadian and British beers, whiskies, and prices lower than those in The Empress itself. Some locals hang out here. Live entertainment on weekends.

❧ *Charles Dickens Pub, 633 Humboldt Street, (250) 361–2600. Hours: 11:00 A.M.–midnight daily. Wheelchair accessible. Credit cards: Visa, MasterCard, American Express, enRoute, Diners.*

The nearby PESCATORE'S FISH HOUSE & GRILL is believed by some to be the finest fish restaurant in Victoria. It certainly is the most lively and hip in decor, ambience, staff, and creative cuisine. Diego Rivera/Frida Kahlo–style murals and paintings decorate the walls, huge fans hang from the ceiling and turn romantically slowly, and menus are available in Japanese, German, French, and English.

Pescatore's offers a set menu as well as ultra-fresh shellfish and other specials written on a blackboard over the bar. Those might include Prince Edward Island mussels, Queen Charlotte Island manilla clams, Nova Scotia deep-sea lobster, and Vancouver Island Dungeness crab—possibly the best in the world.

Try their blue-plate specials, which include for lunch such bargains as grilled red spicy salmon on exotic greens with grilled potatoes and blueberry salsa for $7.95.

The extensive excellent wine list is broken down by food groups. Yes, it makes sense. Look for what you are eating, and the wine lists suggests those most appropriate to accompany your food.

Pescatore's Fish House & Grill, 614 Humboldt Street (250–385–4512, Fax: 250–385–5562). Hours: summer 11:30 A.M.–11:00 P.M. Monday–Saturday, 5:00 P.M.–11:00 P.M. Sunday. Winter earlier closing. Wheelchair accessible. Credit cards: Visa, MasterCard, American Express, Diners.

JADE TREE, at 606 Humboldt, is the lease known deal shop in Victoria, possibly anywhere. It features British Columbia jade, all of which is mined from one mountain on northern Vancouver Island, and some of which is sent to China to be carved. The quality is high, and the prices are low, unbelievably so.

The Jade Tree also carries imported Chinese jade; rhodonite, a beautiful pink jadelike rock (scientifically manganese silicate); and hematite, a gunmetal-colored stone known as Alaska black diamond that is found in British Columbia, Quebec, Ontario, and Newfoundland. Jewelry made from these goodies makes great gifts to take home as B.C. souvenirs. Affordable for all of us.

Jade Tree, 606 Humboldt Street, (250) 388–4326. Hours: summer 10:00 A.M.–6:30 P.M., winter 10:00 A.M.–5:30 P.M., open at noon Sunday all year. Wheelchair accessible. Credit cards: Visa, MasterCard, American Express, enRoute.

SYDNEY REYNOLDS, on the corner right next door to the Jade Tree, is one of Victoria's best chinaware shops. Located ideally for tourists, it was originally a saloon in 1908, a bank in 1909, and became a shop in 1929. You can easily find several selections of teacups and saucers from $14.95, mint trays from $14.95, and Woodburns chocolates for only $1.25, as well as more expensive collectors' china, including Lomonosov porcelain dolls and St. Petersburg and Ukrainian dolls.

Sydney Reynolds, 801 Government Street, (250) 383–2081. Hours: 9:00 A.M.–9:00 P.M. Monday–Saturday, 10:00 A.M.–7:00 P.M. Sunday. Wheel-

ARMADILLO BARS
Barbara Housser of Sam's Deli, Victoria

Ingredients
⅔ cup Karo syrup
1 ice cream scoop honey
6 cups natural smooth peanut butter
14 cups Rice Krispies
chocolate chips

Preparation
Warm Karo syrup and honey and add to peanut butter. Add Rice Krispies and mix thoroughly with your hands. Press firmly into pan and cover with chocolate chips. Place in 325° F oven for four minutes. Spread the melted chocolate over the top somewhat evenly. Refrigerate. Don't overdo the chocolate chips on top, or the chocolate will crack when cut. This makes a large restaurant pan of squares. For less, just halve the recipe.

chair accessible. Credit cards: Visa, MasterCard, Carte Blanche, Diners. Japanese spoken.

The sidewalk tables at SAM'S DELI have the best view of the inner harbour at the lowest price in town, even though we hate to tell too many people this. Sam's friendly and gracious young staff begs you not to feed the birds that flitter in for your yummy crumbs.

Local businesspeople and government workers come here for daily lunch specials, chicken potpie, spinach lasagne with salad, or a half tuna sandwich with thick, chunky clam chowder, particularly in the winter when fewer visitors are around. We find the shrimp sandwich irresistible and unequaled anywhere. It's so big we share it, sometimes accompanied by a Caesar salad. It's a good 1.5 inches thick with shrimp, lettuce, alfalfa sprouts, avocado, tomato, and lettuce on brown, white, or rye, all for $6.00. Other usual deli meats are available, plus good Caesar salad, and bagels with lox. Try the asparagus sandwich, too.

Each sandwich is made as you order it at the counter, and the maker asks you ingredient by ingredient if you want that, a little more, teensy bit less, Dijon or regular mustard, on and on. The line might go all the way out into the street, but you and your sandwich are still special and the most important for now. How these servers retain their cool is beyond us. But then, they're Canadian.

Vancouver natives Bruce and Barbara Housser opened Sam's in 1976 and have been running it ever since. They find and employ the best of university students year-round, whether business warrants it or not, and we should support them for this sensitivity.

And it's a great place for a plain old cup of coffee and carrot cake at teatime. Indoor and outdoor seating. One of our favorite spots.

❧ *Sam's Deli, 805 Government Street, (250) 382–8424. Hours: Monday–Saturday 7:30 A.M. on, Sunday from 9:00 A.M. Wheelchair accessible. Rest rooms at back left, not the cleanest, but handy. Credit cards: Visa, MasterCard.*

CANADIAN IMPRESSIONS, 811 Government Street, offers a large range of Canadian products, including B.C. jade animals, weatherproof jackets and hats, umbrellas (great in an emergency), Canadian sweaters (we have bought four here over the years), gifts, and an interesting native art gallery upstairs on the balcony that wraps around the walls of the store. Most of the best native artists are represented here, including Roy Vickers, Joseph Wilson, Sue Colman, Danny Dennis, Peter Dawson, and Manuel Salazár. You can also buy English toffees, Scottish shortbread, maple syrup, smoked Pacific salmon, and even moccasins.

❧ *Canadian Impressions, 811 Government Street, (250) 383–2641. Hours: 8:00 A.M.–11:00 P.M. daily. Downstairs wheelchair accessible, but gallery not. Credit cards: Visa, MasterCard, American Express, Diners, JCB. Japanese spoken.*

SUPER SHIRTS is a pretty good Victoria souvenir shirt shop, featuring jackets, sweats, and T-shirts.

❧ *Super Shirts, 815 Government Street, (250) 383–6422. Hours: 8:00 A.M.–11:00 P.M. daily. Wheelchair accessible. Credit cards: Visa, MasterCard, American Express, JCB.*

TIMBER RIDGE ADVENTURE CLOTHING offers drool-over Koolah oilskin jackets with leather collars at $250.00, handsome Rennie country-plaid flannel shirts from $49.99 on sale; Banff jackets, handprinted shirts, and leather backpacks from $39.99. Don't miss the Kanata blankets from $65.00.

❧ *Timber Ridge Adventure Clothing, 817 Government Street, (250) 384–1897. Hours: 8:00 A.M.–11:00 P.M. daily. Wheelchair accessible. Credit cards: Visa, MasterCard, American Express, enRoute, JCB.*

Cross Courtney Street and continue up Government. You will notice several people trying to earn a living wearing sandwich boards painted with restaurant and pub ads at this corner. Humor them, please.

COPITHORNE & ROW—GIFTWARE MERCHANTS, at 901 Government Street, is a fine-china and crystal shop with affordable souvenirs as well as rare collectors' pieces including Empress hotel mugs, Dunoon mugs, Sheraton Simpson, St. George china, Irish Crest, Waterford, Wedgwood, and Herend. You can find English floral bone china mint trays starting at $9.95, delicate

COPITHORNE & ROW—VICTORIA'S OLDEST BRICK BUILDING

bone china roses from $5.95 or six for $25.00, and Ming Shu mugs featuring Chinese astrology designs.

Copithorne & Row will mail gifts and guarantee safe delivery. You do not pay until your purchase arrives safely. Imagine!

❧ *Copithorne & Row—Giftware Merchants, 901 Government Street, (250) 384–1722. Hours: 9:00 A.M.–9:00 P.M. daily except Sunday in summer, 9:00 A.M.–5:30 P.M. daily in winter. Sunday 9:30 A.M.–6:30 P.M. Wheelchair accessible, but it's a squeeze. Credit cards: Visa, MasterCard, American Express, JCB.*

The INDIAN CRAFT SHOPPE has the usual fairly inexpensive souvenir stuff, including authentic Cowichan sweaters (always look for the label that says AUTHENTIC COWICHAN SWEATER), aprons, spoons, Canadian maple leaf patches and decals, and soothing natural and native music on tape and CD. This is also the only store left where you can get those ridiculous little falling-snow globes.

Fine points: The Indian Craft Shoppe and Copithorne & Row occupy Victoria's first brick building, built in 1858 as a hotel. The Tudor facade is relatively new.

✤ *Indian Craft Shoppe*, 905 Government Street, (250) 382–3643. *Hours: summer 8:30 A.M.–9:00 P.M. daily, winter 9:00 A.M.–5:30 P.M. Wheelchair accessible. Credit cards: Visa, MasterCard, American Express, Diners, JCB.*

DOCKSIDE GIFTS caters more honestly to tourists and is one of Victoria's most "elegant" T-shirt shops for infants through adults, featuring souvenir Victoria designs as well as lots of shirts and tote bags with lovely, locally painted flower patterns, and fleece vests and jackets.

✤ *Dockside Gifts*, 907 Government Street, (250) 389–0995. *Hours: summer 8:00 A.M.–11:00 P.M., winter 9:30 A.M.–6:00 P.M. and until 9:00 P.M. Friday and Saturday. Wheelchair accessible. Credit cards: Visa, MasterCard.*

While somewhat visitor-oriented, STONE'S FINE JEWELLERY does lots of business with locals also. Their presentation and display of jewelry is most peaceful, elegant, and unpretentious, with something for everyone. Stone's features B.C. and Chinese jade, pink and gray stones, and fine fiery opals, as well as more expensive, quality jewels. Prices range from $29 to $18,000.

✤ *Stone's Fine Jewellery*, 911 Government Street, (250) 383–0062. *Hours: summer 8:00 A.M.–9:00 P.M., winter 9:00 A.M.–6:00 P.M. Wheelchair accessible. Credit cards: Visa, MasterCard, American Express, Diners, JCB. Japanese, French, and German spoken.*

If you are a chocolate fan, lover, junkie, or aholic, an absolute must-visit is ROGERS' CHOCOLATES. No question. Period. Particularly for the chocolate creams.

In business in Victoria for more than one hundred years, Rogers' chocolates have been enjoyed by various residents of both the White House and Buckingham Palace. Savor one of their fabulous chocolate creams, filled with a multitude of flavors from mandarin orange to peppermint, raspberry, coffee, or more chocolate, for just $2.50, tax included. They're big enough to share.

Rogers' products range from the creams and chocolate-coated ginger to Victoria truffles, creams miniatures, milk chocolate almond brittle, thin mints, candied nutcorns, and even dark and light (not meant as low-fat) fruit cakes. Available in combo packs, some with Murchie's teas and coffees, all can be ordered by mail. Once you get on the mailing list, you can join us in salivating over the pictures. They also guarantee shipment anywhere.

Fine points: The Queen Ann Revival–style Rogers Building is a heritage building designed in 1903 by architects Thomas Hooper and Edward Watkins under direction of Charles Rogers, the store's eccentric founder. A young gentleman, disguised as a classic beefeater, greets you and answers questions. Keep your eyes open for the resident ghost.

❧ *Rogers' Chocolates.* 913 Government Street (250–384–7021 or 800–663–2220; Fax: 250–384–5750). Web: www.islandnet.com/rogers; E-mail: rogers@islandnet.com. Hours: summer 9:00 A.M.–10:00 P.M. daily, winter 9:00 A.M.–9:00 P.M. Wheelchair accessible. Credit cards: Visa, MasterCard, American Express, Diners, JCB.

The EDINBURGH TARTAN SHOP, at 921 Government Street, is definitely the most elegant of Gidden Industries' shops. Edinburgh exudes Celtic elegance and ambience.

You can find Scottish family trees, names, coats of arms, and tartans. If they don't have yours, they can get it quickly. This is a life-enhancing experience, even if this heritage is not yours.

We love their tartan blankets at two for $150 (you have to buy both), charming English children's clothing, clan crests, Celtic jewelry, London Fog coats, Scottish tweeds, clan reference books, and everything else you could imagine connected with clans.

Fine points: The building dates from 1899, when it housed Victoria's largest department store.

❧ *Edinburgh Tartan Shop,* 921 Government Street, (250) 388–9312. Hours: 10:00 A.M.–6:00 P.M. Wheelchair accessible. Credit cards: Visa, MasterCard, American Express.

You will find a new experience at LUSH, a newly expanded branch of a successful English fresh, handmade cosmetics company that has turned this corner into a downtown hot spot. *Time Out* says "entering Lush is like having sex." Not so sure that's true, but the soothing aromas and spoons to scoop all-natural cosmetics into your own container or cutting off your own chunk of herbal soap do lead to romantic and self-indulging fantasies. Many of the products look, feel, and smell good enough to eat, or at least salivate over. Try Lush's Grass Roots shampoo, Lip Service, or the Bath Bombs. One of our favorites.

❧ *Lush,* 1001 Government Street, (250) 384–LUSH. Hours: 9:30 A.M.–6:00 P.M., Friday and Saturday until 7:00 P.M., Sunday 11:00 A.M.–6:00 P.M., open later in summer. Wheelchair accessible. Credit cards: Visa, MasterCard, American Express.

THE BOARDWALK features T-shirts galore and union made-in-Canada hats, ties, shortcake, and Harley-Davidson stuff.

❧ *The Boardwalk,* 1007 Government Street, (250) 389–1555. Hours: 9:00 A.M.–11:00 P.M. summer, 9:30 A.M.–6:00 P.M. winter. Wheelchair accessible. Credit cards: Visa, MasterCard.

AVOCA HANDWEAVERS, possibly our favorite store, has been creating nurturing, stylish fabrics in Ireland since 1723, and now they are available in Victoria, thank heavens, god, and goddess.

We walked in one day and mentioned to the proprietor that there must be a fire in the back. She replied that what we detected was a small piece of peat burning to remind us of that smell familiar throughout the Irish countryside. The scents, the clothes, the hats, posters, jewelry, brass door knockers, cookbooks, and walking sticks all take us back in heart and time.

We find some of the most beautifully feminine Irish women's clothing here, such as capes, coats, jackets and skirts, and men's Irish tweed jackets and hats, as well as handwoven mohair blankets and scarves. Waterproof coats and waxed cotton jackets run $99, and you can find authentic Aran knit sweaters here for $99—best price anywhere. A definite must.

Avoca Handweavers, 1009 Government Street, (250) 383–0433. Hours: summer 9:00 A.M.–9:00 P.M., Sunday 10:00 A.M.–8:00 P.M.; winter 9:00 A.M.–5:30 P.M., Sunday noon–5:00 P.M. Wheelchair accessible. Credit cards: Visa, MasterCard, American Express. French and Japanese spoken.

SOUVENIRS & GIFTS GALORE offers the usual visitor-oriented stuff, plus licorice of all sorts, mint Humbugs, plastic place mats, Precious Moments china figurines, nativity scenes, and Little Moments.

Souvenirs & Gifts Galore, 1013 Government Street, (250) 385–7123. Hours: summer 9:00 A.M.–10:30 P.M., winter 9:00 A.M.–6:00 P.M. Wheelchair accessible. Credit cards: Visa, MasterCard, American Express.

PICCADILLY SHOPPE, Victoria's most elegant T-shirt shop, stocks lots of University of Victoria (UVic) T-shirts and hats, as well as those of the Vancouver Canucks (hockey) and the Vancouver Grizzlies (basketball) teams.

Piccadilly Shoppe, 1017 Government Street, (250) 384–1288. Hours: 9:00 A.M.–10:00 P.M. daily, closes earlier in winter. Wheelchair accessible. Credit cards: Visa, MasterCard, American Express.

IRISH LINEN STORES, a traditional Irish linen store here since 1910, has almost too-Irish shamrock bow ties for $9.95, linen pincushions for $9.95, hankies, crocheted doilies and place mats, dainty white aprons, printed tea towels, and handwoven scarves. Irish Linen Stores and Avoca Handweavers complement each other.

Fine points: 1017 and 1019 Government Street are part of the Galpin Block, constructed in 1884.

❧ *Irish Linen Stores, 1019 Government Street, (250) 383–6812. Hours: summer 9:00 A.M.–7:00 P.M., winter 9:00 A.M.–5:30 P.M. Wheelchair accessible. Credit cards: Visa, MasterCard, American Express, JCB.*

Until recently, METRO-TODAY'S CLOTHING carried very jazzy/elegant sports clothes for women. It has now switched to catering to tourists and sells jazzy-colored, native design T-shirts, Mondetta clothes, and other souvenir shirts and Canadian products tourists might like. Metro still sells the Not-Yet-Famous Tilley Hat, the white-brimmed hat with brass studs you see all over Vancouver Island, particularly on the tennis court or cricket field, for $39.99, and Cuban hand-rolled cigars.

❧ *Metro-Today's Clothing, 1023 Government Street, (250) 386–0005. Hours: 9:00 A.M.–9:00 P.M., winter 9:00 A.M.–6:00 P.M. Wheelchair accessible from Government Street. Credit cards: Visa, MasterCard, American Express, Diners, Discover, JCB.*

EATON CENTRE, part of the huge Canadian chain, is a multilevel mall covering the entire block between Government, Fort, Douglas, and View Streets. The mall was built around Eaton's Department Store, which closed in 1999 and is supposed to reopen in November 2000 as a Sears-run version of Eaton's. This redevelopment project, completed in 1990, keeps the mall downtown. Eaton Centre houses 110 stores, some excellent and some predictable. On extremely rainy days it seems as if half of Victoria hangs out here.

Public rest rooms, elevators, and telephones are located on the ground floor, halfway between the Government and Douglas Street sides. If you enter from Fort Street, they are almost straight ahead.

There is also a newish government liquor store toward the eastern (Douglas Street) entrance near Pacific Coast Savings Credit Union.

Eaton Centre also has a food court that offers the usual sandwiches and hamburgers, plus Greek, Japanese, and Korean foods, and Smiths bookstores.

❧ *Eaton Centre, Fort, Douglas, and View Streets. Hours: 9:00 A.M.–9:00 P.M. Wheelchair accessible. Credit cards: acceptance varies by store.*

BRITISH IMPORTERS features elegant British men's clothing with standout labels of Kenneth Cole, Hugo Boss, Calvin Klein, Danbridge, and everything from tweeds to neon purple jackets, English shoes, and custom braces (suspenders).

❧ *British Importers, 1101 Government Street, (250) 386–1496. Hours: 9:30 A.M.–5:30 P.M. Monday–Saturday, noon–5:00 p.m. Sunday. Wheelchair accessible including ramp to lower level. Credit cards: Visa, MasterCard, American Express.*

The best thing about the ELEPHANT AND CASTLE is its ambience. Indoors it resembles an English pub with heavy upholstered chairs and wooden tables, and outside its cafe tables offer one of the best people-watching views in Victoria.

The bar is exceptional and serves fifty-five single malt Scotch whiskeys, one Welsh malt whiskey, fifty-eight imported beers, and six beers on draft.

Few locals go here, and the food is rather standard. The menu reads well, although the combinations of foods occasionally astound, like a Cajun Halibut Caesar Salad at $4.50 or the Teriyaki Beef Pasta Salad with soup for $6.75. Hamburgers and fries and fish and chips seem to work.

꙳ *Elephant and Castle, 100 Eaton Centre at Government and View Streets, (250) 383–5858. Hours: summer 11:00 A.M.–midnight or 1:30 A.M. on warm nights, winter 11:00 A.M.–9:00 P.M. Wheelchair accessible, with accessible rest room on level of Eaton Centre entrance. Credit cards: Visa, MasterCard, American Express, Diners, enRoute.*

AWear, a huge, jazzy, Gap-like British clothing chain recently moved into the marvelously cavernous Royal Bank building on Government between View Street and Trounce Alley, brings even more pizzazz to downtown, with local W. & J. Wilson, Polo Ralph Lauren, and Eddie Bauer all in the same block.

Cross View Street and continue on Government to W. & J. WILSON CLOTHIERS SINCE 1862. This wonderful and warm store, in an 1870s building that was renovated in 1912 as an example of Edwardian simplicity, has wood paneling and thick carpets and is the oldest family-owned clothing store in Canada. Tom and Kathy Thompson and Lisa and Scott are the current generations managing Wilson's, with the charm and delight that only proud family members can muster.

Mum goes to Europe and imports the clothes herself. Her taste is classic exquisite, and ranges from Geiger and Bianca from Germany to Castleberry and Rodier, Burberry and Mansfield coats, Tilley hats, and Cambridge and Austin Reed clothes.

It's a pleasure just to enter this store and experience its ambience. Then, surely, you will find something you must have.

Be sure to visit their new Adventure Clothing shop, featuring Liberty of London and Tilley Endurables, at Fort and Broad Streets, opposite the south side entrance to Eaton Centre.

꙳ *W. & J. Wilson Clothiers, 1221 Government Street, (250) 383–7177. Hours: 9:30 A.M.–5:30 P.M. Monday–Saturday, 11:00 A.M.–4:00 P.M. Sunday. Wheelchair accessible. Credit cards: Visa, MasterCard, American Express, JCB.*

Our handwriting is bad enough that our notes on the ELECTRIC JUICE BAR seem to read "Eclectic Juice Bar," which this fun veggie cafe/deli might also be called. You can get Seattle's Best Coffee, great grilled panini (sandwiches) for $4.00, low-fat muffins, bagel and cream cheese for $1.87, smoothies with no bad junk in them, vitamins, and good garden burgers. Humorous bright paintings decorate the bright yellow walls.

✦♿ *Electric Juice Bar, 1223 Government Street, (250) 380–0009. Hours: 7:30 A.M.–6:30 P.M. Monday–Saturday, 10:00 A.M.–5:00 P.M. Sunday. Wheelchair accessible, including rest room. Credit cards: Visa, MasterCard.*

ROCKY MOUNTAIN CHOCOLATE FACTORY is temptation central for candied apples covered with M&Ms and truffles as well as ice creams, gourmet gelato, sorbets made with intriguing ingredients, and homemade fudge.

✦♿ *Rocky Mountain Chocolate Factory, 1225 Government Street, (250) 382–8811. Hours: summer 10:00 A.M.–10:00 P.M., winter 10:00 A.M.–6:00 P.M. Wheelchair accessible. Credit cards: Visa, MasterCard, American Express.*

ROOTS, at 1227 Government Street, provided all those sleek-looking sports clothes for Canada's 1998 Winter Olympics athletes. It specializes in made-in-Canada sweat suits and other athletic clothing, denim, soft leather shoes and boots for adults and kids, and leather bags and jackets. New products include watches, yo-yos, and shirts with Asian and fake Asian script. In 1973 owners Don Green and Michael Budman designed a shoe called the "Negative Heel," like a sixties' earth shoe, for ultimate walking comfort. We have bought boots, sandals, and loafers here and find them, along with our Hush Puppies and Doc Martens, to be the most comfortable shoes we've ever worn. One of our favorites.

✦♿ *Roots, 1227 Government Street, (250) 383–4811. Hours: 9:30 A.M.–6:00 P.M. Monday–Saturday, noon–5:00 P.M. Sunday. Wheelchair accessible. Credit cards: Visa, MasterCard, American Express.*

SASQUATCH TRADING COMPANY LTD. offers an unusually good collection of Cowichan art crafts, including masks, and 1,500 genuine Cowichan sweaters bought directly from the reserve. You'll also find leather gloves, suede vests, slippers and moccasins, drums, carvings, and cowhide rugs.

✦♿ *Sasquatch Trading Company Ltd., 1233 Government Street, (250) 386–9033. Hours: summer 8:30 A.M.–9:00 P.M. daily, winter 8:30 A.M.–5:30 or 6:00 P.M. Wheelchair accessible. Credit cards: Visa, MasterCard, American Express, Diners, Carte Blanche, JCB.*

STREET fills the need for a hot teenagers' and early twenties' boutique with great back-to-school sales if you time it right. Fashion labels include Levi's, Ikeda, Guess, Big Star, Esprit, Razzy, Diesel, London's Pepe Jeans, and Joe Boxer shorts. ❧ *Street, 1241 Government Street, (250) 383–0424. Hours: summer 9:30 A.M.–9:00 P.M., winter 9:30 A.M.–6:00 P.M. Wheelchair accessible. Credit cards: Visa, MasterCard, American Express.*

Cross Yates Street and continue on Government to STARBUCKS COFFEE, large and comfortable, with reliable coffee.
Fine points: Erected in 1883 as Pritchard House, the building was completely remodeled in 1946 and was recently redone by Starbucks.
❧ *Starbucks Coffee, 1301 Government Street, (250) 383–4448. Hours: 7:00 A.M.–10:00 P.M. daily. Wheelchair accessible. Credit cards: Visa, MasterCard.*

Payless Shoes, the same everywhere, has moved in next to Starbucks.
PACIFIC TREKKING, 1305 Government Street, is one of the best places for people who walk, hike, and travel to find quality outdoor travel gear. This is an unusually welcoming and friendly store where you are greeted at the door, and there is an information counter to the right of the door where you can ask questions ranging from hiking trails and climate to the location of the nearest rest room. Novices are made to feel comfortable and brilliant. Even if you don't engage in active sports, check out the fabulous new colors of fleece and microfleece nightshirts.

Pacific Trekking's clothes are suited to serious outdoors activities or everyday wear. You will find a huge supply of Gore-Tex products (both sold and repaired here), tents, boots, a kids' room, an upstairs trail center, a great travel book selection, and entire rooms devoted to boat and rain gear. Assistance is available in every room.
Fine points: Watch for Pacific Trekking's Labor Day Rental Sale, at which is sold stuff that's been broken in by occasional users.
❧ *Pacific Trekking, 1305 Government Street, (250) 388–7088. Hours: 10:00 A.M.–6:00 P.M. Monday–Saturday, noon–5:00 P.M. Sunday. First floor is wheelchair accessible. Credit cards: Visa, MasterCard, American Express, JCB.*

THE GAP is The Gap is The Gap. The new Gap building filled a gap in this block and a clothing gap in Victoria. It has all the Gap clothes found in the United States, with slight emphasis on warmer clothes, for good reason. Gap Kids is upstairs. Great sales in August and September.

❧ *The Gap*, 1319 Government Street, (250) 920–9925. Hours: 9:30 A.M.–5:30 P.M. Monday–Wednesday, open until 9:00 P.M. Thursday–Saturday; 11:00 A.M.–5:00 P.M. Sunday. Downstairs (adults' clothing) accessible. Credit cards: Visa, MasterCard, American Express.

Christmas runs year-round at the ORIGINAL CHRISTMAS VILLAGE, where there is an emphasis on German and former Soviet Union national decorations like Ukrainian dolls and ornaments.

Owner Falk Reinhold, who imports directly and tries to keep prices low, seeks to blend the feel of Germany's Christkindl market with the charm of Victoria. While inside, you may feel as if you've taken a quick trip to Bavaria. *Fine points:* This store has an extremely strict policy with children, so read the many signs carefully to find out your responsibilities. The owners recommend that you plan thirty minutes to carefully tour the inside.

❧ *Original Christmas Village*, 1323 Government Street, (250) 380–7522. Hours: 9:00 A.M.–5:30 P.M. daily. Street floor is wheelchair accessible but crowded. Credit cards: Visa, MasterCard, American Express.

SA-NUU-KWA GALLERY offers a rare chance in downtown Victoria to watch native carvers at work and purchase west coast native art, sterling silver jewelry, handcarved memories, masks, prints, baskets, soapstone, and smoked salmon.

❧ *Sa-Nuu-Kwa Gallery*, 606 Johnson Street, (250) 480–5515. Hours: 10:00 A.M.–5:00 P.M. Monday–Saturday, noon–4:00 P.M. Sunday. Wheelchair accessible. Credit cards: Visa, MasterCard.

A sister boutique to the original in Vancouver, NICOLE ADRIENNE features fashionable dyed knitwear, much of which is made in Indonesia.

❧ *Nicole Adrienne*, 1327 Government Street, (250) 920–4246. Hours: 10:00 A.M.–6:00 P.M. daily, until 9:00 P.M. Friday; 2:00–6:00 P.M. Sunday. Wheelchair accessible. Credit cards: Visa, MasterCard.

Cross Government Street toward the west and walk down the other side, and you'll come to COWICHAN TRADING COMPANY, one of a group of privately owned stores that sells authentic Cowichan products. This one has the usual tourist souvenirs and some interesting additions, such as soapstones and an extensive choice of Cowichan sweaters, hats, masks, aprons, pot holders, as well as Canadian windsocks and native handcarvings. You can get Cowichan knitting wool for $7.50 (eight ounces) and rabbit pelts for less than $6.00.

⚘ *Cowichan Trading Company,* 1328 Government Street, (250) 383–0321. *Hours: summer* 9:00 A.M.–10:00 P.M. *daily, winter* 9:00 A.M.–5:30 P.M. *Sunday. Wheelchair accessible from two doorways. Credit cards: Visa, MasterCard, American Express, enRoute, JCB.*

Fine points: The building numbered 1316–1328 on Government Street was built between 1879 and 1888, originally in Victorian style, but later "modernized" with stucco.

BADGE KINGDOM, at 1322 Government, sells military memorabilia, as well as family or military crests; military posters; Canadian Mountie, U.S., and Canadian military uniforms; and historic sports and military patches from both the United States and Canada. The shop also does framing in the back.

⚘ *Badge Kingdom,* 1322 Government Street, (250) 385–7522. *Hours:* 9:30 A.M.–5:00 P.M. *Monday–Saturday; closed Sunday. Wheelchair accessible. Credit cards: Visa, MasterCard, American Express.*

We think KABOODLES is one of the most fun shops in Victoria. It's primarily a kids' toy store that appeals to grown-ups, and the skillful and artful displays tempt any age. Kites, windsocks, Legos, Gund bears, games, bubbles, stickers, Mr. Bean, and Brio goodies will lure you right in. We all need bubbles in our lives.

⚘ *Kaboodles,* 1320 Government Street, (250) 383–0931. *Hours: Monday–Tuesday* 9:30 A.M.–6:00 P.M., *Wednesday–Saturday* 9:30 A.M.–8:00 or 9:00 P.M., *Sunday* 11:00 A.M.–6:00 P.M. *Wheelchair accessible. Credit cards: Visa, MasterCard, American Express.*

ROBERTA'S HATS may be our favorite fun hat store anywhere. Young saleswomen wearing hats, natch, make you feel special and can always find a hat that's you. This is one hat store where you won't feel self-conscious.

Roberta's has everything from Australian Outback hats to berets and fake leopard skin, plus kids' hats. Don't let the men stand outside—they'll like this one, 'cause there's something for them, too. The ladies at Roberta's take hats seriously and do hat reblocking and cleaning, a rarity these days. "If you're not interested in purchasing a new hat, we can help your old one."

⚘ *Roberta's Hats,* 1318 Government Street, (250) 384–2788. *Hours: Monday–Saturday* 10:00 A.M.–5:30 P.M., *Sunday noon–5:00 P.M. Wheelchair accessible. Credit cards: Visa, MasterCard, American Express.*

SEED OF LIFE NATURAL FOODS is a small, good, solid natural foods store with a whole wall of vitamins and supplements, and some metaphysical books. *Seed of Life Natural Foods, 1316 Government Street, (250) 382–4343. Hours: 9:00 A.M.–6:00 P.M. Monday–Saturday, noon–5:00 P.M. Sunday. Wheelchair accessible. Credit cards: Visa, MasterCard.*

You will indeed have SWEET MEMORIES after trying Connie and Shukry Regep's goodies. The Regeps, who are originally from Michigan and Czechoslovakia, respectively, have developed a favorite spot of locals and visitors.

You can watch Connie baking waffle cones in the front window, after which you have to go in and see what else they have made: their own ice cream and frozen yogurt. The Regeps make such personalized flavors as tin roof, moose trader, turtle (caramel pecans and chocolate), caribou caramel (caramel ripple with chocolate caramel cups), orange creamsicle (remember 50/50s?), and chocolate banana.

There are no seats here. The best you can do is to lean your fanny against the brick windowsill in front or walk around with your treat.

Fine points: Sweet Memories has been voted the best yogurt and hard ice cream shop in Victoria by locals several times, and the building was originally part of the 1892 New England Hotel, designed by John Teague, architect of city hall. *Sweet Memories, 1312 Government Street, (250) 383–1312. Hours: summer noon–9:00 or 10:30 P.M. ("as long as there are people out there"), winter noon–5:30 P.M. Closed Christmas through February. Wheelchair accessible. Credit cards: none.*

COMMAND POST MILITARIA & ANTIQUES sells and pays cash for German and Nazi military paraphernalia and sells British and Canadian military and mounted police medals, along with patches, navy ship hats, uniforms, knives, and old flags. Since moving from a previous location it appears to be emphasizing antiques and dolls rather than the Nazi stuff although a sign in the window begs for German World War II supplies. Tells you somthing. *Command Post Militaria & Antiques, 1306 Government Street, (250) 383–4421. Hours: 9:00 A.M.–5:00 P.M. daily. Wheelchair accessible. Credit cards: Visa, MasterCard.*

FIELDS SHOES, recently expanded, is a great store for no-fuss, real work and cowboy boots for both workers and cowboys as well as for hip teens and others. Brands include Caterpillar, Boulet western boots, Ecco, Birkenstock, Timberland, motorcycle boots, and some belt buckles. Even men will like this store. It makes you want to touch the good-smelling leather.

Fine points: The building was erected in 1891 by the Canadian Pacific and designed by Thomas Hooper.

❧ *Fields Shoes, 1300 Government Street, (250) 388–5921. Hours: 10:00 A.M.–6:00 P.M. Monday–Saturday, closed Sunday. Wheelchair accessible. Credit cards: Visa, MasterCard.*

EDDIE BAUER has been at this Government Street location for more than seventy-seven years. A large, beautiful store for women and men, this Eddie Bauer has an annual special sale on backpacks in late August–early September— a good deal for school. Clothes and salespeople are typically friendly.

Fine points: The building was designed by Francis Rattenbury in 1897 for the Bank of Montreal and is a precursor of his Empress hotel design.

❧ *Eddie Bauer, 1254 Government Street, (250) 383–1964. Hours: 9:30 A.M.–9:00 P.M. Monday–Saturday, 9:30 A.M.–5:30 P.M. Sunday. Wheelchair accessible. Credit cards: Visa, MasterCard, American Express.*

TORREFAZIONE ITALIA, at 1234 Government, is an excellent, almost elegant coffee house perfectly wedged between Polo Ralph Lauren and Eddie Bauer. The outside tables—difficult to get in summer—are prized for people watching, and for coffee drinkers who smoke. This Torrefazione cafe recently was awarded four smiles by the on-line newsletter *Coffee Experts* in a two-way tie for the best coffee in Victoria and has just enjoyed redecoration in mauve and blue, creating a more subtle and darker atmosphere.

As you enter the cafe, you feel as if you are in modern Italy. The excellent coffee and friendly service combine with the sofas to the left, the cafe tables with their comfortable wooden chairs, and the country Italian pottery to create an ambience unmatched. Clean rest rooms, too.

Coffee and coffee beans are the main thrust here, although crisp biscotti, limited sweets, and terrific panini (from Italian Foods Imports on Blanshard) are gobbled by locals on the run. Lots of local business is transacted during coffee breaks here. Some days we've thought of staying all afternoon.

You simply approach the counter, give your order (which may also include orange or lemon San Pellegrino water), move to the right, and either wait or sit until your order is ready. Even a cup of decaf coffee is made individually, often by manager Italo Porcella himself, so patience here is a worthwhile virtue.

❧ *Torrefazione Italia, 1234 Government Street, (250) 920–7203. Hours: 7:00 A.M.–6:00 P.M. Monday–Thursday, 7:00 A.M.–9:00 P.M. Friday–Sunday. Wheelchair accessible. Credit cards: Visa, MasterCard.*

POLO RALPH LAUREN is a typically elegant Polo Ralph Lauren boutique with typically friendly Canadian staff and service. The cozy dark wood paneling on the walls makes you want to snuggle up and stay a while.

Fine points: Francis Rattenbury won the Bank of Montreal's building design competition with this chateau-style classic in 1897. It is a precursor of his Empress hotel design.

❧ *Polo Ralph Lauren, 1200 Government Street at the corner of Bastion Square (View Street), (250) 381–7656. Hours: 9:00 or 10:00 A.M.–6:00 P.M. Monday–Saturday, noon–5:00 P.M. Sunday. Not wheelchair accessible. Credit cards: Visa, MasterCard, American Express, JCB.*

Bastion Square, to the west of Government Street, is a pedestrian mall that connects to View Street east of Government.

At 50 Bastion Square, the nearby **RE-BAR** serves "modern [read healthy, vegetarian] cuisine" and is extremely popular with locals for its seasonal and regional cuisine at breakfast, including scrambled eggs or omelets between $8.00–$9.50, and at lunch for sandwiches or salads (and terrific quesadillas). Funky with wild colored walls, Re-Bar also has an excellent fresh juice bar featuring exotic fruit and vegetable juices, baked goods, Northwest's best coffees, dinner, and Sunday brunch, all cafeteria-style.

❧ *Re-Bar, 50 Bastion Square, (250) 361–9223. Hours: Monday–Thursday 7:30 A.M.–8:00 P.M., Friday until 9:30 P.M., Sunday 8:30 A.M.–3:30 P.M. Not wheelchair accessible. Credit cards: none. Beer and wine.*

At the **MARITIME MUSEUM OF BRITISH COLUMBIA**, 28 Bastion Square, you can see many interesting examples of the ships and discoveries that are important parts of British Columbia's history.

In the museum's cavernous halls you'll see a full-scale model of the stern of Captain Cook's ship; the dugout *Tilicum* with cabin and sail in which John Claus Voss sailed around the world from Oak Bay between 1901 and 1904; a model of the *Beaver;* a set of three chronometers; and *Trekka,* the smallest (20 feet, 6 inches) sailboat to circle the globe (1955–59). Maps, equipment, an 1847 photo of the Songhee war party, and a feast of other memorabilia delight history and maritime fans.

Fine points: Originally the Provincial Court House built in 1889 where the old city jail once stood and public hangings took place, this building, designed by H. O. Tiedman and Francis Rattenbury, became the Maritime Museum in 1965.

❧ *Maritime Museum of British Columbia, 28 Bastion Square, (250) 385–4222. Hours: 9:30 A.M.–4:30 P.M. Admission: adults $5.00, seniors older than sixty-five $4.00, students $3.00, children six to eleven $2.00, under six free, families $13.00. Wheelchair accessible. Credit cards: none.*

THE MISTY GARDEN RESTAURANT, tucked cozily off Bastion Square, is a charming new vegetarian restaurant featuring breakfast, lunch, and dinner. Owners Christine Spelling and Chef Mark Bailey fulfill their dream.

The Misty Garden Restaurant, 26 Bastion Square, (250) 381–2422. Hours: 9:00 A.M.–11:00 P.M. daily. Credit cards: none.

PARADISO DI STELLE, coffee bar serves great soups and sandwiches, homemade gelato, and baked goods. Outdoor seating with fabulous water view.

Paradiso di Stelle, 10 Bastion Square, (250) 920–7266. Hours: 7:00 A.M.–5.00 P.M. Monday–Friday, 8:00 A.M.–5:00 P.M. Saturday, and 9:00 A.M.–5:00 P.M. Sunday. Credit cards: Visa and MasterCard.

Stroll down the rest of Bastion Square toward the stairs, and then we'll bring you back up the south side.

Notice Burnes House, 18–26 Bastion Square, which was built in 1887 as a reputable hotel. It also served as a brothel and a warehouse.

LIQUID, 15 Bastion Square, formerly known as Harpo's and The Planet, is a Victoria musical landmark where Jimi Hendrix, B. B. King, Jann Arden, Jeff Healey, and the Crash Test Dummies have all performed. Live local and touring bands Sunday–Wednesday, DJs Thursday–Saturday.

ENTRANCE TO BASTION SQUARE AT GOVERNMENT STREET

Fine point: This is the oldest steel-framed building in Victoria.

➷ *Liquid,* 15 Bastion Square, (250) 385–5333. Hours: 9:00 P.M.–2:00 A.M. weekdays, 8:00 P.M.–2:00 A.M. Friday–Saturday, 8:00 P.M.–midnight Sunday. Not wheelchair accessible. Credit cards: Visa, MasterCard, American Express.

ANTHONY'S OLD TIME PORTRAITS is back to offer lots of fun if you want to dress up in old-timey costumes for a quickie photo—ready in five minutes. You can fulfill a fantasy of looking like a gangster or moll, pioneer, Charlie Chaplin, R. C. M. P., or a Victorian lady or gentleman.

➷ *Anthony's Old Time Portraits,* 19 Bastion Square, (250) 383–2290. Hours: noon–6:00 P.M. daily. Credit cards: Visa, MasterCard.

Robyn Burton's DIG THIS—GIFTS AND GEAR FOR GARDENERS, below street level at 45 Bastion Square, is an original gardeners' paradise with plants, soil, nutrients, quality tools, and garden furniture. With a slogan of "adopt a plant," the fun staff also sells raucous gardeners' T-shirts. With a horticulturist on duty, Dig This offers complete support service for city gardeners. And from this therapy a beautiful plant grows!

Fine points: Upstairs in the law chambers building the public is welcome to view historic photos in the hall. The Architectural Institute of British Columbia has offices in suite 203 and runs architectural walking tours. The building, a Francis Rattenbury product, was built in 1901 to provide law offices across the street from the courthouse.

➷ *Dig This—Gifts and Gear for Gardeners,* 45 Bastion Square, (250) 385–3212. Hours: Monday–Saturday 9:30 A.M.–5:30 P.M., Sunday noon–5:00 P.M. Not wheelchair accessible. Credit cards: Visa, MasterCard.

CAMILLE'S FINE WEST COAST DINING, below 45 Bastion Square, offers a splendid dining experience featuring local crab cakes, duck confit, filet of salmon at $19.00 and rack of lamb at $25.00. David Mincey and Paige Robinson have earned an international reputation for elegant dining in a warm setting. We prefer the entry-level room, surrounded by wine bottles. The staff's wine knowledge is excellent, and the desserts are worth succumbing to.

➷ *Camille's Fine West Coast Dining,* below 45 Bastion Square, (250) 381–3433. Hours: dinner 5:30 P.M.–10:00 P.M. Not wheelchair accessible. Credit cards: Visa, MasterCard, American Express. Fully licensed.

GARRICK'S HEAD PUB, an old-fashioned British-style pub, is part of the Bedford Hotel, with patio tables facing Bastion Square. Sandwiches, meat pies, hamburgers, fish and chips, and daily specials comprise Garrick's better-than-usual pub grub, mostly less than $8.00. Great variety of ales and beers. Friendly and fun hangout. *Fine point:* The 1885 building was originally the law office of B.C. premier Theodore Davie (B.C. Premier 1892–1895).

❧ *Garrick's Head Pub, 69 Bastion Square, (250) 384–6835. Hours: Monday–Tuesday 11:00 A.M.–11:00 P.M., Wednesday–Saturday 11:00 A.M.–1:00 A.M., Sunday 10:00 A.M. –10:00 P.M. Wheelchair accessible through Bedford Hotel. Credit cards: Visa, MasterCard, American Express.*

Go up around the corner of Government Street and to the right into **Breeze**, a hip, popular clothing store featuring sample sales, Esprit clothes, watches, sunglasses, good deals on Hush Puppies shoes in several colors, Unlisted bags, Calvin Klein, and Hot Sox. This place is always busy with local and visiting young and young at heart.

❧ *Breeze, 1150 Government Street, (250) 383–8871. Hours: summer 10:00 A.M.–10:00 P.M. Monday–Saturday, noon–8:00 P.M. Sunday; winter 10:00 A.M.–6:00 P.M. Monday–Saturday, noon–6:00 P.M. Sunday. Wheelchair accessible. Credit cards: Visa, MasterCard, American Express.*

SESAME-CITRUS DRESSING

David Mincey of Camille's Fine West Coast Dining, Victoria

Some of the ingredients are available at import and specialty food shops.

Ingredients

½ cup fresh orange juice concentrate

1 cup lime juice

½ cup Balsamic vinegar

½ cup brown sugar

2 tbsp. Ketjap Manis

1 tsp. Sambal Oelek

1 tbsp. grainy Dijon mustard

¼ cup chopped cilantro

2 tbsp. sesame oil

¼ cup soy sauce

3 cups olive oil

Preparation

Blend all ingredients in a blender except olive oil. When blended, slowly add oil to mixture while blending some more, until thick.

Note from David: "This does make a lot of dressing, but it keeps for weeks in the fridge. We use this in our famous Warm Duck Salad, tossed with baby greens, fresh ginger, orange segments, and hot confit of duck. It works with many types of salad—try with fresh tomatoes, shrimp or pan-seared scallops, bacon, bell peppers, etc."

The **Bedford Regency Hotel**, at 1140 Government Street, with claims of being one of the great "Small Luxury Hotels of the World," is situated in the middle of everything, with a whale-watching tour service at the entrance. All rooms have goose-down comforters and complimentary coffee, and most have Jacuzzi tubs, double-headed showers, and woodburning fireplaces (See "Where to Stay").

The Bedford's restaurant serves breakfast (included with room), lunch, dinner, and sumptuous buffets, as well as daily afternoon tea year-round.

Bedford Regency Hotel, 1140 Government Street, (250) 384–6835. Hours: Hotel, twenty-four hours; Garrick's Head Pub, 11:00 A.M.–11:00 P.M. Wheelchair accessible through Government Street entrance only. Credit cards: Visa, MasterCard, American Express. Fully licensed.

Elegant **OLD MORRIS TOBACCONIST**, purveyors of "smokers requisites since 1892," sells Cuban cigars, both those made totally in Cuba and those made in Canada from Cuban tobacco. Americans who may or may not believe in doing business with Cuba flock to this store to buy what is contraband in their country.

Old Morris also sells house blends, private blends, and personal blends (at your request), as well as a fine selection of pipes for all seasons.

As you enter the shop, notice the burning flame in the center of the room, and don't walk into it. Green tile floors, a heavy wood look, toy airplane mobiles, a portrait of Queen Elizabeth behind the cash register, and English chocolates all combine to give you a unique experience.

Even if you, like us, do not endorse the use of tobacco in any form, you might want to visit this store just to see the well-preserved architecture. There's also a good variety of newspapers available at the door.

Fine points: Built in 1882, the building was redesigned by Thomas Hooper in 1909 to provide founder E. A. Morris with Edwardian "res- trained elegance."

GREEN CURRY
David Mincey of Camille's Fine West Coast Dining, Victoria

Ingredients

  3 bunches cilantro, leaves only

  4 large shallots

  1 oz. fresh ginger, peeled

  10 small cloves garlic

  3 tbsp. soy sauce

  2 tbsp. lemon juice

  ½ lb. fresh basil

  1 tbsp. cumin

  2 medium jalapeños, seeded

  4 cans coconut milk

Preparation

Puree all ingredients in food processor until fine. Add mixture to the coconut milk in pot and whisk well. Reduce by half over medium heat.

Note from David: "We use this sauce in our claypot dish with grilled seafood, Shanghai noodles, and Asian greens. It also makes a great pasta sauce or sauce for prawns, chicken, or any vegetarian stir-fry."

❧ *Old Morris Tobacconist, 1116 Government Street, (250) 382– 4811. Hours: 9:00 A.M.–6:00 P.M. daily, Friday until 9:00 P.M., Sunday noon–5:00 P.M. summer. Wheelchair accessible. Credit cards: Visa, MasterCard, American Express.*

In business since 1894, MURCHIE'S TEA AND COFFEE at 1110 Government, with a tea and coffee store next door where you can buy tins and gift packages, is the ultimate tea destination of British Columbia. You can rely on Murchie's to sell the best of everything. We take many late afternoon rests and sustenances here, preferably at the outdoor tables if the weather allows.

In the tearoom you can enjoy everything from orange or currant scones with clotted cream and jam to sandwiches, salads, and daily specials such as vegetarian or meat lasagna. Biscotti and special teatime-size sweets and tarts tempt locals as well as visitors. Espresso drinks and a full range of teas, including a few decaffeinated, warm the soul. Murchie's does not sell decaf coffee, although it claims its coffee has only 30 percent of the caffeine of regular coffee.

Here's the routine: You stand in line to place your order; don't be discouraged, the line moves fast. There's a second line at the far end of the counter. Go directly there. If you are in a hurry, try the ready-made tuna, egg salad, or turkey sandwiches priced at less than $6.00. The Greek salad is especially good.

Local ladies often come for their afternoon tea and sit on the mezzanine (two steps up), while visitors like to people-watch at the front. An extremely friendly staff enhances your experience. Get on the mailing list. Rest rooms are excellent and are downstairs at the back of the tearoom. Turn left at the bottom of the stairs.

Fine points: The 1907 building, designed by William R. Wilson, is beautifully preserved.

❧ *Murchie's Tea and Coffee, 1110 Government Street, (250) 383–3112. Hours: 7:30 A.M.–7:00 P.M. Monday–Wednesday, 7:30 A.M.–9:00 P.M. Thursday–Friday, and 8:00 A.M.–6:00 P.M. Saturday–Sunday. Partly wheelchair accessible (rest rooms wheelchair accessible from Langley Street). Credit cards: Visa, MasterCard.*

MUNRO'S BOOKS, 1108 Government Street, is a book lovers' heaven, plain and simple. The heritage building's warm, hardwood floors immediately set the quiet tone for what's ahead: the ultimate book experience. Even if you rarely buy books, come on in here, and you will love it.

Special large sections featuring Canadiana, Victoria, and Vancouver Island are to the left of the door; cooking and travel are farther back on the left; and a fantastic children's reading room hides at the left back. Politics, philosophy, and everything else work their way up the right side of the store. This is a great place to pick up Canadian cookbooks.

MUNRO'S BOOKSTORE AND MURCHIE'S TEA AND COFFEE ON
GOVERNMENT STREET

Owner James Munro is usually there working alongside the staff. A leading figure in Victoria known for his generous support of the arts, historic
preservation, and the environment, he treats his staff and books as gently and
respectfully as he does the environment.

Be sure to notice Carole Sabiston's fabulous banners hanging on the walls,
the larger of which are titled *The Four Seasons Suite.* Carole's textile assem-
blages appear throughout Canada, the United States, and the United
Kingdom. She is a member of the Royal Canadian Academy of Arts and
recently received the prestigious Saidye Bronfman Award for excellence in the
arts. In 1992 she received the order of British Columbia. Coincidentally, she
is married to Jim Munro.

Terrific sale tables occupy the center of the store toward the back. We always
find something irresistible here.

Fine points: The building was designed by Thomas Hooper and built as the
Royal Bank in 1909–10. When James Munro renovated it in 1984, he uncov-
ered and retained the original plaster ceiling.

❧ *Munro's Books,* 1108 *Government Street,* (250) 382–2464 *or* (888) 243–2464; *Fax:* (888) 382–2832. *E-mail: munrobooks@ampsc.com. Hours: 9:00 A.M.– 6:00 P.M. Monday– Wednesday, 9:00 A.M.–9:00 P.M. Thursday–Saturday, 11:00 A.M.–5:00 P.M. Sunday. Wheelchair accessible, although ramp is a little steep. Credit cards: Visa, MasterCard, American Express, JCB.*

JAMES BAY TRADING COMPANY, 1102 Government Street, is a somewhat upscale souvenir shop with attractive sweaters, leathers, slippers, caps, and much more. Leather fanny packs start at $50, ladies leather gloves at $59, indigo leather backpacks at $260, and beautiful Cowichan-style blue or green and beige sweaters at $177. Check out the duck decoys and native jewelry, as well as packaged smoked salmon, maple sugar, and film.
Fine point: James Bay is housed in the Lascelles-Southgate Building erected in 1869, with the second story and tower added in 1887.
❧ *James Bay Trading Company,* 1102 *Government Street,* (250) 388–5477. *Hours: 9:30 A.M.–10:00 P.M. Monday–Saturday, 9:30 A.M.–8:00 P.M. Sunday. Wheelchair accessible. Credit cards: Visa, MasterCard, American Express, JCB.*

The SPIRIT OF CHRISTMAS is Victoria's most elegant Christmas store. Even for those who don't dote over Christmas ornaments and decorations, it's a real treat to walk in here. We dreaded it and then found ourselves walking around saying, "Wow, look at this!" and similar smart remarks.
Everything Christmas is available here, from playing cards to wind chimes and ornaments. You can watch handpainting of ornaments in the back and have personalized rubber stamps made.
Fine points: This heritage building was the first school in British Columbia. Later, in 1856, the legislative assembly met here.
❧ *Spirit of Christmas,* 1022 *Government Street,* (250) 385–2501. *Hours: summer 9:30 A.M.–9:00 P.M. daily, winter 9:30 A.M.–6:00 P.M. Wheelchair accessible. Credit cards: Visa, MasterCard, American Express.*

SEEING IS BELIEVING recently moved here from Eaton Centre with its load of tourist-oriented, whimsical "possible gifts for impossible people." You will find car dice, games, wild lamps, Ravesburger puzzles, and Pokémon shirts.
Fine points: Between 1885 and 1987 this was the Bank of British Columbia, designed by Warren Williams, architect of the Dunsmuir Craigdarroch Castle. Famed poet Robert Service ("The Shooting of Dan McGrew") once worked for the bank and lived upstairs.

❧ *Seeing Is Believing,* 1020 Government Street, (250) 382–8578. Hours: 9:00 A.M.–9:00 P.M. daily. Not wheelchair accessible. Credit cards: Visa, MasterCard, American Express.

DESIGNERS INTERNATIONAL BY MADISON AVENUE may move next door but still carries fine ladies' furs, leathers, silks, watches, and accessories from Versace, Fendi, Chloe, Bally, Yves St. Laurent, and Cartier. This building dates from 1890. ❧ *Designers International by Madison Avenue,* 1010 Government Street, (250) 384–2435. Hours: summer 9:30 A.M.–10:00 P.M., winter 9:30 A.M.–5:30 P.M. Wheelchair accessible. Credit cards: Visa, MasterCard, American Express.

MOOSE has thousands of hilarious and prank magnets, glow-in-the-dark stuff, and R. C. M. P. (Royal Canadian Mounted Police) collectibles. ❧ *Moose,* 1010 Government Street, (250) 381–9945. Hours: summer 9:00 A.M.–11:00 P.M. daily; winter 10:00 A.M.–6:00 P.M. Sunday–Thursday, 10:00 A.M.–8:00 P.M. Friday–Saturday. Wheelchair accessible. Credit cards: Visa, MasterCard, American Express, JCB.

HILL'S INDIAN CRAFTS has a marvelous collection of truly authentic First Peoples' crafts, wood arts, drums, and colorful shirts, which make fabulous gifts. The sales staff is knowledgeable and answers dumb questions graciously, thank heavens. ❧ *Hill's Indian Crafts,* 1008 Government Street, (250) 385–3911. Hours: summer 9:00 A.M.–9:00 P.M., winter 9:00 A.M.–5:30 P.M. Wheelchair accessible. Credit cards: Visa, MasterCard, American Express, JCB.

ARTINA'S JEWELLERY is an exquisite gallery shop of tasteful native and British Columbia silver and jewelry and whimsical, colorful ceramic necklaces by Libby Nicholson. ❧ *Artina's Jewellery,* 1002 Government Street, (250) 386–7000. Hours: 9:30 A.M.–5:30 P.M. daily. Wheelchair accessible. Credit cards: Visa, MasterCard, American Express, JCB.

BEAR RIVER is another good tourist souvenir shop with stuffed bears and animals, souvenir and nature shirts, hats, mugs, maple syrups, and other local products. ❧ *Bear River,* 1000 Government Street, (250) 361–9900. Hours: 9:00 A.M.–9:00 P.M. daily. Wheelchair accessible. Credit cards: Visa, MasterCard, American Express.

BIG DOGS offers kids, adults, and big-size active wear featuring the Big Dogs logo.

❧ *Big Dogs, 910 Government Street, (250) 361–4244. Hours: 9:30 A.M.–5:30 P.M. Monday–Thursday, 9:30 A.M.–8:00 P.M. Friday, 11:00 A.M.–5:00 P.M. Sunday, later weekend evenings in summer.*

ISLAND SPIRIT sells some of the best quality souvenirs in town. Once called Beautiful British Columbia, this shop is now locally owned and has disposable cameras, candles, real Butchart Gardens calendars and books in several languages, the ever-present sweat clothes, and interesting British Columbia jade.
❧ *Island Spirit, 910 Government Street, (250) 281–3711, Fax: (250) 381–4430. Hours: 8:30 A.M.–6:00 or 9:00 P.M. Wheelchair accessible. Credit cards: Visa, MasterCard, American Express.*

Right next door to their Island Shop, Maria Chambers's and Chellan Clark's TIGER SHOP offers "nonfiction sweats," including UVic sweats, usually at a discount. T-shirts, too.
❧ *Tiger Shop, 910 Government Street, (250) 381–4241. Hours: summer 8:30 A.M.–10:00 P.M. daily, winter 8:00 A.M.–6:00 P.M. Wheelchair accessible. Credit cards: Visa, MasterCard, American Express.*

WEST PACIFIC TRADERS is a new, high quality, and pleasant souvenir shop down some stairs below sidewalk level with lots of the usual, plus Rogers' chocolates, Tilley hats (you must have one), and cold drinks.
❧ *West Pacific Traders, corner of Government and Courtney, (250) 381–4001. Hours: summer 8:00 A.M.–11:00 P.M., winter 9:00 A.M.–9:00 P.M. Not wheelchair accessible. Credit cards: Visa, MasterCard, American Express, Discover, JCB, Diners.*

Even devotees of Pagliacci's cheesecake like the CHEESECAKE CAFE. A new family restaurant upstairs has a full-range menu from pastas to burgers, fish and chips, beautifully displayed sweets, seafood, and salads. It has a new reputation as good and reliable, despite plastic menus.
❧ *Cheesecake Cafe, corner of Government and Courtney, (250) 382–2253. Hours: Monday–Thursday 11:00 A.M.–midnight, Friday–Saturday 11:00 A.M.–1:00 A.M., Sunday 10:00 A.M.–11:00 P.M., Sunday brunch 10:00 A.M.–2:30 P.M. Not wheelchair accessible. Credit cards: Visa, MasterCard, American Express.*

Cross Courtney and continue south on Government to GRABBAJABA FINE COFFEE, a locally popular cafe to grab a cup of java. Coffeepots labeled with the day's special blends are set on hot plates for you to serve yourself. You can also find an iced mocha, because Grabbajaba is on the shady side of Government Street.

❧ *Grabbajaba Fine Coffee, 816 Government Street, (250) 388–3770. Hours: summer 7:30 A.M.–midnight, winter 7:30 A.M.–7:30 P.M. Wheelchair accessible, but rest room is not. Credit cards: none.*

You can see into the windows on Government of the subterranean CUSTOM HOUSE ART GALLERY, but the entrance is actually on Wharf, at the corner opposite the Tourism Victoria Information Centre. Down a few stairs you will find mass-produced art replicas, posters for all tastes, and woodwork.
Fine points: You will find a handy mailbox located outside the Custom House Gallery on Government and a public telephone across the street in front of Sam's.
❧ *Custom House Art Gallery, 811A Government Street or 801 Wharf, (250) 381–1022. Hours: 9:00 A.M.–6:00, 9:00, or 11:00 P.M. Not wheelchair accessible. Credit cards: Visa, MasterCard, American Express.*

If you are in need of immediate sustenance, feet rest, a fancy drink, or a meal slightly more elegant than Sam's Deli, cross Humboldt with the light to MILESTONE'S. While this restaurant has one of the absolute best views in Victoria, it even has excellent food and young local staff. Amazing!
Popular with locals as well as visitors, this is the ultimate umbrella-drink spot in town. Horrendous pink and orange alcoholic margaritas or daiquiris and Long Island or Eclectic iced tea snow cones come in actual fish bowls, usually with more than one straw.
Milestone's specializes in tasty pastas ($7.95 and up) and salmon but also has burgers ($6.25), salads, and daily specials.
The outdoor cafe downstairs (open only in warm months) is right on the Inner Harbour Causeway facing the Empress Hotel and Parliament buildings, and it costs slightly less than the upstairs dining room. We have been extremely happy with their very local fish and huge chips ($8.95) and a Caesar salad ($4.95; with chicken or shrimp, add $2.95), splitting both. Not your healthy meal prize, but great fun.
❧ *Milestone's, 812 Wharf Street, (250) 381–2244. Hours: Monday–Thursday 11:00 A.M.–10:00 P.M., Friday 11:00 A.M.–11:00 P.M., Saturday 10:00 A.M.–11:00 P.M., Sunday 9:00 A.M.–10:00 P.M. including brunch. Dining room not wheelchair accessible, but downstairs cafe on the Causeway is, from Wharf Street. Credit cards: Visa, MasterCard, American Express, Diners. Fully licensed.*

A stroll along WHARF STREET's 5 short blocks can fill a whole morning or afternoon, or you can just cover a few blocks and get the flavor (although you might miss some of the colorful shops). We'll take you up the east side of the street and then back down the water side.

NAUTICAL NELLIES RESTAURANT & OYSTER BAR is a surprisingly good tourist-oriented restaurant with an excellent fillet of salmon burger or halibut clubhouse ($9.98) including soup or salad, pastas, burgers, oyster shooters in vodka and Tabasco ($3.98), aged steaks from $14.28 to $28.98, whole Dungeness crab ($26.78), and Nova Scotia lobster ($29.98). The view of the Inner Harbour is terrific from here.

❧ *Nautical Nellies Restaurant & Oyster Bar, 1001 Wharf Street at Broughton, (250) 380–2260. Hours: winter 11:00 A.M.–10:30 P.M., summer till 11:30 P.M. Fully licensed. Wheelchair accessible. Credit cards: Visa, MasterCard, American Express.*

House of Traditions, at 1111 Wharf Street (250–361–3020), offers a near-fantasy collection of lace gowns of all kinds, as well as dolls. Soon you will walk by a heritage building of the Ministry of Small Business, Tourism & Culture Discover British Columbia, 1117 Wharf Street (250–356–6363).

The VICTORIA BUG ZOO is a budding biologist's heaven offering live weird little things called insects to look at while learning sustainable respect for tiny animals. All the insects, including scorpions, millipedes, tarantulas, African beetles, and Australian walkingsticks, are behind glass. An entomologist will answer your questions gently

---

CHOCOLATE-COVERED TARANTULAS
*Carol Maier,
President/Owner/
Entomologist, Victoria
Bug Zoo*

Ingredients

8 squares semisweet baker's chocolate

2 cups chow mein noodles

1 cup mini-marshmallows

½ cup nuts, sliced or chopped

½ cup raisins

¼ cup coconut, shredded

Preparation

Carol Maier describes how to prepare her recipe: "Melt chocolate in a saucepan on the kitchen range or in an appropriate-size bowl in a microwave set on medium. Gentle heat is recommended. While the chocolate is melting, mix the other ingredients together. When the chocolate is thoroughly melted, pour it over the other stuff and stir gently to coat everything with chocolate.

"Spoon tarantula-size globs (for want of a better term) onto a cookie sheet or a sheet of wax paper. Lubricating the cookie sheet with a little cooking oil might help prevent sticking but isn't really necessary. The individual portions should be about the size of the body of a young adult *Brachypelma smithi*.

"In cool climates they can be left to cool at room temperature, but in warmer climates they should be placed in the refrigerator until hard."

and knowledgeably. Delilah the yellow mantis keeps owner Carol Maier company at the front desk. You can also buy unique gifts such as fake tatoos, posters, books, jewelery, and specialty honeys here. One of our favorites.
❧ *Victoria Bug Zoo, 1107 Wharf Street, (250) 384–2847. Hours: 9:30 A.M.–5:30 P.M. Monday–Saturday, 11:00 A.M.–5:30 P.M. Sunday. Wheelchair accessible. Credit cards: Visa, MasterCard, American Express.*

A new branch of the KEG STEAKHOUSE & BAR, this one is elegant and offers great, slightly expensive steaks cooked to perfection from blue rare to "Chicago style," pastas, and salads. A few outdoor tables have been added to take advantage of the spectacular Inner Harbour view.
Fine points: Just up the block from Keg are J. R.'s India Curry House, Siam Thai, and Koto Japanese restaurants, offering interesting ethnic alternatives in case the steak house doesn't appeal to you.
❧ *Keg Steakhouse & Bar, 500 Fort Street at Wharf, (250) 386–7789. Hours: 4:30–10:30 P.M. Fully licensed. Partly wheelchair accessible. Credit cards: Visa, MasterCard, American Express.*

D'ARCY MCGEES finally answers Victoria's need for an Irish pub, somewhat jazzed up that it is. Sharing that fabulous Inner Harbour view, D'arcy McGees offers Irish and Canadian beers and ales, Irish pub grub, and the required fish and chips. Music on weekends.
❧ *D'arcy McGees, 1127 Wharf Street, (250) 380–1322, Fax: (250) 380–1335. Hours: 11:00 A.M.–10:00 P.M. weekdays, till midnight weekends. Fully licensed. Wheelchair accessible. Credit cards: Visa, MasterCard, American Express.*

Garlic lovers' delights at the GARLIC ROSE range from breakfast—muffins ($1.50), omelets ($6.50), and waffles ($5.95)—to burgers (including the Garlic Rose with garlic and herbs for $6.50), and salads, pizzas, shellfish, Mediterranean spiced fish, kabobs, and steaks. There's also a full vegetarian menu.
Owner Moses Hanna has lived in forty countries and now says he has settled in heaven—Victoria. You get lots of food, no matter what you order. Service is sometimes slow and nonchalant. Superb view from outside tables in good weather.
Fine points: From here to 1213 Wharf Street is the Reid Block, completed in 1863.
❧ *Garlic Rose, 1205 Wharf Street, (250) 384–1931. Hours: summer 8:30 A.M.–midnight or so, winter 8:30 A.M.–10:00 P.M. Wheelchair accessible. Credit cards: Visa, MasterCard. Fully licensed.*

CHRISTMAS HOUSE, at 1209 Wharf, feels like Christmas at home instead of glitz. As you walk in you see a basket of stuffed bears on the floor with a sign that reads: WANTED: GOOD HOMES FOR WELL-BEHAVED BEARS, LYN-D-ZINE'S BORN IN VICTORIA BEARS MADE FROM RECYCLED FUR COATS, ALL HOUSE TRAINED. They're $75 and worth it.

Here in Victoria's oldest Christmas store, you can also get locally handcrafted Christmas stockings and ornaments quite reasonably, a collector's set of four 4-foot Dickens carolers for only $795, Department 56 village figures, Christopher Radko glass, hand-crafted Canadian collectibles, a whole display of Frosty Frolic Land in the corner, as well as Christmas music CDs and tapes. Most inviting of all is the old English chair near the door "for tired shoppers."

❧ *Christmas House, 1209 Wharf Street, (250) 388–9627. Hours: summer 9:30 A.M.–9:00 P.M. daily, winter 9:30 A.M.–5:30 P.M. Wheelchair accessible. Credit cards: Visa, MasterCard, American Express.*

FAST FRAMES is a poster and print shop that specializes in those and in quick framing so you can take your prize home framed. It's fun to walk in and browse.

❧ *Fast Frames, 1213 Wharf Street, (250) 383–4212. Hours: 9:30 A.M.–5:30 P.M. Wheelchair accessible. Credit cards: Visa, MasterCard.*

TATTOO ZOO, next door, specializes in piercing and tattooing of all kinds. Several binders of plastic-coated pages allow you to select a design if you don't have your own. Options range from native to Celtic (which amazingly resemble each other) plus lots of hooded sweats and T-shirts. Personal note: We were treated with respect and politeness by the young staff.

❧ *Tattoo Zoo, 1215 Wharf Street, (250) 361–1952. Hours: 11:00 A.M.–6:00 P.M. Monday–Saturday, noon–4:00 P.M. Sunday. Wheelchair accessible. Credit cards: Visa, MasterCard.*

For a quick lunch, snack, or dinner, try LOLA'S PIZZA. This hip pizza place offers vegetarian options, pizza by the slice, delivers whole pizzas, and recycles all cans and bottles near the door. Fifteen-inch pizzas are only $10.00 plus $1.50 per topping; 18-inchers start at $13.00.

Fine points: 1215–1219 Wharf Street was built in 1891 by James Yates.

❧ *Lola's Pizza. 1219 Wharf Street, (250) 389–2226. Hours: 11:00 A.M.–3:00 A.M. Monday–Saturday, 11:00 A.M.–1:00 A.M. Sunday. Wheelchair accessible. Credit cards: none.*

The new RAVENSONG NATIVE ART GALLERY features dramatic native work from master jeweler Bill Helin's Tsimshian art and Paul Kennedy's Native North American collections including jewelry, paintings, carvings, and Tsimshian gold and silver.

❧ *Ravensong Native Art Gallery, 1221 Wharf Street, (250) 382–ARTS or (888) 382–ARTS. Hours: 10:00 A.M.–6:00 P.M. daily. Wheelchair accessible. Credit cards: Visa, MasterCard, American Express.*

Cross Wharf Street toward the water, and we will continue back on the water side of the street.

At GRANDPA'S ANTIQUE PHOTO STUDIOS you can pose for a photo as any old-time character whose costume Grandpa has in the back or front room. Photo time and prints range from $26 to $99, with poster-size and postcards available (in several languages). Have fun.

❧ *Grandpa's Antique Photo Studios, 1252 Wharf Street, (250) 920–3800. Hours: Monday–Thursday 10:00 A.M.–4:00 P.M. Not wheelchair accessible. Credit cards: Visa, MasterCard.*

You can recover or celebrate at CHANDLER'S SEAFOOD RESTAURANT. This elegant, impressive restaurant with its rich dark wood interior is right next door to the Victoria Regent Hotel. It has been voted Best of the City seafood restaurant for several years.

Chandler's outdoor decks nearly hang over the water, enabling you to see, hear, and feel seaplanes arriving from Washington and Vancouver. This is a great place to soak up old Victoria.

Some of the excellent dishes you might try include half a local Dungeness crab ($13.95); seafood brochettes with salmon, prawns, and halibut on a skewer ($10.95); Atlantic lobster; clams and mussels ($14.95); salmon cakes ($7.95); and chicken ($14.95–$19.95). King salmon runs from $16.95 to $23.95, while a whole Dungeness crab goes for $29.95.

Fine points: The 1896 building was commissioned by James Yates, a Hudson's Bay Company carpenter who started a bar and made a fortune. It was first used to wholesale liquors, cigars, and blankets to Yukon miners and later served as a ship chandlery until 1979.

❧ *Chandler's Seafood Restaurant, 1250 Wharf Street at the bottom of Yates Street, (250) 385–3474. Hours: 11:30 A.M.–10:00 P.M. daily. Partly wheelchair accessible. Credit cards: Visa, MasterCard, American Express, enRoute.*

The Victoria Regent Hotel is convenient for commuters and visitors from Vancouver or Seattle because seaplanes land practically off the deck. Many rooms include kitchens, and continental breakfast is included. (See "Where to Stay.")

Newish BRAVO ON WHARF sets the mood with zebraskin rugs in the street-level lounge, and the stone walls drop almost three stories to the dining room.

Abstract lamps hang from the bar level all the way down to the tables. Quite a visual from above, but completely inaccessible for the handicapped.

Elegant fusion and Thai foods include grilled Thai squid on glass noodles ($11.00), braised salmon ($15.00), pork shank with grilled pears ($13.00), New York steak with portobellos ($14.00), and crab and shrimp cakes ($8.00).

❧ *Bravo on Wharf, 1218 Wharf Street, (250) 386–2900. Hours: 11:30 A.M.–11:00 P.M. daily. Not wheelchair accessible. Credit cards: Visa, MasterCard, American Express, Diners. Fully licensed.*

OCEANSIDE GENERAL STORE is a privately owned small convenience store with Island Dairy ice cream, candy, snacks, dips, cool drinks, and water.

❧ *Oceanside General Store, 1208 Wharf Street, (250) 361–3316. Hours: 10:00 A.M.–11:00 P.M. Wheelchair accessible. Credit cards: none.*

Global Currency Exchange also at 1208 Wharf Street (250–398–0520) offers convenient but expensive money exchange, so if you can hold off, wait until you get to a bank for a better rate.

Fine points: Global's building was constructed in 1882 for Roderick Finlayson, who built Fort Victoria; the Finlayson Building was divided into shops in 1944.

A cozy, quickie cafe, the BLUE CARROT is part of a group of eateries that also includes the Wharfside Eatery. This one is inexpensive: great sandwiches at $4.95 or Black Forest ham and asparagus at $5.95; pizzas such as Canadian back bacon, shrimp, and scallops from $5.95 to $6.95; homemade and huge cookies.

❧ *Blue Carrot, 1208 Wharf Street, (250) 360–1808. Hours: summer 7:00 A.M.–6:00 P.M., winter 7:00 A.M.–3:00 P.M. Not wheelchair accessible. Credit cards: Visa, MasterCard, American Express.*

The WHARFSIDE EATERY is a favorite local hangout for lunch, afternoon tea ($14.95), or after work. Lots of young people come here for a good beer. The decor will cheer you just for its humor with huge hanging fake flowers, Spanish tile floors, ceiling fans, and a wooden cutout of Nasty Jack with his theoretical pirate patch.

The Wharfside features a daily light lunch at $7.95 in addition to its full-range menu of burgers, pastas, salads, seafood, and chicken that will please you and the kids. The beautiful enclosed deck faces the Inner Harbour water for gorgeous year-round dining or drinking. Umbrellas for shade upon request.

❧ *Wharfside Eatery, 1208 Wharf Street, (250) 360–1808. Hours: 11:30 A.M.–midnight daily, afternoon tea 2:00–5:00 P.M. Wheelchair accessible. Credit cards: Visa, MasterCard, American Express. Fully licensed.*

We now continue on to STORE STREET, which is practically an extension of Wharf Street, and in 1 block several business establishments are actually part of MARKET SQUARE. Here they are.

CAFE MEXICO, 1425 Store Street, serves Mexican food in a fun, colorful, and appropriately raunchy atmosphere. Cafe Mexico is most popular for its lunchtime buffet at $6.95 (there's a lighter, low-fat alternative menu from $4.99-$7.99). You'll also find calamari, carne chipotle, and tortillas filled with prawns, scallops and mushrooms with white wine sauce, sour cream, and avocado. And, yes, burgers.
❧ *Cafe Mexico, 1425 Store Street, (250) 386-5454. Hours: Sunday–Thursday 11:30 A.M. on, Friday–Saturday 11:30 A.M.–midnight. Wheelchair accessible. Credit cards: Visa, MasterCard, American Express, Diners. Beer and wine.*

SWEETWATER'S NITECLUB is a happening club for twenty–fortysomethings with music and "proper dress required," whatever that is. Another sign looks for $: WE WELCOME ALL AMERICANS—IT'S PARTY TIME, FOLKS. The owners claim it is the safest and most enjoyable club in town.
❧ *Sweetwater's Niteclub, 27–560 Johnson Street, (250) 383-7844. Hours: 8:00 P.M.–2:00 A.M. Mostly wheelchair accessible. Credit cards: Visa, MasterCard. Fully licensed.*

"Getting You Out There"—that's the motto of OCEAN RIVER SPORTS, and, man, can they! Ocean River sells and rents kayaks, hiking and walking boots, backpacks, and tents. It also has a kids room and gives kayaking lessons and tours. An excellent selection of travel books includes specific active interests such as hiking, biking, sailing, kayaking, and almost anything else you can think of. The staff treats visitors and kids extremely well. Get on the mailing list.
Fine points: You can get to Market Square from the back door.
❧ *Ocean River Sports, 1437 Store Street, (250) 381-4233. Hours: Monday–Thursday, Saturday 9:30 A.M.–5:30 P.M., Friday 9:30 A.M.–8:30 P.M., Sunday 11:00 A.M.–5:00 P.M. Mostly wheelchair accessible from Store Street. Credit cards: Visa, MasterCard, American Express.*

The corner of Store and Pandora Streets is CASA DE MALAHATO CUBAN CIGARS LTD., a cigar emporium and smoking room that appears to do very well with its special-interest audience. There are plans to enlarge the smoking area where people come to puff billows, lick their lips, and enjoy their habit, often newly acquired.

Most of the cigars here are Cuban, but some are made in Canada of Cuban tobacco. Make very sure you are getting specifically what you expect. Brands you might recognize include Cohiba, Partages, Romeo y Julietta, and Bolivar.

❧ *Casa de Malahato Cuban Cigars Ltd., 1441 Store Street, (250) 383–0812 or (800) 882–6881; Fax: (250) 383–0822. Not wheelchair accessible. Credit cards: Visa, MasterCard, American Express, JCB. Web: www.fujipub.com/casa; E-mail: casa@fujipub.com.*

If you do enter Market Square near here, you will run smack into great temptations: the Bavarian Bakery, Fat Phege's Fudge Factory, pizza, and tacos and burritos. Your choice.

If you stay on Store, you'll come to FOWL FISH CAFE & OYSTER HOUSE, which majors in local fish and shellfish, as well as chicken. Oysters, in most ways imaginable, are excellent.

❧ *Fowl Fish Cafe & Oyster House, 1605 Store Street, (250) 361–3150. Hours: lunch and dinner. Wheelchair accessible. Credit cards: Visa, MasterCard, American Express. Fully licensed.*

MILLENNIUM is an excellent underground jazz club, Victoria's latest rage.

❧ *Millennium Jazz Club, 1605 Store Street, (250) 360–9098. Hours: 9:00 P.M.–2:00 A.M. Not wheelchair accessible. Credit cards: Visa, MasterCard.*

Artimages Gallery on Store Street level and **The Fran Willis Gallery** offer local artists' work, jewelry, and cards.

While you are in the neighborhood, be sure to drop by SWANS at the corner of Pandora Street (1 block south of Fisgard) and Store Street (which continues to Wharf Street on the west side of Market Square). This is a neatly restored heritage building that houses a pleasant small hotel, pub and brewery, restaurant, an excellent wine and beer shop, and a nightclub. SWANS CAFE & PUB is an extremely popular thirtysomethings hangout, with Caesar salads, huge burgers and fries, piled-high nachos, local halibut and chips, shepherd's pie, and occasionally a lowish-fat chicken taco tostada and other salads. In-house brewed ales are the best, of course. Food prices are reasonable. Ask for a window table for best view (The Gorge is across Store Street) and people-watching.

❧ *Swans Cafe & Pub, 506 Pandora Street, (250) 361–3310. Hours: 11:00 A.M.–2:00 A.M. Wheelchair accessible. Credit cards: Visa, MasterCard, American Express.*

You can park at Pandora and Store Streets for $1.50 in quarters for three hours.

East on Pandora is ALLEY ANTIQUES, which specializes in Chinese and Japanese antiques and collectibles, old cameras, bottles, books, and Oriental painting supplies.

*& *Alley Antiques, 536B Pandora Street, (250) 384–9393. Hours: 9:30 A.M.–6:00 P.M. Wheelchair accessible. Credit cards: Visa, MasterCard, American Express.*

Locals frequent and recommend KAZ JAPANESE RESTAURANT for its traditional Japanese cuisine including sushi, tempura, noodle soups, and many less known, adventurous, and interesting entrees.

*& *Kaz Japanese Restaurant, 1619 Store Street, (250) 386–9121. Hours: lunch Monday–Saturday 11:30 A.M.–2:30 P.M; dinner Monday–Friday 5:00–9:00 P.M., Saturday 5:00–10:00 P.M. Wheelchair accessible. Credit cards: Visa, MasterCard. Beer, wine, sake.*

We enjoy the SOUR PICKLE CAFE, a cafe with Mt. Royal bagels, healthy muffins, huge sandwiches, juices, organic coffee, with breakfast or lunch starting at $2.99. Some sidewalk tables.

*& *Sour Pickle Cafe, 1623 Store Street, (250) 384–3593. Hours: 7:30 A.M.–11:30 P.M. Wheelchair accessible. Credit cards: none.*

Susan Toby's and Maria Henson's INSIDE OUT HOME AND GARDEN LTD. offers a charming and earthy array of home accessories with a twist. Perfect lamps (for Kathleen's taste), furniture, Native paddles, and other semielegant oddities abound.

*& *Inside Out Home and Garden Ltd., 1627 Store Street, (250) 388–0661; Fax: (250) 388–0662. Hours: 9:30 A.M.–5:30 P.M. Monday–Saturday, 11:00 A.M.–5:00 P.M. Sunday. Wheelchair accessible. Credit cards: Visa, MasterCard.*

SPECIAL STREETS OF DOWNTOWN VICTORIA. This walk will take you up and down the charming streets that run east and west and across Government Street all the way to Chinatown. We will also guide you through Antique Row, Chinatown, Old Town, and Market Square.

The first street you come to going north (up) Government Street is Courtney. Up to the right are several sources of food. On the left side going up you will see the BUN SHOP, where great, inexpensive sandwiches served on soft panini-style buns/rolls are perfect to take on picnics, ferry rides, and tours. The red chairs and white tables out on the sidewalk mark the spot. The Bun Shop serves salmon, tuna, egg salad, ham, turkey, cheeses, and salads, all for less than $5.50. Next door you can get twenty-four flavors of local Dairyland ice cream. *Bun Shop, 600 Courtney Street, (250) 385–3511. Hours: summer 7:30 A.M.–9:00 P.M., ice cream parlor open until 11:00 P.M.; winter 7:30 A.M.–5:00 P.M. Wheelchair accessible. Credit cards: Visa, MasterCard.*

Just a block off the beaten track, HUGO'S GRILL AND BREWHOUSE has converted itself from an ultraelegant steak house to a terrific grill with its still-fabulous steaks and eight great pizzas (about $10.00), pastas from primavera ($12.95) to smoked chicken linguini, AAA beef stroganoff ($14.95), and Tahi prawn and seafood. Appetizers include Thai veggie spring rolls, crab cakes, crispy calamari, pan-fried Fanny Bay oysters, and crispy scallion ginger St. Louis side ribs ($8.95). Soups and salads are always good with real green goddess among dressing choices, and then you can get into the divine steaks (up to $29.95), spring salmon, chicken, and mixed grill.

At lunch you can try Montreal smoked beef on rye ($7.95), or their spectacular Hugo burger or salmon burger ($8.95), all of which come with choice of salads or pommes frites. Their pub and brewhouse are right up Courtney Street. Lots of fun, friendly staff led by manager Michele Linley, and great food all around. A la carte brunch on Sunday.
Hugo's Grill & Brewhouse, 619 Courtney, (250) 920–4844, Fax: (250) 920–4842; Web: www.hugoslounge.com. Hours: 11:00 A.M. on. Fully licensed with their brews on tap. Partly wheelchair accessible. Credit cards: Visa, MasterCard, American Express.

Across Courtney Street, **Harbour Sweets** offers candies, **Harbour Cones** sells ice cream and smoothies, and **Le Soleil** makes custom jewelry.

On the north side of Courtney, enjoy Gordon Street. On the left (west) side you will find the FLAG SHOP. (Watch the slight step down at the door.) The Flag Shop manufactures and sells flags of all nations and makes them for personal or public causes and beliefs. It also sells pins, crests, patches, and decals. Truly a fun place to explore and temporarily transport yourself elsewhere. Don Flynn, Jim Webb, and Jim and Chantal answer questions most graciously.
Flag Shop, 904 Gordon Street, (250) 382–3524. Hours: 9:00 A.M.–5:30 P.M. weekdays, 10:00 A.M.–4:00 P.M. Saturday. Not wheelchair accessible. Credit cards: Visa, MasterCard, American Express.

The sandwich-board person on Government Street for LA CUCINA—DA PASTA PLACE passes out coupons enticing you to an "all-you-can-eat" pasta buffet that includes good-looking pastas and Italian salads for $6.95. What they fail to mention is that the offer is good only at lunchtime, from noon to 2:30 P.M.

In the small dining room with mauve vinyl tablecloths and at the pleasant sidewalk tables, you can order focaccia sandwiches, lots of pastas, and children's portions of pasta for $5.00.

At dinner, minestrone soup costs $4.95, penne with stir-fry veggies is $11.50, spinach cannelloni with farmer's cheese $12.50, chicken breast cacciatore $13.95, and seafood calzone $15.25.

La Cucina—Da Pasta Place, 920 Gordon Street, (250) 381–4558. Hours: 12:30–2:00 P.M., 5:00–10:00 P.M. Wheelchair accessible. Credit cards: Visa, MasterCard, American Express. Fully licensed.

If you want to try Vietnamese food, you might walk around the corner to Langley Street and the best Victoria has to offer, LE PETIT SAIGON, an authentic Vietnamese experience with exotic full carnivore and vegetarian menus. Many locals dine here both at lunch and dinner.

Le Petit Saigon, 1010 Langley Street, (250) 386–1412. Hours: lunch 11:00 A.M.–2:00 P.M., dinner from 5:00 P.M. Wheelchair accessible. Credit cards: Visa, MasterCard, American Express. Fully licensed.

Just up from the corner is VALHALLA PURE OUTFITTERS FACTORY OUTLET, 615 Broughton. This Canadian company's outdoor gear is made in British Columbia. The quality is top of the line, and the prices reflect the workmanship. Rock Butt shorts go for $44, and sturdy, handsome waxed cotton baseball caps are $20. You can get hiking boots, Teva sandals, Valhalla packs, Eco clothes of recycled material, and sleeping bags. Valhalla also features a wide array of gear for rock and ice climbing.

Valhalla Pure Outfitters Factory Outlet, 615 Broughton Street, (250) 360–2181. Hours: Monday 9:30 A.M.–6:00 P.M., Tuesday–Saturday 9:30 A.M.–9:00 P.M., Sunday 10:00 A.M.–6:00 P.M. Wheelchair accessible. Credit cards: Visa, MasterCard, American Express, Diners, JCB.

Fine points: There's a parking garage here on Broughton and Broad Streets.

DELANE is an unpretentious, elegant leather boutique featuring mostly Canadian-made fashionable jackets for men and women, wallets, bags, luggage, accessories, and clothing. Great sales in August and September.

Delane, 619 Broughton Street, (250) 383–7922. Hours: Monday–Saturday 10:00 A.M.–5:30 P.M., Thursday–Saturday 10:00 A.M.–9:00 P.M., summer. Wheelchair accessible. Credit cards: Visa, MasterCard, American Express.

For a near-European experience, duck into CHOCOLATIER BERNARD CALLEBAUT, an elegant Belgian candy store with shiny copper and brass counters. Bernard Callebaut chocolates are well known throughout Canada (there are also stores in the States, in Seattle and Phoenix). Forty-seven varieties of handmade chocolates are made weekly with fresh cream, butter, chocolate, and no preservatives.

❧ *Chocolatier Bernard Callebaut, 623 Broughton Street, (250) 380–1515. Hours: 9:30 A.M.–5:30 P.M. Monday–Saturday, noon–4:00 P.M. Sunday. Wheelchair accessible. Credit cards: Visa, MasterCard, American Express, Diners.*

It's worth the trip another block up Broughton to the GREATER VICTORIA PUBLIC LIBRARY. This fabulous library, built in 1980, has active children's and teens' sections to the right of the entrance, excellent card and computer catalogues, and a most hospitable staff. The espresso cart in the courtyard is quite good.

❧ *Greater Victoria Public Library, 735 Broughton Street, (250) 384–3182. Hours: Monday, Wednesday, Friday, Saturday 9:00 A.M.–6:00 P.M.; Tuesday, Thursday 9:00 A.M.–9:00 P.M. Wheelchair accessible.*

If you don't want to go up a block to the library, cross Broughton and start at the far end of the block. TONY'S TRICK & JOKE SHOP, at 688 Broughton, is a don't-miss spot. Magicians/owners Tony and Ann Eng truly are "In Business For Fun." While they do a land-office business supplying professional magicians' needs, the place is a town headquarters for every kid and grown-up fascinated by illusion and fantasy.

❧ *Tony's Trick & Joke Shop, 688 Broughton Street, (250) 385–6807. E-mail: tonyeng@pinc.com. Hours: 10:00 A.M.–5:30 P.M. Monday–Saturday, noon–4:00 P.M. Sunday. Wheelchair accessible. Credit cards: Visa, MasterCard.*

HIME SUSHI hosts many Japanese visitors and local businesspeople who pack in for the reasonable daily lunch specials from $6.45 to $8.45, the Bento lunch box specials at $8.25, and sushi plates, which may combine New York steak, teriyaki, and tempura. Slow, seven-course dinners are only $19.95.

❧ *Hime Sushi, 680 Broughton Street, (250) 388–4439. Hours: 11:30 A.M.–9:00 P.M. Monday–Saturday. Wheelchair accessible. Credit cards: Visa, MasterCard, American Express, enRoute, JCB. Sake, beer, wine.*

The WINE BARREL, 644 Broughton, is a friendly and interesting wine and wine accessories shop owned and managed with enthusiasm by Dr. Wilf Krutzmann, a veterinarian who prefers cheering people more than animals these days. Here you can buy from a great selection of B.C.'s best wines at winery prices.

Wilf has provided a place to get wine information from all over the world as well as wine glasses; gourmet goods to serve with wine, such as Gigi biscotti; Cuisine Perel chocolate sauces; wine soup; wine racks and corkscrews; Schoffeitt spices; and gift wrap.

Until recently, one could not sell wine in British Columbia unless one's store was actually attached in some way to a government liquor store. After a long, public struggle with the government, Wilf finally triumphed and obtained one of the few private wine shop licenses in June 1998. Victoria Mayor Bob Cross cut the ribbon at the broadly publicized reopening of the Wine Barrel, where Wilf is now able to sell wine as well as accessories.

Wilf also conducts fabulous and informative Friday evening wine tastings and wine tours throughout North America. One of our favorite places.

*♣ **Wine Barrel,** *644 Broughton Street, (250) 388–0606; Web: www.bcwine. com/thewinebarrel. Hours: 10:00 A.M.–7:00 P.M. Monday–Saturday; noon–5:00 P.M., sometimes later Sunday. Wheelchair accessible. Credit cards: Visa, MasterCard, Diners, enRoute.*

SWEET DREAMS BOUTIQUE presents a sumptuous corner at Broad Street with down comforters, pillows, bedding, and everything for romantic comfort. ***Fine points:*** The 1884 building was designed by Thomas Trounce.

*♣ **Sweet Dreams Boutique,** *636 Broughton Street, (250) 383–6133. Hours: 9:30 A.M.–5:30 P.M. daily, later sometimes. Wheelchair accessible. Credit cards: Visa, MasterCard, American Express.*

Across Broad Street on the corner is **FIORI,** Lisa D. Hageman's new elegant boutique of unusual imported home accessories. Expect to see hand-printed Parisian fabric, towel sets ($198), linen robes ($197), custom-made bedding, and a Medici-style red tapestry duvet ($792).

*♣ **Fiori,** *1002 Broad Street, (250) 381–8825; Fax: (250) 381–8835. Hours: 11:00 A.M.–6:00 P.M. Monday, 10:00 A.M.–6:00 P.M. Tuesday–Saturday, 1:00–5:00 P.M. Sunday. Wheelchair accessible but crowded. Credit cards: Visa, MasterCard.*

EBIZO SUSHI, a popular local hangout at lunchtime, serves an extensive sushi menu and lunch specials such as lemon grass chicken at $8.95 with soup, rice, and condiments, or beef or salmon teriyaki at $8.95. Many locals say this is the best sushi in Victoria.

*♣ **Ebizo Sushi,** *604 Broughton Street, (250) 383–3234. Hours: lunch 11:30 A.M.–3:00 P.M. Tuesday–Saturday; dinner 5:00–9:30 P.M. Tuesday–Thursday, 5:00– 10:00 P.M. Friday and Saturday. Some tables wheelchair accessible. Credit cards: Visa, MasterCard. Sake, beer, wine.*

The CALIFORNIA WRAP, SMOOTHIE, AND JUICE BAR defines these delectables for non-Californians. Wraps have everything that could go in a sandwich or on a pizza, wrapped in plain flour, sun-dried tomato, or spinach tortillas; smoothies blend fruit and yogurt into a drink or a meal.

❧ *California Wrap, Smoothie, and Juice Bar, 602 Broughton Street, (250) 382–9727; Fax: (250) 995–8423. Hours: 10:00 A.M.–8:00 P.M. daily. Not wheelchair accessible. No credit cards.*

Below Government Street on Broughton is the new one-of-a-kind WHALE STORE, which offers killer whale and marine life–watching tours and "anything you can think of with whales on it." Look for whale-decorated aprons, boxer shorts, towels, photos, shirts, and much more.

❧ *Whale Store, 532 Broughton, (250) 383–ORCA; Web: www. whale-store.com or www.islandnet. com/-oceanx. Hours: summer 8:00 A.M.–9:00 P.M. daily, winter 11:00 A.M.–5:00 P.M.; reservations 7:00 A.M.–11:00 P.M. Wheelchair accessible. Credit cards: Visa, MasterCard, American Express, JCB.*

Go back a short block to **Broad Street,** one of our favorites. Its old-world ambience and the quality boutiques and restaurants make it a true pleasure to visit, both here and on the other side of Eaton Centre. We'll begin on the west side of Broad Street, south of Eaton Centre.

SPIRAL LIVING, at 1006 Broad, is a new favorite store of many Victorians. It features design, style, and high-quality accessories for living, many with a spiral-design theme. We favor the lamps and candleholders, while our children adore the French soaps, candles, small rugs, linens, perfumes, and aromatherapy supplies. Noriko

---

PAGLIACCI'S FAMOUS TOMATO SAUCE
Lana Millott of Pagliacci's, Victoria

Ingredients

  1 tbsp. garlic

  ¼ cup olive oil

  1-100 oz. tin crushed tomatoes

  8 oz. tin tomato paste

  10 oz. tomato puree

  1 ½ tsp. fennel seed

  2 tsp. black pepper

  1 tbsp. salt

  ½ tsp. chiles, crushed

  2 tbsp. sugar

  2 tbsp. parsley

Preparation

  Sauté garlic in olive oil. Add crushed tomatoes, tomato paste, tomato purée. Season with fennel seed, basil, black pepper, salt, crushed chiles, sugar, and parsley. Bring to simmer. Cook for two hours.

A HAUNTED CITY

"Victoria is a haunted city," said the late Robin Skelton, emeritus professor from University of Victoria, poet, and coauthor of A Gathering of Ghosts.

A woman in a flowing white dress haunts Oak Bay Golf Course. In early evening she walks across the course; later in the evening she is seen staring out to sea. She first appeared in 1936, shortly after the strangling murder of Doris Gravlin, a nurse found buried in a sand trap on the course. Suspicion fell on her husband, Victor, a local newspaper reporter, who drowned himself while the police were investigating. Doris appears always to young couples walking on or driving by the golf course and usually disappears in a dwindling pool of light. The sightings occur about twice a year and have been reported by responsible, non-hysterical couples.

Several tourists visiting the Point Ellice House have thanked the management for the pleasant woman (always in a blue dress) who gave them directions when there were no docents on duty. Others have reported being scolded by an ethereal woman who ordered them to leave the premises, including two young nurses who camped out one night. The descriptions match that of a younger beautiful Kathleen O'Reilly, the party-loving daughter of Peter and Caroline O'Reilly, born there in 1867. She passed up numerous eligible suitors and returned after World War I to live in the house until her death in 1945, lonely and unhappy. It was rumored that this ghost story was cooked up by family members trying to promote the house as a tourist attraction, but the reports of visitations continued after it was sold to the province in 1974.

The ancient Tod farmhouse has its specter, an Indian woman in chains. James Dunsmuir's mansion at Hatley Park (Royal Roads University) is visited by the spirit of a little old lady. A bearded man in a long greatcoat appears some October mornings sitting on the curb outside the McPherson Theatre. To believers he is called "The Frenchman" because in the 1880s a young Frenchman was shot dead,

Zimmerman designs much of the graceful wrought-iron work. Her husband, Blair, manages the shop while Noriko manages their son, whose photo you see in many of the picture frames on display.

❧ *Spiral Living, 1006 Broad Street, (250) 381–1510; Fax (250) 595–3239. Hours: 9:30 A.M.–6:00 P.M. daily, later in summer. Wheelchair accessible. Credit cards: Visa, MasterCard, American Express.*

supposedly in an argument during a poker game held after hours in the area. Legend has it that youthful Alexander Dunsmuir of the coal company was present, and to cover up both the murder and scandal, the body was placed sitting on the curb, propped against a tree. Dissatisfied that his death was unsolved, the Frenchman returns to haunt the scene.

One ghost was the busy resident of the upstairs office of world-famous Rogers' Chocolates on Government Street. Quite regularly lights and the radio went on when no one was present, and footsteps going

TOMBSTONES AT
ROSS BAY CEMETERY

up and down the stairs and moving about were heard by employees working late in the store. The eccentric candy maker, Charles Rogers and his wife, Leah, lived upstairs in what is now the office for about fifteen years. Charles Rogers died in 1927 still heartbroken over the suicide of their only son in 1903. His wife sold the business and then gave the fortune to her church and other charities, finally living in abject poverty in a small James Bay house with no electricity until her death at eighty-eight in 1958. She was buried at Ross Bay Cemetery but was so poor there was no money for a headstone. The restless phantom of the offices soon arrived. Convinced that Leah's spirit might be angry that she had no grave marker, the Rogers's Chocolate Company recently bought a headstone for Leah Rogers' grave. Apparently satisfied, the ghost no longer visits the store.

SIMPLY THE BEST CLOTHING does not overstate this elegant European boutique with the best clothing *and* the best pen collection in western Canada. Clothing labels include Nautica, Breitling, the Paul & Shark Yachting line, Calvin Klein, hand-painted ties to $500, and $150 cashmere socks.

But it's the pens that grab you, ranging in price from $30 to $100,000. Feast your eyes and wallets on Montegrapas, Omas, Lamy, Aurora, Pelikan, and

Rotiring. You can obtain a pen commemorating Jerusalem's 3,000th birthday for $12,000, and a set of twenty-four UNICEF signature pens for $60,000. And don't forget your raincoat with zip-out opossum lining. Watch makers include Porsche, Breitling, and Phillippe.

❧ *Simply the Best Clothing, 1008 Broad Street, (250) 386–6661. Hours: Monday–Saturday 9:30 A.M.–6:00 P.M., Sundays close to Christmas. Wheelchair accessible. Credit cards: Visa, MasterCard, American Express, JCB.*

WINCHESTER GALLERIES features contemporary Canadian and historical paintings.

❧ *Winchester Galleries, 1010 Broad Street, (250) 286–2773. Hours: 10:00 A.M.–6:00 P.M. Wheelchair accessible. Credit cards: Visa, MasterCard, American Express.*

CASWELL LAWRENCE FINE ART GALLERY offers West Coast art, sculpture, painting, pottery, and jewelery. Heather Wheeler and Maureen Flanagan offer the work of Craig Vincent, Carol Evans, Graham Herbert, and soapstone sculptor Nancy Street.

❧ *Caswell Lawrence Fine Art Gallery, 1014 Broad Street, (250) 388–9500; Fax: (250) 388–9511; Web: www.caswell-lawrence.com. E-mail: gallery@ caswell-lawrence.com. Hours: 9:30 A.M.–5:00 P.M. Monday–Saturday, 11:00 A.M.–5:00 P.M. Sunday. Wheelchair accessible. Credit cards: Visa, MasterCard, American Express.*

On the east side of Broad Street, still south of Eaton Centre, we'll start with FLOWERS ON TOP, a fabulous downtown florist with flowers displayed on the sidewalk, bringing cheer to everyone, even on a gloomy day. Victorians love giving flowers to each other and themselves.

❧ *Flowers on Top, 1005 Broad Street, (250) 383–5262. Hours: when you see the flowers out. Wheelchair accessible. Credit cards: Visa, MasterCard.*

RONSONS, which proclaims itself "Rockport Headquarters," also carries Mephisto, Aerosoles, Birkenstock, and Easy Spirit shoes. August/September sales always seem to include better men's styles than women's.

Fine points: In 1884 the Weiler Brothers built 1005–1009 as a furniture factory and warehouse. It was converted to shops and offices in 1972.

❧ *Ronsons, 1005 Broad Street, (250) 380–6500. Hours: 9:30 A.M.– 6:00 P.M. daily. Wheelchair accessible. Credit cards: Visa, MasterCard, American Express.*

One of Victoria's most popular restaurants and watering holes is PAGLIACCI'S, at 1011 Broad. Howie Siegel, his brother David, and Alan Difiori (thank heavens someone was Italian!) opened this magnetic, charismatic, Jewish–Italian–Brooklyn–San Francisco restaurant in 1979 because they couldn't find cappuccino or cheesecake after a Sunday movie.

Thousands of Victorians and visitors rejoice at their good luck. This place is so popular that they don't take reservations; you just line up on the sidewalk, patiently. Good conversation usually mingles, focaccia bread passes, and occasionally a surprise beverage shows up in coffee cups.

Pagliacci's is always the place we go for our first and last nights in Victoria. It's that good and that much fun. Besides, it's our kids' favorite.

At dinner, everything is good, some things creamier and garlickier than others. The names of menu highlights get you laughing before you even order: the Toots Shor New York steak, the Mae West, Prawns Al Capone, Girl from Ipanoodle, and the Hemingway Short Story. Their queen of dishes is pasta with mushrooms, artichokes, Cajun spices, and cream at $17.95. Good wine list.

There are booths if you need one, and tables get moved out of the front window at about 9:00 P.M. to make room for the band Sunday–Wednesday. The music is always highest quality, fun, and local. One of our favorites. Thanks to Chef Lana Millott for her famous tomato sauce recipe (see page 79).

❧ *Pagliacci's, 1011 Broad Street, (250) 386–1662. Hours: lunch 11:30 A.M.–3:00 P.M.; tea, espresso drinks, and sweets 3:00–5:00 P.M.; dinner 5:30–10:00 P.M. Wheelchair accessible. Credit cards: Visa, MasterCard. Fully licensed.*

Local ADVENTURE CLOTHING, LTD., an elegant activewear outpost of J. Wilson, is a great addition to this block, replacing the Benetton chain. Adventure offers Tilley Endurables and Liberty of London among other brands.

❧ *Adventure Clothing, Ltd., 1015 Broad Street, (250) 384–3337 or (877) 381–3337 toll free; E-mail: sean@islandnet.com. Hours: Monday–Friday 9:30 A.M.–5:30 P.M., Monday–Saturday, 11:00 A.M.–4:00 P.M. Sunday. Not wheelchair accessible. Credit cards: Visa, MasterCard.*

This brings you to Fort Street and the Eaton Centre mall across Fort. We'll now proceed down the north side of Fort across Government to Wharf Street, then return up the south side back to Government.

KOTO HOUSE, a Japanese restaurant and sushi and salad bar, features traditional Japanese and American foods. Beautifully displayed specialty dishes include obento, tofu tempura, and salmon katsu. There are fifteen to twenty main courses at dinner, and ten to thirteen sashimi varieties, all including soup, salad, and rice.

❧ *Koto House, 510 Fort Street, (250) 382–1514. Hours: lunch 11:30 A.M.–2:00 P.M.; dinner 5:00 P.M. on, Saturday–Sunday 5:00 P.M. on. Wheelchair accessible. Credit cards: Visa, MasterCard, American Express.*

SIAM THAI RESTAURANT is a convenient Thai restaurant with interesting dishes such as garlic pepper pork at $8.95 or Pad Talay with prawns, squid, scallops, fish, and veggies in oyster sauce at $13.95. There's an entire vegetarian menu such as hot and spicy vegetarian noodles with egg, vegetables, and tofu at $7.95.

❧ *Siam Thai Restaurant, 512 Fort Street, (250) 383–9911. Hours: lunch 11:30 A.M.–2:00 P.M.; dinner 5:00 P.M. on, Sunday 5:00 P.M. on. Wheelchair accessible. Credit cards: Visa, MasterCard, American Express.*

Cross Fort Street to the south side to CROWN PUBLICATIONS INC. For information lovers it is well worth the trip from Government Street to see this exclusive source for British Columbia government documents, including mining and topographical maps, nautical charts, B.C. acts and regulations, ministry of forestry reports, ministry of education curriculum and travel guides, and resource books.

Check out the interesting supply of guides to resources and living in B.C., on such topics as gardening, natural history, aboriginal history, environment, and the outdoors. Crown accepts mail, special, phone, and fax orders.

❧ *Crown Publications Inc., 521 Fort Street, (250) 386–4636. Hours: Monday–Friday 8:30 A.M.–5:00 P.M., Saturday 9:30 A.M.–5:00 P.M. Wheelchair accessible. Credit cards: Visa, MasterCard, American Express.*

Cross Langley Street and proceed up Fort Street to the Temple Building at 525 Fort. The city of Victoria's *Downtown Heritage Registry* calls the 1893 elegant sandstone building "one of the most architecturally significant" in the city. It was the first independent project of Samuel Maclure, father of Victoria's Edwardian movement. This great heritage building houses the Victoria Chamber of Commerce and WENDY RUSSELL ANTIQUES, one of the coziest and most personal antiques shops in town. Just two steps down, it reflects the owner's tastes in estate and antique jewelry, and small objets d'art.

❧ *Wendy Russell Antiques, 525 Fort Street, (250) 385–9816. Hours: Monday–Saturday 10:00 A.M.–5:00 P.M. Not wheelchair accessible. Credit cards: Visa, MasterCard, American Express.*

Now we're back to Government Street. Cross it and continue up the south side of Fort. This block has interesting boutiques and galleries, and Antique Row begins 2 blocks east of here. Fort Street is now one-way up (east).

A good first stop, at least to look, is BADEN-BADEN, a "casual, classic European elegance" boutique that features German designers and German imports. The owners go to Germany and buy directly, in the style of that famous resort of Baden-Baden. Their wares include beautiful blouses, shirts, jackets, and sweaters.

❧ *Baden-Baden, 611 Fort Street, (250) 380–1063. Hours: Monday–Saturday 9:30 A.M.–5:30 P.M. Wheelchair accessible. Credit cards: Visa, MasterCard, American Express.*

LENS & SHUTTER is absolutely the most convenient camera shop to fill all your camera, film, and developing needs. They have everything, including one-hour developing services; batteries; used cameras and lenses; filters from most manufacturers, such as Nikon, Leica, Minolta, Vivitar; and bags and cases of all sizes.

❧ *Lens & Shutter, 615–617 Fort Street, (250) 383–7443. Hours: Monday–Saturday 9:30 A.M.–5:30 P.M. Wheelchair accessible. Credit cards: Visa, MasterCard, American Express.*

Next door, KNIGHTSBRIDGE GIFT SHOPS LTD. is a classic gift shop featuring knickknacks and Limoges porcelain.

❧ *Knightsbridge Gift Shops Ltd., 623 Fort Street, (250) 385–1312. Hours: 9:30 A.M.–5:30 P.M. Monday–Saturday, 11:00 A.M.–5:00 P.M. Sunday. Wheelchair accessible. Credit cards: Visa, MasterCard.*

The new **Golden Chopsticks Restaurant** surprised us with its clean, sparkling interior, having replaced a tearoom that had seen better decades. Exciting lunch specials range from $6.95 to $9.95, including soup, and dinner may include the usuals plus chop suey, deep-fried garlic spare ribs, Szechuan everything, pepper and salt squid or bean curd, and Ma Po Tofu. Family dinners for up to six people, including deliveries to downtown hotels, are $47.95.

❧ *Golden Chopsticks Restaurant, 627 Fort Street, (250) 388–3148. Hours: Monday–Saturday 10:00 A.M.–9:00 P.M., Sunday 11:00 A.M.–9:00 P.M. Wheelchair accessible. Credit cards: Visa, MasterCard.*

SCARAMOUCHE GALLERY is a gift shop and gallery where you might find turquoise jewelry, glassware, Nova Scotia seagull pewter, local pottery, native art, Robin Righton's raku pottery, and loads of cat things.

❧ *Scaramouche Gallery, 635 Fort Street, (250) 386–2215. Hours: summer 9:00 A.M.–9:00 P.M., winter 9:00 A.M.–6:00 P.M., Sunday 10:00 A.M.–5:00 P.M. Wheelchair accessible. Credit cards: Visa, MasterCard, American Express, Diners, Discover, JCB.*

FRANKLIN & COMPANY offers elegant gifts including the very best in stemware and ceramicware. Richard Franklin brought his world-class experience to Victoria and shows Royal Doulton, Royal Worcester, Waterford, Spode, and much more.

❧ *Franklin & Company, 637 Fort Street, (250) 361–3337; Fax: (250) 361–3307. Hours: 9:30 A.M.–5:30 P.M. Monday–Saturday, noon–4:00 P.M. Sunday. Wheelchair accessible. Credit cards: Visa, MasterCard, American Express.*

PABOOM is a new gallery of wild modern home accessories, such as standing candelabra, see-through flower place mats ($1.95), day-glo flower pots, and mod kitchen utensils—all at great prices.

❧ *Paboom, 641 Fort Street, (250) 380–0020. Hours: 10:00 A.M.–6:00 P.M. Monday–Wednesday, and Saturday, 10:00 A.M.–9:00 P.M. Thursday–Friday, 11:00 A.M.–5:00 P.M. Sunday. Wheelchair accessible. Credit cards: Visa, MasterCard.*

This Fort Street location is the main dispensary for McGILL & ORME PHARMACY, a large Canadian pharmacy. It is extremely handy for visitors. You can get everything you need from Band-Aids to aspirin and much more. One of our favorites.

❧ *McGill & Orme Pharmacy, 649 Fort Street, (250) 384–1195. Hours: Monday–Saturday 9:00 A.M.–6:00 P.M., Sunday and holidays 11:00 A.M.–6:00 P.M. Wheelchair accessible. Credit cards: Visa, MasterCard.*

As you cross Broad Street, notice that Eaton Centre takes up the block to the left with some stores we will explore on our way back down Fort Street.

AVENUE CHINA & CHINTZ INTERIORS is a small, cheerful shop that always charms us with the baptismal gowns in the window, elegant china, and its demitasse cup collections.

❧ *Avenue China & Chintz Interiors, corner of Fort and Broad, (250) 595–1880. Hours: 9:30 A.M.–5:30 P.M. Wheelchair accessible. Credit cards: Visa, MasterCard.*

Be sure to visit ALCHERINGA GALLERY, the best and most expensive native arts gallery in Victoria. It features tribal art from the Canadian Northwest coast, the island of New Guinea, and aboriginal Australia. B.C. First Peoples artists whose work you usually find here include Robert Davidson, Reg Davidson, Richard Hunt, Tony Hunt, Corrine Hunt, and several other Hunts. Masks, posters, books, and prints are all available from $100 to $10,000. You are welcome to come in, browse, sit on benches, read, contemplate, and learn.

Fine points: This is one of Victoria's oldest buildings, which opened in 1879 as a grocery store.

❀❧ *Alcheringa Gallery, 665 Fort Street, (250) 383–8224. Hours: Monday– Saturday 9:30 A.M.–7:00 P.M., Sunday and holidays noon–5:00 P.M. Wheelchair accessible. Credit cards: Visa, MasterCard, American Express.*

As you cross Douglas Street, a rather wide street, you approach the part of Fort Street that is marked on city street signs as ANTIQUE ROW, even though there aren't any antiques for another block. Antique Row has many other interesting shops and restaurants, which we will help you explore.

A handy international newsstand, REGAL NEWS supplies newspapers from B.C. and all of Canada, southern China, Washington, D.C., Europe, London, Scotland, and Asia, and also has the usual newsstand items of candy, snacks, cigarettes, and cool drinks.

❀❧ *Regal News, 701 Fort Street, (250) 383–5225. Hours: 7:30 A.M.–5:30 P.M. daily. Wheelchair accessible but tight. Credit cards: none.*

If you need those photos done now, ONE-HOUR PHOTO EXPRESS is truly a one-hour film development place. Services include passport photos, negative prints from slides, and camera repairs; they also sell batteries and accessories.

❀❧ *One-Hour Photo Express, 705 Fort Street, (250) 389–1984. Hours: Monday–Saturday 8:30 A.M.–5:00 P.M. Wheelchair accessible. Credit cards: Visa, MasterCard, American Express, JCB.*

Voted Victoria's Best copy place, J & L COPY & FAX lives up to its reputation. Helpful, friendly service makes problem solving easy. You can receive or send faxes, make copies, get business cards in a couple of days, use their computer, print out from your own disk, get typesetting done, and have résumés prepared. One of our favorites.

❀❧ *J & L Copy & Fax, 777 Fort Street, (250) 386–3333. Hours: Monday–Friday 7:00 A.M.–7:00 P.M., Saturday 9:00 A.M.–5:00 P.M. Wheelchair accessible. Credit cards: Visa, MasterCard. One hour free parking at City of Victoria Parkades.*

We love DILETTANTES CAFE, 787 Fort Street, a fabulous small, lively restaurant that is both elegant and casual in its food, service, and decor. First, read their definition of *dilettante* to get their perspective. Dilettantes is so popular that it recently added a full bar and expanded dining space and added "Mediterranean nights" on Tuesday and Wednesday.

The varied menu always includes innovative but not cutesy vegetarian dishes, fresh local fish, pastas, and decadent desserts. Try their vegetable wonton soup at either $5.95 or meal size at $6.95, a huge Niçoise salad at $8.50 (one of our favorites), or the sometimes daily special of fettucine with smoked wild salmon and clams at $10.95.

Dilettantes also serves coffee-break goodies including Mount Royal bagels, eggs and hash browns, and peanut-butter-and-banana sandwiches. Weekend brunch might include French toast, eggs Benedict, pancakes, or black bean huevos rancheros. Lunch can be chicken quesadillas to halibut burgers and everything in between. Ultimate West Coast eclectic cuisine. One of our favorites.

❧ *Dilettantes Cafe, 787 Fort Street, (250) 381–3327. Hours: Monday– Saturday breakfast, lunch, and dinner; Sunday brunch until 2:00 P.M. Wheelchair accessible. Credit cards: Visa, MasterCard, American Express. Beer and wine.*

Eyecatching AMOS & ANDES IMPORTS offers eclectic ethnic handmade clothing and bags including Ecuadorian sweaters, dresses and shirts, some loose or plus sizes, Asian Creations, and Caribbean Pacific labels, all with some humor.

❧ *Amos & Andes Imports, 795 Fort Street, (250) 480–5183. Hours: 10:00 A.M.–5:30 P.M. daily. Wheelchair accessible. Credit cards: Visa, American Express.*

Antique Row

Now cross Blanshard and enjoy the real ANTIQUE ROW. Any of the antiques dealers will give you a copy of their brochure, *Victoria's Antique Shops.*

Of course, the first business you come to on Antique Row is not exactly an antique—it's Starbucks Coffee. The few sidewalk tables are often occupied by regulars, but try those squeezed in on the Fort Street side to sit in the shade.

At PACIFIC ANTIQUES, Leonard Clarke specializes in wonderful conversation as well as eighteenth- and nineteenth-century English, Irish, and oriental furniture, silver, glass, and porcelain. He also has 450 pieces of British brass cabinet hardware. Clarke, who has lived in Canada for more than twenty years, serves as honorary life president of the Irish Antique Dealers and is now president of the Antique Dealers Association of Western Canada.

❧ *Pacific Antiques, 805 Fort Street, (250) 388–5311. Hours: 9:30 A.M.–5:30 P.M. daily. Wheelchair accessible. Credit cards: Visa, MasterCard, American Express.*

MVP SPORTS CARDS serves as a hangout for sports fans of all ages and sexes and sells sports hats, cards, Christmas ornaments, wall clocks, novelty phones, and everything you can imagine connected to hockey, baseball, basketball, and football, plus NASCAR memorabilia. Posted prices include 7 percent GST. Leave the kids here and go to Starbucks.

MVP Sports Cards, 807 Fort Street, (250) 380–1958. Hours: 9:00 A.M.–5:30 P.M. Monday–Saturday, noon–4:00 P.M. Sunday and holidays. Wheelchair accessible. Credit cards: Visa, MasterCard.

The CANADA MONETARY EXCHANGE has an interesting and eclectic collection of coins, stamps, gold, silver, Northwest coast native carvings, autographs, signed movie star photos, Baccarat paperweights, currency exchange, and precious metals.

Canada Monetary Exchange, 809–811 Fort Street, (250) 386–2222. Hours: Monday–Friday 9:00 A.M.–4:00 P.M. Wheelchair accessible. Credit cards: none.

If you want to send some fresh Canadian salmon home, get it at the NEPTUNE SEAFOOD MARKET here on Fort Street. A local favorite, Neptune specializes in family-caught fish, including B.C. smoked sockeye salmon, swimming crabs, lobsters, mussels, scallops, and oysters. You can have these delicacies packed to ship home. Try the smoked salmon pâté made with cream cheese.

Neptune Seafood Market, 813 Fort Street, (250) 383–5621. Hours: Monday–Saturday 9:00 A.M.–6:00 P.M. Wheelchair accessible. Credit cards: Visa, MasterCard.

RECOLLECTION ANTIQUE AND COLLECTIBLES MALL represents sixty antiques dealers of all tastes and price ranges.

Recollection Antique and Collectibles Mall, 817A Fort Street, (250) 385–1902. Hours: 10:00 A.M.–5:30 P.M. Monday–Saturday, noon–4:00 P.M. Sunday. Wheelchair accessible. Credit cards: Visa, MasterCard, American Express.

ATLAS STEREO TV RADIO sells all that stuff plus fuses and Sharp calculators, Sony, Hitachi, and JVC everythings.

Atlas Stereo TV Radio, 821 Fort Street, (250) 385–2712. Hours: Monday–Saturday 9:00 A.M.–5:30 P.M. Wheelchair accessible. Credit cards: Visa, MasterCard, American Express.

CASPIAN PERSIAN CARPETS is also just what it says. The owners buy, trade, and sell new and old carpets; make appraisals and repairs; and do cleaning.

❧❧ *Caspian Persian Carpets, 825 Fort Street, (250) 383–3434. Hours: 9:30 A.M.–5:30 P.M. daily. Wheelchair accessible. Credit cards: Visa, MasterCard, American Express.*

VAN ISLE COIN & STAMP is also just what it says, specializing in buying and selling gold wafers, Krugerrands, maple leafs, collector coins, stamp supplies, junk silver coins, and silver bars.
❧❧ *Van Isle Coin & Stamp, 831 Fort Street, (250) 382–6331. Hours: Monday– Saturday 9:00 A.M.–5:00 P.M. Wheelchair accessible. Credit cards: Visa, MasterCard.*

ANGELA FASHIONS offers cramped but intriguing displays of dramatically feminine dresses and shoes intended for weddings, bridal parties, mothers of the bride, and formal wear. Smartly, for everyone's sake, there is a children's play center in the corner.
❧❧ *Angela Fashions, 833 Fort Street, (250) 480–0114. Hours: Monday– Saturday 10:00 A.M.–5:00 P.M. Wheelchair accessible. Credit cards: none.*

Voted Best Antique Shop by the *Victoria News* in 1995, FRED NEWBERRY ANTIQUES is both friendly and formal. It features handcrafted decoys, English and oriental antiques, collectors' pieces, silver, china, and art deco.
❧❧ *Fred Newberry Antiques, 835 Fort Street, (250) 388–7732. Hours: Monday–Saturday 10:00 A.M.–5:00 P.M. Wheelchair accessible. Credit cards: Visa, MasterCard.*

At ROMANOFF & CO. ANTIQUES, 837 Fort Street, Paul Freeman represents a new generation of antiques dealers with pizzazz and flair. While this store is new, its plum walls, lighted glass display cases, and carved wooden chairs make it one of the most warm and elegant places in the area.

Romanoff's features china dolls, silver, art glass, bronzes, estate jewelry, paintings, historical prints, ancient coins, watches, and artifacts. His brother Ian Freeman owns Penny Black Antiques, Stamps, & Coins, and his parents own the 1800 Shop next to Penny Black, both on Langley behind Murchie's Tea and Coffee.

Romanoff's has added more Tuskers Collectible Toys "sold to help African wildlife," Steiff bears, mechanical toys, and collectors' toys from around the world. Romanoff's toy sales support the David Sheldrick Wildlife Trust.
❧❧ *Romanoff & Co. Antiques, 837 Fort Street, (250) 480–1543. Hours: Monday–Saturday 10:30 A.M.–5:30 P.M., in summer. Sunday noon–5:00 P.M. Wheelchair accessible. Credit cards: Visa, MasterCard, American Express.*

VINTAGE BOOKS majors in general history (you remember him), fine bindings, and antiquarian books. Along with Poor Richard's, Vintage has the best history collection in town.

❧ *Vintage Books, 839 Fort Street, (250) 382–4414. Hours: Monday–Saturday 11:00 A.M.–5:00 P.M. Wheelchair accessible. Credit cards: Visa, MasterCard.*

Music and music-culture lovers will enjoy WARD MUSIC, reputed to be *the* music shop. Ward has "Canada's largest selection of sheet music," the best-stocked drum department on Vancouver Island, instruments and music to supply tastes from grunge to symphony, a school instrument-renting program, and terrific air-conditioning. One of our favorites. And kids hang out here, which is a good sign all around.

❧ *Ward Music, 911 Fort Street, (250) 385–3413. Hours: Monday–Saturday 9:30 A.M.–6:00 P.M. Mostly wheelchair accessible. Credit cards: Visa, MasterCard.*

Next have a look in VICTORIA LIMITED EDITIONS for fine collectibles from a Coca-Cola limited-edition set of full bottles at $2,995.95 and Goebel collectors-club miniatures to Waterford, Royal Doulton, Minton, Royal Albert, Lladro, Villeroy and Boch Christmas scene miniatures, crystal, china, and limited-edition plates.

❧ *Victoria Limited Editions, 919 Fort Street, (250) 386–5155. Hours: 9:30 A.M.–6:00 P.M. Wheelchair accessible, but tight squeeze. Credit cards: Visa, MasterCard.*

Voted Best Lunch by *Victoria News* readers, the woman-owned BLUE FOX CAFE at 919 Fort is colorful, cheerful, and terrific. Megan and her then week-old son came here for her "coming out" lunch. And, of course, she ran into friends.

Lunch ranges from lush burgers to creamy shrimp Caesar salad and everything in between. Potatoes at anytime are exceptional. Good espresso drinks. David thinks the gigantic homemade veggie burgers are the best in town, while Jerry goes gaga over the seafood club sandwich (smoked salmon and shrimp).

Breakfast may be the best in town also, with the omelets rivaled only by those at John's Place. Pancakes with fruit are humongous, yogurt and fruit likewise, toast may be on their homemade bread (Yes!), cinnamon rolls to die for, all reasonably priced. Kathleen thinks the veggie omelet is the best anywhere.

There's usually a line outside on weekends, and it's nearly impossible to get in between noon and 1:00 P.M., but it's worth the wait, honest. The menu is written on most walls in primary colors plus some, and the chintz tablecloths' colors cover the spectrum, superimposed with Far Side cartoons at each place. Enjoy! One of our favorites.

❧❧ *Blue Fox Cafe, 919 Fort Street, (250) 380–1683. Hours: Monday–Friday 7:30 A.M.–4:00 P.M., Saturday 8:00 A.M.–4:00 P.M., Sunday 9:00 A.M.–3:00 P.M. Wheelchair accessible. Credit cards: Visa, MasterCard. Beer and wine.*

BABAK'S ORIENTAL CARPETS is just what it says, with the perennial GOING OUT OF BUSINESS or CLEARANCE SALE signs.
❧❧ *Babak's Oriental Carpets, 931 Fort Street, (250) 480–7114. Hours: Monday–Saturday 10:00 A.M.–5:30 P.M., Sunday 2:00 P.M.–5:00 P.M. Wheelchair accessible. Credit cards: Visa, MasterCard, American Express.*

The ARTFUL NEEDLE is a fine couture boutique, not a tattoo parlor. When you enter this shop you instantly feel as if you walked into a French couture salon. "Fabric is our canvas" is the house motto here. Seamstresses make full garments, do alterations, and sell some needlepoint supplies.
❧❧ *Artful Needle, 959 Fort Street, (250) 385–5505. Hours: Monday–Friday 9:00 A.M.–5:00 P.M., Saturday 9:00 A.M.–1:00 P.M. Wheelchair accessible. Credit cards: American Express.*

After you pass the office buildings at the Vancouver Street corners, you will be on the busiest block of Antique Row.
OLD 'N' GOLD purchases and sells jewelry, watches, clocks, collectibles, and a few antiques.
❧❧ *Old 'n' Gold, 1011 Fort Street, (250) 361–1892. Hours: 10:00 A.M.–5:00 P.M. Monday–Saturday. Not wheelchair accessible. Credit cards: Visa, MasterCard, American Express.*

Listed in "Northwest Best Places," this pink VILLA ROSA RISTORANTE features Northern Italian cuisine, including salmon Tuscana with Chianti and cracked pepper and butter at $10.95–$14.50, Italian salads, pastas at around $9.50, vegetarian specials, pizzas, and cannelloni at $13.50. Try the grilled veal in Marsala wine ($15.50) or roast lamb ($14.50). Owned by the folks who bring us the San Reno's Greek restaurant with fabulous veggie pizza.
❧❧ *Villa Rosa Ristorante, 1015 Fort Street, (250) 384–5337. Hours: lunch Monday–Friday, dinner daily. Outdoor tables wheelchair accessible. Credit cards: Visa, MasterCard, American Express. Fully licensed.*

Food lovers must at least go into CAPTAIN COOK'S BAKERY LTD., a great bakery with fine hot and cold deli foods at the back counter, including flatbreads (pizza), stuffed peppers, meats and vegetables, Greek salad, tortellini, fruit, cole slaw, meat and cheese pasta salads, meat pies, salamis, and daily specials. A huge range of breads from ryes and raisin breads to twists, sweet and sourdough, and traditional Europeans tempts, as well as sweets and pastries galore. Often voted Victoria's Best Donut Shop, Captain Cook's now has a full-service restaurant upstairs with a huge wall and ceiling mural depicting Captain Cook's adventures.

Sometimes you need to take a number, because this place buzzes. Tearoom and rest rooms are upstairs, too. Victorians hang out with tea, lunch, or coffee at ample outside tables. Try the low-fat muffins. One of Kathleen's favorites.

❧ *Captain Cook's Bakery Ltd., 1019 Fort Street, (250) 386–4333. Hours: Monday–Saturday 6:30 A.M.–6:30 P.M. Outside and main level wheelchair accessible, upstairs is not. Credit cards: Visa, MasterCard.*

At David Robinson Antiques (1023 Fort Street, 250–384-6425), you have to ring for service and entry to see the furniture, clocks, oriental rugs, paintings, silver, copper, brass, and porcelain. No one answered when we tried. Notice the beautiful Tudor-style building.

FORT STREET CYCLERY was voted Best of Victoria in *Victoria News*. This shop offers long-ride foods, clothes, equipment, sunglasses, parts, Bell helmets, and everything else you might need. Mountain-bike brands include Raleigh, Haro, Maxam, GT, Wheeler, Iron Horse, Parkforce, Phoenix. Have a look at the fat-tired Schwinns. Rides information daily.

❧ *Fort Street Cyclery, 1025 Fort Street, (250) 384–6665. Hours: Monday–Saturday 10:00 A.M.–6:00 P.M., Sunday noon–5:00 P.M. Mostly wheelchair accessible. Credit cards: Visa, MasterCard.*

VOSS ART & ANTIQUES LTD. offers picture frames, collectibles, clocks, games, and Chinese artifacts.

❧ *Voss Art & Antiques Ltd., 1025 Fort Street, (250) 386–1850. Hours: 10:00 A.M.–5:00 P.M. Tuesday–Saturday, Wheelchair accessible. Credit cards: Visa, MasterCard.*

At the CLOTHES HORSE—DESIGNER FASHION BOUTIQUE you will find "Gently Used Fashions and Fancies," ladylike, previously owned fashions that include Esprit, Alfred Sing, Liz Claiborne, Bally, Anne Klein, Taxi, and Ports. Have a look.

❧ *Clothes Horse—Designer Fashion Boutique, 1037 Fort Street, (250) 383–8773. Hours: 10:00 A.M.–5:30 P.M. daily. Wheelchair accessible. Credit cards: Visa, MasterCard, American Express.*

Vancouver Island Soup located in the MOSAIC building makes soup. Surprise! The MOSAIC is a newly converted condominium complex with retail shops on the street floor.

ROGER'S JUKE BOX RECORDS sticks with oldies. Classic 33 rpm albums are stacked in cartons inside the store, and 50-cent album crates line the sidewalk in front. A sixties-feeling kinda place.

✤↺ *Roger's Juke Box Records, 1071 Fort Street, (250) 381–2526. Hours: 10:00 A.M.–5:30 or 6:00 P.M. Wheelchair accessible. Credit cards: Visa, MasterCard.*

Now we cross Fort Street to the north side to enjoy the best antiques block of all.

KUDOS features slightly recycled fashions including lots of leather. All consignment clothes are natural fiber and cater to the health-wise. There's plenty here for serious wear or costumes.

✤↺ *Kudos, 1048 Fort Street, (250) 384–1119. Hours: 10:00 A.M.–5:00 P.M. daily. Wheelchair accessible. Credit cards: none.*

J & J WATCH AND CLOCK REPAIR has a surprisingly interesting collection of new and old wall clocks, pocket watches, and wristwatches. Watchmaker Canh N. Ho repairs all clocks made with a smile and will change a watch battery while you wait.

✤↺ *J & J Watch And Clock Repair, 1046 Fort Street, (250) 361–4480. Hours: 9:30 A.M.–5:30 P.M. daily. Wheelchair accessible. Credit cards: Visa, MasterCard.*

CHARLES BAIRD ANTIQUES is a welcome addition to Antique Row. Charles Baird moved his highly esteemed shop to here in 1997, and a venture into this beautiful, narrow shop (8.5 feet wide) is an elegant treat, as is Baird's sense of humor.

✤↺ *Charles Baird Antiques, 1044A Fort Street, (250) 384–8809. Hours: Monday–Saturday 9:00 A.M. to 5:00 P.M., closed Sunday. Wheelchair accessible. No credit cards, "but will accept checks, small children, dogs, old autos."*

In VANITY FAIR ANTIQUE MALL, forty antiques dealers sell their collections and provide an interesting experience and hours of entertainment. Everything is here. We have found exceptional books and old kitchen utensils, dolls, memorabilia, china, spoons, and more in rooms and rooms of great stuff and artwork. Victorians regularly vote this place Best Antique Shop.

✤↺ *Vanity Fair Antique Mall, 1044 Fort Street, (250) 380–7274. Hours: Monday–Saturday 10:00 A.M.–5:30 P.M., Sunday 11:00 A.M.–4:00 P.M. Wheelchair accessible. Credit cards: Visa, MasterCard.*

At DOMUS ANTICA GALLERIES, Helga Past specializes in eighteenth- and nineteenth-century furniture, porcelain, glass, paintings, brass, and pewter. You must see the copper collection!

❦ *Domus Antica Galleries, 1038–1040 Fort Street, (250) 385–5443. Hours: 10:30 A.M.–5:00 P.M. Wheelchair accessible. Credit cards: Visa, MasterCard, American Express.*

THE GLASS MENAGERIE has the most amazing collector-plate collection we've ever seen, from traditional British classics to Elvis and Beauty and the Beast, plus other collectibles and antiques.

❦ *The Glass Menagerie, 1036 Fort Street, (250) 475–2228. Hours: 10:30 A.M.–5:30 P.M. Monday–Saturday, 11:00 A.M.–4:00 P.M. Sunday. Wheelchair accessible. Credit cards: Visa, MasterCard.*

The OLD VOGUE SHOP has wonderful $1.00 books, fifties kitchen equipment, Depression era glass and jewelry, delicate vintage clothing, estate linens, porcelain, and pottery, plus a few fifties toys.

❦ *Old Vogue Shop, 1034 Fort Street, (250) 380–7751. Hours: Monday–Saturday 10:30 A.M.–5:30 P.M. Wheelchair accessible. Credit cards: Visa, MasterCard, American Express.*

SALLY BUN, a spinoff of the Sally Cafe, is ideally convenient for shoppers and local workers alike. Here you can enjoy light snacks including dim sum–style buns filled with sun-dried tomatoes, artichokes, and pesto; pizza makings; chocolate; mushrooms; or daily surprises. Soup and salad attract lots of locals, as do the coffee and outrageous cinnamon buns, splitable for two for breakfast.

❦ *Sally Bun, 1030 Fort Street, (250) 360–1889. Hours: Monday–Saturday 10:00 A.M.–5:00 P.M. Wheelchair accessible. Credit cards: Visa, MasterCard.*

Three different stores, one location: FANNY DAVIS MALL ANTIQUES AND GENTLY USED FURNITURE, APPLEWOOD ANTIQUES, and ANTIEK MOR&LES, make a true emporium of great collectibles, restorations, solid wood period furniture, and old photos, including some by Man Ray.

❦ *Fanny Davis Mall Antiques and Gently Used Furniture, 1028 Fort Street, (250) 360–1889. Hours: Monday–Saturday 10:00 A.M.–5:00 P.M. Wheelchair accessible. Credit cards: Visa, MasterCard.*

JEFFRIES & CO. SILVER SMITHS LTD. carries an almost blinding array of exquisite silver tea services, serving dishes, candelabra, and other treasures.

Jeffries & Co. Silver Smiths Ltd., 1026 Fort Street, (250) 383–8315. Hours: Monday–Saturday 8:00 A.M.–5:00 P.M. Not wheelchair accessible. Credit cards: Visa, MasterCard, American Express.

JEAN HUTTON CUSTOM FRAMING truly does do "Framing with a flair" as advertised. The shop frames everything either plainly or ornately and sells fine-art reproductions, posters of interesting artists from David Hockney to Paul Klee, and food posters, too.

Jean Hutton Custom Framing, 1016 Fort Street, (250) 382–4493. Hours: Monday–Saturday 10:00 A.M.–5:00 P.M. Wheelchair accessible. Credit cards: Visa, MasterCard.

The best Chinese restaurant in Victoria is, indisputably, J & J WONTON NOODLE HOUSE at 1012 Fort. This is the most creative Chinese cuisine we have ever experienced. The entire kitchen is glassed in so you can watch the cooks, a restaurant fad rarely indulged in by Chinese restaurants. Co-owner/chef Joseph Wong spent a month in China learning more exciting cooking techniques and specialty dishes.

Of course, noodles are the focus, as in soups, meins, and funs. Try the daily luncheon specials. Lunch costs from $5.95 up, and delightful dinner dishes range from $3.95 to $10.95. Full vegetarian menu available at all times. Air-conditioned. Be sure to try the ginger-garlic fried chicken! One of our favorites.

J & J Wonton Noodle House, 1012 Fort Street, (250) 383–0680. Hours: Tuesday–Saturday 11:00 A.M.–2:30 P.M., 3:30–8:30 P.M. Wheelchair accessible. Credit cards: Visa, MasterCard. Beer and wine.

Wedged between two of Victoria's best restaurants is an interior design and home accessory studio called ROOM BY ROOM BY ROOM, which has elegant funk from picture frames to candle lamps and soji screens.

Room by Room by Room, 1010B Fort Street, (250) 388–6780. Hours: Monday–Saturday 10:00 A.M.–5:00 P.M. Wheelchair accessible. Credit cards: Visa, MasterCard.

DA TANDOOR, lauded by many as Victoria's best Indian restaurant, features vegetarian, poultry, lamb, seafood, and Tandoori kabobs. We have tried many dishes here and all were excellent, but one or two have been slightly dry. Da Tandoor also sells Indian and Pakistani jarred foods and chutneys.

Da Tandoor, 1010 Fort Street, (250) 384–6333. Hours: dinner after 5:00 P.M. daily. Wheelchair accessible. Credit cards: Visa, MasterCard. Beer and wine. Reservations recommended.

Cross Vancouver Street to IDAR JEWELLER & GOLDSMITH, where one-of-a-kind, elegant, modern, handmade and designed-here jewelry is created and displayed in a small, dramatic shop.

❧ *Idar Jeweller & Goldsmith, 946 Fort Street, (250) 383–3414. Hours: Monday–Friday 8:30 A.M.–5:30 P.M., Saturday 9:30 A.M.–4:30 P.M. Wheelchair accessible. Credit cards: Visa, MasterCard, American Express, and all currencies.*

CAFE BRIO—CUCINA DOMESTICA, one of Victoria's newer trendy restaurants, now serves West Coast and seasonal Italianate cuisine for lunch and dinner, with patio service in the summer, and what a great crowd-viewing spot that is!

At lunch you might try linguini with rock prawns at $12, pork loin at $12, or sea bass at $11. Dinner might feature braised rabbit on pepardelle herbed risotto at $16, sea bass at $19, steak and roasted root vegetables at $17, free-range chicken at $19, or venison steak at $20.

❧ *Cafe Brio—Cucina Domestica, 944 Fort Street, (250) 383–0009. Hours: lunch and dinner. Wheelchair accessible. Credit cards: Visa, MasterCard, American Express. Fully licensed.*

PACIFIC EDITIONS exhibits, distributes, and sells the best of Northwest Coastal native fine art and limited-edition prints, silver objects, and jewelry. Custom framing is also available here.

❧ *Pacific Editions, 942 Fort Street, (250) 388–5233. Hours: Monday–Saturday 9:30 A.M.–5:00 P.M. Credit cards: Visa, MasterCard.*

Catchily named SENZUSHI is said by many to be the best sushi restaurant in Victoria. You will also enjoy its attractive decor.

❧ *Senzushi, 940 Fort Street, (250) 385–4320. Hours: 11:00 A.M.–10:00 P.M. Wheelchair accessible. Credit cards: Visa, MasterCard. Beer and wine.*

We think BLOOMFIELD'S FLOWERS & POTTERY is Victoria's greatest pot shop (clay, that is). You will find a lovely collection of painted Spanish plates and pots and locally painted ones of all sizes. It is also a charming place to stop for cut flowers.

❧ *Bloomfield's Flowers & Pottery, 938 Fort Street, (250) 382–4747. Hours: 9:30 A.M.–6:00 P.M. Monday–Saturday, 11:00 A.M.–4:00 P.M. Sunday. Wheelchair accessible. Credit cards: Visa, MasterCard.*

LUND'S AUCTIONEERS & APPRAISERS is a great place to find treasures, including fine-art estate sales and collectibles. Some galleries buy furniture here, then repaint and resell it. Auctions take place weekly on Tuesday at 1:00 and 7:00 P.M.

You may preview the next week's sale goods Saturday from 10:00 A.M. to 4:00 P.M., Monday 9:00 A.M. to 6:00 P.M., and Tuesday from 9:00 A.M. until sale time.
❧ *Lund's Auctioneers & Appraisers, 926 Fort Street, (250) 386–3308. Hours: see above. Wheelchair accessible. Credit cards: Visa, MasterCard.*

Cross Quadra to the SPICE JAMMER. Some locals think this is the best Indian restaurant around, serving a variety of foods. At lunch, sandwiches are all three-tiered, such as a BLT with soup and tossed salad for $4.95! Tandoori kabobs at dinner are $7.95, and samosas vary by filling, including vegetarian. The menu makes easy sense, and the food and decor are just as straightforward. One of Megan's favorites.
❧ *Spice Jammer, 852 Fort Street, (250) 480–1055. Hours: Monday–Friday 11:30 A.M.–2:30 P.M., 5:00–9:00 P.M.; Saturday noon–3:00 P.M., 5:00–10:00 P.M.; Sunday 8:30 A.M.–3:00 P.M., 5:00–9:00 P.M. Wheelchair accessible. Credit cards: Visa, MasterCard.*

MIROIRS is an elegant new shop that features "The most beautiful mirrors in the world," meaning a few antiques and hundreds of Canadian reproductions of classic European mirrors. John Doyle has created a pleasant ambience with oriental rugs to warm red walls.
❧ *Miroirs, 832 Fort Street, (250) 361–3382; cell: (250) 216–7820; E-mail: miroirs@hotmail.com. Hours: 11:00 A.M.–5:30 P.M. Tuesday–Saturday. Wheelchair accessible, but tight. Credit cards: Visa, MasterCard.*

At WELLS BOOKS, the Wells Group, which is primarily Jeri Bass and Diane Wells, presents expertise and comfort as well as excellent collections of nautical and transportation books—books on trains, planes; automobiles; the sea and ships; transportation; cooking; wine; Canadian, British, and European history, and children's books. Wells also sells antiquarian collections, leather-bound books, fine bindings, and plastic book jacket covers for around $3.00.
❧ *Wells Books, 828–832 Fort Street, (250) 360–2929. Hours: 10:00 A.M.–5:00 P.M. daily. Mostly wheelchair accessible. Credit cards: Visa, MasterCard.*

BRITANNIA & CO. ANTIQUES is just what it says it is, with some prestigious pieces.
❧ *Britannia & Co. Antiques, 828 Fort Street, (250) 480–1954. Hours: 10:30 A.M.–5:30 P.M. Monday–Saturday. Wheelchair accessible. Credit cards: Visa, MasterCard, American Express.*

Go in to experience CLASSIC SILVERWARE in the Chelsea Building. In contrast to some other antiques shops, this one's sign welcomes you and means it: WE'RE OPEN. FEEL FREE TO COME IN AND BROWSE.

Margaret Kuyvenhoven and Ita Laninga specialize in discontinued silverplated flatware at affordable prices, vintage linens, lace, old baptismal gowns, tablecloths, and bedding. A friendly place.

❦ *Classic Silverware, 826 Fort Street, (250) 383–6860. Hours: Monday–Saturday 10:00 A.M.–5:00 P.M. Wheelchair accessible. Credit cards: Visa, MasterCard.*

CAIRO COFFEE MERCHANTS, a designer coffee bean (roasted daily) boutique, also carries proper teapots, mugs, packaged spices, Bombay chutneys, and imported teas. You can mix your own tea blends.

❦ *Cairo Coffee Merchants, 774 Fort Street, (250) 386–3937. Hours: Monday–Saturday 9:00 A.M.–5:30 P.M. Wheelchair accessible. Credit cards: none.*

Be sure to try NEW SAIGON VIETNAMESE RESTAURANT unless you are MSG sensitive. Clean and pleasantly decorated with Vietnamese prints and live plants, New Saigon offers truly authentic Vietnamese cuisine, such as grilled garlic meatballs with meat brochette and rice sticks ($5.75), fish hot pot ($10.95), pork hot pot marinated in fish sauce with caramel sauce ($8.95), noodle soups, and green papaya salad ($5.50).

❦ *New Saigon Vietnamese Restaurant, 772 Fort Street, (250) 385–5516. Hours: 11:00 A.M.–3:00 P.M., 5:00–9:00 P.M. Monday–Saturday. Wheelchair accessible. Credit cards: Visa, MasterCard, en Route, American Express.*

Locals come to PATISSERIE DANIEL daily for exceptional salads and lunches, pastries, cakes, low-fat goodies, vegetable crostini, tomato rosemary flatbread, and dressings made with peach vinegar. One of our favorites.

❦ *Patisserie Daniel, 768 Fort Street, (250) 361–4243. Hours: Monday–Friday 8:00 A.M.–5:30 P.M., Saturday 9:30 A.M.–5:30 P.M. Wheelchair accessible. Credit cards: Visa, MasterCard.*

Even women will have a pleasant surprise at B.C. SHAVERS & HOBBIES, a wonderful emporium of things traditionally masculine: shavers (and hair dryers) repairs; sharpening of knives, scissors, and tools; model trains, race cars; air brushes; compressors; paints; metal detectors; model boats and planes; and electric shavers. It also sells a huge collection of puzzles and railroad books, X-acto craft tools, and collectibles from Star Trek to old car and airplane models. A good place to break the molds, so to speak. One of our favorites.

✤⇣ *B.C. Shavers & Hobbies, 742 Fort Street, (250) 383–0051. Hours: Monday–Thursday, Saturday 9:00 A.M.–5:30 P.M.; Friday 9:00 A.M.–9:00 P.M. Wheelchair accessible. Credit cards: Visa, MasterCard, American Express.*

At RUSSELL BOOKS, Diana and Russell del Pol and daughter hold forth at their 9,000-square-foot, three-floor book emporium with remarkable collections of calendars (Marilyn Monroe fans, run!); cards; new, used, and antiquarian books; and historic prints and posters. Browsers of all stripes are welcomed by a member of the family, which includes adult children Andrea, Brandon, Sean, and Chad. One of Jerry's favorites.

✤⇣ *Russell Books, 734 Fort Street, (250) 361–4447. Hours: Monday–Saturday 9:00 A.M.–5:30 P.M., Sunday noon–5:00 P.M. Wheelchair accessible. Credit cards: Visa, MasterCard, American Express.*

Unless you think you're only going to tempt yourself, be sure to take a number the minute you walk into the GOLDEN SHEAF BAKERY. The deep, fully packed meat pies, cookies, breads (including chipmunk health bread), and gorgeous sweets for all occasions make you want to stay.

✤⇣ *Golden Sheaf Bakery, 730 Fort Street, (250) 383–9725. Hours: Monday–Friday 7:00 A.M.–5:30 P.M., Saturday 7:30 A.M.–5:30 P.M. Wheelchair accessible. Credit cards: Visa, MasterCard.*

DOT'S DISCOUNT is discount designer clothing at its finest. Dot's is crowded with women's clothes tastefully displayed and women tastefully clothed. It's wedged between two great Victorian bakeries, so you can celebrate after your purchase.

✤⇣ *Dot's Discount, 724 Fort Street, (250) 383–2683. Hours: Monday–Saturday 9:30 A.M.–6:00 P.M., Sunday noon–5:00 P.M. Wheelchair accessible. Credit cards: none.*

How do Victorians survive? DUTCH BAKERY & COFFEE SHOP, another successful sweet shop, tempts the browsing weary. Voted Best Bakery in Victoria in 1996, this is another fabulous temptation full of homemade chocolates, pastries, meat pies (from $1.55), buttery cookies ($2.70 a dozen), and wedding and birthday cakes made the same day you order. Breakfasts until 12:30 P.M.

✤⇣ *Dutch Bakery & Coffee Shop, 718 Fort Street, (250) 385–1012. Hours: Tuesday–Saturday 7:30 A.M.–5:30 P.M. Wheelchair accessible. Credit cards: none.*

STEVENSON'S SHOE CLINIC calls itself "the essential Birkenstock repair center" (although others do it). Mephisto, Clark, Rockport, Ecco, and Timberland shoes and Samsonite luggage all are fixed here happily and promptly.

Stevenson's Shoe Clinic, 714 Fort Street, (250) 383–8615. Hours: Monday–Friday 8:00 A.M.–5:30 P.M., Saturday 8:45 A.M.–5:00 P.M. Wheelchair accessible. Credit cards: Visa, MasterCard.

In case the walk across Douglas Street wears you out, COMPANY'S COMING sells the company's muffins and pastries and fresh-ground coffees. For an early morning or late afternoon pick-me-up, Lena and Joe Anderson's cheerful blue-and-white check decor and cafeteria style make it a quick stop.

Company's Coming, 670 Fort Street, (250) 383–7044. Hours: Monday–Friday 7:00 A.M.–5:30 P.M., Saturday 8:00 A.M.–5:30 P.M., Sunday 9:00 A.M.–5:00 P.M. Wheelchair accessible. Credit cards: none.

Do not miss INTERACTIVE GAMES & STUFF. Jack Pinder's young business is doing wonderful business with wonderful stuff for kids of all ages. Buy a biosphere just like the one taken on a Russian space shuttle or Total yo-yos like the ones Tommy Smothers uses from $5.00 to $150.00. A gigantic collection of jigsaw puzzles attracts serious puzzle fans. He also sells magnificent chess sets, enormous kites, game books, and origami paper. One of Jerry's favorites.

Interactive Games & Stuff, 654 Fort Street, (250) 480–3979. Hours: Monday–Saturday 9:30 A.M.–5:30 P.M., Sunday noon–5:00 P.M., until 8:00 or 9:00 P.M. in summer. Wheelchair accessible. Credit cards: Visa, MasterCard.

Next door is CRABTREE & EVELYN, a branch of this internationally popular home for fragrances, soaps, potpourri, jams, chutney, and teapots.

Crabtree & Evelyn, 640 Fort Street, (250) 381–6344. Hours: Monday–Saturday 9:30 A.M.–5:30 P.M., Sunday noon–5:00 P.M., later in summer and holiday season. Wheelchair accessible. Credit cards: Visa, MasterCard.

VANESSA JEWELLERS is an "engagement ring center," in case the impulse strikes you. Vanessa's also sells unusual design clocks including ones that look like CDs, footballs, and soccer balls, as well as watches. The store does watch repairs and goldsmithing, too.

Vanessa Jewellers, 636 Fort Street, (250) 383–4542. Hours: Monday–Saturday 9:30 A.M.–5:30 P.M., Sunday 1:00–5:00 P.M., later in summer and holiday season. Wheelchair accessible. Credit cards: Visa, MasterCard, American Express.

PASTEL'S, at 203 Eaton Centre, serves many local workers and shoppers as a handy, healthy, sandwich, soup, and salad cafe with bagels, buns, and muffins; bottled waters; teas; and espresso drinks. Limited seating inside, lots of patio tables facing Fort.

❧ *Pastel's, 203 Eaton Centre, (250) 383–5113. Hours: 9:30 A.M.–5:30 P.M., later in summer and holiday season. Not wheelchair accessible. Credit cards: Visa, MasterCard.*

Tired feet ought to stop at FOOTLOOSE LEATHERS, where the emphasis is on "shoes that are good for your feet." Keith and Kirsten Greiner sell comfortable shoes such as Gage-Cole, Birkenstock, Mephisto, Ecco, Doc Martens, and John Fleuvogs, as well as orthopedic shoes that look good and feel good. Keith also makes custom shoes personally. One of Kathleen's favorites.

❧ *Footloose Leathers, 628 Fort Street, (250) 383–4040. Hours: Monday–Saturday 9:30 A.M.–5:30 P.M., Sunday 11:00 A.M.–5:00 P.M., later in summer and holiday season. Not wheelchair accessible. Credit cards: Visa, MasterCard.*

SCALLYWAGS is an elegant children's boutique (yes, it's the same as the one in The Empress hotel) featuring children's clothes, dolls, teddy bears, and stuffed dolls galore. Go in just for the fun of it.

❧ *Scallywags, 624 Fort Street, (250) 360–2570. Hours: Monday–Saturday 9:30 A.M.–5:30 P.M., Sunday 10:00 A.M.–5:00 P.M., later in summer and holiday season. Wheelchair accessible. Credit cards: Visa, MasterCard.*

If you want to explore more of Eaton Centre, go ahead. We're going to continue. View Street runs east and west right outside the northern doors of Eaton Centre. Many of the shops on the north (non–Eaton Centre) side of View Street below Broad also face on Trounce Alley, which you must explore. It intersects here. This private street, designed and developed by Thomas Trounce, used to be closed off once a year to keep it from technically becoming a public way.

This side of Trounce Alley was built in 1889 by developer/architect Thomas Trounce. It has served as a bank, YMCA, and Victoria Stock exchange. A duplicate building across the alley burned down in 1910.

THE TAPA BAR, a delightfully Spanish reworking of Vin Santo Urban Bistro, offers tapas and entrees from Four Bean Salad with salted cod ($4.00), calamari fritos ($5.00–$7.00), Bisteck Madagascar ($12.00), swordfish cebiche ($3.00), or mussels, chicken, and chorizo fondue to pastas and thin crust pizza. A pitcher of sangria is only $14.00. Green-and-white checked cloths cover outdoor tables while bold paintings hang on mustard walls inside.

➷ *The Tapa Bar,* 620 Trounce Alley, (250) 383–0086. Full bar. Hours: Monday–Thursday 11:30 A.M.–10:00 P.M., Friday–Saturday 11:30 A.M.– midnight. Wheelchair accessible. Credit cards: Visa, MasterCard, American Express.

Visit ALL IN BLOOM for the cheer, as well as for the home and garden accessories. Shelagh Macartney owns and hosts this boutique chock-full of the perfect sun/shade hat, smocks, gifts with a floral theme, books, unique papers and cards, ribbons, gardening tools and gloves, teensy rubbed-color plant pots from $7.95 to $13.95, and mosaic-covered vases. Don't miss The Near Naked Man ironing board cover (Kathleen bought two), sushi candles, and Virgin and Slut soaps and lip balm.

Just as important, Shelagh's shop is the hilarious communications community/social center for a whole segment of Victoria. Even if you don't need anything, go in just to enjoy her and her customers.

➷ *All in Bloom,* 616 Trounce Alley, (250) 383–1883. Hours: Monday–Saturday 10:00 A.M.–5:30 P.M., Sunday noon–4:00 P.M. Wheelchair accessible. Credit cards: Visa, MasterCard, American Express, and "no library cards," says Shelagh.

In case you missed them elsewhere, here's another NUSHIN BOUTIQUE LTD., an elegant European-style ladies' boutique featuring Louis Feraud of Paris clothes.

➷ *Nushin Boutique Ltd.,* 606 Trounce Alley, (250) 381–2131. Hours: Monday–Saturday 10:00 A.M.–5:30 P.M., Sunday noon–4:00 P.M. Wheelchair accessible. Credit cards: Visa, MasterCard, American Express.

On the other (south) side of Trounce Alley, the shops also face View Street, such as fabulously eclectic POMEGRANATE, where Sue and Rea have assembled a truly exotic collection of personal accessories and clothing from Africa and Asia in what looks like a bazaar (and not bizarre). Tasteful clothing from long black chiffon scarves with brilliant yellow tigers to shirts and skirts, jewelry, folk art, masks, crafts, fabrics, baskets, and much more. Kathleen often finds a scarf here.

➷ *Pomegranate,* 614 View Street, (250) 388–0488. Hours: Monday–Saturday 10:00 A.M.–5:30 P.M., Sunday noon–5:00 P.M. Wheelchair accessible. Credit cards: Visa, MasterCard, American Express, JCB.

INSTINCT ART AND GIFTS offers New Age spiritual gifts, incense, tapes, and books with interesting native and Celtic jewelry in a very peaceful and nonaggressive atmosphere. Dumb questions answered graciously here.

➷ *Instinct Art and Gifts,* 622 View Street, (250) 388–5033. Hours: Monday–Saturday 10:00 A.M.–5:30 P.M., Sunday noon–5:00 P.M. Wheelchair accessible. Credit cards: Visa, MasterCard.

PASTA WITH PRAWNS IN TOMATO-CREAM SAUCE
Gerri Schelini of The Tuscan Kitchen, Victoria

Ingredients

8–16 oz. pasta, preferably
    rustichella

12–16 oz. prawns, fresh or frozen

2 cloves garlic, crushed

2 tbsp. olive oil

tomato sauce, in 2–3 ratio to
    1 cream

cream

Roma tomatoes, chopped (optional)

parsley, chopped

sea salt

freshly ground pepper

sun-dried tomatoes (optional)

capers (optional)

splash of white wine

Preparation

For fresh prawns, cook in boiling water until pink-orange, cool, and peel. For frozen cooked prawns, thaw in small bowl with gently running cold water for a few minutes and drain.

Gently and briefly sauté garlic in oil. Add prawns and turn flame up a little, then toss prawns to cook evenly. Add sun-dried tomatoes and capers if you wish. Add a splash of white wine, stir lightly, and add tomato sauce. Turn the flame down and gently simmer a few minutes. Add cream. Cover and let the flavors develop for a few more minutes. Don't allow to boil.

Follow package cooking time for pasta; toss with prawn mixture and serve. Serves four.

If you want to "kick it up a notch," add a little hot sauce. To make it extra special, try half squid ink and half fettucine egg noodles. The squid ink lends a seafood flavor, and the contrast of colors is nice. A simple salad of greens or cooked greens with Balsamic vinegar is a nice accompaniment.

Buon appetito.

We're now at Broad Street, north of Eaton Centre.

On the back (north) side of Eaton Centre, facing View and Broad Streets, food lovers absolutely must visit The Tuscan Kitchen and Haute Cuisine Cookware.

Gerri and Mauro Schelini's THE TUSCAN KITCHEN specializes in Italian food stuffs, Italian ceramics, tools, gadgets, pots and pans, herbs, Dean & DeLuca spices, confections, twenty Balsamic vinegars, and loads of Italian cookbooks.

❧ *The Tuscan Kitchen, 653 View Street, (250) 386–8191; E-mail: tuscan.kitchen@home.com. Hours: 10:00 A.M.–6:00 P.M., and later Monday–Saturday, noon–5:00 p.m. Sunday. Wheelchair accessible. Credit cards: Visa, MasterCard.*

A must-stop is the WEST END GALLERY, at the northeast corner of View and Broad. West End Gallery features Canadian artists and hosts the annual Canadian Glass Show, featuring the work of more than sixty artists. Try to see the work of Grant Leier and Barton Nixie.

❧ *West End Gallery, 1203 Broad Street, (250) 388–0009; Fax: (250) 388–0099. Hours 10:00 A.M.–5:30 P.M. Monday–Friday, 10:00 A.M.–5:00 P.M. Saturday, noon–4:00 P.M. Sunday. Not wheelchair accessible. Credit cards: Visa, MasterCard.*

MONK OFFICE SUPPLIES is a convenient source of everything you need to write a letter, glue, or cut and paste. Copies made for only 5 cents. You can also get maps and travel supplies.

❧ *Monk Office Supplies, 1200 Broad Street, (250) 382–1615. Hours: Monday–Friday 8:30 A.M.–5:00 P.M., Saturday 9:00 A.M.–5:00 P.M. Wheelchair accessible. Credit cards: Visa, MasterCard.*

HAUTE CUISINE COOKWARE is Victoria's best kitchen accessories shop and one of the most enjoyable, period. Stephanie Clark has assembled the finest of everything: Le Creuset, Emile Henry porcelain cookware, iron grills, loads of peppermills including brass, woks (12 inches–30 inches)—including the largest wok and peppermill on the island—Martha Stewart parody books, magnetic poetry for your fridge, Bodum coffee presses, aprons, place mats, napkins, the perfect garlic press and wine bottle openers, a superior selection of cookbooks, tea kettles, and designer teapots. One of our favorites.

❧ *Haute Cuisine Cookware, 1210 Broad Street, (250) 388–9906. Hours: Monday–Saturday 10:00 A.M.–6:00 P.M. Wheelchair accessible, but be careful. Credit cards: Visa, MasterCard.*

We usually check in at the VITAMIN SHOP, a health shop to end them all, featuring 4,000 items of everything you need away from home or at home: vitamins, Natural Factors, Good Health Guides, Quest, Nature's Way, Herbal Select teas, Gaia herbs, and consultations.

❧ *Vitamin Shop, 1212 Broad Street, (250) 386–1212. Hours: Monday–Friday 9:00 A.M.–6:00 P.M., Saturday 9:30 A.M.–5:30 P.M., Sunday 11:00 A.M.–5:00 P.M. Wheelchair accessible. Credit cards: Visa, MasterCard.*

Locals like EUGENE'S GREEK RESTAURANT ON BROAD, which offers dining inside or at a couple of sidewalk tables, plus takeout. Because of its business-area location, cafeteria-style service is quick whether you order souvlaki, gyros, spanakopita, tiropita, Greek salad, or baklava. You can also get comfort foods such as chicken pie for $3.50 and "criss cut" fries at $2.25. Souvlaki (kabobs) pork is only $5.50 and lamb $5.75. Go to the counter in back and order your food. The food and decor are simple, good, and direct. One of David's favorites.

❧ *Eugene's Greek Restaurant on Broad, 1280 Broad Street, (250) 381–5456. Hours: Monday–Friday 8:00 A.M.–8:00 P.M., Saturday 10:00 A.M.–8:00 P.M. Wheelchair accessible. Credit cards: Visa, MasterCard. Beer and wine.*

A truly local gift shop featuring all Canadian products, UNIQUE GIFTS & MORE has cat everythings from cat journals to cards, Daniel's Belgian chocolates, all cards on recycled paper, and aromatherapy supplies.

❧ *Unique Gifts & More, 1282–1286 Broad Street, (250) 381–2132. Hours: Monday–Friday 9:30 A.M.–5:30 P.M., Saturday 10:00 A.M.–5:30 P.M. Wheelchair accessible. Credit cards: Visa, MasterCard, American Express, enRoute.*

BAGEL STREET CAFE is a newish chain cafe with excellent bagels (try chocolate chip!) and creative schmears (cream cheese mixes), teas, good coffees, and a large variety of add-on goodies.

❧ *Bagel Street Cafe, 1294 Broad Street, (250) 381–4141. Hours: Monday–Friday 7:00 A.M.–6:00 P.M., Saturday 9:00 A.M.–6:00 P.M., Sunday 9:00 A.M.–5:00 P.M. Wheelchair accessible. Credit cards: Visa, MasterCard. Smoking at outside tables.*

UNIVERSAL TATTOO is the oldest tattoo studio in Victoria (nearly twenty years) and offers Celtic, tribal, native, military, portrait, family crest, fix-up, custom, and esoteric tattoos. You can keep environmentally sound by paying an extra $100 to use vegetable-based inks. Just to keep you happy while you wait, Zain and Gary have pool tables and pinball machines for you to play.

❧ *Universal Tattoo, 1306 Broad Street, (250) 382–9417. Hours: 11:00 A.M.–7:00 P.M. daily. Wheelchair accessible. Credit cards: Visa, MasterCard.*

PLUM offers soft ladies' apparel to size sixteen, but art lovers will enjoy STARFISH GLASSWORKS at the northwest corner of Broad and Yates. You can watch glassblowing noon–6:00 P.M. Wednesday–Sunday. Lisa Samphire, Marna Tudor, and Gary Bolt are the artist-owners and feature thirty-five other Canadian glass artists.

❧ *Starfish Glassworks, 630 Yates Street, (250) 388–7827; Fax: (250) 388–7828; Web: www.starfishglass.bc.ca. Hours: 10:00 A.M.–6:00 P.M. Tuesday–Saturday, noon–6:00 P.M. Sunday. Upstairs gallery not wheelchair accessible. Credit cards: Visa, MasterCard.*

Cross Yates Street, and in the next block of Broad you'll come to SUN & SURF SWIMWEAR, dudes' and dudettes' headquarters. Hot stuff for surfing, which you can here, believe it or not. You'll find Billabong; Mr. Zogs; Sex Wax (calm down, parents); skateboards; Redsand, O'Neill, and Speedo swimsuits; wet suits; surfer, body, and bowling magazines; and Frisbees. Cool sunglasses.

❧ *Sun & Surf Swimwear, 1314 Broad Street, (250) 920–5511. Hours: Monday–Thursday, Saturday 10:00 A.M.–6:00 P.M.; summer Fridays 10:00 A.M.–8:00 P.M.; Sunday 11:00 A.M.–5:00 P.M. Partly wheelchair accessible. Credit cards: Visa, MasterCard, American Express.*

Voted Best Fish & Chips in Victoria by *Monday Magazine* readers, the OLD VIC FISH & CHIPS is deep-fried heaven. One piece of cod, with chips of course, costs $5.95. Halibut starts at $7.45, and you can get assorted breaded shellfish for $8.50, chicken breast strips and chips for children for $4.95, and mushy peas for only $1.50. The usual lunch special consists of one piece of cod and chips with coffee, tea, or small pop for $6.45. Warm oak booths and brass plates on the walls give this place a cheerful British atmosphere.

❧ *Old Vic Fish & Chips, 1316 Broad Street, (250) 383–4536. Hours: Monday–Saturday 11:00 A.M.–7:00 P.M. Wheelchair accessible. Credit cards: Visa, MasterCard. Beer and wine.*

Martin Barnett and Patsy Frederick's RISING STAR BAKERY & NATURALLY GOOD CAFE produces all the delightfully light breads for afternoon tea at both The Empress and Point Ellice House. While this funky Jewish bakery is not strictly kosher, this is a health-foods cafe despite the huge, fluffy cinnamon buns; focaccia Mexican (an ethnic confusion that works); soups; sandwiches; teas; and coffees. Patsy also runs the Gingerbread Bakery in Cook Street Village.

❧ *Rising Star Bakery & Naturally Good Cafe, 1330 Broad Street, (250) 388–9411. Hours: Monday–Friday 7:00 A.M.–7:00 P.M., Saturday–Sunday 8:00 A.M.–4:00 P.M. Wheelchair accessible. Credit cards: none.*

Cross Broad Street and continue down the east side, taking a quick peek into G FAMILY GROCERY, a handy place to pick up any little convenience needs. ❧ *G Family Grocery, 1317 Broad Street, (250) 382–5143.*

BROAD STREET CAMERAS & REPAIRS is an old-timey, dignified, traditional camera shop that repairs almost any camera you bring in and sells film and any other equipment you may need. On-site black-and-white film development is also offered.
❧ *Broad Street Cameras & Repairs, 1309 Broad Street, (250) 384–5480. Hours: Monday–Friday 9:30 A.M.–5:30 P.M., Saturday open at 10:00 A.M. Wheelchair accessible. Credit cards: Visa, MasterCard.*

ROBINSON'S OUTDOOR SPORTING GOODS STORE supplies Victorians with fishing equipment galore, including poles, licenses, outfits, crab traps (only $22.99), plus lots of advice and tips.
❧ *Robinson's Outdoor Sporting Goods Store, 1307 Broad Street, (250) 385–3429. Hours: 9:30 A.M.–5:30 P.M. Wheelchair accessible. Credit cards: Visa, MasterCard.*

Now we're back at Yates. Up Yates from Broad, on your left (north side), you will find Lyle's Place and the English Sweet Shop. LYLE'S PLACE is definitely the hip place for new and used CDs, cassettes, concert tickets, and to find out what's happening.
❧ *Lyle's Place, 726 Yates Street, (250) 382–8422. Hours: 10:00 A.M.–6:00 P.M. daily, Sunday noon–5:00 P.M. Wheelchair accessible. Credit cards: Visa, MasterCard.*

Two highlights of Yates Street for sugar lovers with an affinity for traditional British candies are the English Sweet Shop and the British Candy Shoppe.
The ENGLISH SWEET SHOP is the self-claimed "sweetest shop in town since 1932." This old-fashioned English candy shop also claims to carry "the largest selection of imported toffees and sweets in the Northwest."
❧ *English Sweet Shop, 738 Yates Street, (250) 382–3325. Hours: 9:30 A.M.–5:30 P.M. Wheelchair accessible. Credit cards: Visa, MasterCard.*

A block down Yates Street (on the other side), the BRITISH CANDY SHOPPE is an extremely up-to-date, colorful, and vibrant British import candy shop where locals and visitors of British origin line up for their favorite comfort candies from home, some even waiting for just the right-shaped jelly bean expected in on a certain day. You simply select your candy bar, biscuits, or loose candy from huge glass jars, pay, and reminisce to your heart's and dentist's content.

❧ *British Candy Shoppe, 635 Yates Street, (250) 382–2634. Hours: 9:30 A.M.–5:30 P.M. Wheelchair accessible. Credit cards: Visa, MasterCard.*

If you cross Yates at Broad and want to go down Yates, on the south side are Silverwood and Growlie's Restaurant.

SILVERWOOD is a new direct-import shop featuring masks, mirrors, jewelery, sculpture, and incense from Thailand, Bali, Indonesia, and India.

❧ *Silverwood, 619 Yates Street, (250) 389–6119. Hours: 10:00 A.M.–6:00 P.M. Monday–Saturday, 11:00 A.M.–5:00 P.M. Sunday. Wheelchair accessible. Credit cards: Visa, MasterCard.*

Nongrowling GROWLIE'S RESTAURANT is a small, local, comfy diner featuring charbroiled beef and chicken burgers with soup, salad, or pan fries for only $5.55, a vegetarian menu, and New England clam chowder with garlic toast at $2.95. Prices include GST, there is a public phone, and local beers are best priced. Lots of locals come here.

❧ *Growlie's Restaurant, 615 Yates Street, (250) 383–2654. Hours: Monday–Saturday 8:00 A.M.–6:30 P.M. Wheelchair accessible. Credit cards: Visa, MasterCard. Beer and wine.*

There's another Honey Bun at 605 Yates, a chain of bakeries with Chinese fast food(!) ranging from $1.59 to $3.99 including MSG.

Cross Yates. If you love or even like the smell of leather, LEATHER WORLD is it. Handmade belts, soft backpacks, hair barrettes, purses, fanny packs, silver-spiked black leather collars, string ties, and wallets, much of which is made here. You will also find 1,500 different styles of belt buckles from Harley-Davidson and BSA to personal names, or with cars, fishing, and Canadian themes. One of our favorites.

❧ *Leather World, 610 Yates Street, (250) 388–7825. Hours: 9:30 A.M.–5:30 P.M. daily. Wheelchair accessible. Credit cards: Visa, MasterCard.*

BERNSTEIN & GOLD is one of the most elegant and least snobbish shops selling home furnishings, table linens, and fine china. Beautiful.

❧ *Bernstein & Gold, 608 Yates Street, (250) 384–7899. Hours: Monday–Saturday 10:00 A.M.–5:30 P.M., Sunday noon–5:00 P.M. Wheelchair accessible. Credit cards: Visa, MasterCard, American Express.*

And here we are at Starbucks again. Once through Starbucks, you cross Government Street on Yates, you will again pass Fields Shoes, and then go down the north side of Yates. There is a parking garage on the south side of Yates.

Must-see MIRARI INTERIORS is a design studio where you are welcomed to explore handmade artistic and Italian modern furniture and wild, sensuous lamps, ultimate dog bowls and trinkets, shapely ironwork, and jazzy designed St. Moritz watches. New additions include Montreal-made Rugby North American Italian leather jackets, pants, and men's handbags.

❧ *Mirari Interiors, 576 Yates Street, (250) 380–1114. Hours: 10:00 A.M.–5:30 P.M. Monday–Saturday, noon–5:00 P.M. Sunday. Wheelchair accessible. Credit cards: Visa, MasterCard, American Express, Diners.*

STEAMER'S PUB serves as a gathering place for local twenty-, thirty-, and fortysomethings with loads of excellent local beers, great food including huge salads from $2.95, tasty pastas, and fish and chips, all at great prices, plus sidewalk table seating in good weather. Good Canadian rock and Celtic bands play here frequently. Pool tables in the back. A favorite.

❧ *Steamer's Pub, 570 Yates Street, (250) 381–4340. Hours: 11:30 A.M. on. Mostly wheelchair accessible. Credit cards: Visa, MasterCard.*

You must venture upstairs to a theatrical-feeling space with high ceilings, HUGHES LTD., an elegant, with-it clothes boutique for men and women featuring Canadian designers Lida Baday, Jacqueline Conoir, Ron & Normand, Martinique, Lilith, Sandwich, Tombolini, Diesel Style Lab, Pelo, DKNY, InWear, TSE cashmere, K.S., and Joan & David.

❧ *Hughes Ltd., 564 Yates Street, (250) 381–4405. Hours: 10:00 A.M.–5:30 P.M. Monday–Saturday, noon–5:00 P.M. Sunday. Downstairs wheelchair accessible. Credit cards: Visa, MasterCard, American Express.*

ALEXANDRIA has elegant home furnishings "for your nearby loft"—we wish—including classic and modern furniture, textiles, area rugs, and accessories.

❧ *Alexandria, 560 Yates Street, (250) 381–5590. Hours: 10:00 A.M.–5:00 P.M. Monday–Friday, 10:00 A.M.–4:00 P.M. Saturday. Wheelchair accessible. Credit cards: Visa, MasterCard.*

Don't miss Victoria's finest men's couture clothing boutique, OUTLOOKS FOR MEN. Dale Olsen's shop is the place to play pool and get the latest men's fashions at Victoria prices. A limited stock of high-quality labels such as Kenneth Cole, Part Two, Willie Rodriguez, Jack Victor, and Mezzrow draws locals and visitors of all ages and lifestyles. One of David's favorites.

❧ *Outlooks for Men*, 554 Yates Street, (250) 384–6121. Hours: Monday–Thursday 10:00 A.M.–5:30 P.M., Friday 10:00 A.M.–9:00 P.M., Sunday noon–4:00 P.M. Wheelchair accessible. Credit cards: Visa, MasterCard, American Express, Diners.

CARNABY STREET is Rosina Usatch's near cultural museum of a boutique, specializing in ethnic clothing, tribal jewelry, antique carpets, and rare textiles. Believe us, you have never seen such a collection! Dresses/robes/gowns dazzle in beautifully dramatic color combinations from black to brilliant reds, purples, along with greens, and teal blue, many of which are available in large sizes, from $75 to $400. You'll also find Ecuadorian sweaters for winter warmth. The fine carpet gallery has a Russian/Persian boudoir atmosphere. Ask nicely. All price tags have both Canadian and American prices. One of Kathleen's favorites.
Fine points: The building dates back to 1888.
❧ *Carnaby Street*, 538 Yates Street, (250) 382–3747. Hours: summer 9:30 A.M.–7:00 P.M. or later, especially Friday and Saturday nights. Partly wheelchair accessible. Credit cards: Visa, MasterCard, American Express.

Lots of local government workers and businesspeople drop into FERRIS' OYSTER BAR & GRILL to get food to go or lunch on the deck in back, where there's a seafood BBQ every Sunday from noon to 10:00 P.M. Blood-red walls with bold paintings, rough plank floors, a narrow wooden bar, white oak tables and chairs, a potted cactus on each table, and stained-glass windows give the partial feeling of a true pub.
Fine points: Built in the 1850s, this was the first masonry building on Yates Street. The founder, James Webster, was shot dead in 1862 when the killer mistook him for someone else.
❧ *Ferris' Oyster Bar & Grill*, 536 Yates Street, (250) 360–1824. Hours: Monday–Thursday, Sunday noon–10:00 P.M., Friday–Saturday noon–11:00 P.M. Wheelchair accessible. Credit cards: Visa, MasterCard. Fully licensed.

As you reach the lower end of Yates Street, you get into Old Town Victoria. As you cross Waddington Alley, you will come upon the VICTORIA INTERNATIONAL YOUTH HOSTEL, a clean, cheerful hostel welcoming all ages with some private rooms; 108 beds from $15.00 for youth hostel members to $19.50 for nonmembers. You can also get tourist information from a friendly host. (See "Where to Stay.")
❧ *Victoria International Youth Hostel*, 516 Yates Street, (250) 385–4511. Hours: 7:00 A.M.–midnight, doors locked at 2:30 A.M. Partly wheelchair accessible. Credit cards: Visa, MasterCard. One hundred percent nonsmoking and nondrinking.

At RESTAURANT MATISSE, John Phillip and Chef Philippe Renaudat have re-created a little bit of Paris night here in Victoria. They serve either a la carte or table d'hôte. The latter may include lobster bisque, carpaccio d'ombre chevalier, fillet of beef or roast lamb, and crême brulée for $36.50–$38.50. Try the excellent bouillebaise of local fish, crab, and other shellfish in a pernod broth ($23.95). Carnivores enjoy the steak tartare ($13.50), duck ($22.95), or rabbit available two ways ($20.95).

🌺 *Restaurant Matisse, 512 Yates Street, (250) 480–0883. Hours: opens 5:30 P.M. Wednesday–Sunday. Wheelchair accessible. Credit cards: Visa, MasterCard, American Express.*

Down from the parkade you will find three worth-its. The first is STOCKS & STONES, a great name for a design firm, which you'll find just inside the lobby. Helen and Sarah Killington feature lamps, oak and small statuary, and run their design business from here.

🌺 *Stocks & Stones, 535 Yates Street, (250) 920–0644. Hours: Monday–Saturday 10:00 A.M.–5:00 P.M. Not wheelchair accessible. Credit cards: Visa, MasterCard, American Express.*

Pizza Hut, at 533 Yates, brings its usual pizza and pasta to Victoria, just up the street from PERIKLIS RESTAURANT, at 531. Periklis offers authentic Greek cuisine featuring lamb, steak, chicken, ribs, seafood, souvlaki, dolmadakia, taramosalata and pita, Greek salata, and special Greek combinations. Weekend nights Greek and belly dancers perform with an occasional appearance by Zorba and the Bad Greeks.

Owner/manager Paul Vasilakopoulos and family have been here for more than twenty years, "so we must be doing something right." In keeping with Periklis the Greek's political nature, Periklis the Restaurant is frequented by B.C. politicians, such as former premier Mike Harcourt.

🌺 *Periklis Restaurant, 531 Yates Street, (250) 386–3313. Hours: lunch Monday–Friday 11:30 A.M.–5:00 P.M., dinner daily 5:00 P.M.–11:00 P.M. Wheelchair accessible. Credit cards: Visa, MasterCard, American Express. Fully licensed.*

SÜZE LOUNGE & RESTAURANT replaced a funky coffee and tea house at 515 Yates. To update the atmosphere and convert the space, owners Jay Gildenhuys and Graham Storey sandblasted the historic brick walls, added paintings and warm, dark wooden furniture, and built a gorgeous bar with several table lamps strategically placed to create intimate lighting and a peppy ambience. The name Süze comes from a Picasso collage, and the entire restaurant appears to be put together in a Picasso-esque style.

You might try the excellent grilled Belgian endive salad, chicken and artichoke cannelloni, pad Thai, or pear and blue cheese pizza.

SÜZE Lounge & Restaurant, 515 Yates Street, (250) 383–2829. Hours: lunch, dinner, Sunday brunch, late-night dining daily. Bar level is wheelchair accessible. Credit cards: Visa, MasterCard, American Express. Fully licensed.

We are now going to explore Johnson Street, but first, turn into Waddington Alley, the only street in Victoria with wood block paving. In an even smaller alleyway off Waddington, between Yates and Johnson, you'll find IL TERRAZZO DI CECCONI'S, best-known as just Il Terrazzo. It is worth finding. The menu is available in English, French, German, and Japanese.

The decor is novella Italian Canadian with bright colors, bright people, big plants, lots of windows, and a cheerful outdoor feeling indoors. Il Terrazzo's food is excellent West Coast Italian, if we may be so bold.

Try the stuffed calamari, which are succulent and cost $8.95, or the prawns, mussels, polenta, and Asiago baked in their wood-burning oven. Seven-inch pizzas are $9.00. At dinner we had mouthwatering sautéed oysters and pollo arosto—a marinated, wood-oven baked, half free-range chicken (probably the whole thing was free range) at $16.95. There was also stuffed veal scaloppini at $16.95, osso buco at $18.95, or tender melt-in-your-mouth bistecca con pesto at $18.95. The pastas and wine list are both excellent. One of our favorites.

Il Terrazzo Di Cecconi's, 555 Johnson Street, (250) 361–0028. Hours: lunch from 11:30 A.M. and dinner from 5:00 P.M. daily. Wheelchair accessible. Credit cards: Visa, MasterCard, American Express. Fully licensed.

We will now take you up both sides of JOHNSON STREET, which is one-way up (east).

WILLIE'S BAKERY bakes bread and other goodies for its parent, the group that includes Il Terrazzo and Pescatore's. The soups and sandwiches are fabulous deals at about $4.00. Kathleen loves the tuna Niçoise with watercress. Excellent coffees, and try to get there in time to enjoy the popular pan au chocolate. The site was originally Willie's Bakery and finally has returned to its intended best use. Don't miss one of our favorites, the B & B upstairs.

Fine points: This little Italianate building was erected in 1887 for baker Louis Wille (sic).

Willie's Bakery, 537 Johnson Street, (250) 381–8414. Web: www.isabellasbb. com/willies./ Hours: Monday–Thursday 7:00 A.M.–6:00 P.M., Friday and Saturday open at 8:00 A.M. but close later. Wheelchair accessible. Credit cards: Visa, MasterCard, American Express.

DOG'S DAY BAKERY is the pet of entertainer Janis Mullan and Penny Stone. Blethering Place Tea Room owner and Janis's mother, Maureen Mullan, helped develop the recipes for baked-here chocolate- and wheat-free doggie bagels, carob-covered cookies, and the coming "Cat-a-teria." Pet lovers and lovers' pets must visit. You can also order from home via the Web site. Dogs come right in.
❧ *Dog's Day Bakery, 543 Johnson Street, (250) 386–3647 (FUN–DOGS); Web: www.dogsdaybakery.com. Hours: 9:00 A.M.–9:00 P.M., summer, 10:00 A.M.–6:00 P.M. winter. Wheelchair accessible. Credit cards: Visa, MasterCard, American Express.*

SKY HIGH KITES features stunt kites from around the world, wind socks, boomerangs, croquet equipment, yo-yos, kids' balls, games, and harmonicas.
❧ *Sky High Kites, 547 Johnson Street, (250) 382–4999. Hours: 10:00 A.M.–5:30 P.M. daily. Wheelchair accessible. Credit cards: Visa, MasterCard, American Express.*

STILL LIFE sells fun vintage, used, and new clothing, with something for almost everyone, including Blundstone Australian footwear.
❧ *Still Life, 551 Johnson Street, (250) 386–5655. Hours: Monday–Saturday 10:30 A.M.–6:00 P.M., Sunday close at 5:00 P.M. Wheelchair accessible. Credit cards: Visa, MasterCard.*

At BUTTON BOUTIQUE you can explore (and acquire) historic and unique buttons; Canadian-made buttons; notions; and stitchery tools. Kim and Michael Stremel offer buttons of nuts, stone, bone, and antlers, as well as pairs or single buttons, and stitchery magazines in several languages. One of Kathleen's favorites.
❧ *Button Boutique, 561 Johnson Street, (250) 384–8781; E-mail: buttons@island.net; Web: www.buttonedup.com. Hours: 10:00 A.M.–6:00 P.M. Monday–Saturday, noon–5:00 P.M. Sunday. Not wheelchair accessible. Credit cards: Visa, MasterCard.*

Rap and New Age music junkies will love BOOMTOWN, which sells new and used, with even some rentals.
❧ *Boomtown, 561 Johnson Street, (250) 380–5090. Hours: Monday–Wednesday 10:00 A.M.–6:00 P.M., Thursday–Friday until 7:00 P.M., Saturday 1:00–8:00 P.M. Not wheelchair accessible. Credit cards: Visa, MasterCard, American Express.*

Visit **A & A GALLERY**, a unique art gallery that feels like the open art studio it is, in which owner/artist Andy Shutse Lou does stunning freehand Chinese brush painting and framing. The son of a famous Beijing artist and trained in the United States, Lou gives art lessons Tuesday evening and Saturday. Ask to see his workshop on the mezzanine.

A & A Gallery, 561 Johnson Street, (250) 380–9461. Hours: 10:00 A.M.–5:30 P.M. Partly wheelchair accessible. Credit cards: Visa, MasterCard, American Express.

SACRED HERBS is a head shop that focuses on promoting the "sacred herb," hemp, in all forms, including Hempy's clothes and smoking equipment. There's been only one problem with authorities—when a policeman confiscated a marijuana plant growing in the window (!) and scolded them not to do that again.

Sacred Herbs, 561 Johnson Street (no phone). Hours: Monday–Saturday 11:00 A.M.–6:00 P.M., Sunday 1:00–5:00 P.M. Wheelchair accessible. Credit cards: none.

At **DRAGONWARE** expert seamstress and native Victorian Judy Bishop provides costumes and dancewear for individuals and costuming for theatrical and dance studios. Our favorite is the tutus she makes for the 300-pound man who delivers singing telegrams and wears them out every three months. "Men just don't know how to take care of their clothes!" Judy says.

Dragonware, 561 Johnson Street, (250) 381–3355. Hours: Monday–Saturday 10:00 A.M.–5:30 P.M., Sunday noon–4:00 P.M. Wheelchair accessible. Credit cards: Visa, MasterCard.

Julia Bump's store motto is "Why be normal?" and at **ZYDECO** you'll see what she means. This delightfully wacky shop offers the unusual from all over the world: literary best-sellers *Roadkill Cookbook* and *What Bird Did That?*; the born-again Christian car magnet fish with "Darwin" in it; hard-to-get Ray Troll fishing shirts from Alaska with artwork and titles like "Twist and Trout"; and a bonanza of Christmas stocking stuffers or party favors. Locals also shop here, for good reason.

Fine points: The building dates from 1879.

Zydeco, 565 Johnson Street, (250) 592–6308. Hours: Saturday–Tuesday 10:00 A.M.–6:00 P.M., Wednesday–Friday 10:00 A.M.–8:30 P.M. Wheelchair accessible. Credit cards: Visa, MasterCard.

ZINNIA WORLD NOTIONS is an interesting little shop full of unusual imported jewelry, oriental rugs recycled into pillows, oils and perfumes, and teas from India, all at reasonable prices. Owner Dustin Hanoski traveled to Asia and Mexico gathering handmade crafts and has taken great care to make sure artists and craftspeople are not ripped off in the selling process.

❧ *Zinnia World Notions, 569 Johnson Street, (250) 385–9915. Hours: Monday–Saturday 10:00 A.M.–6:00 P.M., Sunday noon–5:00 P.M. Wheelchair accessible. Credit cards: Visa, MasterCard, American Express.*

Victoria's jazz aficionados gather at ENDANGERED SPECIES MUSIC to discover and buy old record albums. Owner Brian Deneault is doing what he loves—music.

❧ *Endangered Species Music, 575 Johnson Street, (250) 995–0099. Hours: Monday–Saturday 10:00 A.M.–5:30 P.M., Sunday noon–5:00 P.M. Wheelchair accessible. Credit cards: Visa, MasterCard.*

LONE WOLF GALLERY is "Jill and Jack's" pride, joy, and goal to present a "stress-free" store featuring Zen gardens, small water fountains, local artists working on-site, and a mix of North American carving and artwork.

❧ *Lone Wolf Gallery, 577 Johnson Street, (250) 380–4004. Hours: 10:30 A.M.–5:30 or 6:00 P.M. Monday–Saturday, 11:00 A.M.–5:00 P.M. Sunday. Wheelchair accessible. Credit cards: Visa, MasterCard.*

PACIFIC WOODS OUTFITTERS CENTRE is a newish upscale active adventure store with hiking footwear including "Chlorophylle" boots, backpacks, and lots of books about hiking and nature.

❧ *Pacific Woods Outfitters Centre, 581 Johnson Street, (250) 388–0470. Hours: Monday–Friday 9:30 A.M.–5:30 P.M., Saturday 9:30 A.M.–9:00 P.M., Sunday 11:00 A.M.–5:00 P.M. Wheelchair accessible. Credit cards: Visa, MasterCard.*

The Royal Jubilee Hospital Auxiliary's THRIFT SHOP is a secondhand bargain shop and a great place to find women's and men's clothing and other goodies for your home or apartment.

❧ *Thrift Shop, 585 Johnson Street, (250) 386–7111. Hours: Monday–Friday 10:00 A.M.–4:00 P.M., Saturday 10:00 A.M.–5:00 P.M. Wheelchair accessible. Credit cards: none.*

More head shops and cultural headquarters for alternative Victoria can be found at OFF THE CUFF and OFF THE CUFF TOO, where you can buy hemp clothes, lava lamps, Harley-Davidson see-through panties, smoking equipment of all sorts, T-shirts of most alternative bands and causes, books on hemp and opium growing, hemp paper, and incense.

Fine points: The building was a pharmacy from 1876 through 1957.

✦✧ *Off the Cuff and Off the Cuff Too, 587 Johnson Street, (250) 386–2221. Hours: 10:00 A.M.–11:00 P.M. Not wheelchair accessible. Credit cards: Visa, MasterCard.*

Directly across Johnson Street from Waddington Alley and Java is MARKET SQUARE, which is now a huge, restored complex of forty-five small shops and restaurants with distinct personalities, many on Johnson and Pandora Streets. Try everything in Market Square, if you have time. Created in the 1970s from old Victorian structures, Market Square's core buildings included the Grand Pacific Hotel (also known as Russ House and later Drake Hotel) at the corner, dating from 1879, and the Scott & Peeden Building next door on Store Street, erected in 1896. Tenants included houses of prostitution, saloons, gunsmiths, and an opium factory.

CROCODILE BAR & GRILL is one of the hot new kids on the block, at the southwest corner of Market Square, with some reasonably priced entrees and great lunches. Specialties include grilled Ahi tuna ($21.50), Arctic Char fillet ($18.50), pan-roasted breast of duck ($22.50), Moroccan chicken ($16.50), or a whole rack of lamb with mango ($25.50).

Calabrian (thin crust) pizzas with baby lobster or goat cheese and chorizo sausage ($9.95); great pastas such as lemon-pepper linguini with mushrooms, spinach, vine-ripened tomato, eggplant, and zucchini sautéed in pesto ($8.50); and sandwiches from Ahi tuna burgers to a French lamb baguette ($9.50) are some of the offerings.

The happening place on this block is in the Crocodile Lounge in the cellar, where you can listen to live jazz Friday and Saturday nights from 8:30 p.m. to 1:00 A.M. Brunch on Saturday and Sunday has a fabulous Italian bacon and gorgonzola frittata ($10.95).

✦✧ *Crocodile Bar & Grill, 560 Johnson Street, (250) 386–5252. Hours: 11:00 A.M.–midnight daily, brunch 11:00 A.M.–4:00 P.M. Saturday–Sunday. Fully licensed. Mostly wheelchair accessible. Credit cards: Visa, MasterCard, American Express.*

Robert Smith, of SILVER SMITH, offers the largest selection of silver jewelry in town, including his own custom designs in silver and gold. In the summer he displays native original art and crafts, and in the winter he shows icons and spectacular, massive turquoise bracelets.

Fine points: The cast-iron fountain at the 560 Johnson Street entrance was moved from a traffic circle near The Empress hotel.

✦✧ *Silver Smith, 560 Johnson Street, (250) 383–7979. Hours: 10:00 A.M.–5:00 P.M. daily. Wheelchair accessible. Credit cards: Visa, MasterCard.*

Fascinating **ROYAL HOLOGRAPHIC ART GALLERY** makes your eyes and mind swirl. Here you can get holographic everything (except a driver's license) made by fifty different artists, from watches at $44.95 to sunglasses and framed pictures.

❧ *Royal Holographic Art Gallery, 560 Johnson Street, (250) 384–0123. E-mail: royal@islandnet.com; Web: www. islandnet.com/~royal/index.htm. Hours: Monday–Friday 10:00 A.M.–5:30 P.M., Saturday 11:00 A.M.–5:00 P.M., Sunday noon–4:00 P.M. Wheelchair accessible. Credit cards: Visa, MasterCard, American Express, Diners.*

Kids love **BAGGINS** for Tango Rose, Rebel Beach, unusual Converse shoes, Hollywood jeans, and Parsley & Sage shirts and tops. An experience for those older than fourteen.

❧ *Baggins, 540 Johnson Street, (250) 388–7022. Hours: summer 10:00 A.M.–8:00 P.M., winter 10:00 A.M.–5:30 P.M. Wheelchair accessible. Credit cards: Visa, MasterCard, American Express.*

OLD TOWN NEWS sells Canadian, American, and some European newspapers, as well as snacks, cold drinks, and postcards.

❧ *Old Town News, 560 Johnson Street, (250) 380–6548. Hours: 8:00 A.M.–9:00 P.M. daily. Wheelchair accessible. Credit cards: none.*

Try **LA CACHE** for a restful combination of print dresses, painted cups and saucers, bed linens, tablecloths, place mats, and giftware—all from classic French styling to casual twenties looks, and all color-coordinated to mix and match.

❧ *La Cache, 562 Johnson Street, (250) 384–6343. Hours: Monday–Saturday 10:00 A.M.–6:00 P.M., Sunday 11:00 A.M.–5:00 P.M. Not wheelchair accessible. Credit cards: Visa, MasterCard, American Express.*

Now walk into giant **MARKET SQUARE** and explore its many levels. Be sure to notice the new mural down the stairway by Chris Johnson of the Chippewas of the Nawash Band.

WOOFLES—A DOGGY DINER is a miniscale gourmet doggie-treat shop with wheat-free pizza bites, carob-dipped hearts, and Chateau Woof de Pup bottles of goodies. Dogs welcomed.

❧ *Woofles, 560 Johnson Street, (250) 385–WOOF. Hours: 10:00 A.M.–6:00 P.M. daily. Wheelchair accessible. Credit cards: Visa, MasterCard.*

OUT OF HAND GALLERY handles pottery and jewelry from British Columbia as well as work of other Canadian artists. A great place to buy a Canadian original.

❦ *Out of Hand Gallery, 566 Johnson Street, (250) 384–5221. Hours: summer 10:00 A.M.–7:00 P.M., Saturday until 6:00 P.M., Sunday noon–5:00 P.M.; winter 10:00 A.M.–5:00 or 6:00 P.M. Not wheelchair accessible. Credit cards: Visa, MasterCard, American Express.*

GRIFFIN BOOKS is a good general bookstore with excellent impulse buys and a good collection of Canadian authors' work.

❦ *Griffin Books, 560 Johnson Street, (250) 383–0633. Hours: 10:00 A.M.–5:30 P.M. Monday–Saturday, 11:00 A.M.–4:00 P.M. Sunday. Wheelchair accessible. Credit cards: Visa, MasterCard.*

WIMSEY BOOKS is a haven for lovers of mystery and crime novels, both new and used.

❦ *Wimsey Books, 560 Johnson Street, (250) 380–1764. Hours: summer 10:00 A.M.–7:00 P.M., winter 10:00 A.M.–5:00 or 6:00 P.M. Wheelchair accessible by elevator. Credit cards: Visa, MasterCard.*

Don't miss RUBBER RAINBOW, one of Canada's most written-about stores. The Rubber Rainbow sells condoms—plain, simple, colorful, funny, serious, and, yes, tasteful. Founded here by Carol Nicholson and her daughter Chelsea, who runs this shop, there are now eleven Rubber Rainbows in Seattle, Vancouver, Whistler, and Honolulu.

Rubber Rainbow (not to be confused with Double Rainbow, Americans) is so nicely and humorously presented that mothers and daughters, fathers and sons, and the crisscross, feel comfortable exploring it together.

New products include flavored glow-in-the-dark body paint, aprons, and a new International Condom Collection with Hershey chocolate, grape, lemon, mint, and other flavors. Rubber Rainbow owners and staff answer all questions frankly and graciously.

❦ *Rubber Rainbow, 560 Johnson Street, (250) 388–3532. Hours: 11:00 A.M. on. Wheelchair accessible from Johnson Street gate. Credit cards: Visa, MasterCard.*

People walk or ride from all over town to get to GREEN CUISINE, a totally vegetarian restaurant with a hot buffet, salad bar, in-house organic bakery, juices, and espresso drinks (made with soy milk if you prefer). You go through the buffet line and pay for your food by weight. One of our favorites.

❦ *Green Cuisine, 560 Johnson Street (lower level), (250) 385–1809. Hours: 11:00 A.M.–8:00 P.M. daily. Wheelchair accessible by elevator. Credit cards: Visa, MasterCard, American Express.*

Check out BEAD WORLD for everything you need for bead stringing, the Mayan and Central American Imports shops, and the other food places on every level. Public washrooms are on the lower level, at the northeastern corner of the complex. Children of all ages will enjoy Foxglove Toys.

Back out on Johnson Street, the next store you come to is JEUNE BROTHERS OUTDOOR EQUIPMENT, one of Victoria's best outdoor equipment stores carrying Sierra designs, North Face, rentals, tents, kayaks, and a great selection of travel guides. Its store next door, Jeune Brothers Tent and Awning, Ltd. (250–385–7751), sells canvas of all sizes and colors (even to cover your yacht), boat toppings, lawn swings, and a few flags. These two stores cover many of your leisure-time needs.

❧ *Jeune Brothers Outdoor Equipment, 570 Johnson Street, (250) 386–8778. Hours: 10:00 A.M.–6:00 P.M. daily. Opens earlier on weekends. Wheelchair accessible. Credit cards: Visa, MasterCard, American Express.*

BOSUN'S LOCKER has everything for the serious or wanna-be boater, from jackets to rigging and teflon coating (we could all use a little of that), hinges, lots of rope, West Coast charts, and batteries.

Fine points: This 1899 building was famous in the 1930s as a walk-up house of prostitution.

❧ *Bosun's Locker, 580 Johnson Street, (250) 386-1308. Hours: Monday–Friday 8:30 A.M.–5:30 P.M., Saturday 9:00 A.M.–5:00 P.M. Wheelchair accessible. Credit cards: Visa, MasterCard, American Express.*

Every city has a pawn shop, so here is UNIVERSAL TRADING PAWNBROKERS, with guitars, jewelry, the usual. Try it if you like it.

❧ *Universal Trading Pawnbrokers, 584 Johnson Street, (250) 383–9512. Hours: 10:00 A.M.–5:30 P.M. daily. Wheelchair accessible.*

After you cross Government Street going up (east), you come to an exceptionally good block for kids, starting with OLDE TOWNE SHOE REPAIR, with the DOC MARTENS FIXED sign in the window. Mike Waterman, a former banker who ditched that profession fifteen years ago to "do his own thing" and work with his hands, is a native Victorian who loves to talk to his customers while he works. In his whopping 356-square-foot shop he will repair your leather purse on the spot or explain the anatomy of Doc Martens shoes and actually fix them, saving Doc lovers hundreds of dollars. One of Jerry's favorites.

❧ *Olde Towne Shoe Repair, 605 Johnson Street, (250) 386–8333. Hours: Monday–Friday 9:00 A.M.–5:30 P.M. Wheelchair accessible. Credit cards: none.*

At FRIENDS OF DOROTHY'S CAFE, a glass display case enclosing a red-sequined slipper greets you at the door as you enter this cozy, interesting restaurant devoted to *The Wizard of Oz*. With the movie playing continuously, the cafe's motto is, of course, "I have the feeling we're not in Kansas anymore." Surprise! Lunch and dinner are in the $6.25–$13.45 range. The menu covers the waterfront, Victoria style, with breakfast served all day, including the "Yellow Brick Road" of poached eggs, Cajun sausages, toast and fries, and new healthier and vegetarian offerings. Gay friendly. Lots of locals.

❦ *Friends of Dorothy's Cafe, 615 Johnson Street, (250) 381–2277. Hours: 11:00 A.M.–8:00 P.M. Tuesday–Thursday, til 9:00 P.M. Thursday and Friday, and 11:00 A.M.–4:00 P.M. Sunday. Wheelchair accessible. Credit cards: Visa, MasterCard.*

Fine points: 615–625 Johnson was originally the Canada Hotel, built in 1874 with bay windows.

A new hit in Victoria is the vegan LOTUS POND VEGETARIAN RESTAURANT. Try Shiitake Delight, of lightly battered shiitake mushrooms sautéed in spicy basil sauce ($12.95); Lemon Mock Chicken ($10.95); soups and noodle dishes; and wheat-free selections. Several Buddist and Chinese publications on sale. Lunchtime natural vegan buffet and dim-sum menu.

❦ *Lotus Pond Vegetarian Restaurant, 617 Johnson Street, (250) 380–9293. Hours: 11:00 A.M.–9:00 P.M., Tuesday–Sunday. Wheelchair accessible. Free delivery; discount for pick-up orders. Credit cards: Visa, MasterCard.*

The name of SNOWDEN'S BOOKS does not refer to Princess Margaret's ex-husband, Tony. Here Victoria's own Jerry Snowden sells his incredible collection of new and used paperback books at discount prices. Great place to find a cheap read.

❦ *Snowden's Books, 619 Johnson Street, (250) 383–8131. Hours: 10:00 A.M.–5:00 P.M. daily, Monday half day. Wheelchair accessible. Credit cards: Visa, MasterCard.*

PACIFIC WESTERN CRAFTS AND THE BEAD SHOP offers a terrific assortment of beads for all needs of the do-it-yourself designer.

❦ *Pacific Western Crafts and the Bead Shop, 621 Johnson Street, (250) 480–1497. Hours: Monday 10:00 A.M.–5:00 P.M., Tuesday–Friday 10:00 A.M.–7:00 P.M., Saturday 10:00 A.M.–6:00 P.M. Wheelchair accessible. Credit cards: Visa, MasterCard.*

DARK HORSE BOOKS has, primarily, books on witchcraft, Wicca, science fiction, and fantasy, both new and used, mostly paperbacks. Heaven if those are your interests.

➷☞ *Dark Horse Books, 623 Johnson Street, (250) 386–8736. Hours: 10:00 A.M.–6:00 P.M. Wednesday–Saturday, noon–5:00 P.M. Sunday. Wheelchair accessible. Credit cards: Visa, MasterCard.*

GAMES WORKSHOP, is a Warhammer strategy-game shop. Only.

➷☞ *Games Workshop, 625 Johnson Street, (250) 361–1499. Hours: 10:00 A.M.–6:00 P.M. Monday–Wednesday, 10:00 A.M.–9:00 P.M. Thursday–Saturday, noon–5:00 P.M. Sunday. Wheelchair accessible. Credit cards: Visa, MasterCard, American Express.*

CURIOUS COMICS AND IMAGE is a terrific comic book store with great Calvin and Hobbes murals at the door, lots of books about comics, DC comics, Star Wars, and comics T-shirts. It also sells computer games.

➷☞ *Curious Comics and Image, 631 Johnson Street, (250) 384–1656. Comic hot line: (250) 384–1053. Hours: 9:30 A.M.–6:00 P.M. daily, Sunday 11:00 A.M.–5:00 P.M. Wheelchair accessible. Credit cards: Visa, MasterCard.*

And you will find even more comics at YELLOW JACKET COMIC BOOKS & TOYS, which has all current comics galore and life-size *Star Wars* cardboard cutouts for $34.95. Another kids' heaven.

➷☞ *Yellow Jacket Comic Books & Toys, 649 Johnson Street, (250) 480–0049. Hours: 9:30 A.M.–5:30 P.M. Monday–Saturday, 11:00 A.M.–5:00 P.M. Sunday. Wheelchair accessible. Credit cards: Visa, MasterCard.*

Chinatown

Now we come to Victoria's 1-block CHINATOWN. The ornate, elegant Gate of Harmonious Interest, built in 1882 and restored and lovingly painted in 1996–97, marks your official entry into the area.

While Victoria's Chinatown is small by San Francisco or Vancouver standards, it is intense, colorful, vibrant, and growing, along with Victoria's and Vancouver's Chinese immigrant populations. Many Hong Kong Chinese moved to Vancouver before China's takeover of Hong Kong from the British. Victoria's Chinatown is still the hub of the Chinese community who shop here and in a few stores adjoining the recognized center.

➷☞ *Hours: Most shops and restaurants in Chinatown stay open as long as there are customers, so we cannot be specific; they like to keep flexible. Many of them do not have telephones or listed phone numbers, and few take credit cards.*

GATE OF HARMONIOUS INTEREST, CHINATOWN, FISGARD STREET

The first store on the left, at Government and Fisgard, is QUONLEY'S GIFTS AND GROCERY. Beach mats at two for $2.99 and back scratchers on the sidewalk outside immediately signal Chinatown. Inside you will find lovely wind chimes, lacquered boxes, Chinese and Japanese traditional shoes and slippers, and basic groceries. China tea sets, incense, best-deal rice bowls, and Chinese and Japanese candies are complemented by Anglo foods such as ice cream cones and sandwiches to go.

Quonley's Gifts and Grocery, 1628 Government Street, (250) 383–0623. Wheelchair accessible.

Fine points: There is a public telephone in the pagoda on the sidewalk here.

561 FISGARD is a tourist-oriented shop featuring Chinese trinkets and jewelry, but mostly press-on T-shirts with imitation Disney and other cartoon designs. *Wheelchair accessible.*

ADVANCED BUSINESS CENTRE, 559 Fisgard, is actually a handy one-hour photo place with frames, postcards, and Chinese gift cards. *Wheelchair accessible.*

The JANK COMPANY is the cleanest, best grocery store (and more) in Chinatown. Displays of Chinese vegetables such as choy sum, gai lan, yu choy, eggplant, kohlrabi, snow peas, and surian (a soft Thai pineapple-like fruit) beckon you from the sidewalk. Inside, at least eight varieties of dried mushrooms and seaweed, rice bowls (as low as 99 cents), canned and dried imported Asian foods galore, tofu, dried pea snacks, waters, juices, and candies grab your money.

♣❧ *Jank Company, 555 Fisgard Street. Mostly wheelchair accessible.*

We find the CHINATOWN TRADING COMPANY, 551 Fisgard, to be a fabulous emporium of Chinese imports. The abundance, good taste, variety, and display of world imports here is astounding. Great inexpensive souvenirs and Christmas stocking stuffers, home accessories, embroidered flower bun warmers at only $2.99, hundreds of teapots, kitchen utensils, madras bedspreads, baskets, papier-mâché, chimes, more baskets, and even rugs fill this historic building's maze of rooms.

In a display case toward the back you can see a rare private collection of actual Chinese workers' artifacts, including dominoes, work and play tools, lanterns, and books from the original Chinatown. Peek into the old-time gambling/banking center hidden in the corner.

♣❧ *Chinatown Trading Company, 551 Fisgard Street, (250) 381–5503. Mostly wheelchair accessible. Credit cards: Visa, MasterCard.*

The last room of the Chinatown Trading Company exits onto Fan Tan Alley, which we will visit as soon as we complete our trip down this side of Fisgard and come back up the other side.

FAN TAN CAFE is a small restaurant that does a nice job catering to visitors with its good Hong Kong cuisine, hamburgers for kids (or anyone else) in a pinch, combination plates, and great prices. Lunch is served until 4:30 P.M. A Victoria *Times-Colonist* restaurant reviewer named Fan Tan one of her top ten restaurants of 1999, although we find the food to be inconsistent. Enjoy the red and black Miro-like interior and paintings, and the starry lights in the ceiling.

♣❧ *Fan Tan Cafe, 549 Fisgard Street, (250) 383–1611. Wheelchair accessible. Hours: noon–2:30 A.M. Monday–Saturday, noon–9:00 P.M. Sunday. Credit cards: Visa, MasterCard, American Express. Fully licensed.*

ORIGINAL CHINESE SCHOOL ON
FISGARD STREET

The front half of TIKI PICTURE FRAMING & GALLERY has beautiful Chinese linens, cushion covers, hankies, kimonos, doilies, and bun warmers, as well as Baoding iron balls, whose directions you follow to soothe acupuncture points. The back half has a good supply of watercolors, oils, paper, canvases, brushes, cards, and Chinese prints and scrolls.

❧ Tiki Picture Framing & Gallery, 545 Fisgard Street, (250) 384–3742. Hours: 10:00 A.M.–5:00 P.M. Wheelchair accessible. Credit cards: Visa, MasterCard.

A large Chinese clientele frequents KIMBO RESTAURANT, a Chinese family-style restaurant with formica tables and padded chrome chairs. Worth a try.

❧ Kimbo Restaurant, 543 Fisgard Street, (250) 383–5251. Wheelchair accessible. Credit cards: Visa, MasterCard. Fully licensed.

FAN TAN GALLERY is a cozy non-Chinese emporium of home decor accessories with a collection of pillows, baskets, handmade rugs of all sizes from Turkey and India, local furniture, and Mexican pots. The house cat might surprise you by staying asleep in the folded rugs. If you are thinking of buying a rug here, be sure to ask if it is colorfast, and listen carefully to the answer.

❧ Fan Tan Gallery, 541 Fisgard Street, (250) 382–4424. Hours: Monday–Saturday 10:00 A.M.–5:30 P.M., extended hours at Christmas. Entry floor is wheelchair accessible. Credit cards: Visa, MasterCard.

DALE'S GALLERY is another non-Chinese gallery of beautifully tasteful prints and watercolors by local artists such as Elizabeth Griffiths and Brian Crovet, plus framing services.

❧ Dale's Gallery, 537 Fisgard Street, (250) 383–1552. Hours: 10:00 A.M.–5:30 P.M. Monday–Saturday, noon–4:00 P.M. Sunday. Wheelchair accessible. Credit cards: Visa, MasterCard, American Express.

The CHINESE-CANADIAN CULTURAL ASSOCIATION at 535 Fisgard serves as a community center of sorts and is generally closed to the non-Chinese public. Photos of Mao Zedong, founder of the People's Republic of China, and former Canadian prime minister Pierre Elliott Trudeau still hang on the walls.

Fine points: The building was constructed in 1901 by Lee Cheong and Lee Wong with an elegant facade and a passageway to tenements in back.

BEAN AROUND THE WORLD is an excellent Anglo coffeehouse at the end of this group of buildings. Popular with real coffee lovers, Bean serves only organic coffee and is gay friendly. Lots of friendly characters work and gather here, for chocolate mousse or coconut cream pie and Italian ice creams.

❧ *Bean Around the World, 533 Fisgard Street, (250) 386–7115. Hours: early to late.*

TAMAMI SUSHI majors in sushi and teriyaki specialties such as salmon or New York steak, with combination plates ($13.95–$17.95) available.
❧ *Tamami Sushi, 509 Fisgard Street, (250) 382–3529. Hours: 11:30 A.M.–2:30 P.M. and 5:00–10:00 P.M. Tuesday–Saturday, 5:00–10:00 P.M. Sunday. Wheelchair accessible. Credit cards: Visa, MasterCard.*

Cross Fisgard Street, and we'll bring you back up the other side, first to Clicks Furniture for ultimate deco, and then to the ORIENTAL BOOK & GIFT SHOP, an old, interesting shop in an old, interesting building. Catering primarily to Chinese customers, this shop carries Chinese language books and maps, tea sets, games, and serving dishes.
❧ *Oriental Book & Gift Shop, 532 Fisgard Street, (250) 385–2424. Wheelchair accessible. Credit cards: none.*

WAH YUEN GROCERY has improved tremendously recently. Chinese delicacies and cooking utensils are worth a visit.
❧ *Wah Yuen Grocery, 534 Fisgard Street, (250) 383–2813. Wheelchair accessible. Credit cards: none.*

At DON MEE'S SEA- FOOD RESTAURANT (up- stairs) the word *Chinese* is left out of the name but probably is assumed. This is the most elegant Chinese restaurant in town, featuring traditional Cantonese- and Szechuan-style seafood, chicken and beef, and a traditional dim sum lunch daily. Live, swimming lobsters and crabs greet you and await your order. The family dinners start at $12.55 per person. Climb the stairway to the second floor entrance. Free delivery after 5:00 P.M.
❧ *Don Mee's Seafood Restaurant, 538 Fisgard Street (upstairs), (250) 383–1032. Hours: from lunch on, daily. Not wheelchair accessible. Credit cards: Visa, MasterCard, American Express, Diners. Fully licensed.*

TRADEWINDS is a small Chinese import shop with lots of miniatures, teacups, and personal soaps.
❧ *Tradewinds, 544 Fisgard Street, (250) 381–5422. Wheelchair accessible. Credit cards: Visa, MasterCard.*

HUNAN VILLAGE CUISINE offers wake-you-up Hunan-style hot and peppery cuisine (heat can be altered) featuring seafood such as local oysters, crab, and cod in season, and duck. Lunch ranges upward from $6.45, dinner from $8.45, combination dinner from $12.85. Free delivery within 6 miles, which most hotels and motels are.

❧ *Hunan Village Cuisine, 546 Fisgard Street, (250) 382–0661. Wheelchair accessible. Credit cards: Visa, Master-Card, American Express. Beer and wine.*

KWONG TUNG SEAFOOD RESTAURANT serves Hong Kong–style Cantonese and Szechuan cuisine with dim sum served daily. Lunch combination plates range from $7.25, dinner from $12.95, group meals from $10.25 for two or more. Fresh crab. Free delivery after 5:00 P.M. within 4 miles.

FAN TAN ALLEY

❧ *Kwong Tung Seafood Restaurant, 548 Fisgard Street (upstairs), (250) 381–1223. Hours: lunch and dim sum 11:00 A.M.–3:00 P.M., dinner from 5:00 P.M. Not wheelchair accessible. Credit cards: Visa, MasterCard, American Express. Beer and wine.*

FISGARD MARKET is a small, traditional Chinese full-service grocery with Chinese specialties such as vegetables, mangoes, papaya, coconut milk, and cold drinks.

❧ *Fisgard Market, 550 Fisgard Street, (250) 383–6969. Wheelchair accessible.*

We find MAGPIE GIFT STUDIO to be the most elegant shop/studio in Chinatown, featuring Chinese and Japanese antiques, paper lanterns, sculptural lamps, statues, and artful designer jewelry.

❧ *Magpie Gift Studio, 556 Fisgard Street, (250) 383–1880. Wheelchair accessible. Credit cards: Visa, MasterCard.*

BBQ Bakery is a small, local, formica-table Chinese restaurant frequented by local Chinese and neighborhood workers. It won several local awards in the 1980s. *Fine points:* Originally the Chinese Benevolent Association building (designed by John Teague in 1885), it was later the first Chinese School, replaced by a cigar factory.

BBQ Bakery, 560 Fisgard Street. Hours: 10:00 A.M.–8:30 P.M. Monday–Saturday, 10:00 A.M.–6:45 P.M. Sunday. Wheelchair accessible. Credit cards: none. Beer and wine.

Mild Chinese cuisine catering to North American tastes is the focus at Foo Hong Chop Suey. Lots of chop suey, chow mein; lunch specials from $4.75 and dinner for less than $10.00.

Foo Hong Chop Suey, 564 Fisgard Street, (250) 386–9553. Hours: 11:30 A.M.–3:00 P.M., 4:30 P.M.–9:00 P.M. Wheelchair accessible. Credit cards: none. Beer and wine.

Ocean Garden Restaurant serves bland Cantonese and Szechuan specialties including fresh oysters, crabs, and clams in season; lunch specials from $4.95, special dinners for two from $17.50. Lots of Chinese and other locals eat here daily. Free delivery; discount if you pick up and take out.

Ocean Garden Restaurant, 568 Fisgard Street, (250) 360–2818. Hours: 11:30 A.M. on. Wheelchair accessible. Credit cards: Visa, MasterCard. Beer and wine.

Now walk one-half block back down the south side of Fisgard to Fan Tan Alley. Like Waddington and Trounce Alleys, Fan Tan Alley was cut through the block to provide "street" frontage for more buildings. New owner and civic leader William J. MacDonald created the alley in 1881. Some of the buildings along here date from the 1880s, including an opium factory that remained legal until 1907.

Between 1912 and 1920 Chinese owners hired architects and replaced older structures with the current brick buildings, most housing retail stores on the ground floor and tenements above. Obviously sunlight and fresh air were not considerations. At its narrowest point the alley is only 4 charming feet wide. Fan Tan, by the way, is a Chinese gambling game.

Heart's Content is a happening boutique/shop that feels like London-west, featuring jazzy hip clothes including an excellent supply of Doc Martens shoes and boots, Ray Troll T-shirts at $24, well-priced skirts and dresses, and fun sun hats. One of our favorites.

❧ *Heart's Content, 18 Fan Tan Alley, (250) 380–1234. Hours: 11:00 A.M.–5:30 P.M. Wheelchair accessible. Credit cards: Visa, MasterCard.*

DRAGON SONG MUSIC COMPANY is a fascinating home to historic, ethnic, acoustic, and imported musical instruments. Oriental rugs accentuate displays of African and Celtic Bodhran drums, as well as old sound equipment.
❧ *Dragon Song Music Company, 16 Fan Tan Alley, (250) 385–4643. Hours: 10:00 A.M.–6:00 P.M. daily, closed 12:30–1:00 P.M. for lunch. Wheelchair accessible. Credit cards: Visa, MasterCard.*

At the NEW TOWN BARBER an ancient Chinese gentleman and, occasionally, a younger man cut hair the old-fashioned way, slowly, and in an ancient building.
❧ *New Town Barber, 10 Fan Tan Alley, (250) 382–3813. Hours: 9:30 A.M.–5:00 P.M. Wheelchair accessible. Credit cards: none.*

We visit the TURNTABLE at least once a month to scan the fabulous collection of high-quality old records, CDs, and tapes from George Carlin to Elvis and Frank Sinatra, plus every acid rock and rap available. Psychedelic and current concert posters paper the ceiling and walls in the little space left. Gary Anderson and friends will play anything you bring up to the counter. They also stock an interesting small collection of Celtic and Canadian Celtic music. One of our favorites.
❧ *Turntable, 3 Fan Tan Alley, (250) 382–5543. Hours: 10:00 A.M.–5:30 P.M., sometimes later. Not wheelchair accessible. Credit cards: Visa, MasterCard, American Express.*

For a new or familiar experience, stop in at TRIPLE SPIRAL METAPHYSICAL, the ultimate cozy source of metaphysical and pagan supplies, from incense and candles to books, tapes and CDs, jewelry, cards, fabulous paintings and collages, drums, scented oils, and ritual tools. Owner Alison Skelton gives tarot readings, astrological analyses, palm readings, and natural magic instruction.
❧ *Triple Spiral Metaphysical, 3 Fan Tan Alley, (250) 380–7212. Hours: 11:00 A.M.–5:00 P.M. Readings by appointment. Not wheelchair accessible. Credit cards: Visa, MasterCard.*

TURTLE EXPRESS is an interesting, cozy southeast Asian import shop you shouldn't miss. It features original handcrafted jewelry, handpainted material, and accessories.
❧ *Turtle Express, 3 Fan Tan Alley, (250) 384–2227. Hours: 11:00 A.M.–5:30 P.M. daily. Not wheelchair accessible. Credit cards: Visa, MasterCard, American Express.*

Whirled Arts features imports from Central and South America, including bags, clothing, and chatchkas, and holds candlewax readings.

Whirled Arts, 3 Fan Tan Alley, (250) 386–2787. Hours 11:00 A.M.–5:30 P.M. Not wheelchair accessible. Credit cards: Visa, MasterCard, American Express.

RESIDENTIAL NEIGHBORHOODS

Now we begin our look at neighborhoods beyond the downtown area, starting with James Bay.

JAMES BAY. James Bay was originally named for Governor James Douglas, who built his home and lived there in the 1850s. James Bay itself included the area where the inner harbour and The Empress hotel now stand, since the bay was filled in during 1903–4. Most of the flat part was Beckley Farm, once producer of vegetables for Victoria and now remembered in name almost solely as a pleasant retirement home.

Today James Bay includes the Parliament buildings and waterfront; everything south to Dallas Road, including Ogden Point, where cruise ships and the

MILE "0" OF TRANS-CANADA HIGHWAY, DALLAS ROAD AND
DOUGLAS STREET

Royal Victoria ferry dock, and over to Beacon Hill Park; the James Bay Inn at 270 Government Street and Emily Carr's home at 207 Government Street; and the community center of James Bay on Menzies Street. Many Victorian homes remain and are worth a drive or carriage tour. Almost all of the waterfront along Dallas Road and Beacon Hill Park are wheelchair accessible.

In James Bay village, at the intersection of Menzies, Simcoe, and Toronto Streets (1 block west and 3 blocks south of The Empress hotel), you will find a government liquor store, a small shopping center with beautifully expanded Thrifty Market, Harvey's (where you can get almost anything you could possibly need from envelopes and film to fuses, newspapers, magazines, postcards, and stamps), and a cleaners. Don't miss the Hungarian deli in the same complex, or Cup a Joe, across Toronto downstairs from the drugstore and the Bank of Montreal, for great breakfast and lunch from $2.95 on up.

At this intersection enjoy the Bent Mast, one of our favorite neighborhood bar/restaurant/hangouts, the recently expanded James Bay Coffee & Books for excellent scones and humongous cinnamon buns (white or whole wheat), coffees and teas, a laundromat right next door so that you can enjoy coffee while you do your laundry, a lovely flower shop, a teensy bicycle shop, and, of course, fish and chips and burgers, Pacific Coast Savings, and the Banana Belt Cafe at 281 Menzies. The James Bay Tearoom and Restaurant is also in James Bay at 332 Menzies Street.

COOK STREET VILLAGE. Cook Street Village is on—surprise—Cook Street, a few blocks east of Beacon Hill Park. Like many Victoria neighborhood villages, it primarily supplies locals with lovely foods and flowers, as well as more mundane necessities. Huge chestnut trees canopy the street and set the cozy mood.

The 300 block of Cook Street hosts dueling coffee chains, with Moka House on the east side and Starbucks directly across the street, both enjoying regulars. Moka House has music some nights and generally healthier food, including fabulous sandwiches and pastries. On the Starbucks side, PicAFlic rents movies and videos and has an unusual collection of foreign films.

You might want to try SOPHIA'S RESTAURANT, specializing in hearty Greek and Italian food with indoor and beautiful sidewalk tables. Roast lamb, chicken, steak, pizza, seafood, and a salad bar—something for everyone—plus live entertainment Friday and Saturday from 7:00 to 10:00 P.M. Free delivery after 5:00 P.M. *Sophia's Restaurant, 343 Cook Street, (250) 386–1455. Wheelchair accessible. Credit cards: Visa, MasterCard. Fully licensed.*

Kay's Korner at 337 Cook (250–386–5978) features "experienced goods" and a sense of humor. A great place for experienced treasures.

The Cook Street Market Place, 333 Cook, sells groceries and many other things worth investigating. World of Flowers is here, and Rising Star Bakery, breadbaker for The Empress hotel and Point Ellice House afternoon teas, has a branch here. The Village Card Shoppe (250–383–1943) sells charming cards and notes, knickknacks, and lottery tickets, and offers full postal services. The Flying Beagle Pub at the corner of Cook and Oxford Streets is the most beautiful neighborhood pub in Victoria. Also check out Cassis Bistro, at 253 Cook (see page 138).

Be sure to drop in to the excellent Fairfield Bookshop for the best in used books, and check out Surroundings next door for restored local antiques and imported furnishings.

On the west side of Cook at number 252, Cook Street Fish and Chips (250–384–1856) serves a breakfast special all day for $3.45 and a lunch special salmon sandwich with soup or fries for $4.95. It also has outdoor seating. Starbucks serves its usual great coffees and munchies.

Wine lovers should check out Cook Street Village Wines at 242 for B.C. wines and ice wines, as well as local entertainment from Glenn Barlow, Richard Pyatt, and Ian Sutherland. The Electric Juice Cafe offers quality health drinks and foods.

FAIRFIELD. Fairfield is a pleasant residential neighborhood that was cut from Governor James Douglas's Fairfield Farm. It extends from the eastern side of Beacon Hill Park to Gonzales Bay and includes Ross Bay Cemetery between Fairfield and Dallas Roads. Many Arts and Crafts–style houses remain on Trutch Street. It's worth a trip to see, especially in April when the Yoshina cherry trees blossom with an abundance of soft pink pompons.

Fairfield Plaza on Fairfield Road has a collection of excellent food places such as Nature's Fare, where you can stock up on organic foods and bread from the Italian Bakery, and Bagga Pasta.

FERNWOOD. The Fernwood neighborhood focuses on its center at Fernwood Road and Gladstone Avenue, and when you get there, you'll see why. It looks and feels like a small English village with a very un-square square. Named for Fernwood Manor, the first Victoria mansion built outside of the James Bay area in 1860, it was once the 300-acre estate of Benjamin Pearse. Now younger people are renovating older homes, and the neighborhood has an almost secret, with-it sense of self and eccentricity.

The BELFRY THEATRE, at 1281 Gladstone Avenue (250–385–6815), was built around 1890 and was once the Emmanuel Baptist Church. Originally formed on a 1974 six-month government grant to help three people develop a theater company, the Belfry (no bats, we hope) is now one of Canada's premier small theaters.

The other most obvious building in Fernwood is the country English-looking **GEORGE & DRAGON PUB & RESTAURANT**. Dishing up food, firewater, and fun, this place is a mecca for locals and visitors alike. The atmosphere is casual, with heavy tables and lots of wood, and sunny outdoor tables facing south. Appetizers include Dragon Eggs—deep-fried jalapeño peppers stuffed with jack cheese at $8.75; bangers and mash at $6.95; world tastes of Indonesia and Thailand; and Mona's meat loaf at $7.95. Live-music weekends.

🌺 *George & Dragon Pub & Restaurant, 1302 Gladstone Avenue, (250) 388–4458. Hours: Monday– Saturday 11:00 A.M.–midnight, Sunday 11:00 A.M.–11:00 P.M. Not wheelchair accessible. Credit cards: Visa, Master-Card. Beer and wine.*

BELFRY THEATRE, FERNWOOD

At the **THIN EDGE OF THE WEDGE**, the yellow and brick walls (not road) with dramatic paintings and cat photos and the black-and-white checked flooring combine with soft couches and the best cafe magazine and book selection anywhere to make you want to stay all day or evening. No one is rushed here. Open-mike poetry nights attract loads of neighbors.

The Thin Edge is developing a reputation for the best pizza in Victoria, serving its sumptuous creations by the slice ($3.00 and huge) or by the pie (one size fits all—$20.00). Flavors include the standards plus La Chihuahua with refried beans, black beans, salsa, and ground beef optional; Arty Choke with pine nuts and the obvious; the Five-O with Canadian ham, pineapple, and peach; Spanakopitza with spinach, feta, tomato, red onion, and cracked pepper; and the Buckingham with fresh basil, onions, broccoli, cheddar cheese, and cracked peppercorns.

Italian sodas, espresso drinks, and unusually excellent draught, local, and imported beers (mug $3.75, pitcher $13.00—yes!) quench any kind of thirst.

🌺 *Thin Edge of the Wedge, 1311 Gladstone Avenue, (250) 386–8446. Hours: 11:00 A.M.–11:00 P.M. weekdays, until about 1:00 A.M. weekends. Wheelchair accessible. Credit cards: Visa.*

To make its pizzas, the Thin Edge uses dough from Breadstuffs Bakery (250–380–7727) next door, a newly enlarged bakery selling out most days. Besides the best pizza dough, Breadstuffs also turns out excellent breads. But it's the breakfast goodies, including the awesome walnut cinnamon buns, cookies, and squares, that do in a lot of locals. One of our favorites.

Across Fernwood and beside the Belfry Theatre is Gladstone Square, which feels European, complete with gazebo and kiosk, Front Row Video with a full range of movies and cult classics, Gordies Music, a tattoo parlor, and a new cafe related to Thin Edge pizza.

Down at 2000 Fernwood you'll find Play It Again—Quality Consignments (250–380–0049). There are also several tucked-away offices housing nonprofit foundations in this wonderfully eclectic neighborhood. One of our favorites.

OAK BAY VILLAGE. Oak Bay Village is a truly self-sufficient village community with its own town council. It includes what used to be the Uplands Farm and the Tod Farm, the latter of whose house stands today. When 243 property owners in Oak Bay petitioned the city of Victoria to be annexed in 1906, they were turned down, and later that same year Oak Bay incorporated as a city.

Oak Bay is known for gentility, British influence, nice weather, a beautiful marina, its village center, large Edwardian-style homes, the Oak Bay Beach Hotel, and the Marina Restaurant complex. We strongly encourage you to take a bus tour or car through the area and sample neighborhood living. (Bus 1 Willow or 2 Oak Bay). *Fine points:* You can take the Oak Bay Explorer bus from Belleville Street or in front of The Empress.

Now we will take you through the attractions of Oak Bay and down its main street, coincidentally called Oak Bay.

One highlight experience of Oak Bay for visitors is the BLETHERING PLACE TEAROOM & RESTAURANT (2250 Oak Bay, 250–598–1413). Loads of locals frequent this cozy and comfortable Tudor-style tearoom with teas served from 11:00 A.M. to 7:00 P.M. or just about any other time if you ask. Light tea is $8.95 and full tea is $11.95.

Right around the corner from the Blethering Place, eaters and food lovers must check out Colin Campbell Village Butcher and Oak Bay Seafoods Fresh Fish & Game (back behind the butcher shop). Colin Campbell personally cuts, ages, and sells exquisite meats and poultry ranging from game hens and Scotch eggs to baron of beef, and Tuxford and Tehbutt cheeses. Fresh Fish & Game offers salmon pâté, smoked pheasant sausage, venison pepperoni and sausage, and venison and maple breakfast sausage, to say nothing of the freshest fish around.

Tucked downstairs in Monterey Mews between the provisions shops and the tearoom are Upstairs Downstairs, selling dollhouses and everything a collector

THE BLETHERING PLACE TEA ROOM & RESTAURANT

could want; Oak Bay Models, with cars, trains and planes; and the Celtic Cottage, with Irish and Scottish foods, candies, and jewelry.

In the same building but back on Oak Bay Street, Nushin Boutique has another shop featuring elegant European clothes. Painted Words Art Supplies & Books Ltd. at 2238 Oak Bay is more than just the local art supply store. It's a cultural community center providing all the art supplies you may have forgotten to bring to capture that gorgeous local scene. At the Grafton Bookshop, Jill Grafton serves as a community secondhand and antiquarian bookstore for what she calls "a reading neighborhood." Wonderful! Pure Pizzazz sells women's clothing, and Ottavio Italian Bakery & Delicacies bakes and sells the obvious as well as Torrefazione Italia coffee, fabulous and unusual French cheeses, truffle oils and pastes, and Sagra olive oil.

Oak Bay Books is a small, charming, local, independent bookstore. Please visit. Rogers' Tudor Sweet Shoppe features Rogers' famous chocolates, British specialty sweets, and Jackson's of Piccadilly teas. You can pop into Pharmasave for any little remedies you might need, on your way to Ivy's Bookshop, a rare surviving, competing, and charming independent local bookstore.

Starbucks has moved conveniently in right next to Ivy's in the Oak Bay Building, and just west is a small version of chain Bagel Street Cafe.

A block farther west on Oak Bay, don't miss two worthwhile culinary stops: The White Heather Tea Room and Small City Bistro.

Cross Oak Bay Street to the interesting Oak Bay Flower Shop, a handy one-hour photo, Athlone Gourmet Coffee, Village Chocolatier, and Coastal Cookbook Company, all within the ATHLONE COURT complex at Oak Bay and Hampshire Road. Here you will also find the Hampshire Grill, Fairway Market, and Timeless Toys.

For a light, inexpensive lunch, try Side Street Bistro on Hampshire Road off Oak Bay for excellent soups, small pizzas, and whole-grain sandwiches.

A new wonderful find is the WHITE HEATHER TEA ROOM on Oak Bay, where you can either indulge in lunches of a "sconewish," a cheese and chive scone filled with chicken, egg salad, or cream cheese and roasted peppers, with soup or salad ($6.95); salads; or tea choices.

White linen tablecloths and serviettes and oriental rugs set the tone for your tea and White Heather's humor, from "The Wee Tee" at $6.95 to the "Not So Wee Tea" ($9.95) and The Big Muckle Giant Tea ($27.95) for two people. Don't miss the Welsh cakes cooked to order on the grill from 2:00 to 4:00 P.M. at only $1.50 for four "cakes." Remember the chicken a la king from your youth? It's here ($7.95)!

☙ *White Heather Tea Room, 1885 Oak Bay, (250) 595–8020. Hours: 8:30 A.M.–5:00 P.M. Tuesday–Saturday, 10:00 A.M.–5:00 P.M. Sunday, including Sunday brunch. Wheelchair accessible. Credit cards: Visa, MasterCard.*

A couple of doors west is SMALL CITY BISTRO, a proper bistro with a proper menu featuring specialties including beet and barley salad with pistachios ($7.00), polenta fries with chipotle aioli or roasted veggie sandwich ($7.00), and burgers ($8.00), all including soup or salad, and all in sumptuous portions.

Dinner may include tempura vegetables with soy wasabi aioli ($13), crispy southern-fried oysters ($15), caramelized fillet of salmon ($16), prawn and scallop mousse ravioli ($15), duck confit on roasted vegetable risotto ($17), and lamb ragout ($19). The new patio in back is perfect in good weather months.

☙ *Small City Bistro, 1871 Oak Bay, (250) 598–2015. Hours: 11:30 A.M.–3:00 P.M. and 5:00–10:00 P.M. or midnight daily. Beer and wine. Wheelchair accessible. Credit cards: Visa, MasterCard.*

Across from Windsor Park on Windsor at Newport (1 block off Beach Drive) is a Tudor-style building in which you will find a W. & J. Wilson boutique, as well as a prize tearoom, WINDSOR HOUSE TEA ROOM AND RESTAURANT. Here you can enjoy traditional soups and Caesar salads, Welsh rarebit, a deep-dish chicken potpie, spinach crepe, or the Queen's Plate of quiche Lorraine, all at $7.95.

The pink linen tablecloths, white serviettes, and old English ambience set the mood for your afternoon tea, ranging in price and quantity from $6.95 to $25.95, the latter for two.

✥ *Windsor House Tea Room and Restaurant, 2540 Windsor Street at Newport, (250) 595–3135. Hours: 11:00 A.M.–5:00 P.M. Monday–Saturday. Wheelchair accessible. Credit cards: Visa, MasterCard.*

Heading back eastward on Oak Bay you will find Jack Burgess Ltd. ladies' wear, Snugglepots children's store, the Bee Hive wool shop for knitting and crocheting supplies, Oak Bay Hardware, and the wonderful, small Village Bakery & Deli, where you can get shepherd's pie at $1.50, cannelloni, beef and cabbage or vegetarian rolls at $2.50, Cornish pasties at $1.85, beef stew, and an assortment of great salads, from Greek to tortellini.

Colleen Gibson (CG) Designs—The Gallery shows interesting local-scene paintings and frames; China and Chintz offers its usual tempting home furnishings and accessories; Maresa Boutique offers women's clothing. Now you are back facing the Blethering Place Tearoom and Restaurant, just in time to indulge yourself and try a light or full tea. Enjoy!

You may also want to try afternoon tea in the summer at the elegant Oak Bay Beach Hotel, 1175 Beach Drive (Bus 2 Oak Bay). The ambience is warm and sedate British, which in this case are not contradictions. The Marina Restaurant, right at the Oak Bay marina, offers excellent West Coast cuisine, a marvelous sushi bar, and sumptuous Sunday brunch, with a full and intriguing bar lounge, all with one of the most romantic views in greater Victoria. We'll come back to this restaurant again.

Where to Stay in Oak Bay

OAK BAY BEACH HOTEL, 1175 Beach Drive, $136–$226, fifty-one units, historic elegant beachfront resort, antique furnishings, seaview dining, pub, conference facilities, nearby golf and tennis; (250) 598–4556 or (800) 668–7758.

Where to Stay at University of Victoria

UVIC HOUSING AND CONFERENCE SERVICES, Sinclair at Finnerly Road, $32–$65, May 1 to August 31 only, 999 units, shared baths, some kitchens, breakfast included, no pets; (250) 721–8396.

SIGNIFICANT OTHERS

Significant Others, in this case, refers to restaurants and other places of interest not located in the hard-core downtown mecca but that we highly recommend. They are worth the effort it might take to get there.

Even the daily Victoria *Times-Colonist* restaurant reviewer rated FOSTER'S EATERY as the best new restaurant of 1999, so our opinion of Foster's may have nothing to do with the fact that it is owned by our son-in-law, Sean Sloat.

Foster's is a Victoria version of a New York or San Francisco cafe/bistro with hand-painted walls, sculpted iron fixtures, and bold local art works on the walls, and plenty of magazines and newspapers to occupy guests.

The light menu may include, if you're lucky, the spinach and warm red-potato salad with bacon, oven-dried tomatoes, and goat cheese with Balsamic dressing and crème fraîche drizzle ($8.25), and great panini, all of which are unusually tasty, served on grilled focaccia and less than $8.25. If you feel like a more conventional sandwich, try the Really Good BLT on toasted multi-grain or sourdough bread ($6.50); the chicken club with double smoked bacon, Dijon mayo, and aged cheddar ($9.25); or the delectable Pacific Club of layered shrimp, smoked tuna, watercress, and red onion ($9.50). All panini and sandwiches come with soup or salad.

The all-time favorite of most customers is the roasted mushroom lasagna with fresh roasted mushrooms, ricotta, mozzarella, white-wine spinach, garlic, and Parmesan with greens or soup ($7.95). *Times-Colonist* critic Lee Crossley wrote that the caramelized onion and goat cheese tart ($8.25) "still makes me weak in the knees whenever I think of it."

Foster's uses only local organic Salt Spring Roasting Company coffees. Even the decaf is superb. Without many sauces to judge, soups can be a good measure of a restaurant's depth and quality. Here they are all made from fresh vegetable or chicken stock and rate with the very best. The south-facing patio in back is divine in good weather. One of our favorites.

♣✄ *Foster's Eastery, 1117 753 Yates Street, (250) 382–1131; Fax: (250) 382–1187. Hours: 8:00 A.M.–7:00 P.M. winter, 8:00 A.M.–10:00 P.M. summer. Beer and wine. Wheelchair accessible. Credit cards: Visa, MasterCard, American Express.*

At marvelous CASSIS BISTRO on Cook Street, John Hall and David Abersak use only local fish and Vancouver Island meats, so you are in for a real treat. Appetizers may include seared rare chinook salmon with roasted asparagus on frisee salad ($9.00), rockfish brandade and garlic crostini on warm young spinach salad ($8.75), or "country-style" duck confit and apple pâté ($9.00).

PORK MEDALLIONS "DANIEL"
Stephen Wilson and John Hall of Cassis Bistro, Victoria

Ingredients

1 pork tenderloin

salt and pepper

2 tbsp. cold butter, unsalted

1 tbsp. grated ginger

1 tsp. shallots, minced

1 tbsp. fireweed honey

$\frac{1}{3}$ cup brandy

$\frac{1}{3}$ cup veal stock

3 tbsp. cream

1 tsp. fresh lemon juice

Preparation

Clean pork tenderloin and cut into 2-oz. portions; flatten into medallions between plastic wrap. Season both sides of medallions with salt and pepper. Sauté in 1 tablespoon of the butter for one minute each side. Remove from pan and let rest, but keep warm.

In same pan, add grated ginger and minced shallots. Sauté until translucent. Add honey and caramelize. Deglaze with brandy and reduce until almost dry. Add veal stock and cream. Reduce until desired consistency is reached and remove from heat.

Whisk in 1 tablespoon of the butter and the lemon juice.

Arrange medallions on plates and pour sauce over them. Serve with buttermilk mashed potatoes and enjoy.

Serves two.

Main dishes typically are baked orzo and Asiago au gratin with garlic truffle oil croutons and asparagus over oven-dried tomato and fennel ($15), a special risotto, Sooke Hills rainbow trout with Salt Spring Island mussels and spring onion ragout ($22), bouillabaisse, pork loin chop Daniel in deference to John's mentor from Chez Daniel ($21), and a mouthwatering medallion of beef strip with Blossom's blue cheese butter ($24). Whew!

❧ *Cassis Bistro, 253 Cook Street, (250) 384–1932. Hours: dinner 5:30 to about 10:00 P.M. Wheelchair accessible. Credit cards: Visa, MasterCard. Fully licensed.*

ESTEVAN VILLAGE is about half a mile north of Oak Bay and is an even smaller community shopping area. Culinary highlights of the neighborhood are the

Willow Tree Cafe; the local coffee, huge sandwich, and banana split hangout with sidewalk tables; and Paprika Bistro, the beloved baby of George and Linda Szasz.

PAPRIKA BISTRO looks very California, with two cozy small rooms and warm mustard walls hung with Avis Rasmussen's appealing primary-color paintings and prints. No one checks to see if you really have tickets to enjoy the "Pre-Theatre Dinner" at $25, which includes possibly organic greens salad, wild coho salmon with citrus beurre blanc or George's chicken curry, and crème brûlée or the daily sorbet.

Specialty appetizers include warm Roquefort crouton with grilled pear ($7.50), shaved duck foie gras on organic greens ($7.95), and veal sweetbreads ($8.95). Dinner entrees delight with Nana Szasz's veal goulash ($17.95), seafood bangers and mash ($19.50), grilled lamb sirloin ($19.95), smoked sablefish ($21.50), and ultimate classic shortribs ($20.95). Worth finding, for sure.

Paprika Bistro, 2524 Estevan, (250) 592-7424; Fax: (250) 592-1316. Hours: from 5:00 P.M. Monday–Saturday. Beer and wine. Wheelchair accessible. Credit cards: Visa, MasterCard.

Rib lovers and lovers of just good, basic food with a flair must check out ISABEL'S RIBS on Douglas Street, about a block past The Bay department store. Its storefront appearance is slightly deceptive, but Isabel's offers the best ribs and rib pieces we have ever enjoyed. A stained-glass window featuring a wine bottle and grapes contributes to a room with brown, British-style cross boards on the walls and flowered tablecloths covered with glass. The place is usually packed with local regulars, but there is additional seating on the mezzanine.

Isabel is Portuguese-Canadian and has multinational, "real food" culinary talents. Kathleen loves the "rib pieces" at lunch, which are those tasty little ribs at the narrow end of the rack, served with salad and french fries and absolutely the best garlic bread in Victoria. With all rib orders you have your choice of BBQ, hot BBQ, or honey-garlic sauce. Servers deliver finger bowls of warm lemon water with each order, thank heavens! Fabulous sandwiches featuring Dungeness crab, shrimp, steak, lox, and veggies complete the lunch menu, all served with fries or tossed salad.

It's not all ribs, though. Jerry loves the shrimp tortellini or veggie lasagna ($8.95), which come with Caesar salad and garlic bread, as do all pasta orders. You can also combine chicken and ribs ($15.95), sautéed tiger prawns and ribs ($18.95), lobster tail and ribs ($23.95), or just plain New York steak ($15.95), peppercorn steak ($16.95), pan fried oysters ($15.95), baked salmon in filo stuffed with mushrooms and spinach ($16.95), sautéed oysters and prawns ($16.95), or Isabel's Combo of sautéed oysters, prawns, scallops, and salmon ($18.95). Run, don't walk. One of our favorites.

❧ *Isabel's Ribs, 1813 Douglas Street, (250) 386–2722. Hours: 11:30 A.M.–2:30 P.M., 5:30 P.M. on. Beer and wine. Main dining room is wheelchair accessible, rest rooms and mezzanine are not. Credit cards: Visa, MasterCard, American Express.*

Many locals regard BAAN THAI as the best Thai restaurant on Vancouver Island. Specialties include pla lard prik (pan fried fish) at $12.95, swimming rama (beef with peanut sauce) at $10.95, veggie specials at $6.95, and excellent pad Thai (rice noodles with shrimp, tofu, and chicken if you wish) at $6.95. All dishes may have tofu substituted for meat. You also have your choice of hotness, and we recommend mild. Medium burns our lips, but if that sends you to heaven, go for it. Be sure to try this one!

❧ *Baan Thai, 1117 Blanshard, (250) 383–0050. Hours: Monday–Friday noon–2:30 P.M. and 5:00 P.M. on, Sunday noon on. One low step to doorway. Credit cards: Visa, MasterCard, American Express, enRoute.*

HERALD STREET CAFFÉ, a favorite restaurant of many Victorians, features truly creative West Coast cuisine with ample portions, local seafood, meats, and vegetables. Recipient of prestigious American and Canadian awards for Best Wine List and Best American Wine List, it is also the favorite of *Monday Magazine* readers and many radio and television polls.

Chef Paul Bell and crew obviously have exceptional palates and few boundaries. Two of their most popular dishes at lunch are the lamb tenderloin sandwich with grilled zucchini and red peppers on house-made breads (which themselves are to die for—try the brown bread with herbs), plus potato crisps and roasted potatoes; and the smallish crab cakes that are available every day, not just Friday, in pesto and salsa. Both are just $9.95 and come with soup or salad, which, here, is a difficult decision. Indulge in the dessert crepes with chocolate and mandarin orange sauce.

Chocolate-pudding walls are the perfect, warm background for local, vibrant, wildly colorful paintings, and huge vases of sunflowers and yellow and orange chrysanthemums combine to make you feel as if you are part of a painting. Elegantly casual.

Enormous thanks to Paul Bell for generously sharing the recipe for his special version of rack of lamb.

❧ *Herald Street Caffé, 546 Herald Street, (250) 381–1441. Hours: lunch Wednesday–Saturday 11:30 A.M.–3:00 P.M., Sunday brunch 11:00 A.M.–3:00 P.M., dinner Sunday–Thursday 5:30–10:00 P.M., Friday–Saturday 5:30 P.M.–midnight. Wheelchair accessible. Credit cards: Visa, MasterCard, American Express, Diners, enRoute. Fully licensed.*

ONION AND GOAT CHEESE TARTS
Sean Sloat of Foster's Eatery, Victoria

Ingredients

6 yellow onions

1 cup crème fraîche

2 oz. goat cheese

1 clove garlic, minced

1 tbsp. thyme, chopped

4 eggs

6 tart shells, prebaked or thawed

salt and pepper

Preparation

Julienne the onions and caramelize in a pan. Add crème fraîche and most of the goat cheese, minced garlic, chopped thyme, and salt and pepper. Fold in eggs.

Fill prebaked or thawed tart shells with mixture and top with dollop of goat cheese nestled in filling. Bake at 300° F for approximately twenty minutes.

Serves four to six.

The CANOE CLUB BREWHOUSE AND RESTAURANT, the newest hot addition, is located at the foot of historic Chinatown (east of Fisgard, across Wharf) in a restored heritage 1894 powerhouse, right on the waterfront. Visit it just to experience the prize location.

Enjoy house-made brews and a contemporary menu featuring seared Ahi tuna, mussels in dark ale broth with herbs and cream, lamb, and antipasto platters.

❧ *Canoe Club Brewhouse and Restaurant, 450 Swift Street, (250) 361–1940. Hours: Sunday–Thursday 11:00 A.M.–midnight, Friday–Saturday 11:00 A.M.–1:00 A.M. Wheelchair accessible. Credit cards: Visa, MasterCard. Beer and wine.*

The JAMES BAY TEAROOM AND RESTAURANT is a local and international favorite place for British cuisine and afternoon tea. In a charming small building with flowers hanging outside, enjoy a breakfast of kippers and eggs; lunch of traditional sandwiches, soups, or meat pies; dinner of poached local salmon or roast beef with Yorkshire pudding; tempting sweets; and, of course, everything that goes with traditional, proper tea. Dinner specials are about $10.

❧ *James Bay Tearoom and Restaurant, 322 Menzies at Superior, (250) 382–8282. Hours: breakfast Monday–Saturday 7:00–11:30 A.M., Sunday 8:00 A.M.–12:30 P.M.; lunch Monday–Saturday 11:30 A.M.–4:30 P.M.; tea daily 1:00–4:30 P.M.; dinner daily 4:30–9:00 P.M. Wheelchair accessible. Credit cards: Visa, MasterCard. Beer and wine.*

SANTIAGO'S CAFE, an oasis of fun and hip Spanish ambience, serves an enormous selection of tapas, sangrias, umbrella drinks, colors, and flan. Try it for someone's birthday. It's a hilarious experience.

❧ *Santiago's Cafe, 660 Oswego south of Belleville, (250) 388–7376. Hours: 11:00 A.M.–11:00 P.M. Restaurant is wheelchair accessible, rest rooms are not. Credit cards: Visa, MasterCard, American Express.*

JOHN'S PLACE is generally recognized as the ultimate Victoria diner—or any diner for that matter. Images of Marilyn Monroe dominate the walls (along with several other fifties and sixties favorites), vinyl benches dominate the booths, pies and cakes dominate your view at the door, and fantastic basic food dominates the menu. Enjoy the funk and junk with a crowd of cross-cultural, cross-generational, mellow with-its.

FRESH SALT SPRING ISLAND MUSSELS WITH GARLIC, PRESERVED LEMON, AND WHITE WINE
George Szasz of Paprika Bistro, Victoria

Ingredients
    1 lb. fresh Salt Spring Island mussels, scrubbed and debearded
    ½ onion, diced
    ½ tomato, diced
    1 tbsp. preserved lemon, sliced, or juice of ½ lemon
    ¼ cup white wine
    3 sprigs Italian parsley, chopped
    2 tbsp. salted butter

Preparation
    Place all ingredients into a small saucepan with a tight-fitting lid. Bring to a boil. With a slotted spoon, remove mussels to serving bowl. Discard any with broken or unopened shells. Reduce stock slightly. Check seasonings. Pour stock over mussels.

GOULASH SOUP
George Szasz of Paprika Bistro, Victoria

Ingredients

3 tbsp. lard or vegetable oil

1 medium onion, diced

½ lb. beef or veal shank, cut into 1-inch cubes

1 tsp. salt and pepper

1 tsp. caraway seeds, crushed

1 tsp. strong paprika

4 cups beef stock or water

1 green pepper, diced

2 small tomatoes, diced

1 medium carrot, diced

1 medium parsnip, diced

½ lb. potatoes, diced into ½-inch pieces (about two potatoes)

Preparation

Heat lard or oil in a large, heavy-bottomed pot. Sauté the onion until it turns translucent, then add the meat and brown it lightly on all sides. Sprinkle with salt and pepper and the caraway seeds.

Add 2 cups of the stock and blend. Add the green peppers, tomatoes, carrots, and parsnips and bring to a simmer. Cover and simmer for one hour, adding more stock as necessary to keep the meat covered.

Peel and dice the potatoes and add them to the soup. Simmer until the potatoes are done. Serve and enjoy!

At breakfast you have to try the waffles or pancakes with or without fruit, or create your own omelet (our favorite is cooked fresh asparagus, mushrooms, and feta cheese), or eggs Benny with the best potatoes anywhere. Lunch and dinner go on until at least 9:00 P.M., with excellent Japanese noodle soups, authentic enchiladas, piled-high pastas, and crisp salads. John's banana bread melts in your mouth. One of our favorites.

❧ *John's Place, 723 Pandora Street, (250) 389–0711. Hours: 8:00 A.M.–9:00 P.M. daily. Wheelchair accessible. Credit cards: Visa, MasterCard. Beer and wine.*

Many mornings we go to the OGDEN POINT CAFE, a spectacular waterfront cafe at the breakwater where cruise ships dock.

RACK OF LAMB STUFFED WITH RADICCHIO, ENDIVE, AND SPINACH WITH BUTTERNUT PUREE
Paul Bell of Herald Street Caffé, Victoria

Ingredients
Stuffing:
½ lb. mixed endive and radicchio, washed and drained
½ lb. English spinach (leaves only)
1 tbsp. extra virgin olive oil
salt and pepper to taste
1 clove garlic, chopped
1 tbsp. vinegar

Lamb:
8 racks of lamb, 4 cutlets per rack, trimmed of all fat and sinew, chined
salt and pepper
1 tbsp. extra virgin olive oil

Butternut puree:
1 butternut pumpkin squash, peeled, seeded, and cut into pieces
2 tbsp. butter
salt and pepper
fresh ginger, chopped, to taste
sprigs of thyme

Preparation
Stuffing:
Blanche the endive, radicchio, and spinach and rinse under cold water, drain, and chop coarsely. Sauté the greens in olive oil with salt and pepper for five minutes. At the last minute, add the garlic and vinegar. Remove from heat and set aside to cool.

Lamb:
Insert a long, thin knife just off center of the meat on the rack (closer to the bone) to cut a pocket in the meat. Stuff the lamb with the greens and season with salt and pepper.

Heat a little oil and sear the racks on all sides. Transfer to a roasting rack and cook in a preheated 400° F oven for twenty minutes. Remove from oven and allow to rest for twenty minutes.

Puree:
Cook butternut squash in boiling, salted water until tender. Drain well and puree in food processor with the butter, salt, pepper, and fresh ginger.

To serve, cut racks into cutlets and arrange them on heated individual plates. Pour some of the cooking juices over the cutlets. Serve with butternut puree. Garnish with a sprig of thyme.

A central gas fireplace highlights the restaurant upstairs from the Dive Centre with awesome views of the Pacific Ocean, and there's indoor and outdoor seating in good weather. Gail Patterson quit being a legal secretary and Bob Lumbley quit being a fisherman to create something for divers and the rest of us.

Locals out on their daily walks stop by and stay. Here are some of the reasons why: breakfasts of steamed eggs, waffles, fruit, yogurt, and muesli; excellent coffees and teas; Caesar, spinach, or Greek salads at about $5.50; daily soups and "the best clam chowder in Victoria" every day at about $4.50; sandwiches at $5.95 (with a side green salad, add $1.50); shepherd's pie, and spinach and mushroom turnovers; and best of all, desserts to die for, including choices for diabetics and those requiring lactose-free and fat-free sweets. No preservatives or salt added. One of Kathleen's favorites.

❧ *Ogden Point Cafe, 199 Dallas Road at Montreal Street and the Ogden Point Piers, (250) 386–8080. Hours: summer 7:00 A.M.–10:00 P.M., winter 7:00 A.M.–7:00 P.M. Wheelchair accessible by ramp from paved path to breakwater. Credit cards: Visa, MasterCard. Smoking on the sundeck.*

Victorians' favorite fish and chips place, BARB'S PLACE, floats at Fisherman's Wharf. With only a couple of tables, this place does a huge business among local businesspeople who take a break and come down to the water, fishers, and

OGDEN POINT CAFE AND DIVE CENTRE WITH *PRINCESS MARGUERITE III* IN BACKGROUND

visitors alike. The menu is short, to the point, and painted on the outside wall above the order windows. Come early and buy fish directly off the boats. Ice cream, too. One of our favorites.

✤☙ *Barb's Place, 310 St. Lawrence, (250) 384–6515. Hours: spring–fall 10:00 A.M.–8:00 P.M. Not wheelchair accessible. Credit cards: none.*

Be sure to get across Johnson Street Bridge (the blue bridge) to OCEAN POINTE RESORT. Cross the bridge (approach from Pandora or Wharf Streets as Johnson is one-way east) and take the immediate right (west end) by foot (a ten-minute stroll from Wharf Street) or wheel and the sidewalk/road will take you to Ocean Pointe for a few hours' minivacation.

Ocean Pointe's Boardwalk Restaurant and Terrace offer an exceptional Sunday brunch and view of the Inner Harbour, providing the ultimate taste and romance experiences for that time of day. Plan to stay a while so that you can sample the omelet station, the Chinese station, rows of salads from Thai to green and green Thai, the carving station with roasts galore, and the most orgiastic selection of desserts, including cheesecakes from Ely's in Chicago and Moevenpick ice cream. All this for less than $25, with complimentary parking. One of our favorites.

✤☙ *Ocean Pointe Resort, 45 Songhees Road, (250) 360–2999. Reservations required (250–360–5889). Hours: Two seatings: 11:30 A.M. and 1:30 P.M. Wheelchair accessible by elevator. Credit cards: Visa, MasterCard, American Express, Diners. Fully licensed.*

If you are interested in buying B.C. wines to take home, try the OCEAN POINTE RESORT WINE SHOPPE. Wine aficionados will enjoy this unusual collection of rare B.C. wines, including Lang, Cedar Creek, Gray Monk, Summerhill, Blue Mountain, Mission Hill's Library Releases, Calona, and St. Hubertus. The shop also offers wine seminars Sunday afternoons after brunch. Be sure to enter the wine shop's contest to win a trip to the Okanagan Wine Festival.

✤☙ *Ocean Pointe Resort Wine Shoppe, 45 Songhees Road, (250) 360–5804. Hours: Tuesday–Sunday noon–8:00 P.M. Wheelchair accessible by elevator. Credit cards: Visa, MasterCard, American Express, Diners.*

Marina Restaurant and Marina Cafe-Deli, both at 1327 Beach Street, are two of Victoria's best culinary rendezvous. MARINA RESTAURANT properly boasts an exquisite view of the Oak Bay Marina and the lower mainland; it is almost a pleasant surprise that the food and service here are just as good. Extremely popular with its regulars, the Marina Restaurant specializes in local shellfish and fish, local pastas, salads, house-made breads and desserts (very

OCEAN POINTE RESORT & A COMMUTER SEAPLANE,
INNER HARBOUR

local), with an interesting and imaginative local sushi bar, and elegant Sunday brunch at about $20. Monday is pasta special night ($6.95).

❧ *Marina Restaurant, 1327 Beach Street, (250) 598–8555. Hours: lunch 11:30 A.M.–2:30 P.M. Monday–Saturday, dinner 5:00–10:00 P.M. Sunday–Thursday, 5:00–11:00 P.M. Friday and Saturday, Sunday brunch buffet 10:00 A.M.–2:30 P.M. Mostly wheelchair accessible. Credit cards: Visa, MasterCard, American Express, Diners, enRoute. Fully licensed. Reservations highly recommended.*

The MARINA CAFE-DELI is a hidden inexpensive spot with all-day full breakfasts and exotic salads and sandwiches. It's worth the wander to find this place, to say nothing of the view, equaled only by the Marina Restaurant upstairs. You walk down the stairs between the gift shop and the Marina Restaurant and follow the cafe flags around the deck to the waterside of the building. Don't give up. The view, a hot espresso, and thou, baby.

The panini sandwiches are great to share along with a salad. We chose the rice and garbanzo salad with apples, oranges, and light curry. The breakfasts (50 cents to $5.00) are huge and hearty. Cafeteria style. One of our favorites.

❧ *Marina Cafe-Deli, 1327 Beach Street, (250) 598–3890. Hours: summer*

7:00 A.M. on, winter 8:00 A.M.–5:00 P.M. Not wheelchair accessible. Credit cards: Visa, MasterCard, American Express, Diners, enRoute. Beer and wine.

MOUNT ROYAL BAGEL FACTORY makes and supplies most of the better bagel-serving restaurants on Vancouver Island. The address is slightly misleading, because you actually find it by turning off Quadra Street onto Grant. It's a little joint on the left and well worth the effort.

❧ *Mount Royal Bagel Factory, 1115 North Park, (250) 380–3588. Hours: 7:00 A.M.–7:00 P.M. daily. Wheelchair accessible. Credit cards: none.*

PABLO'S DINING LOUNGE, slightly off the beaten track in a charming Victorian house southwest of the Inner Harbour, serves as a haven of "French" cuisine, including seafood, lamb, beef, poultry, and terrific paella (which, of course, is Spanish). You will savor succulent local rack of lamb and enjoy music with your dinner Wednesday–Saturday. The Spanish coffee is strong and potent. Entrees range from $14 to $30.

❧ *Pablo's Dining Lounge, 225 Quebec Street, (250) 388–4255. Hours: 5:00– about 11:00 P.M. daily. Not wheelchair accessible. Credit cards: Visa, MasterCard, American Express. Fully licensed.*

MARINA RESTAURANT AND MARINA CAFE-DELI
AT THE OAK BAY MARINA

WOODEN SHOE DUTCH GROCERIES & DELICATESSEN, on Quadra Street near Hillside Avenue, features Dutch and other imported cheeses, Indonesian foods, Dutch meats, cookies, pickles, "bunwiches" to order, biscuits, cooking equipment, fifty varieties of licorice, Delft pottery and housewares, wooden and leather clogs, books, and tapes. An unusual deli and worth the trip.

❧ *Wooden Shoe Dutch Groceries & Delicatessen, 2576 Quadra Street, (250) 382–9042. Hours: Monday–Saturday 9:30 A.M.–5:30 P.M., until 7:00 P.M. Friday. Wheelchair accessible. Credit cards: Visa, MasterCard.*

Our favorite place for pizza is the SAN REMO RESTAURANT on Quadra Street. The San Remo serves interesting Greek specialties with occasionally bland vegetables, but loads of people go there for the pizza and salads. The vegetarian specials are outstanding and filling for several people.

❧ *San Remo Restaurant, 2709 Quadra Street, (250) 384–5255. Hours: lunch Monday–Saturday, dinner daily. Wheelchair accessible from Quadra Street. Credit cards: Visa, MasterCard, American Express. Full bar.*

As winemakers in northern California's Sonoma Valley say, "It takes a lot of beer to make good wine." Here are two places where you can stoke up for whatever you have to do.

When you're over the blue bridge, you'll find SPINNAKER'S BREWERY PUB & RESTAURANT on Catherine Street an excellent on-site microbrewery and restaurant. From downtown Victoria cross the Johnson Street (blue) Bridge and turn left on Catherine Street.

While you wait for a table in the foyer, you can peer through the window and watch some brewing going on. Spinnaker's offers beers-of-the-day for drinking in the pub and restaurant. Breakfast is a real waker-upper with hearty foods to get your day going. At lunch or dinner try the fluffy fish and chips, Caesar salads, or huge burgers. To get a view of the Inner Harbour, ask for a table near the window. Inquire about daily food and brew specials. Both are excellent and are local favorites.

❧ *Spinnaker's Brewery Pub & Restaurant, 308 Catherine Street, (250) 386–2739. Hours: breakfast 7:00–11:00 A.M., lunch 11:00 A.M.–4:00 P.M., dinner 4:00–11:00 P.M., brewpub 11:00 A.M.–11:00 P.M. Wheelchair accessible. Credit cards: Visa, MasterCard, American Express, Diners.*

Right in town, microbrew lovers should visit the VANCOUVER ISLAND BREWERY, one producer of "The Island's Own Beer!" This microbrewery, which has quadrupled in employees and volume in ten years, makes Victoria lager, Piper's pale ale, Hermann's dark lager, and Victoria Weizen authentic wheat beer, to critics' raves like Michael Jackson's in Simon & Schuster's *Pocket Guide to Beer.* Even better, you can take a tour of the new state-of-the-art brewery during the summer at 11:30 A.M. and at 1:00 and 3:00 P.M., with tastes and a stop at a colorful, fun gift shop.

❧ *Vancouver Island Brewery, 2330 Government Street, (250) 361–0005. Hours: Monday–Wednesday 11:00 A.M.–6:00 P.M., Thursday–Saturday till 7:00 P.M. Wheelchair accessible. Credit cards: Visa, MasterCard.*

THINGS YOU REALLY SHOULD SEE

There are a few more attractions not covered in any of our neighborhood tours that you really should visit.

The ART GALLERY OF GREATER VICTORIA attracts exhibits of international renown and shows them in an almost homey, comfortable, friendly, and accessible atmosphere. It has the largest collection in British Columbia, holding 10,000 works.

Permanent exhibits include works by contemporary B.C. and other Canadian artists, such as Emily Carr, other North American and European works, and possibly Canada's finest collection of Japanese and Chinese art. Visit the only Shinto shrine in North America.

Once the temporary residence of B.C.'s lieutenant governor, the 1889 mansion was purchased by retailer David Spencer in 1903 and given to the Art Gallery of Greater Victoria in the 1950s.

Every August the gallery puts on an art festival on Moss Street, where you can watch artists, or do the painting yourself if you're so inclined, ending the day in a wonderful beer party in the museum parking lot. Lots of fun, lots of locals, low cost.

❧ *Art Gallery of Greater Victoria, 1040 Moss Street, (250) 384–4101. Hours: Monday–Saturday 10:00 A.M.–5:00 P.M., Thursday until 9:00 P.M., Sunday 1:00–5:00 P.M. Admission: members free, adults $5.00, seniors and students $3.00, children twelve and younger free. Monday is Pay What You Can Day. Wheelchair accessible. (Buses 10 Haultain; 11, 14 UVic up Fort Street, get off at Moss.)*

The B.C. AVIATION MUSEUM, heaven for aviation buffs, is basically a hangar where volunteers restore airplanes and construct engine displays as well as exhibit aircraft, from as early as 1911 to post–World War II.

❧ *B.C. Aviation Museum, 1910 Norseman Road, Victoria International Airport, Sidney, B.C., (250) 655–3300. Hours: summer 10:00 A.M.–4:00 P.M. daily, winter 11:00 A.M.– 3:00 P.M. daily. Admission: adults $4.00, seniors $3.00, children* *to twelve free accompanied by an adult, group rates on request. Wheelchair accessible. Credit cards: none. Directions: Take Highway 17 (Pat Bay Highway), take Airport turnoff (McTavish Road), and turn right on Canora Road to museum driveway.*

BEACON HILL PARK, bound by Douglas Street, Dallas Road, Southgate Street, and Heywood, is one of the most relaxing places we know. The flowers are breathtaking year-round; there are lots of daytime-safe paths to walk; lots of activities for kids; the lakes are peaceful; the birds, ducks, and squirrels talk to you; and, if you're lucky, so does the one remaining swan in Goodacre Lake. The park runs all the way to Dallas Road and the Strait of Juan de Fuca, facing Washington's Olympic Mountains.

For the kids there's an excellent Children's (petting) Farm with baby goats, sheep, and potbelly pigs; a wading pool near the Dallas Road entrance; and just north of the rest rooms and public telephone there's a fun, colorful playground with a pretend train and lots of climbing equipment.

Watch cricket matches on the southeast side, Victoria Lawn Bowling Club matches on the east side, and soccer matches on the southwest side of the park. Or make use of a fine pitch-and-putt golf course. There's lots of parking along the parks roads, on side streets, or on Dallas Road.

In the Queen's Garden toward the southeast corner of the park, two plaques commemorate Queen Elizabeth's visits to the site, but the shrubs and trees seem to refuse to grow and look a bit forlorn.

Please pay attention to signs throughout Beacon Hill Park, which basically say please don't feed the animals.

Following the road southeast from the Children's Farm toward the totem and Dallas Road, notice the forty Japanese Sakura cherry blossom trees planted April 21, 1990, in hopes that "Friendship Will Bridge the Pacific Ocean."

The world's tallest totem pole is located at the southeast corner of Beacon Hill Park, adjoining the most natural part of the park. Carved by Mungo Martin, David Martin, and Henry Hunt, the totem is 127 feet, 7 inches tall. It was dedicated July 2, 1956. Lie on your back and experience the magnitude of this work and symbol, as Kathleen did for the photo.

❧ *Beacon Hill Park is bound by Douglas Street, Dallas Road, Southgate Street, and Heywood, beginning 1 block from Belleville (250–361–0364). Directions: Bus 5 or walk. All facilities are wheelchair accessible.*

Most people want to see the BUTCHART GARDENS (Benvenuto Avenue, Central Saanich). Beginning in 1904, Jenny and Robert Pim Butchart began to develop and beautify what used to be a worked-out quarry for their Portland Cement Company. Ever since the family has lived out its commitment to horticulture and beauty by cultivating hundreds of thousands of plants and flowers. Easy-to-walk paths take visitors through the exquisite sunken garden (once a limestone quarry); the ultimate rose garden, where each plant is labeled; the serene Japanese garden; and the classic Italian garden, which are all interspersed with sculptures.

Pick up leaflets in eighteen languages near the new visitors center and the Benvenuto Seed and Gift Store and guide yourselves over the 130 acres. Visitors center staff will answer all questions graciously about the plants grown here and the local area.

From June 15 to September 30, thousands of colored lights hidden among

WORLD'S TALLEST TOTEM POLE, BEACON HILL PARK AT DALLAS ROAD

the flowers illuminate the entire gardens. Sing-alongs with the Butchart Gardeners happen Monday through Saturday nights from June 1 to September 30. A Lights Up! dance and variety show takes place weeknights from mid-June to early September, and spectacular fireworks light up the sky Saturday nights in July and August. The Christmas decorations are worth the trip. Take the bus to avoid traffic jams.

All Butchart Gardens dining facilities are excellent and range in price from economical to expensive. The Coffee Bar serves light snacks; the Blue Poppy Restaurant cafeteria serves terrific sandwiches, salads, hot dishes, and afternoon tea at reasonable prices; and the Dining Room in the old Butchart residence ("Benvenuto") serves elegant lunches and dinners. A great espresso bar and ice cream stand is at the top of the sunken garden.

The Benvenuto Seed & Gift Store sells gorgeous calendars, books, gardening implements, videos of the gardens, seeds of flowers growing there, gift cards, teapots and cups, and an abundance of other appropriate stuff. You can also get catalogues and plant identification help.

❀ *Butchart Gardens, Benvenuto Avenue, Central Saanich (250–652–5256 recorded; 250–652–4422 business; 250–652–8222 dining reservations). Hours: open 9:00 A.M., gates close at different times all year, from early in winter to 10:30 P.M. summer. Admission: summer adults $16.50, juniors thirteen to seventeen $8.25, children five to twelve $2.00; winter less. Mostly wheelchair accessible. Credit cards: Visa, MasterCard, American Express. Beer and wine. In summer months, try to go early in the morning or late in the afternoon to avoid biggest crowds. Take B.C. Transit Bus 75 for a little more than $2.00.*

Scottish immigrant Robert Dunsmuir built CRAIGDARROCH CASTLE as a monument to himself and the fortune he made in Vancouver Island coal, fulfilling the promise he made to his wife, Joan, before they left Scotland. *Craigdarroch* means "rocky oak place" in Gaelic, which it was before he cut the trees down to build his status symbol.

Currently owned by the Craigdarroch Castle Historical Society, it seems most attractive when the grass is green or at night in full moonlight. Built with Vancouver Island sandstone and brick, the castle has four floors, thirty-nine rooms, and eighteen fireplaces. In 1890 it cost $200,000 to build, including the grounds.

BUTCHART GARDENS

CRAIGDARROCH CASTLE

The castle also served as the veterans hospital from 1919 to 1921 and as Victoria College, affiliated with McGill University of Montreal, from 1921 to 1946. The gift shop sells charming English and Scottish trinkets, candies, biscuits, cards, postcards, and interesting books.

Craigdarroch Castle, 1050 Joan Crescent, (250) 592–5323. Hours: summer 9:00 A.M.–7:00 P.M. daily, winter 10:00 A.M.–4:30 P.M. daily. Admission: adults $8.00, students $5.50, children six to twelve $2.50, donation for younger. Not wheelchair accessible. Credit cards: Visa, MasterCard, American Express. (Buses 11, 14 up Fort Street).

Many locals take their daily walks through Beacon Hill Park and along DALLAS ROAD (Bus 5 or walk), the latter for a particularly exhilarating view of the water and the Olympic Mountains. Many commemorative landmarks along the way note such sites or occurrences as Russian and Canadian boating accidents; Marilyn Bell's 1956 swim across the Juan de Fuca Strait from Port Angeles, Washington, to Victoria, British Columbia; Indian village sites; Horseshoe Bay; evidence of the retreat of the Third Ice Age; Japanese friendship; a water fountain for dogs; and Mile 0 of the Trans-Canada Highway.

Walking or driving along Dallas Road to the east of Beacon Hill Park is breathtaking. Sometimes the ocean climbs the breakwater, and often you can watch hang gliders imitating birds. A must.

EMILY CARR HOUSE, located on Government Street, 4 blocks south of the Parliament buildings, memorializes the birthplace of Canada's most beloved painter and writer. Emily Carr rebelled against her strict English upbringing and followed her heart, roaming the British Columbia wilds, painting, writing, and taking in artists, writers, and other guests at the House of All Sorts around the corner on Simcoe Street (also the name of one of her most famous books). In her later years she wrote her best known work, *The Book of Small.* A lovely place to visit with a most interesting gift shop and pleasant and helpful docents. Signs in the "literary garden" surrounding her house relate Carr's written work to plants in the family garden.

❧ *Emily Carr House, 207 Government Street, (250) 383–5843. Hours: 10:00 A.M.–5:00 P.M. daily mid-May to mid-October; call for an appointment the rest of the year. Admission: adults $5.35, students and seniors $4.28, kids five to twelve $2.50, family $12.84. Christmas season: $5.00 includes special treats and special programs. Partly wheelchair accessible. Credit cards: Visa, MasterCard.*

GOVERNMENT HOUSE (1401 Rockland Avenue, 250–387–2080) is the official residence of the lieutenant governor, the Crown's ceremonial appointee who represents the queen and who occasionally steps in to communicate in a crisis. You can walk throughout the grounds, but you cannot tour the house. (Bus 1 Richardson and a walk).

In good weather, hundreds of local brides and grooms have their wedding pictures taken in the gardens of Government House. Year-round, other locals protest the vast cost of maintaining the office and grounds of a somewhat political and powerless appointment.

The original Government

EMILY CARR HOUSE,
GOVERNMENT STREET

House was purchased by the province from the heirs of George Cary, British Columbia's first (and unbalanced) attorney general. It burned down in 1899, as did its successor in 1977, after which the current mansion was built.

HORTICULTURE CENTRE OF THE PACIFIC cultivates wonderful demonstration gardens that fascinate amateur and professional gardeners or the simply curious beauty fan. Browse through perennial flower displays, the Asiatic and Oriental lily collection, the rose garden with a hundred different varieties of miniature roses, and a rhododendron vale.

Horticulture Centre of the Pacific, 505 Quayle Road, (250) 479–6162. Hours: dawn to dusk daily. Mostly wheelchair accessible. Directions: Highway 17 (Pat Bay Highway), turn onto Highway 17A, turn left off Beaver Lake Road, and the center will be on your left. Admission: $3.00. (Bus 21 and a walk.)

Where to Stay

All accommodations in Victoria appear in order of proximity to Victoria's Inner Harbour, since it is the geographic focal point of most visitors' stays. Those listed first are closest to the inner harbour.

Downtown Victoria

Hotels

Splurge

The Empress, 721 Government Street (250–384–8111 or 800–441–1414; www.fairmont.com—click on *Empress*), $129–$419; 464 units; little dogs at $50 per stay; since 1909 world famous symbol of Victoria; center of Inner Harbour; lounge, dining, high tea; special packages.

Abigail's Hotel, 906 McClure Street (250–388–5363; www.abigailhotel.com), January–February $119–$197, March–April and October 15–December $159–$263, May–October 15 $199–329; 22 units, including 6 in coach house; gourmet breakfast; classic Tudor design; no pets.

Chateau Victoria Hotel, 740 Burdett Avenue (250–382–4221; 800–663–5891; www.chateauvictoria.com), March–April $79–92, May–June $117–$250, July–October 14, $139–$260, rest of year reduced rates; 177 units; roof-top restaurant; pool; bar; exercise room; no pets.

Queen Victoria Inn, 655 Douglas Street (250–386–1312; www.queenvictoria inn.com), October 15–April $75 for two, including breakfast; May–October 14 $165; AAA and senior discount; 146 units, all with balconies; indoor pool; many kitchens; no pets.

Royal Scott Inn, 425 Quebec Street (250–388–5463 or 800–663–7515; www.royalscot.com), summer $199–359, off-season $129–$269; 176 units; restaurant; indoor pool; near U.S. ferries; shuttle; no pets.

Victoria Regent Hotel, 1234 Wharf Street (250–386–2211 or 800–663–7472; www.regenthotel.victoria.bc.ca), June 15–October 15 $149–$359, remainder $119–269; 41 units; by the water; restaurant; some fireplaces; packages; no pets.

Laurel Point Inn, 680 Montreal Street (250–386–8721 or 800–663–7667; www.laurelpoint.com), June 15–September $155–$250, penthouse $675; October–May 15 $125–$185, penthouse $485; May 16–June 15 special $155–$250; 200 units; indoor pool; glass balconies; Japanese tubs; ocean views; lounge, dining; no pets.

Ocean Pointe Resort, 45 Songhees Road (250–360–2999 or 800–667–4677; www.oprhotel.com), June–mid-October $249–$409, rest of year varies at lower rates; 250 units; looks back across harbor; terrace; spa; bar; tennis; wine shop; no pets.

Best deals

Days Inn on the Harbour, 427 Belleville Street (250–386–3451 or 800–325–2525; www.daysinnvictoria.com), May–June $135–$165, July–September $173–$203, October–April $105–$125; 71 units; kitchens; near U.S. ferries; great view of the Inner Harbour and The Empress (ask for the fourth floor facing the water); no pets.

Bedford Regency Hotel, 1140 Government Street (250–384–6835 or 800–665–6500; www.victoriabc.com/bedford.html), May 14–October 17 $165–$250, rest of year $95–$150; 40 units; continental breakfast; in heart of shopping; no pets.

Ramada Huntingdon Manor, 330 Quebec Street (250–381–3456 or 800–663–7556; www.bctravel.com/huntingdon), May12–June 15 $133–$213, June 16–September 26 $153–$233, September 27–October 15 $119–$199, rest of year $83–$163; 116 units; jacuzzi; lounge, restaurant; art gallery; near U.S. ferries; no pets.

Harbour Towers Hotel, 345 Quebec Street (250–385–2405 or 800–663–5896; www.harbourtowers.com), April 16–May $220–$370, June–October 15 $260–$460, rest of year $180–$290; 185 units; restaurant; pool; sauna; shuttle; harbor and water views; no pets.

Best Western Inner Harbour, 412 Quebec Street (250–384–5122 or 800–528–5122; www.victoriahotels.com), June–September $159–$219, May and October $109–$159, rest of year $89–$119; 74 units; continental breakfast; outdoor pool, sauna, Jacuzzi; no pets.

Clarion Hotel Grand Pacific, 450 Quebec Street, (250–386–0450 or

800–663–7550; www.hotelgrandpacific.com), $116–$224; 145 units; pool; restaurant; fitness facility; no pets; expanding to about 300 units in spring 2001.

Coast Harbourside Hotel & Marina, 146 Kingston Street (250–360–1211; www.coasthotels.com), summer $250 and up, rest of year lower; 132 units; pool; bar and grill; pets with $20-per-day charge.

James Bay Inn, 270 Government Street (250–384–7151; www.jamesbayinn.bc.ca), May–June $80–$150, July–September $106–$245, rest of year lower; 48 units; historic; lounge, restaurant; no pets.

Quality Inn Downtown, 850 Blanshard Street (250–385–6787 or 800–661–4115), formerly Green Gables Inn; May–June 15 $99–$109, June 16–September $135–$169, rest of year $79–$89; 56 units; Old Bailey Pub and Green Room Cafe; no pets.

Strathcona Hotel, 919 Douglas Street (250–383–7137 or 800–663–7476; www.strathcona.com), May–June $61–$94, July–September $79–$119, October–April $54–$74; 85 units; pub was first in Victoria after prohibition; Big Band John's bar, Cuckoo's Nest sports lounge, Sticky Wicket restaurant, rooftop dining in spring and summer; no pets.

Swans Hotel, 506 Pandora Avenue (250–361–3310 or 800–668–7926; www.swanshotel.com), May–June $125 and up, July–September $159 and up, rest of year starts at $99; 29 units; restored historic building; microbrewery and pub downstairs.

Best Western Carlton Plaza, 642 Johnson Street (250–388–5513 or 800–663–7241; www.bestwestern.com), May–September $149–199, rest of year starts at $79; 103 units; expanded heritage hotel; restaurant, bar; no pets.

Bed-and-Breakfasts

There are dozens of nice B&Bs in Victoria, and here is a list of those that are in designated heritage houses, or architectural or historic special places. For reservations or information on others, call (250) 479–1986, (250) 655–7173, (604) 733–2777, (604) 825–7416, (604) 738–7207, or (800) 561–3223.

Holland House Inn, 595 Michigan, (250) 384–6644

Haterleigh, 243 Kingston Street, (250) 384–9995

Andersen House, 301 Kingston Street, (250) 388–4565

Gatsby's, 309 Belleville, (250) 388–9191

Beaconsfield Inn, 998 Humboldt, (250) 384–4044

Ryan's, 224 Superior, (250) 389–0012

Humboldt House, 867 Humboldt, (250) 383–0152

Dogwood Manor, 1124 Fairfield, (250) 361–4441

Berry House, 114 St. Andrews, (250) 744–9128

Inn on St. Andrews, 231 St. Andrews, (250) 384–4508
Edwardian Inn, 135 Medana, (250) 380–2411
Prior House, 600 St. Charles, (250) 592–8847
Meridian House, 116 Eberts, (250) 360–0747
Dreemskerry, 1509 Rockland, (250) 384–4014
Craignmyle, 1037 Craigdorroch, (250) 595–5411
Blue Bird, 1052 Craigdorroch, (250) 598–8981
Oak Bay Guest House, 1052 Newport, (250) 598–3812

CHAPTER 4

EXPLORING OUTSIDE VICTORIA

ry to squeeze out a little time to explore beyond Victoria proper. Within thirty minutes by car or bus, you can visit Elk Lake, stop in at fresh vegetable stands, see the B.C. Aviation Museum, and stroll Sidney on the eastern, nontouristy side of the island.

Going up the west side of the island, you can easily experience Vancouver Island's full range of beauty in a short day trip, or longer if you have time. Find your way to Royal Roads University, hike trails, and visit Sooke and its regional museum, all within forty minutes of Victoria. While Sooke has long been an independent community and is the home of the world-renowned Sooke Harbour House, it's nearly a suburb of Victoria, with sensible people commuting back and forth every day.

Farther afield, enjoy rain forests and beaches, visit Point-No-Point, and forage along the West Coast Trail and Port Renfrew tide pools within two hours of Victoria.

VICTORIA TO SIDNEY

A day trip to Sidney is a fun and quick way to find out what life on Vancouver Island outside Victoria is like. Just thirty minutes away you can experience small-town Canada, with beautiful scenery to boot.

If you're driving, head north on Blanshard Street, which becomes Highway 17 (Patricia Bay Highway), which will take you to Sidney. If you prefer to have someone else do the driving, you can take Buses 70, 72, or 75.

You might want to stop along Highway 17 at the SAANICH ARTIFACTS SOCIETY, where you can see thousands of local artifacts; possibly the largest collection of working steam engines in Canada; an operational sawmill; and a blacksmith shop, where several trained blacksmiths produce souvenirs you can buy. You can also stroll on several miles of lush nature trails around the property and see Pioneer Chapel, a log cabin, and a nature pond. Catch the summer fair on Father's Day weekend, with demonstrations, hayrides, and country food. Or on the second weekend after Labor Day, see the fall threshing show.

❧ *Saanich Artifacts Society, 7321 Lochside Drive, Saanichton (250–652–5522). Hours: 9:30 A.M.–noon daily, June–August 9:30 A.M.–4:00 P.M. daily. Wheelchair accessible.*

One of our favorite stops for peace of mind along the way is BEAVER LAKE/ELK LAKE PARK, about twenty minutes north of Victoria on Highway 17. First you will see the signs to Beaver Lake, and then the sign to Elk Lake comes up quickly with a short left-turn lane. Careful.

Elk Lake is a particularly popular sailboarding and rowing lake. More Canadian rowing medalists from the 1996 Olympics trained at Elk Lake than anywhere else in the world. Go Canada!

When you turn off to Sidney, you will find yourself on Beacon Avenue, the main street of Sidney, which looks on the surface like a midwestern U.S. town. Look further.

You may want to browse along BEACON AVENUE, which has interesting shops (including branches of several Victoria boutiques), bookstores, and cafes. On the other hand, you may want to make a beeline for the tiny wharf and the famous SIDNEY FISHERMAN'S MARKET, where you wade in through fishermen's water and debris to buy the freshest local seafood ever. The pier is extremely people-friendly, with local kids and adults dropping their crab nets (and occasionally a small child) over the edge.

The Stir Six Coffee and Sushi Bar at the end of the pier does a bang-up business in ice cream, coffee, light snacks, and sushi made to order, as locals buy coffee or a snack for their commutes to nearby islands on the Sidney Island Ferry or the forty-five-year-old Portland Island Ferry. Parking spaces are few, so nab one in parking lots to the north of the pier.

SIDNEY MUSEUM, at the entrance to Port Sidney Marina, contains the large personal collection of artifacts donated by Saanich Peninsula pioneers May and Joe John. The permanent exhibits include models, skeletons, and murals depicting the story of local whales and the evolution of whales, a relief map of Vancouver Island, and photographs of local history, particularly that of the Coast Salish Aboriginal Peoples and European and Oriental settlers who arrived later.

❧ *Sidney Museum, 9801 Seaport Place, (250) 656–2140. Hours: summer 10:00 A.M.–5:00 P.M. daily. Credit cards: Visa, MasterCard. Public rest rooms.*

At MINERAL WORLD AND SCRATCH PATCH, kids can look at rocks, participate in discovery and touching almost with abandon, and expend some high

SIDNEY BANDSTAND, BEACON AVENUE

energy on the playground equipment in front while you scour the nearby shops adjoining the gorgeous marina.

✸℧ *Mineral World and Scratch Patch, 9891 Seaport Place, (250) 655–4367. Hours: March–New Year's Day 10:00 A.M.–4:00 P.M. daily, May 1–Labor Day 10:00 A.M.–5:00 P.M. Admission: by donation. Wheelchair accessible.*

DEEP COVE CHALET (11190 Chalet, 250–656–3541) is one of Victorians' favorite out-of-town restaurants and romantic dinner destinations, with a German and French menu emphasizing local seafood, lamb, and game. Sunday brunch is a reservations-only proposition at about $30, as is dinner. For a more economical excellent meal, SQUID ROE (9818 Third Street, north of Beacon Avenue, 250–656–1822) serves breakfast from $1.99, land-hearty lunches, dinners, snacks, and a range of non- and alcoholic beverages in a pub atmosphere. Both are accessible, and fully licensed. The BLUE PETER PUB & RESTAURANT (2270 Harbour, 250–656–4551) is less expensive and intimate but has excellent fresh seafood, steaks, and pastas, as well as an outdoor patio overlooking the marina.

For fun transportation around Sidney on land, try CELEBRATION CARRIAGE SERVICES (250–655–3672) for five scenic tours about town. They range from a ten-to-fifteen-minute minitour to the Grand Sidney Special through town to

Tsehum Harbour, a former governor general's house. Just wait at the carriage stand outside Port Sidney Marina, late afternoon and early evening, Thursday–Sunday.

Around Sidney on water, try a SIDNEY HARBOUR CRUISE (250–655–5211) for a trip from Port Sidney Marina to Tsehum Harbour, Canoe Cove, Swartz Bay, and back (only $11). Cruises operate daily in summer and on weekends only in spring and fall. Forget it in winter.

The SAANICH PENINSULA VISITOR'S GUIDE, put out by the *Peninsula News Review,* is extremely helpful and available from them at (250) 656–1151 or from the Saanich Peninsula Chamber of Commerce, 9768 Third Street, Sidney, B.C. V8L 3S4; (250) 656–3616. You can get a HERITAGE WALKING TOUR guide from the Heritage Advisory Committee, 2440 Sidney Avenue, Sidney, B.C. V8L 1Y7; (250) 656–1184.

Now here's a quick walking tour of the most interesting part of Beacon Avenue, beginning with the south side and starting from the water end of the street:

The Sidney Bakery, 2507 Beacon, supplies locals with Nanaimo Bars (delectable layered squares of chocolate, coconut, chocolate, yellow icing, and chocolate!), scones, carrot cake, and doughnuts, with special senior discount days on Monday and Thursday. Temptations offers gourmet coffee, great soups, and sandwiches from $2.50 to $4.50, with soup and sandwich at only $4.75. Vintage clothing fans might enjoy the St. Vincent de Paul shop, and travelers should drop in at One Stop Travel Shop at 2495 Beacon. The Phoenix Restaurant serves Chinese food, among other cuisines, with a senior special menu and prices at lunch and dinner.

Baden-Baden, which also has a boutique on Fort Street in downtown Victoria, sells stylish European (primarily German) fashions for women and shares an entryway with Klee Wyck House, which specializes in popular-label shoes. Tivoli Gallery claims to be protected by angels (and probably is) and specializes in Italianate clothes and personal home accessories. Vegetarians and the health-interested can find a home at Sidney Natural Foods.

Starbucks fans can get their fixes at the corner of Beacon and Third Street and then move on to the Village Gallery up the street for local artists' paintings, art supplies, framing, and poster prints.

The pièce de résistance (or should it be nonresistance?) is famous LUNN'S PASTRIES DELI & COFFEE SHOP LTD. (2455 Beacon), which has won more confection awards than any other patisserie and chocolaterie on the west coast of North America. Awards include medals and trophies from England and France, including the International Bakers & Confectioners in London.

Besides enjoying a light lunch here, you can also indulge in frangipan tarts, griottes (cognac cherries in fondant), French candied orange peels, or Kirsch fondant kisses. The deli meat counter has a wide range of German and Hungarian salami sausages rarely seen on the West Coast. Save a few calories in your day for Lunn's. One of our favorites.

Moving westward on Beacon, you can visit Knightsbridge Gift Shops, Ltd. and Tunes & Tees for hip, with-it music and compatible T-shirts.

The Sidney Post Office, built in 1936, is interesting as a sample of local period architecture just east of Touch of Class Ladies Wear. Victoria's Rogers' Chocolates is branching out into the redeveloped old post office building. The Olympia Restaurant at Beacon and Fifth is a local staple serving pizza, steaks, seafood, BBQ ribs, lasagna, Cuban lobster, and Alaskan crab. Monday is pasta night at $4.95.

Kathleen likes Muffet & Louisa for well-priced superb kitchen equipment such as Emile Henry and BIA porcelain and accessories for dining, bed, and bath. Local folks hang out at Alexander's Coffee Bar (set back from the street), where you can also get great bagel sandwiches. Scandia Restaurant features hearty breakfasts all day, liver and onions at $8.99, Wiener schnitzel at $13.95, Danish beef at $10.95, Danish bratwurst at $10.95, Danish Frikadeller meat cakes at $9.95, and a special senior menu.

Sidney calls itself the "Bookstore City," and you can cross Beacon at this point to visit a few of them. Beacon Books at 2372 Beacon majors in exceptional used books with a few China pieces, and you enter the Mystery Bookshop through Beacon Books for mystery and crime novels. Dollars Wild is a bargain store where everything costs $1.00.

Up Fifth Street you might want to check out a great and colorful healthy food-to-go cafe, Vitamin To Go Cafe, or Theo's Greek & Western Cuisine Restaurant, which serves just what it says.

Back on Beacon east of Fifth Street, Cornish's Book & Stationery sells great cards and a few books; Sweet Talk & Lace sells suggestively tempting feathers and lingerie and loungewear; Patricia's Yarn Shop fills knitting and needlework supplies; and Pottery Plus offers imported and local pottery.

As you look up Fourth Street, don't be alarmed at the Canadian Air Force PF 060 airplane apparently poised to take off from the Canadian military recruiting center. Don't worry, it's not going anywhere.

Be sure to visit TANNER'S BOOKS at the corner of Beacon and Fourth Street and its marvelous Children's Book Shop (this one deserves an award, if there were such things). You can't miss its pink and white exterior and stairs. Tanner's is a marvelous, independent emporium with a great inventory of quiet things to do at home or in your hotel room, such as reading books and international newspapers, models of all kinds, greeting cards, candy, snacks, and stationery.

The Sidney Candy Man is jam-packed with Harlan's truffles, wrapped and fresh candy (some in jars you can reach into), and ice cream. There's a coffee bar in back.

We insist you go around the corner on Third Street to the HAUNTED BOOKSHOP. On our last visit we finally ventured in and had a most enjoyable whole afternoon talking with the manager and browsing in this musty, warm shop. The store sells used and rare books, including a few mysteries. The Canadiana collection is exceptional.

Be sure to try CAFE MOZART at 2470 Beacon (250–655–1554) for a dinner of mussels three ways, local sea bass, Northwest Territories caribou medallions, or Saanich ostrich with chanterelle mushrooms.

Where to Stay

Brentwood Bay

Best Value Motel, 1211 Verdier Avenue, corner Highway 17A (250–652–2012); $39–$59; 1 mile to Butchart Gardens.

Saanich

Cherry Bend Motel, 4879 Cherry Tree Bend (250–658–5611); $54–$79; some kitchens; some nonsmoking; no pets.

Saanichton

Quality Inn Waddling Dog, 2476 Mount Newton Cross Road (250–652–1146); $99–$125; English-style inn; pub, restaurant, beer and wine store.
Western 66 Motel, 2401 Mount Newton Cross Road (250–652–4464); $42–$80; no pets.
Super 8 Motel, 2477 Mount Newton Cross Road (250–652–6888); $72–$88; fifty-one units; pets on approval.

Sidney

Dunsmuir Lodge, 1515 McTavish Road (250–656–3166); $79–$129; high on wooded slope, just south of airport; licensed restaurant, lounge; open June–September.
Victoria Airport Travelodge, 2280 Beacon Avenue (250–656–1176); $59–$125; poolside BBQ; licensed dining, pub; lounge, beer and wine store; closest to airport.
Latch Country Inn, 2328 Harbour Road (250–656–6622); $95–$180; restored

1920 house overlooking harbor; adult-oriented; art, antiques; licensed restaurant; no smoking; no pets.

Best Western Emerald Isle Motor Inn, 2306 Beacon Avenue (250–656–4441); $79–$129; sixty-three units; sauna; pets for fee.

Cedarwood Motel, 9522 Lochside Drive (250–656–5551); $89–$160; cottages, suites; close to water; some Jacuzzis; no smoking; small pets OK.

VICTORIA TO PORT RENFREW

If you are driving to the west coast of the island, take Douglas Street north and follow the signs to Highway 1 toward Sooke. (You can also take 1A to Highway 14 for a more local route, but we have never done it without missing a turn.) When you reach Colwood, you'll take the exit from Highway 1 to Highway 14 (Island Highway). Years of construction and dust at this interchange may have been completed by the time you read this. You're on your way.

If you wish to make the trip from Victoria to Sooke by public transportation, take Bus 50 (get a transfer), then Bus 61 from the Western Exchange (transfer) Centre at Colwood ($2.25 each way to Sooke). We enjoy it, but you may feel limited unless you like to walk a lot.

Anywhere along the interchange and parallel to Highway 14 runs the GALLOPING GOOSE TRAIL AND PARK, which begins in View Royal and continues for 42 kilometers (26 miles) along an old Canadian National Railway bed through the lush hills around Colwood, Langford, Metchosin, and Sooke. The trail is great for walking, mountain biking, and horseback riding. It begins at Atkins Avenue and Highway 1A, south of Highway 1. Never far from the highway, this trail helps you feel you're getting away while still being close to Victoria. In spring and summer you can see animals and flowers and enjoy great lookouts. Stay on the main trail. Once you get to Metchosin the trail will take you through several public parks. Dogs OK on leash.

SIX MILE PUB at 494 Island Highway is a great place to stop for a beer, iced tea, lunch, dinner, snack, whatever. Open most the

If you are going to travel into the wilds of Vancouver Island, please be advised that deer, black bear, cougar, wolves, and many other species live in this area. They are wild animals and can be dangerous. Please do not attempt to approach them at any time. Enjoy, but do not disturb.

hours you need it. This "new" pub building was built in 1898, making Six Mile the oldest pub in British Columbia and possibly in western Canada.

Six Mile Pub was originally built in 1855 and called Parson's Bridge Hotel after Bill Parson, who was not a parson but was the builder of the bridge giving access to the Sooke River area. As the hub of local activity, the hotel was always popular, especially with stagecoaches, whose drivers would stop to rest the horses, rest themselves, and, incidentally, drop off the mail.

In 1917 Prohibition closed all Canadian bars. Theoretically. Victoria remained dry until 1952, forcing fun-loving drinkers to go out of town (6 miles) to the Six Mile. Bootleggers unloaded barrels and barrels of liquor, leading to several decades of highly profitable business at the Six Mile Pub, B.C.'s rum-running headquarters.

The Six Mile's current owners, Bill and Donna Phillips, bought it in 1980 and restored its interior as accurately as possible. Their historic photo and memorabilia collections are must-sees.

From the outside it looks like a sedate Tudor establishment. On the inside it looks like many things: each room has a different personality to suit your mood—large banquet, small English with cozy booths, huge bar with small round tables and party atmosphere, an outdoor beer garden/waterfront patio, and herb and flower gardens.

The food is a bit eclectic, but everything is good. Roast beef, fish and chips, salads, penne pasta Alfredo, chicken teriyaki, beef or vegetarian lasagna, shepherd's pie, and easily less than $10. One of our favorites.

Six Mile Pub, 494 Island Highway, (250) 478-3121. Hours: pub 11:00 A.M.–1:00 A.M., lunch 11:30 A.M.–2:00 P.M., dinner 6:00–9:00 P.M. Wheelchair accessible. Credit cards: Visa, MasterCard. Fully licensed.

You will know C*OLWOOD* by its used car lots; Colwood Plaza, a small shopping center; and recognizable restaurants along the road. If you are driving, this is where you take the exit from Highway 1 onto Highway 14. If you are on the bus, you get off here at the Western Exchange Center and get on Bus 61. There are no public phones and no rest rooms at the transfer station; there are a few rain shelters.

F*ORT* R*ODD* H*ILL* H*ISTORIC* P*ARK*, 603 Fort Rodd Hill Road off Ocean Boulevard, was named for an HMS *Fisgard* officer; the batteries and garrison were built from 1895 to 1900. The Fisgard lighthouse was built in 1860 and was the first permanent lighthouse on the Canadian Pacific coast. The band of the 5th (B.C.) Field Regiment, Royal Canadian Artillery, Victoria's oldest military unit, plays Sunday afternoons at 2:00 P.M. in summer.

Fort Rodd Hill Historic Park, 603 Fort Rodd Hill Road, (250) 363-4662. Hours: 10:00 A.M.–5:30 P.M. daily. Admission: free.

After you pass through Colwood, you begin to see the true, deep beauty of the West Coast.

In METCHOSIN, originally called *Smetts-shosin* by natives (meaning "place of stinking fish"—those that washed up dead on the shore), Metchosin Road turns off Sooke Road (Highway 14) just past Colwood. You can visit Witty's Lagoon, Devonian Regional Parks, and Matheson Lake Regional Park for nature trails and right-on-top-of-it looks at West Coast plants and animals.

On the left side of Highway 14, the large, walled Tudor settlement has most recently been ROYAL ROADS UNIVERSITY (250–363–4569, tourist information), originally a mansion built in 1908. The grounds and beautiful gardens are usually open 10:00 A.M.–6:00 P.M. From here it is 24 kilometers (14.4 miles) to Sooke.

GOLDSTREAM PROVINCIAL PARK is accessible up Humpback Road from Highway 14. In November and December you can watch chum salmon run on the lower Goldstream River, just off Highway 1, 20 kilometers (12 miles) west of Victoria. Park naturalists explain the spawning scene. Do not bother the fish, throw anything into the water, or allow animals in the water. In the summer Goldstream is a great place to walk and picnic among the ancient cedar trees and big-leaf maples.

In LANGFORD, the Glen Lake Family Restaurant is obviously the local hangout. If you climb Mount Finlayson in Mount Finlayson Provincial Park, you can experience unequaled views of the entire Victoria area. Finlayson Arm is a good place to start a hike along the Gowlland Range.

Now you just wend your way toward SOOKE, marveling at the natural landscape.

Olde English Pub is thirty minutes out of Victoria on the right side going toward Sooke. The 17 Mile House pub is also popular with locals, but it may be difficult to get off the road in time for these unless you are alert beforehand.

Soon you start to see small bed-and-breakfasts, such as Hartmann House and Cooper's Guest House. Klee Wyk Antiques is on the left. So-called civilization indicators begin to pop up: the Sizzling Fox Restaurant (a medium-priced family restaurant with lots of local clientele) and then a Shell gas/fuel station on the left, followed in another couple of kilometers by the campgrounds of Sunny Shores Resort, Grouches Lair on the Harbour, and Bed & Breakfast by the Sea on the left, then a native art gallery on the left and Nettie's Fruit Stand and a general store on the right.

Two kilometers from Grouches you cross the Sooke River and pass, unless you stop in, a Tudor-style pub on the left. Coming up on the right is Phillips Road, where you want to get off Bus 61 for the Sooke Regional Museum and the Sooke Area Arena.

The newly renovated SOOKE REGION MUSEUM AND TOURISM INFOR-
MATION CENTRE is one of the best small museums we have ever seen.
Charmingly compact and historically accurate, its Moss Cottage (1870) is
Sooke's oldest building and offers entertaining exhibits of local history and mem-
orabilia and a complete history of the salmon and lumber industries in B.C. Be
sure to visit the gift shop and its bargain book box.

The staff of the tourism information center, inside and to the left, will
answer questions, advise you on accommodations and restaurants, and even
make some reservations.

Signs warn: VISITORS BEWARE. WITH THE INCREASING NUMBERS OF TRAV-
ELERS VISITING OUR BEAUTIFUL WEST COAST BEACHES, IT IS UNFORTUNATE
THAT SOME INDIVIDUALS ARE ALSO ATTRACTED WHO MAY AVAIL THEMSELVES
OF VALUABLES LEFT IN LOCKED CARS. PLEASE DO NOT LEAVE VALUABLES IN
UNATTENDED CARS.

The Sooke Region Museum puts on several annual events, including the
Moss Cottage Christmas and tasty salmon barbecues.

*Sooke Region Museum and Tourism Information Centre, 2070 Phillips
Road (right off Sooke Road/Highway 14), (250) 642–6351. Hours: July–August
9:00 A.M.–5:30 P.M. daily, September–June 9:00 A.M. to 6:00 P.M. Tuesday–
Sunday. Wheelchair accessible. Credit cards: Visa, MasterCard.*

Up Phillips Road about .5 kilometer is the Sooke Area Arena, where the
annual FINE ARTS FESTIVAL, the largest juried art show in British Columbia, is
held every August. The committee does an outstanding professional job of
hanging this exhibit in what normally functions as the Sooke Minor Hockey
Association and Sooke Figure Skating Club arena. The festival includes a cafe
with excellent inexpensive sandwiches. The arena is wheelchair accessible;
admission to the show is $5.00.

SOOKE itself is forty minutes west of Victoria. Main attractions include
salmon and halibut fishing, whale watching (loads of charters are available), hiking, and relaxing at nearby beaches and trails.

For centuries there was a Coast Salish settlement that thrived on abundant
local fish, berries, clams, and wild birds. The aboriginal population nearly killed
each other off in tribal wars, leaving few natives when the Europeans arrived
looking for gold and lumber in 1849. The Leech River gold rush in 1864
brought a swell in population to Sooke.

Annual events worth making the trip to Sooke include well-known All Sooke
Day (third Saturday in July), featuring logger sports and a salmon barbecue; the
Share the Spirit native festival; the King's Cup maritime festival; and the Sink or

---

BABE'S NO-BAKE COOKIES
Charlie and Alison (Babe) Warren of Babe's
Honey Farm, Sooke

Ingredients
   1 cup Babe's honey
   1 cup peanut butter
   2 cups quick oats
   2 cups Rice Krispies

Preparation
   Mix by hand and shape into small balls. Kids of all ages love these.

Swim Competition. In addition to the previously mentioned arts festival in August, there is a mountain bike festival in a small, manageable environment.

Try the fish and chips trailer and Babe's honey and vegetable stand on the right going out. The fish, chips, and onions rings are divine, as is everything at Babe's.

Sometimes we go all the way to Sooke just to go to MOM'S CAFE. General manager Glenn Countryman keeps the place what it always has been—a logger- and fisher-friendly, funky joint where an occasional tourist fits in nicely with some of the best breakfasts anywhere. All-day breakfasts include the Logger's (three-egg omelets from $6.50 for two fillings) and the Canadian (lean back bacon and eggs Benedict at $5.95). Oyster and other burgers, bluenose seafood chowder in a bread basket (from $4.50), and salads compete at lunch. Dinner specials range from daily specials such as Stewsday shrimp fettucini with garlic toast and Caesar salad at $9.95 to Gypsy schnitzel with salsa and cheddar or Sunday's roast beef and Yorky. Don't miss Mom's deep-dish pies.

↬ *Mom's Cafe, 2036 Shields Road, Sooke; (250) 642–3314. Hours: "Opens at 6:58 A.M. for your convenience." Wheelchair accessible. Credit cards: Visa, MasterCard. Fully licensed.*

Mom's also has MOM'S WATERFRONT VACATION HOME & COTTAGE (See "Where to Stay"), which provides kayaking, trail and fishing guides.

There are a number of PARKS AND TRAILS in the Sooke area. East Sooke Regional Park is a semiwilderness, 4,500-acre park ideal for both beginning and

SWEET BARBECUE-ROASTED PORK
Charlie and Alison (Babe) Warren of Babe's
Honey Farm, Sooke

Ingredients
1 5-lb. loin roast

1 1-lb., 4-oz. jar apricot preserves

⅛ cup Babe's honey

¼ cup lemon juice

¼ cup soy sauce

½ clove garlic, minced

1 small onion, minced

1 cup ginger ale

⅛ tsp. ginger

⅛ tsp. pepper (optional)

1 1-lb., 13 oz. can (or jar) whole apricots

1 tsp. grated lemon rind

¼ cup grated coconut

parsley sprigs

Preparation
Remove bone from roast (or buy a boneless one) and tie roast with string. Place in a dish. Combine ½ the apricot preserves with honey, lemon juice, soy sauce, garlic, onion, ginger ale, ginger, and pepper and pour over roast. Marinate for four to five hours, turning occasionally.

Remove roast from marinade and reserve marinade. Insert meat thermometer in roast and place roast on spit. Cook over low coals for about 3½ hours or to 185 degrees on meat thermometer, basting frequently with reserved marinade. Spread half the remaining apricot preserves over roast. Heat remaining marinade with remaining apricot preserves and pour over roast. Heat apricots with lemon rind.

Remove roast to hot serving platter. Garnish with apricots and sprinkle with coconut and parsley sprigs.

Serves six to eight.

expert hikers, with beach, coastal and forest trails, petroglyphs, wildflowers, birds, and animals. At the beach you might see large California mussels (which provide natural protection for dog whelks), porcelain crabs, and sea worms. In low intertidal spots watch for purple sea urchins and giant green anemones. You can experience peace close to Victoria. Roche Cove Regional Park gives access to Sooke basin and Galloping Goose Trail. Sooke Potholes Provincial Park is a locally popular swimming and picnicking park on the Sooke River and is an ideal place to watch spawning salmon in the fall. Parking is limited. Whiffin Spit is a natural breakwater between Juan de Fuca Strait and Sooke Harbour. To get there, follow signs to the Sooke Harbour House, a destination restaurant and inn. A few feet past the inn and restaurant is a parking area at Whiffin Spit Park and a twenty-minute walk takes you to the end of the spit with views of the harbor, the Olympic Mountains, seals, seabirds, and wildflowers. Viewable intertidal marine life includes a leaf-shaped crab *(Mimulus foliatus),* a small limpet *(Megatebennus bimaculatus),* sea slugs, and a large red-headed anemone in the gravel. Handicapped access is described as moderate.

Western Canada's finest inn and restaurant, SOOKE HARBOUR HOUSE, at 1528 Whiffin Spit Road, is about forty minutes up the western side of Vancouver Island. As you head toward Sooke on the Island Highway, the sign for Sooke Harbour House is obvious. Wander through the residential neighborhood following the excellent signs until you find it (just a couple of minutes). You are in for a real treat, because co-owners Frederique and Sinclair Philip have just increased the number of rooms at their inn, giving you a better chance to experience it and them. Reservations are a must.

Gourmet magazine rates the inn among the top twenty-five around the world, and its restaurant as the top in the world in the category of authentic local cuisine, number two in the world in "elegant dining room" and number three in the world in "casual dining room," (and it's all the same dining room).

Sooke Harbour House also received the prestigious four-star rating from the Mobil travel guides. It is worth the entire trip if it fits in your budget. If it doesn't, you might consider a splurge. Gourmets, gourmands, chefs, restaurateurs, and food fans from all over the world enjoy the same food here as you do. The inn's decor and setting make you feel at home on the edge of the world. Charges include breakfast and lunch.

Its newest rooms offer understated elegance combined with a local unit's stained-glass shower, wood carvings, and exquisite views from bed.

The whole menu changes daily. On our last visit, the soup was chilled garlic, ginger, English cucumber, carrot juice, and sheep's milk yogurt puree with a baked salmon herb and roast garlic roulade. Among the cold appetizers were uncracked Dungeness crab with a garlic, garden fresh dill, and tuberous begonia butter, and local sidestripe prawns in a ravioli with snow peas and chives, prune plum, yellow and red tomato basil ginger vinaigrette.

Entrees might include wild coho salmon, crisp Port Renfrew ling cod, and organically raised Rainbow Farm free-range chicken. The wine list is superb and rivaled only by Herald Street Caffé's.

ॐ *Sooke Harbour House, 1528 Whiffen Spit Road, (250) 642–3421; Fax: (250) 642–6988; Web: www.sookeharbourhouse.com; E-mail: shh@islandnet.com. Hours: 5:30–9:00 P.M. daily, closed January 6–February 6. Wheelchair accessible. Credit cards: Visa, MasterCard, American Express, Diners, enRoute. Fully licensed.*

As you continue on Highway 14, now called the West Coast Road, you will first come to Gordon's Beach, a roadside beach named after the old Gordon fishtrap, with views of Juan de Fuca Strait and Sheringham Lighthouse.

Try the COUNTRY CUPBOARD CAFE ("Home Cooking with a Flair"), where Jennie Vivian and family serve terrific meals in their A-frame with a deck and patio among the Raggedy Anns, amusing collectibles, and dried flowers. Vegetables are grown along the path to the restaurant. Lunch specialties include huge lean beef or chicken burgers for less than $8.00, and dinner ranges from penne with sautéed vegetables at $10.05 to sautéed chicken and prawns at $16.95, and half-pound New York steaks at $16.95. Jennie's desserts are famous. We dare you to leave without trying the white chocolate Irish Cream cheesecake.

ॐ *Country Cupboard Cafe, 402 Sheringham Point Road at West Coast Road, (250) 646–2323.*

SOOKE HARBOUR HOUSE, SOOKE

Hours: lunch and dinner daily. Not wheelchair accessible. Credit cards: Visa, MasterCard. Beer and wine.

You pass through the unincorporated Shirley District and then arrive at FRENCH BEACH PROVINCIAL PARK, one of our favorites. About one hour from Victoria and 21.5 kilometers (13 miles) from Sooke Centre, this popular sandy beach is good for investigating tidepools at the western end, and there's also a children's playground and campground. French Beach is a favorite feeding spot for migrating gray whales, and there are educational displays near the beach. There is lots of paid parking (price varies, up to $5.00—be sure to take coins and put the ticket on your dashboard), and there are almost one hundred campsites.

French Beach is completely wheelchair accessible, with paved paths (occasionally a little steep), and meshed nets to keep paths through the sand to the water.

Where to Stay in Sooke

Hotels, Motels, and Inns

Sooke Harbour House, 1528 Whiffen Spit Road (250–642–3421); $225–$295; elegant dining; overlooks sea; charming garden terraces; antiques; Jacuzzis; fireplaces; small pets and children OK; wheelchair accessible.

Grouches on the Harbour, 5753 Sooke Road (250–642–3528); $59–$125; cottages in garden setting overlooking harbor; sea views, sundecks; fireplaces; private beach; Jacuzzi; cafe; no smoking.

Manuel Quimper Motel, 6585 Sooke Road (250–642–5644); $64–$122; twenty units; in center of Sooke with views of Sooke Harbour; some Jacuzzis; moorage, fishing charters; no pets.

Lakeside Hideaway, on Poirer Lake (250–642–2577); $125–$155; lakefront cabins for doubles or families.

Point-No-Point, 1505 West Coast Road (250–646–2020); $80–$150; log cabins and suites; all meals; fireplaces, kitchens, some hot tubs; view of water, private beach; afternoon tea.

Fossil Bay Resort, 1603 West Coast Road (250–646–2073); $135–$160; cottages on cliff above waterline; sundecks, hot tubs, fireplaces; adult-oriented; small pets OK with fee.

Bed-and-Breakfasts

Mom's Waterfront Vacation Home & Cottage (250–478–6923); private, one-acre waterfront home and cottage; suitable for families; kayaking, trail, and fishing guides available; call for rates and location.

Hartman House, 5262 Sooke Road (250–642–3761); $100–$120; two units; English style; adult-oriented; German spoken; no smoking, no pets.

Bed and Breakfast by the Sea, 6007 Sooke Road (250–642–5136); $75–$95; private beach; no smoking, no pets; open April–December only.

Seascape Inn, 6435 Sooke Road (250–642–9677); $85–$150; cabins overlooking Sooke Harbour; wharf, fishing charters; no pets.

Ty Collwyn Villa B&B, 6615 Felton Lane (250–642–6702); $125; two-bedroom cottages; hot tubs, beach, indoor pool.

House on the Bay, 7954 West Coast Road (250–642–6534); $110; three units; water view; hideaway; soaker tubs; smoking outside; no pets.

Whiffen Spit Lodge, 7031 West Coast Road (250–642–3041); $80–$110; three units; renovated 1920 country home; Jacuzzi; smoking outside; no pets.

Ocean Wilderness B&B, 109 West Coast Road (250–646–2116); $115–$175; nine units; sea view; hot tub in gazebo; pets OK.

At the western end of French Beach is POINT-NO-POINT RESORT, RESTAURANT & TEAROOM, an absolutely charming natural environment to rent a cabin, enjoy afternoon tea, or have an excellent West Coast cuisine lunch or dinner in the old house converted to a restaurant. At lunch a warm seafood salad with pesto or vinaigrette is $7.95, grilled chicken and mushroom brochette is $7.95, and grilled local salmon on a baguette with pesto mayo and greens is $9.50. The creamy seafood chowder is $5.95. At dinner, try grilled salmon at $15.95 or beef tenderloin with grilled spiced prawns and tomato onion confit at $17.95. One of Kathleen and Jerry's favorites.

✝✿ *Point-No-Point Resort, Restaurant & Tearoom, 1505 West Coast Highway, River Jordan (250–646–2020). Hours: 11:00 A.M.–9:00 P.M. Not wheelchair accessible. Credit cards: Visa, MasterCard. Beer and wine.*

About 3 kilometers (2 miles) beyond Point-No-Point (about 65 kilometers from Victoria) is Sandcut Beach and Sandcut Creek Trail, for which you must park at the road and walk ten minutes down a beautiful rain forest trail (and fifteen minutes back up) to the sand-and-pebble beach (mostly rocks) with romantic waterfalls and sandstone rock formations.

Another 3 kilometers (2 miles) brings you to the Jordan River, and River Jordan, a small logging community with an expansive view of the ocean where the Jordan River empties into the Pacific. This is an excellent spot for surfing, kayaking, and finding Purple Shore Crabs. It's a great picnic area with campsites for tents and vehicles right along the water, all made available by Western Forest Products Ltd., something of a conscience move after raping the forests. Shakies Drive-In on the right is the local and surfer hangout for good fish and chips from

$6.28 to $8.95, a shrimp basket at $7.75, and an oyster dinner at $7.75. You'll also find chicken, the Newfie Burger (cod), and Dairyland ice cream. Deal!

For a more formal meal with tables and chairs, try the BREAKERS CAFE, a cheerful white stucco place with bright flowers and international flags welcoming visitors from around the world. This is an excellent place to hang out and watch surfers and kayakers.

Three kilometers from the Breakers Cafe you reach the parking lot for CHINA BEACH PROVINCIAL PARK and JUAN DE FUCA REGIONAL PARK. China Beach is obviously on the Pacific Ocean side of the road. You can park here and walk fifteen minutes down a pretty steep trail (don't forget you have to walk back up) through lush West Coast rain forest to a long, pristine sandy beach, of course rimmed with logs and California mussel beds. There's a hidden waterfall at the west end of the beach.

The JUAN DE FUCA TRAIL is 49 kilometers (30 miles) long and has two campsites between China Beach and Botanical Beach, intended for all levels of hiking ability (thank heavens); day-use is encouraged.

From here on, notice clear-cutting residue, second-growth forests and other results of reforestation, as well as signs marking fires and replantings. You have to read them quickly, because they're small and cover lots of information.

West of China Beach the road becomes one lane (and rough at times) to Port Renfrew, with several one-lane bridges edged by huge logs, sharp curves, rock slides, wildflowers, clear-cut disasters, and replanted forests. You do not need a four-wheel-drive vehicle to make it to Port Renfrew. We do not mean to scare visitors away, but anyone who gets squeamish with curves or sharp drop-offs on the side of the road had better not go. But if you can make it, the trip is exhilarating and well worth it. We love it and can never wait to go back.

Mystic Beach and Mystic Beach Trail are a thirty-minute hike along a steep rain forest trail to a romantic sandy beach surrounded by sandstone cliffs, shallow waves, and a waterfall. If you can, make it.

In another 2 or 3 kilometers along West Coast Highway you come to the entrance to a winding gravel road to Sombrio Beach, 90 kilometers (54 miles) or two hours from Victoria. This is a favorite of surfers because of the huge Pacific Ocean breakers. The beach is another ten-minute walk from the road. Sombrio Beach is one entry route to the Juan de Fuca Marine Trail, with parking, camping, toilets, and information at the east end of the beach. This is a fairly rugged part of the trail. There are two campgrounds 2 kilometers apart at Bear Beach, although the trail between the two is impassable at high tide.

Twenty kilometers (12 miles) from here, pay attention to the delicate wildflowers on both sides of the road in late summer. The road climbs again, and then take caution—the repair work on a road washout may still be under construction. Thank heavens Vancouver Island lacks California's daily earthquakes! Six kilometers (3.6 miles) from this point is a great place to pull off the road and take photos. The Minute Creek clear-cutting project is one to remember. Three kilometers (2 miles) from Minute Creek we usually lose car radio contact, so if that happens, you know you're getting there.

PORT RENFREW

Arriving in Port Renfrew, on the left is a supply store and the WEST COAST TRAIL Registration Centre, where you must register before embarking along the six-day hike on this remote and glorious trail from here to Bamfield. The authorities are not snooping into your life, but keeping a count of who leaves when to make sure everyone turns up safely eventually. Originally the trail was cut to transport shipwreck victims the 47 miles between Port Renfrew and Bamfield.

Recommended only for experienced hikers and backpackers, the West Coast Trail is part of the Pacific Rim National Park Reserve and is open May 1–September 1. The trail starts across the San Juan River from Port Renfrew. You get to there by taking a ferry from the dock at the end of West Coast Road (Highway 14) at the Port Renfrew Hotel. The West Coast Trail is the only West Coast land connection between Highway 14 and Port Renfrew to Bamfield, Ucluelet, Tofino, and Clayoquot Sound. (The other way to get there is to drive from Victoria north on the Trans-Canada Highway and then west to Port Alberni and keep going.) Reservations recommended, because only fifty-two park-use permits are issued each day. Registration and park-use permits are required.

✿❧ *West Coast Trail (250–728–1282, reservations). Hours: daily from 10:00 A.M.–5:00 P.M. May 1–September 30. Must be at trailhead by noon, or your reservation is forfeited with no refunds. Park fee: about $30.*

"Downtown" Port Renfrew is only 1 kilometer (.6 mile) farther, identified by a gas station and the Galleon Cafe, which has extremely local seafood and ice cream, with a fish tank of neighborhood sea life right in the restaurant. Notice local Gary Pierson's painted mural on the wall showing the 130 shipwrecks off the Pacific Coast of Port Renfrew, which is known as "the graveyard of the Pacific." The public telephone and rest rooms at the cafe are for customers only, so buy something.

At the next little rise you will see the new twenty-two-room WEST COAST TRAIL MOTEL on the left, where Geneva Shen is a font of local lore. A few

WEST COAST TRAIL BOAT AT THE END
OF HIGHWAY 14, THE WEST COAST
ROAD, PORT RENFREW

yards farther on is the $1.2 million LIGHTHOUSE PUB AND RESTAURANT (250–647-5543).

Take a left turn and, at the end of the road, and possibly the world, the old Port Renfrew Hotel—pub, cafe, and rooms—is habituated by true locals with time and stories to spare. Stop for a cup of coffee or something stronger and enjoy. Across the street are a public shower and laundromat (separate) and two portable toilets that serve as public rest rooms.

You may want to try one of the two pubs when you get back from your forty-five-minute hike to BOTANICAL BEACH PROVINCIAL PARK, parking for which you reach by Cerantes Road, a narrow, bumpy gravel road. Drive as far as you can and then walk. Some vehicles can get to within fifteen minutes' walk. World-famous tide pools with lush brown and red algae, anemones, urchins, whelks, mussels, limpets, acorn and goose barnacles, purple sea stars, blood stars, and sea palms attract nature lovers and scientists from around the world. Best viewing when there's a low tide of 4 feet or less. Mill Bay, Botany Bay, and Shoreline trails offer hiking suitable for everyone, including young children and the elderly.

Dr. Josephine Tildon established Botanical Beach as the site of the University of Minnesota's marine station in 1900. She and her colleagues could only get to Botanical Beach's tidepools by steamship from Victoria to Port Renfrew. Such remoteness caused the station's closure in 1907. Fortunately the Nature Conservancy of Canada bought about three acres to preserve the original marine station site, and the area became a provincial park in 1989. Do not disturb or collect marine species!

Where to Stay in Port Renfrew

West Coast Trail Motel, Parkinson Road (250–647–5565; www.westcoasttrail-motel.com); summer $69–$99, off-season $49–$69; twenty-two rooms.

Gallagher's West Coast Camp, Beach Road (250–647–5535); $70; four cottages on San Juan River; no pets; May–October only.

Port Renfrew Hotel, Parkinson Road (250–647–5541); six rooms a few steps from ocean; pub, cafe; fishing charters.

Trail Head Resort, Parkinson Road (250–647–5468); $49 winter and $75 summer; four kitchen units; small campground; sauna; dock, fishing charters; small store.

Arbutus Beach Lodge, 5 Queesto Drive (250–647–5458); $59–$99; beach-front; adults; hot tub; no smoking, no pets.

Beachview B&B, 11 Queesto Drive (250–647–5459); $50–$70; beachfront.

Orca II B&B, 44 Tsonoquay (250–647–5528); $30–$55; 1 block from beach; shared bath; pets on approval.

CHAPTER 5

Up Island

f you can plan to spend more than a few days on Vancouver Island, we hope you will make good use of your time to travel northward. Rare rain forests, rivers and streams, beaches, clean air, open spaces, mountains, fabulous resorts, native relics and art, and interesting local foods await you.

We guide you north from Victoria to Nanaimo on the Trans-Canada Highway (Highway 1) via Cobble Hill, Cowichan Bay, Duncan, Chemainus, and Ladysmith to Nanaimo. Then we describe trips to take farther north on Highway 19 to Campbell River, Port McNeill, and Port Hardy, and west from Nanaimo on Highway 4 to Coombs, Sproat Lake, Port Alberni, Tofino, and Ucluelet, including Pacific Rim National Park and its sultry rain forests.

VICTORIA TO NANAIMO

This blood pressure–lowering trip can take you from one and a half hours to all day, depending on how many stops you make to eat, drink, taste wine, bask, shop, or learn.

To leave the city, take Douglas Street north, which becomes Highway 1 North, also known as the Trans-Canada Highway. From here it is about 54 kilometers (32 miles) to Duncan. Mileage signs here show both kilometers and miles.

The Trans-Canada Highway, which of course begins at Mile 0 at Beacon Hill Park and Dallas Road in Victoria, turns right at Nanaimo and gets on the ferry to Vancouver so it can truly cross all of Canada. Originally cut as a cattle trail over the Malahat pass in the mid-1880s, the highway climbs from Goldstream Park over the summit of 356 millimeters (1,156 feet), enough to pop your ears, before it descends into Bamberton.

The entrance to Thetis Lake Park, a great place for picnics, will come up on the right. Just past Langford, you and the kids can take a break at the **ALL FUN**

WATER SLIDES & RECREATION PARK. Take the Millstream Road exit just 7 miles from downtown Victoria and enjoy a .75-mile water slide complex, two miniature golf courses, driving range, go-cart track, batting cages, bumper boats (these are fun), and more. The Western Speedway, "Canada's largest racing oval," has stock car and late model races plus demolition derbies. Vancouver Island's largest swap 'n' shop is held at the track every Sunday March–October (250–474–1275). There is also a family restaurant called the Yew Tree and an RV park with ninety-five sites, showers, laundromat, lockers, sani-station, store, propane, and firewood; RV park open year-round. (For reservations call 250–474–4546.) Voted "Victoria's Best Place for Family Fun."

✿✆ *All Fun Water Slides & Recreation Park, 2207 Millstream Road, Victoria (250–474–3184). Partly wheelchair accessible. Hours: 11:00 A.M.–7:00 P.M. daily June–September. Credit cards: Visa, MasterCard. No alcohol, no barbecues, no personal flotation devices. Free parking.*

GOLDSTREAM PROVINCIAL PARK is a favorite refuge for Victoria residents and visitors alike. It runs from Highway 1 here through to Highway 1 west of Victoria on the way to Sooke. Fabulous for summer picnicking (no camping), it offers tables under 450- to 500-year-old red cedars, reputed by some authorities to be the oldest trees in Canada, which when cut are used for canoes and totem poles.

From mid-October through November, thousands of chum, coho, and chinook salmon return up the Goldstream River (great to watch), which the Saanich people call "Selekta" to honor the role of the salmon, believed to be their elder brother who transformed people from a magical place under the sea. Traditionally men gaff the salmon with spears, and the women clean, fillet, and smoke the fish over alder fires, a right guaranteed to the Malahat people by treaty in 1850. Across from Goldstream Provincial Park are the reserves of the Malahat, Pauquachin, Tsawout, Tsartlip, and Tseycum bands. *Mostly wheelchair accessible, including rest rooms.*

The trees are so lush here and the water so clear that you can take off your dark glasses in summer—in fact, you'd better, or it will seem like nighttime.

Just 1.6 kilometers (1 mile) past Goldstream you'll get your first spectacular look at Spectacle Lake, Victoria West KOA campground, the Ocean View Motel, and the MALAHAT MOUNTAIN INN restaurant, a marvelous incarnation of the old Malahat Chalet, with up-to-date West Coast cuisine and a fabulous wooden deck facing the water from which you can watch migrating whales while you feast.

✿✆ *Malahat Mountain Inn, 260 Trans-Canada Highway, (250) 478–1944. Wheelchair accessible. Credit cards: Visa, MasterCard, American Express.*

As you approach the Malahat summit, you will see a left turn to Shawnigan Lake (south end) and Shawnigan Lake Provincial Park, where you can hike, picnic, swim, or camp at Shawnigan Lake or Koksilah Provincial Park. Shawnigan Lake is the site of the historic "last spike" of the E&N (Esquimalt & Nanaimo) Railroad and an old restored church, now the Auld Kirk Gallery, and the Shawnigan Historical Museum.

Back on Highway 1, if heights don't bother you, stop at the summit rest area for a spectacular water view. If they do, don't stop here.

THE AERIE resort in Malahat (thirty minutes from Victoria) is said by many to be the most romantic place in the world to have dinner or spend a night. This modern, luxurious inn overlooking Spectacle Lake was created by Austrian natives Maria and Leo Schuster to combine old-world Mediterranean elegance with the Pacific Northwest's natural grandeur. Leo had previously served as executive chef of Donald Trump's hotels, and Maria had owned a luxury resort.

THE AERIE RESORT AND RESTAURANT

The indoor swimming pool, helipad, private hiking trails, and superb restaurant make this a must-try if it fits your budget. If it doesn't, at least go see it. The restaurant's wine list ranks with some of the best. One of our favorites.

The Aerie, 600 Ebedora Lane, Malahat (250–743–7115). Hours: dinner reservations 6:00–9:00 P.M. until last person leaves. Wheelchair accessible. Credit cards: Visa, MasterCard, American Express, Diners. Fully licensed. Directions: Drive Highway 1 toward Nanaimo for about thirty minutes, take the Spectacle Lake exit, and follow signs to The Aerie.

CIDER ALERT!

Merridale Cider *is Canada's only orchard dedicated solely to cider and wine apples. You can catch the orchard in splendiferous bloom in April or watch the fragrant press in October–November, and taste cider varieties of the moment if you go by. A new taste experience in Canada.*

To get to Merridale, take the Trans-Canada Highway and turn west at the northern Shawnigan Lake exit. Go about 2 miles, turn right on Cameron Taggart Road for 1.2 miles, and turn right on Merridale Road to the end.

It's worth the trip to sample and purchase estate-grown, fermented English apple ciders such as scrumpy, cy-ser, Normandy Dry Cider, and Summer Berry Cider.

Be prepared for a true country/dusty experience.

Merridale Cider, 1230 Merridale Road, RR #1, Cobble Hill (250–743–4293). Hours: Monday–Saturday 10:30 A.M.–4:30 P.M. Open daily in the summer.

At the intersection of Shawnigan Lake Road and Cameron Taggart Road, follow the signs into the driveway of DUTCH DELI & MEATS, where Case Langhout personally butchers, ages, smokes, cures, and coddles the best meats around. Cheeses and sausages complete this sublime oasis. We left smelling like smoke and loved every sniff and taste.

Dutch Deli & Meats, Ltd., 1200 Shawnigan–Mill Bay Road, Cobble Hill VOR 1L0; (250) 743–4648. Hours: 9:00 A.M.–5:00 P.M. Wednesday–Friday, 8:00 A.M.–2:00 P.M. Saturday.

LAMB POT ROAST
Merridale Cider, Cobble Hill

Ingredients

2–3 lb. boneless lamb shoulder roast

1 tsp. dried thyme

salt and pepper to taste

3 slices bacon, chopped

4 carrots, sliced

3 onions, sliced

2 celery stalks, sliced

1 cup cider (fermented)

1 cup chicken stock

1 tbsp. tomato paste

2 cloves garlic, minced

2 bay leaves

Preparation

Sprinkle lamb with salt, pepper, and half of the thyme. Roll meat up flat side out and tie tightly with a string.

In a large saucepan or Dutch oven, cook bacon over medium heat until crisp. Brown lamb on all sides in the fat remaining in saucepan. Remove lamb. Add carrots, onion, and celery. Cook over medium heat ten minutes. Stir in cider, stock, tomato paste, garlic, bay leaves, and remaining thyme. Place lamb on top. Cover and bake in 325° F oven for one and a half to two hours, stirring and basting occasionally.

Just before serving, discard bay leaves and add the reserved bacon. Serve with potatoes or rice and your favorite vegetables.

Serves six.

The Bamberton Park/Brentwood Ferry Road turnoff will take you along the water's edge to Mill Bay (5 kilometers) and loads of parks and outdoor recreation.

Along the highway you will come to the Deer Lodge Motel with great views, the Rose Bank Motel, and opportunities for floatplane tours. On the left comes the exit to the north end of Shawnigan Lake and Mill Bay Road. Notice the frequent blue provincial signs designating an artisan's working studio. Please visit and support local artists. Golfers can play at Arbutus Ridge, which you can reach by following Kilmalu Road along the coast north of Mill Bay past Arbutus ridge through Cowichan Bay, Maple Bay, Crofton, and Chemainus.

WEST COUNTRY MUSSELS
Merridale Cider, Cobble Hill

Ingredients
2 dozen mussels
3 tbsp. red pepper, finely chopped
3 tbsp. green pepper, finely chopped
1 tsp. bread crumbs
3 tbsp. red onion, finely chopped
1 tbsp. peanut oil
1 clove garlic, crushed
cup cider (fermented)

Preparation
In a wok or large skillet, heat oil on high heat. Add garlic, onion, peppers, and bread crumbs, stirring constantly. Add mussels. When mussels open, immediately add cider, stir, cover, and steam for three minutes.

Place in serving dish and serve immediately.

Serves four to six.

CHERRY POINT VINEYARDS AND ART GALLERY

We suggest you leave the beaten path and visit a couple of excellent small wineries.

To get to CHERRY POINT VINE-YARDS just five minutes off Highway 1, take the Fisher Road exit south of Duncan, left for a minute on Telegraph, and then right on Cherry Point Road. When you reach the huge wooden wine vat/sign, you've just passed the driveway. Fifty kilometers (30 miles) north of Victoria, Cherry Point Vineyards has thirty-four acres of gently rolling, comfortable, California-like vineyards and sheep ranch. The Swiss chalet–design building, surrounded by lawns, vineyards, and tall cedars, has a hot tub and an elegant patio used frequently for weddings, special dinners, and parties. Wayne and Helena Ulrich have a pleasant tasting room downstairs as well as a prominent local artists' gallery.

Cherry Point's 1998 Auxerrois won the All-Canada Championship Gold Medal, as well as the 1999 and 2000 Wine and Oyster Festival Best White Wine. Watch for their unusual 1999 Agria. Their blends are terrific values at less than $11.

Helena is a fabulous French cook, and her substantial catering operation creates parties in the garden for your needs.

CRAB & LEEK BISQUE A LA CHERRY POINT

Helena Ulrich of Cherry Point Vineyards, Cobble Hill

Ingredients

3 leeks (1½ lb.)
½ cup butter
1 clove garlic, minced
½ cup flour
4 cups chicken stock
½ cup dry white wine
2 cups Half & Half
½ lb. West Coast crabmeat
¼ tsp. salt (optional)
¼ tsp. ground white pepper

Preparation

Remove roots, outer leaves, and green tops from leeks. Split white portion of leeks in half, wash, and cut halves into thin slices.

Melt butter in a Dutch oven over medium-high heat. Add leeks and garlic and cook, stirring constantly until tender (about three minutes).

Add flour, stirring until smooth. Cook one minute, stirring constantly. Gradually add stock and wine. Cook over medium heat, stirring constantly, until mixture is thickened. Stir in Half & Half and last three ingredients.

Serves four.

❧ *Cherry Point Vineyards, 840 Cherry Point Road, RR #3, Cobble Hill (250–743–1272; Web: www.cherrypointvineyards.com). Hours: 11:00 A.M.–4:30 P.M. winter, 11:30 A.M.–6:00 P.M. April–September 30. Wheelchair accessible. Credit cards: Visa, MasterCard.*

Balsamic Vinegar Mayonnaise

Giordano and Marilyn Schulze Venturi of Venturi-Schulze Vineyards, Cobble Hill

Ingredients

2 large egg yolks

juice of ½ lemon or to taste

2 tbsp. Venturi-Schulze Balsamic vinegar

1 tsp. Dijon mustard

enough vegetable oil to make a thick mayonnaise

salt and white pepper to taste

Preparation

Put egg yolks and mustard in a bowl and whisk thoroughly together. Start adding the oil drop by drop at first, then in a stream as you keep beating with the whisk. When you have a very thick sauce, the consistency of sour cream or thicker, add the lemon, Balsamic vinegar, and salt and pepper. Beat again until smooth. Whisk in more oil if the sauce is too thin or runny.

This is excellent with boiled meats and poached or baked West Coast salmon. [We like it on just about anything —K. Hill.]

Serves four.

VENTURI-SCHULZE VINEYARDS, the smallest winery in the Cowichan Valley, is owned and lovingly nurtured by Giordano and Marilyn Schulze Venturi and their children. Their new sparkling wine was served to Queen Elizabeth at Victoria's Empress Hotel during the 1994 Commonwealth Games. Their white wines include a 1992 Schonburger, 1992 Muller-Thurgau, 1992 Madeleine Sylvancer, and a 1993 Siegerrebe. Try their 100 percent pure Balsamic vinegar and fine wines in their one-hundred-year-old farmhouse surrounded by tall fir and maple trees. Venturi-Schulze has just built a gorgeous new winery building and planted more vineyards.

✦ *Venturi-Schulze Vineyards, 4235 Trans-Canada Highway, RR #1, Cobble Hill (250–743–5630). Call ahead.*

In the Cobble Hill area, you will find a fascinating collection of artisans and small, personal farms where you can buy superb products. At Arbutus Ridge Farms (3295 Telegraph Road, Cobble Hill; 250–743–7599), Don and Debra McMurray raise brown free-range eggs and vegetables and make excellent salsa and pesto. *Hours: sunup to sundown daily.*

Jane Van Alderwegen Pottery (3380 Boyles Road, Cobble Hill; 250–743–5839) makes stoneware and porcelain stoneware, both functional and decorative. Phone first.

Dolly and Cordell Sandquist of Country Treasures Cottage Crafts (1133 Fisher Road, Cobble Hill; 250–743–4374) open their cottage for you to enjoy woodcrafts, jams, honey, beeswax candles, pottery, braided rugs, and a Christmas in the Country weekend in mid-November.

At Silverside Farms (3810 Cobble Hill Road, Cobble Hill; 250–743–9149), Jean and Bill Aten grow sweet raspberries and strawberries in July and August (order ahead) and sell homemade jams, jellies, berry vinegars, local honey, and crafts, and fresh berry yogurt cones and Island Farm ice cream.

Peter Versteege's Thistledown Nursery (2790 Cameron Taggert Road, Cobble Hill; 250–743– 2243) offers hanging baskets of flowers, planter boxes, and plants.

Cherry Point Gardens (990 Cherry Point Road, Cobble Hill; 250–743–7335) produces flowers for Tara Vansteenbergen's drying and workshops. Visit peaceful gardens by appointment.

At Cobble Hill Pottery (3375 Boyles Road, RR #1, Cobble Hill; 250–743–2001), John Robertson and Harriet Hiemstra make unique, handcrafted, high-fired pottery. You can watch them work in their studio from 9:00 A.M. to 5:00 P.M. daily.

Cobble Hill Orchard (1310 Fairfield Road, Cobble Hill; 250– 743–9361) grows fresh apples and juices and sells Glen and Wendy Robb's jams, jellies, apple butter, and pies, as well as dried and fresh flowers. Open Friday–Sunday in season, 10:00 A.M.–5:00 P.M. Call to make sure.

BROODING CHICKEN
Giordano and Marilyn Schulze Venturi of Venturi-Schulze Vineyards, Cobble Hill

Ingredients

2 chicken breasts, cut into 2-inch pieces

¼ cup Venturi-Schulze No. 3 or other sweet amber wine

2 tsp. cocoa powder

¼ cup strong coffee

¼ cup cream

1 tbsp. butter

salt to taste

Plus the following, ground to a fine powder in a spice or coffee mill:

8 cloves

1 tsp. allspice

1 tsp. coriander seeds

1 tsp. cumin seeds

seeds from 10 pods green cardamom

10 black peppercorns

½ small nutmeg

½ stick cinnamon

seeds from 4 pods black cardamom

Preparation

In a bowl, combine chicken, ground spices, cocoa, and salt, stirring well to coat. Leave in dry marinade for twenty minutes. Shake chicken and brown in the butter in a frying pan (about two minutes per side). Add the rest of the dry marinade, coffee, and wine and simmer for about three minutes.

Add the cream and cook for five minutes over high heat until chicken is done and the sauce has thickened.

Serves four small portions.

Marilyn Schulze says, "Serve with our No. 3, but beware: This is a stimulating physical experience."

We recommend you stop for lunch at Cowichan Bay, which you can get to from Cherry Point Winery by turning left at the bottom of the driveway on Cherry Point Road. Follow the road farther than you think you should (it turns back inland), turn right on Cowichan Bay (which is Cobble Hill Road on the west side of Highway 1), and follow it down to the water.

If you prefer to try another winery before lunch or dinner, don't miss BLUE GROUSE VINEYARDS. Going north on Highway 1, turn left on Lakeside Road, and Blue Grouse will be on the left. Going south on Highway 1, turn right at the light at Kiksilah Road, and turn left at Lakeside Road. Blue Grouse will be on the right.

Hans Kiltz, a Berlin native with a doctorate in microbiology and a veterinarian specializing in tropical animals, spent twenty years doctoring large animals in Africa and Asia before coming to Canada in 1988 with his Philippine-born wife, Evangeline, to educate their children in a developed country. Salvaging many old vines on this property initially as a hobby, the Kiltzes have developed their project into a successful, sophisticated farmgate winery.

Featured wines: Kerner, Muller-Thurgau, Ortega, Bacchus, Pinot Gris, and Gamay Noir.

Blue Grouse Vineyards, 4365 Blue Grouse Road, Duncan; (250) 743–3834. Hours: Wednesday, Friday–Sunday 11:00 A.M.–5:00 P.M.; January–February by appointment. Wheelchair accessible. Credit cards: Visa, MasterCard.

Head back to Cowichan Bay, conveniently located forty-five minutes north of Victoria, with its picturesque houses on pilings in the water. You might try Myron's By-the-Sea or the Bayshore Fish Market.

Our favorite is the ROCK COD CAFE, a center for believable funk humor and great informal dining with a deck hanging over the water adjoining boat and fishing docks and an indoor stage setting that makes you want to stay from one meal to the next. The rock cod fish is battered (not brutalized) with dill and flour, grilled (one of the two best fish and chips on Van Isle), and served with huge, tasty chips. You can also get a major chicken breast sandwich, plus salads and pastas. Try the Sex in a Pan for dessert, an orgasmic combination of Oreos, chocolate cheesecake, and chocolate sauce.

Rock Cod Cafe, 1759 Cowichan Bay, (250) 746–1550. Hours: open most of the time. Wheelchair accessible. Credit cards: Visa, MasterCard. Fully licensed.

Next door is the don't-miss Cowichan Bay Maritime Centre Museum and home of the Wooden Boat Society, which acquired and renovated the pier in

1988. Watch boat-building and painting and attend workshops if you stick around a while. Take in the annual Cowichan Bay Boat Festival the first or second weekend in June. Contact: Cowichan Wooden Boat Society, P.O. Box 787, Duncan, V9L 3Y1; (250) 746–4955.

Also visit the fascinating Marine Ecology Station, with views of minihabitats and aquaria of coastal marine life.

Be aware that you are experiencing the Cowichan Chemainus Ecomuseum, a 1,000-square-kilometer museum without walls funded by the British Columbia Heritage Trust and the Heritage Canada Foundation.

Check out local art galleries, which include works by residents of the native Coastal Salish band. The first nonnative residents only arrived in 1862 on the HMS *Hecate* with Governor James Douglas in tow. Stroll or wheel along the estuary and Hecate Park to enjoy shorebirds and wildlife.

You can now follow the road along the water or go back up to Highway 1 toward Duncan and Lake Cowichan.

The Old Farm Market and Moby Chix on the east side of the highway are musts. The market features fresh local vegetables, pastas, a deli counter with Coombs meat pies (fabulous), and terrific breads. Moby Chix makes and cuts

COWICHAN BAY

OLD FARM MARKET, DUNCAN

the most interesting superb meats, sausages, and seafoods that we have ever seen. Our favorites.

VIGNETTI ZANATTA is where winegrowing on Vancouver Island began four decades ago. Turn west (left) at the light at Allenby Road, then turn left on Indian Road (which becomes Marshall Road when it crosses Glenora Road). Winery is on the left.

Loretta Zanatta makes wines simply in a solid, personal, old-world Italian method. So far the best are Ortega, a dry fruity white; Glenora Fantasia, a sparkling wine; Pino Grigio; Auxerrois; and the special Damasco. Plan to stop for lunch or dinner at the excellent seasonal Vinoteca, featuring many foods grown right here on the Zanatta's 120 acre farm.

❧ *Vignetti Zanatta, 5039 Marshall Road, RR #3, Duncan; (250) 748–2338; Web: www.zanatta.bc.ca; E-mail: zanatta@seaside.net. Hours: noon–5:00 P.M. Wednesday–Sunday, dinner Thursday–Saturday. Wineshop open March–December. 1:00–4:00 P.M. or call ahead.*

Those of you unaccustomed to aggressive billboard advertising will be startled by the roadside gallery approaching Duncan, the commercial hub of the Cowichan region and an absolute must-stop for native history and totem sightings.

For the Freshwater Eco-Centre at the Vancouver Island Trout Hatchery

(1080 Wharncliffe Road, Duncan; 250–746–6722; 10:00 A.M.–3:30 P.M. daily), turn east on Trunk Road, angle to the right on Marchmont Road, then turn right on Lakes Road to Wharncliffe. Turn right, and you'll find the hatchery, slide shows, discovery games, and learn about native fishing techniques, Japanese fish printing, and fish anatomy.

Where to Stay at Malahat

The Aerie, 600 Ebedora Lane (250–743–7115); $145–$365; twenty units; views of Olympic Mountains and gulf islands; suites individually designed, up to 900 square feet; oriental rugs, fireplaces, Jacuzzis, four-posters; outdoor hot tub; three conference rooms; indoor pool; tennis; spa; gazebo with panoramic view for weddings; helipad, no pets. Dining at The Aerie Restaurant. *Wheelchair accessible. Full bar. Credit cards: Visa, MasterCard, American Express.*
Malahat Oceanview Motel, 231 Trans-Canada Highway (250–478–9231); $78–$90; ocean view, fireplaces, decks; grocery and post office; pets OK.

Where to Stay at Cowichan Bay

Kilpahas Beach Resort, 1681 Botwood Lane (250–748–6222); $75–$130; licensed dining, beer and wine store; indoor pool, saunas; boat and floatplane dock.

VINOTECA ALMOND TORTE
Jim Moody of
Vinoteca/Vignetti
Zanatta, Duncan

Ingredients
1¼ cups flour
1 tsp. baking powder
¾ cup sugar
¾ cup butter
1 package (7 oz.) soft almond paste
4 eggs
½ tsp. almond extract
raspberry sauce, for accompaniment

Preparation
Preheat oven to 350° F. Line bottom of a 9-inch cake pan with a circle of parchment paper. Lightly grease and flour pan and paper. Sift flour and baking powder together and set aside.

In a large bowl, cream together sugar, butter, and almond paste until light and fluffy. Add eggs, one at a time, beating well after each addition. Stir in almond extract. Fold in flour mixture.

Pour batter into prepared cake pan. Bake until golden and until a wooden skewer [or toothpick] inserted into the center comes out clean (forty–fifty minutes). Cool ten minutes in pan, then remove from pan and cool on rack to room temperature.

Serve accompanied with raspberry sauce.

Chef Moody says, "This is a very moist cake that works well in winter with cooked fruit compotes. In the summer, accompany it with fresh fruit, especially raspberries, and of course a glass of Vignetti Zanatta Auxerrois."

Wessex Inn, 1846 Cowichan Bay Road (250–748–4214); $40–$65; Tudor-style on waterfront with sea views, balconies; no pets.

Heading toward DUNCAN, one sign instructs you to turn left for totems, which is very hard to do because of traffic. Wait for the signal and turn left on Cowichan Way to the COWICHAN (KHOWUTZUN) NATIVE VILLAGE, 200 Cowichan Way. An elegant and tastefully designed tribute to First Peoples, the Cowichan (Khowutzun) Native Village affords employment and skills-learning opportunities for natives and learning and pleasure experiences for visitors. As you take guided tours or follow a map yourself, watch native totem carvers, demonstrations of Cowichan knitting, Salish weaving, and decorative beading; enjoy inexpensive delicious native cuisine in the Riverwalk Café (and take home native berry preserves); or experience a traditional lunch of salmon hot off the fire at the Bighouse Restaurant (you'll see native dancers, too!). You can purchase authentic, majestic original native art in the Native Art Gallery or prints and souvenirs in the gift shop.

❧ *Cowichan (Khowutzun) Native Village, 200 Cowichan Way, Duncan (250–746–8119; Web: www.cowichannativevillage.com). Hours: summer 9:30 A.M.–5:00 P.M. daily, winter 10:00 A.M.– 4:00 P.M. daily with reduced prices and programming. Admission: adults $10.00, seniors $8.00, students $6.00, children $5.00, craft activities $1.00–$2.00 extra, families $25.00. Midday salmon barbecue show Tuesday–Saturday at noon July–September, adults $28.50, including admission, seniors and students $26.00, children $22.50, under five $16.75. Wheelchair accessible. Credit cards: Visa, MasterCard.*

Once you get to DOWNTOWN DUNCAN a couple of blocks north, follow the yellow footprints on the sidewalks to take your own tour of the City of Totems. Begun in 1985, the Duncan Totem Poles Project aimed to promote Duncan as a tourist attraction and more than accomplished its goal. On the city side of the 1912 train station, several totems decorate the lawns, and the old station is now a local museum.

Just up Station Street a few doors from the train station visit the JUDY HILL GALLERY & GIFTS (22 Station Street, 250–746–6663) for the best collection of native carvings, masks, jewelry, authentic Cowichan sweaters, books, baskets, and the work of more than a hundred B.C. artists. Hospitable, well-informed staff make browsing or shopping here a pleasure. For superb and affordable fresh food, try Asta Pasta at the corner.

For a local culinary experience, try the ARBUTUS CAFE for breakfast, lunch, or dinner of huge hamburgers; a cod, shrimp, and cheese burger; stir-frys; and wraps—all for less than $8.00.

HAND-CARVED CANOE AT COWICHAN (KHOWATZUN)
NATIVE VILLAGE, DUNCAN

The best dinner spot downtown is GOSSIPS, at 161 Kenneth Street (250–746–6466). Open Tuesday–Saturday.

There's a downtown farmers' market on weekends behind the chamber of commerce in the Blockbuster Video/Overwaitea parking lot off Highway 1.

One of our most pleasant recent discoveries is newish ALDERLEA VINEYARDS LTD., northeast of Duncan. The Dosmans sold their "collision repair business" in Vancouver a few years ago and switched "from crushed cars to crushed grapes," their true passion.

To visit Alderlea, take Highway 1 north of Duncan a couple of minutes to Herd Road. Turn right (east) at the light onto Herd Road, right (south) on Lakes Road, and left on Stamps Road. Alderlea will on your left. It's five to ten minutes from the highway.

Alderlea, the original name of Duncan, welcomes you to bring a picnic or go to the Cowichan Cheese Co. to pick up baguettes and European-style cheeses, such as gouda and St. Paulin. COWICHAN CHEESE COMPANY LTD. (250–715–0400; cheese@cowichan.com) is in a renovated brick church on Norcross Road, off Highway 1 between Duncan and Herd Road.

Back to Alderlea, which is one of only two wineries on Vancouver Island (Venturi-Schulze is the other) that makes its wine solely from grapes grown on its own property—right here. We highly recommend a visit. You can enjoy their Clarinet, Bacchus, pinot gris, Hearth (port-style dessert wine), Pinot Auxerrois, and Angelique blend. A beautiful site.

❧ *Alderlea Vineyards Ltd., 1751 Stamps Road, RR1, Duncan V9L 5W2; phone and fax: (250) 746–7122.*

Just north of Duncan, take Highway 18 west to Lake Cowichan. Follow the road through the Cowichan Valley through Demonstration Forest. The Lake Cowichan area claims title as the "Fly-Fishing Capital of Canada," and for good reason. A fishing path wanders for 31 kilometers (19 miles) along the Cowichan River from Robertson Road clubhouse to Cowichan Lake. Enjoy Lake Cowichan village and Kaatza Station Museum in Saywell Park in the old E&N railway station. There are loads of places to hike, golf, camp, picnic, water-ski, swim, boat, sailboard, and fish along the river and lake. The B.C. Forest Research Station at Mesachie, Gordon Bay Provincial Park at Honeymoon Bay, and the Sutton Creek Wildflower Ecological Preserve are all worth visiting.

Off the Island Highway (Highway 1) to the east are the small coastal communities of Maple Bay and Crofton, which along with Chemainus and tiny Genoa Bay make up the municipality of North Cowichan.

The picturesque village of MAPLE BAY, with a whopping population of 1,848, give or take a few, is 8 kilometers (5 miles) east of Duncan, about halfway up the Sansum Narrows, which separates Vancouver Island from Salt Spring Island. This protected cove is heaven for rowers, kayakers, canoers, water-skiers, and divers. Sansum Narrows is a mecca for fishers of salmon, ling cod, and sea bass. Hiking trails on Maple Mountain and the local museum are both interesting.

CROFTON's 2,500 residents switched jobs to pulp and paper milling in 1957 when the community's economy moved from mining to forestry. Take a mill tour in the summer, or just visit the shops and waterfront in the village for a peaceful stroll. You can take a B.C. ferry between Crofton and Vesuvius on Salt Spring Island as part of a triangle trip with Victoria.

Don't miss the B.C. FOREST MUSEUM PARK, also in Duncan, a fabulous learning and nature experience for the whole family focusing on forestry practices and preservation. There's an exhibit of the history of logging, a miniature town, a logging camp, and a ranger station. Plus twenty-minute rides on a full-size steam train, picnic areas, sawmill, playground, totem poles, and logging truck display. An affiliate of the Royal British Columbia Museum, the Forest Museum has a cozy gift shop, and ice cream and snack bars. Do not approach or feed the wild mink.

❧ *B.C. Forest Museum Park, 2892 Drinkwater, Duncan; (250) 746–1251 or (250) 746–0377. Hours: 9:30 A.M.–6:00 P.M. daily Easter–Thanksgiving (second Monday in October). Steam train runs Victoria Day (Monday before May 24)–Labor Day. Admission: adults $7.00, seniors and students $6.00, children five to twelve $4.00, under five free, families $25.00. Mostly wheelchair accessible. Credit cards: Visa, MasterCard.*

CHEMAINUS'S HERITAGE SQUARE MURAL

As you make your way northward, the North Cowichan Municipal Hall will be on the east side of the highway. Jerry's Diner, which always seems to be full of locals, is great for good, solid meals at good, solid prices. For a more elegant dining experience featuring German cuisine, try the Inglenook Restaurant, 7621 Trans-Canada Highway, Duncan (250–746–4031); open after 5:00 P.M.

Where to Stay in Duncan

Best Western Cowichan Valley Inn, 6474 Trans-Canada Highway (250–748–2722); $76–$89; forty-two units; pool; dining, pub; meeting facilities; near B.C. Forest Museum; pets OK.
Island Welcome Inn, 5325 Trans-Canada Highway (250–745–0331); $37–$57; pets OK.
Silver Bridge Inn, 140 Trans-Canada Highway (250–748–4311); $55–$75; by Cowichan Native Village; small pets OK.

Chemainus

Continue north on Island Highway or take Crofton Road, which becomes Chemainus Road, along the water to charming CHEMAINUS, one of the oldest

European settlements on Vancouver Island. Immigrants moved here to farm in the 1850s. After logging operations decreased and the highway bypassed the town, someone had the bright idea of creating a city of murals and dubbed the place "The Little Town That Could." Now thirty-two murals decorate the exteriors of the town's quaint buildings.

As you take yourself on a tour of the murals, check out the Chemainus Valley Museum, at what was the train station, and the Information Centre (9758 Chemainus Road at Mill Street, 250–246–3944) in an old railroad car (good public rest rooms and telephone here). Across the way is Heritage Square, with its exquisite First Peoples mural, antiques shops, teahouses, small shops, and galleries. Horse-drawn tours start from the park down by the water.

From Chemainus you can take a ferry to Thetis and Kuper Islands to fish, relax, and cruise (on boats, that is). As you leave town going north, we suggest you follow the natural beauty of Old Chemainus Road along the water until it brings you back to Highway 1.

Ladysmith

Once back on Highway 1, you'll know you're in Lᴀᴅʏꜱᴍɪᴛʜ by the startling number of fast-food places; it is actually a charming town once you get into it. In its April 2000 issue, *Harrowsmith Country Life* magazine named Ladysmith one of the ten prettiest towns in Canada.

Ladysmith is located smack dab on the forty-ninth parallel, the line across North America that separates Canada from the U.S.—except on Vancouver Island. It would have been the border if the U.S. had its way in the 1846 treaty negotiations. The town is named after the site of a British victory in the Boer War, and many of its streets are named for British generals in that war.

The older, spruced up part of Ladysmith, up the hill a block west of the highway, has many antiques shops and boutiques for a fun browsers' diversion. Scarra RV Park is convenient if you need it. Buckingham's Browsorium offers eclectic antiques along the highway (when they're open). We enjoy the Printingdon Beanery for great coffee and snacks, and Fraser and Naylor Booksellers. Hemer Provincial Park on Cedar Road has picnic facilities and forest trails along the shore for day hikes and horseback riding, fishing, and canoeing. Stzuminus Park, 5 miles north of Ladysmith, offers camping and hiking trails. You can swim in the warm water of Ladysmith Harbour.

Traveling north from Ladysmith, notice the lavender wildflowers along the road. Signs advertise accommodations and restaurants in Nanaimo, and then you come to the Nanaimo Airport, from which you can get flights to mainland Canada and Washington state. On the west side of the road across from

Nanaimo Airport, be sure to stop (maybe on the way back so you don't get killed twice turning left across the highway) at JOHNSON'S SMART MARKET, a wonderful locally run emporium of fresh unsprayed vegetables, locally caught wild Pacific seafood (including Dungeness crabs for $7.00, sockeye lox, and ling cod), tasteful dried flower arrangements, breads, and condiments. Submarine sandwiches are only $3.95. One of our favorites.

You pass, unless you want to stop, Mountainaire RV Park and Campsite. Check out the Nanaimo River Fish Hatchery for an astounding learning experience.

Even if you don't dare try it, get off the highway and follow the can't-miss signs to the BUNGY ZONE, on the Nanaimo River. Just an hour north of Victoria, it's only a couple minutes off the road and thrilling

A BUNGY ZONE TAKE-OFF.
AAAAAAAHHHH!

just to watch. This is the "only Legal Bridge Bungy Jump Site in North America." Signs all around you warn against jumping if you have most physical problems. You can also watch this from the E&N train, or buy stuff at the shop to pretend you dared.

❧ *Bungy Zone (800–668–7771; 250–753–5867). Hours: daylight except deep winter, opening Valentine's Day (February 14). Admission: jumps range from $50 in winter to $180 combos with I-did-it shirts. Not wheelchair accessible. Credit cards: Visa, MasterCard. Free daily shuttle from Victoria.*

If you have time, follow the signs to Petroglyph Provincial Park, which is not on many maps but has a unique and ancient display of huge rock carvings.

Nanaimo

Nanaimo (Nuh-nigh-mo), known as the Harbour City, is Vancouver Island's second largest city, with 71,000 people and twenty-four parks. It has a beautiful waterfront, though you have to look around the new high-rise apartment buildings and hotels to see it. The wharf, walkways, shops, and cafes at the marina and north of town can't be beat (see map page 202).

The discovery of coal in 1851 brought hopeful settlers to the area, which was originally the site of five separate native villages (called *snenymo*). Incorporated in 1874, Nanaimo is the third oldest city in B.C. and confusing to drive in. Streets go at angles and change names along the way. To drive through town, just follow the signs to Highway 1.

Head down toward the BASTION, built in 1852 by the Hudson's Bay Company as protection from native Haida raids; it's the only remaining such structure in North America. During the summer be sure to catch the Bastion Guards. Held daily at 11:45 A.M., their performances re-create the firing of the noon cannon to eerie bagpipes. Read the wall map near the Bastion for the Nanaimo Heritage Walk and get tourist information from the young, costumed information mavens in the Bastion from 10:00 A.M. to 4:00 P.M. Pioneer Waterfront Plaza is a relatively new creation just below the Bastion.

The Waterfront Walkway begins to the north of the Bastion and will take you to Georgia Park, Swy-A-Lana Tidal Lagoon, and Maffeo-Sutton Park. Georgia Park pays permanent tribute to original native inhabitants with canoe and totem poles. Swy-A-Lana is the only man-made tidal pool in Canada— great summer swimming and picnicking. From Maffeo–Sutton Park you can take a short ferry ride to Newcastle Island, and from the B.C. Ferries dock you can take a twenty-minute ferry ride to gorgeous Gabriola Island.

B.C. Ferries to Victoria and Vancouver leave from the north end of Nanaimo at the foot of Brechin, on which you turn east from the Island Highway.

The E&N Railroad stops way up the hill.

Pioneer Waterfront Plaza is both a resting place (for your feet and bum) and a downstairs waterfront development of cafes, galleries, and small shops, with plenty of metered parking.

A visitor's first challenge is to reach the NANAIMO DISTRICT MUSEUM, 100 Cameron Road, atop a rocky knoll in Piper's Park overlooking the waterfront, a block south of the Bastion. Climb two steep flights of stairs from Front Street or drive around the west side of the knoll on Cameron Road and turn up the curving driveway to the top.

This compact museum is worth the effort and includes re-creations of a Salish village, a mine, and early Nanaimo. Petroglyphs (ancient native designs etched in rock) can be copied by rubbing on paper with pencil. We were particularly fascinated by the history of the charlatan Brother XII and his witchlike mistress, Zee, who formed a cult at nearby Cedar Point and took both dignity and fortunes from their followers between 1927 and 1933 before disappearing.

❧ *Nanaimo District Museum, 100 Cameron Road, Nanaimo; (250) 753–1821. E-mail: ndmuseum@island.net. Not wheelchair accessible. Hours: summer weekdays 9:00 A.M.–5:00 P.M., weekends 10:00 A.M.–6:00 P.M.; winter Tuesday–Saturday 9:00 A.M.–5:00 P.M.*

Check out OLD CITY QUARTER by going up the hill on Bastion from the waterfront, which becomes Fitzwilliam above the highway. Visit the small shops in Fitzwilliam Gate near the top of the hill. The Nanaimo Art Gallery (900 Fifth Street, 250–755–8790) at Malaspina University–College campus hosts important exhibitions from across Canada and is dedicated to involving the community in art and art appreciation. The Festival of Banners brings community artists of all ages and their work to the local and visiting publics by hanging entries from lightposts around Nanaimo.

Serious hiking and canoeing are available at Nanaimo Lakes, Green Mountain, on the Nanaimo River, and at Overton Lakes. Long Lake affords boating, waterskiing, swimming, or fishing. Morrell Nature Sanctuary, behind the army base on Nanaimo Lakes Road, and Piper's Lagoon Park, off Hammond Bay, are bird-watchers' paradises.

NANAIMO'S BASTION

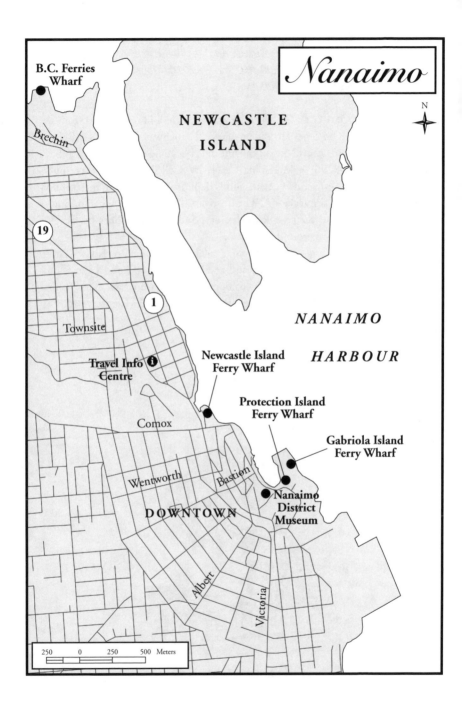

Nanaimo

N

B.C. Ferries
Wharf

Brechin

19

NEWCASTLE
ISLAND

1

Townsite

NANAIMO

HARBOUR

Travel Info
Centre

Newcastle Island
Ferry Wharf

Comox

Protection Island
Ferry Wharf

Gabriola Island
Ferry Wharf

Wentworth

Bastion

DOWNTOWN

Nanaimo
District
Museum

Albert

Victoria

250   0   250   500 Meters

Sportfishing for salmon, cod, or red snapper and shellfish is superb by fishing charter. California and Steller's sea lions come to feed on spawning herring from November to April, and seagulls, cormorants, and bald eagles scavenge for the scraps.

Don't miss the hilarious Bathtub Race on the fourth Sunday in July, the Nanaimo Festival all summer, the Nanaimo Country Fair the third week in August, and the Vancouver Island Exhibition in mid-August.

From a culinary viewpoint, Nanaimo has become increasingly attractive. Artistic fine foods, diners, cafes, dock-fresh seafood and chowders, comfort foods, and fast foods are all plentiful. Stewart Street, along the water, has several good restaurants and cafes, most of which feature local seafood.

We suggest you try WESLEY STREET—A CONTEMPORARY WEST COAST CAFE, across from St. Andrew's United Church, where Jennifer Rollison has produced an oasis of fine dining in Nanaimo, quickly popular with locals as well as visitors in its young life. In this small, charming restaurant and on its flower-covered patio, try the Wesley Street Sampler at lunch with smoked oysters and salmon cakes, pot stickers, and Dungeness crab in filo to really taste the range of appetizers. Sandwiches may include country French ham with Swiss cheese and local greens or soup of the day at $7.75, fresh shrimp croissant at $8.50, or chicken, blue cheese, and walnuts in pita with pasta salad and smoked tomato vinaigrette at $8.00.

Main courses at dinner include Cornish game hen with exotic mushroom and wild rice stuffing and roasted garlic cream at $17, and Fraser Valley venison with fresh rosemary and toasted sunflower seed crust and a candied beet demi. And, soft live jazz accompanies dinner Friday and Saturday nights.

Wesley Street is sensitive to guests' allergies, so please mention them. Huge thanks to Chef Ian Ter Veer for the recipes.

❧ *Wesley Street—A Contemporary West Coast Cafe, #1–321 Wesley Street, Nanaimo; (250) 753–4004. Hours: 11:00 A.M.– 9:30 P.M. Wheelchair accessible. Credit cards: Visa, MasterCard.*

Also try the Mahle House, 2104 Hemer Road at Cedar, in an orange house with local seafood specialties, (250–722–3621; Fax: 250–722–3302; Web: www.island.net/~mahle/.)

Here's a list of **Nanaimo restaurants,** from which you can gather some feeling of what else is available:

Beefeater's Chop House, 1840 Stewart Avenue, (250) 753–2333.
Bluenose Chowder House, 1340 Stewart Avenue, (250) 754–6611; great fish.

BRAISED RABBIT LEG WITH MUSHROOM RISOTTO
Chef Ian Ter Veer and Jennifer Rollison of Wesley Street—
A Contemporary West Coast Cafe, Nanaimo

BRAISED RABBIT LEG

Ingredients

4 rabbit legs

¼ tbsp. chili peppers

3 cloves garlic, chopped

1 tbsp. ginger, chopped

4 4-inch sprigs fresh rosemary

4 4-inch sprigs fresh thyme

4 drops Tabasco

¼ cup Ketjap Manis (from McLean's or Asian food stores)

¼ cup good soy sauce

3 cups good red wine

black pepper, fresh cracked to taste

Preparation

Place rabbit in one layer in nonreactive pan. Mix all the remaining ingredients and pour over rabbit. Marinate for twenty-four hours.

To cook, place rabbit in marinade in 350°F oven for one hour. Remove rabbit from oven and keep warm.

Ladle four ounces of braising liquid per serving into a saucepan and reduce by half. Serve rabbit on risotto and nap with reduced braising liquid.

MUSHROOM RISOTTO

Ingredients

2 cups Arborio rice

1 cup field mushrooms, sliced

1 shallot, sliced

butter

1 cup red wine

1 cup braising liquid (reserved from rabbit)

salt and pepper to taste

Preparation

Blanch Arborio rice in boiling water until firm to bite (fifteen to twenty minutes or to taste). Drain rice. Sauté shallots and mushrooms in butter until all mushroom liquid evaporates. Add wine and braising liquid and reduce by half. Add rice and cook five minutes or until liquid is incorporated into rice and a light sauce remains. Taste and season as needed with salt and pepper.

Presentation

Place rice in center of plate and arrange rabbit leg in center of rice and nap with reduced braising liquid. Garnish with sautéed fresh vegetables.

Bocca on Fitz, 427 Fitzwilliam Street, (250) 753–1799; a small interesting cafe up the hill.

Cafe Casablanca, Dorchester Hotel, 70 Church Street; (250) 754–6835.

Delicato's, 358 Wesley Street, (250) 753–6524; popular, great wraps.

Earl's Restaurant, 2980 Island Highway North, (250) 756–4100; umbrella drinks.

Gateway To India, 202 Fourth Street, (250) 755–4037.

Gina's Mexican Cafe, 47 Skinner Street (250–753–5411).

Grotto Seafood and Sushi, 1511 Stewart Street, (250) 753–3303.

Katerina's Place, 15 Front Street, (250) 754–1351; Greek, view.

Lighthouse Bistro, 50 Anchor Way at Seaplane Terminal, (250) 754–3212.

Sake House, 650 South Terminal Avenue (250) 741–8833.

Where to Stay in Nanaimo

Coast Bastion Inn, 11 Bastion Street (250–753–6801); $89–$148; on inner harbor; water views; restaurant, lounge, pub; sauna, whirlpool, exercise room, hair salon; shuttle; wheelchair accessible.

Best Western Dorchester Hotel, 70 Church Street (250–754–6835); $85–$170; center of harbor, right above water; restaurant, lounge; shuttle; wheelchair accessible; no pets.

Best Western Northgate, 6450 Metral Drive (250–390–2222); $84–$109; restaurant, pub; sauna; wheelchair accessible; pets OK.

Nicol Street Hostel, 65 Nicol Street (250–753–1188); $15.00–$17.50, twenty-five units; kitchens, laundry facility; wheelchair accessible; for the hardy traveler.

NANAIMO TO PORT HARDY

From Nanaimo, the Trans-Canada Highway (Highway 1) takes you to the B.C. Ferries so you can cross the Strait of Georgia to the lower mainland of British Columbia. To drive northward on Vancouver Island, take Terminal Avenue in downtown Nanaimo and head north. It becomes Highway 19 and takes you to Campbell River, Port McNeill, and Port Hardy.

Just north of Nanaimo, first-time visitors and some locals are shocked at the strip-mall developments and WalMart, including the biggest mall on Vancouver Island. To many they seem grossly out of place, but to others they bring urban convenience and consumer goods to the country.

Rhododendron Lake, which you reach by following signs off Highway 19, 7.2 kilometers (4 miles) south of Parksville along a forestry road, is a sense-blowing reserve of wild rhododendrons that date from before the last Ice Age.

CAESAR SALAD EASY BLENDER DRESSING FOR TEN
*Keiko and Hans Kaltenbach of the Beach House Cafe,
Qualicum Beach*

Ingredients
3 egg yolks
5 large garlic cloves
5 strips of anchovy fillets
½ tsp. black ground pepper
pinch of salt
pinch chicken soup–base powder
few drops of Tabasco sauce
few drops of Lea & Perrins Worcestershire sauce
3 cups of vegetable oil or olive oil
¾ cup red wine vinegar

Preparation
Put everything except oil and vinegar in a blender, mix well, then slowly add oil and vinegar to get a creamy consistency. Pour over your favorite greens and sprinkle generously with Parmesan cheese.

Parksville

PARKSVILLE, a popular sportsfishing headquarters, is a city of 9,000 residents 23 miles north of Nanaimo on Highway 19, at the junction of Highway 4 to the West Coast. It's the beginning of Beach Country, where life centers around the waterfront. Artsy shops and galleries and a plethora of cafes, pubs, and restaurants make this a great place to stop, for an hour or a lifetime. (Several resorts are the town's main features. See "Where to Stay.") When the tide is out, the sand and warm water make beachcombing and swimming ideal for the whole family. At the International Sandcastle Competition, builders of all ages race to create between tides.

Freshwater streams west of Parksville offer trout and steelhead fishing, and salmon, halibut, and cod fishing and diving abound offshore. Golfers can choose among four eighteen-hole golf courses. The Brant Festival every April celebrates the arrival of thousands of migrating Brant geese with arts and food all weekend. Check out the History Museum, heritage buildings, and the petroglyphs along Englishman River.

Qualicum Beach

QUALICUM BEACH feels like a modest version of an English or French beach community, with inns and restaurants along the water and expansive beaches with formal walkways and beachcombing (not exactly aerobic). But you can also find swimming, nature hikes, golf, tennis, lawn bowling, and spelunking. Explore the Old Power House Museum and local artists' studios at the Old School House Gallery.

A favorite stopping place here is the BEACH HOUSE CAFE, where Keiko and Hans Kaltenbach produce delightful solid meals with a German twist, such as an excellent traditional Caesar salad at only $4.95; a house-made spaetzle with wild mushrooms at $8.95; a succulent oyster sandwich with fries, slaw, or Caesar salad for just $7.95; and steak and mushroom pie for $8.50.

Beach House Cafe, 2775 West Island Highway, Qualicum Beach, (250) 752–9626. Hours: 11:00 A.M.–10:00 P.M. daily. Partly wheelchair accessible. Credit cards: Visa, MasterCard. Fully licensed.

The Kaltenbachs serve Warsteiner beer and are right next door to the Captain's Inn Motel and Sand Pebbles Inn and Restaurant—in case you make the best decision and stay.

As you wander northward you will pass lots of places you might want to try: the Shady Post Oceanside Pub, the Ben Bow Inn, the Hard Rock Brown Egg Farm, and the Big Qualicum Fish Hatchery and Indian Reserve.

Bowser

If you're hungry when passing through BOWSER, stop at the Cola Diner, a fun fifties restaurant popular with locals. Gardeners may want to visit the Island Sun Greenhouses at Arbutus Bay.

From here on you see many more gorgeous trees than you see people. Most locals like to stop at the FANNY BAY INN, known affectionately as the "FBI," once a hotel and important landmark pub. Owners Dave and Betty Hopkins restored the old lady to its original 1930s look with dark beams, lighter walls, and genuine English pub decor. Visitors and locals mingle like family, with local workers, Harley-Davidson riders, and government workers from Victoria all enjoying big pub food, a roaring fire, dartboards, and the island's largest cribbage board. One of David's favorites.

Courtenay

Next stop is COURTENAY, a sort of gateway to the Comox Valley and end of the E&N railway route linking the area to Victoria. There are no directional

COURTENAY'S E&N TRAIN STATION

signs to the train station and no personnel in it, although the rest rooms are cute and clean. A classic small town that rolls up the rugs early and never unrolls them on Sunday, Courtenay is a quiet place where people live or pass through.

From Courtenay north along Highway 19, the scenery just becomes more beautiful, rugged, and exciting, as does the road.

Campbell River

Thirty miles north of Courtenay and 167 miles from Victoria, CAMPBELL RIVER, with a population of 28,000, is the last major town going north on Highway 19 toward Port Hardy. It is one of Vancouver Island's self-proclaimed "salmon capitals," since record numbers are caught here where the Campbell River flows into Discovery Passage. Once "the end of the road," it is now a distribution center for the northern end of the island. Only five people lived here in 1900, and now vacationers flock here to hike, camp, and fish for sixty- to seventy-pound chinook salmon and take guided fishing tours in search of Tyee (chinook more than thirty pounds). Don't miss the annual Salmon Festival in July for water sports, street dancing, a fishing derby, war canoe races, and salmon galore.

Absolutely worth a stop is the MUSEUM AT CAMPBELL RIVER, across from the Ceremonial Torii Gate at Sequoia Park. It contains a fascinating collection of artifacts and collectibles from Campbell River's early history as well as local First Nations history including carvings, paintings, prints, and jewelry.

☃ *Museum at Campbell River, 470 Island Highway, Campbell River; (250) 287–3103. Hours: summer 10:00 A.M.–4:00 P.M. Monday–Saturday, noon–4:00 P.M. Sunday; winter noon–4:00 P.M. Tuesday–Saturday. Admission: $2.00; $7.50 per family.*

In Campbell River you can take the TimberWest Timber Tour, the Westmin Resources Mine Tour, and a tour of the Quinsam Salmon Hatchery. Nearby trails include Beach Trail, Ripple Rock Trail, Willow Creek Nature Trail and Conservation Area, Canyon View Trail, and the Mitlenatch Island and Bird Sanctuary (250–337–2400).

Strathcona Provincial Park

Highway 28, which runs west from Campbell River, is your best route to enormous STRATHCONA PROVINCIAL PARK, (250–248–3931), the oldest provincial park in British Columbia. It is named for Donald Alexander Smith, First Baron Strathcona, a Canadian pioneer and one of the big guys in construction of the Canadian Pacific Railway. Lord Strathcona drove the last iron spike into the twin steel rails that finally united Atlantic and Pacific Canada on November 7, 1885.

Strathcona Park has animals and birds not living in other parts of Canada. Look from a distance for deer, Roosevelt elk, wolf, and the occasional cougar, chestnut-backed chickadee, red-breasted nuthatch, winter wren and kinglet, gray jay, Steller's jay, band-tailed pigeon, blue grouse, and the unique Vancouver Island white-tailed ptarmigan. Nature walks, short trails, and real hiking trails attract devoted nature lovers from all over the world.

☃ *Strathcona Provincial Park, (250) 248–3931; Strathcona Park Lodge, P.O. Box 2160, Campbell River, B.C. V9W 5C9; (250) 286–8206. Reservations a must.*

Sayward

Forty-three miles north of the "big city" of Campbell River, you come to the old farming and forestry community of SAYWARD, the southern border of the North Island region. Here Island Highway (Highway 19) turns inland for approximately 120 miles.

Now you pass through an area of uninhabited panoramic beauty, snowcapped mountains, and tree-bordered lakes. This is heaven on Earth for naturalists and photographers. Gravel roads lead to Schoen Lake Park, where there is winter skiing, and Nimpkish Lake, where there is boating.

Port McNeill

Then the highway swings back to the east coast of the island at PORT MCNEILL, 124 miles north of Campbell River. Port McNeill has a foot of airstrip for every resident (2,500) and is paradise for recreational anglers. Ferries connect from here to Sointula on Malcolm Island and with Alert Bay on Cormorant Island. Port Alice (gateway to the Pacific by way of Neroutsos Inlet) is 19 kilometers down a scenic winding road.

Port Hardy

Another 28 kilometers (17 miles) up the Island Highway, you come finally to PORT HARDY, the end of the line on Vancouver Island. The largest community in the region, with 5,000 people, Port Hardy was named for VA Thomas Masterman Hardy, in whose arms Admiral Nelson died in the famous Battle of Trafalgar. The first people arrived here 8,000 years ago, and the first white settlers came after 1900. In the years since, it has followed the usual island pattern: coal, lumbering, fishing, sportsfishing, and tourism.

Many visitors come here to take B.C. Ferries's northern route to Prince Rupert, a fifteen-hour daylight trip (in summer) on the Inside Passage to the Queen Charlotte Islands and on to Alaska.

Where to Stay in Parksville

Rathtrevor Resort, 1035 East Island Highway (250–248–2622); $130–$157; condos on Rathtrevor Beach; honeymoon suite; kitchens; fireplaces; hot tub, tennis, volleyball, badminton, two pools, playground; family-oriented; no pets.

Beach Acres Resort, 1015 East Island Highway (250–248–3424); $95–$225; fifty beachfront and forest cottages and town houses on twenty-three acres at Rathtrevor Beach; kitchens; fireplaces; indoor pool, sauna; restaurant, patio; tennis courts, volleyball, badminton, basketball; no pets.

Tigh-Na-Mara Resort Hotel, 1095 East Island Highway (250–248–2072); $89–$164; 142 units, log cottages; and oceanview condos on Rathtrevor Beach; fireplaces; kitchens; Jacuzzis, indoor pool, spa; tennis; restaurant, lounge, playground, summer children's program; pets in off-season only.

Gray Crest Seaside Resort, 1115 East Island Highway (250–248–6513); $89–$159; on Rathtrevor Beach; kitchens; honeymoon suite; pool, whirlpool, sauna; playground; no pets.

ENTRANCE TO PORT HARDY
(Photo Courtesy of Bob Carver)

Holiday Inn Express Parksville, 424 West Island Highway (250–248–2232); $69–$104; eighty-seven units; indoor pool, Jacuzzi; meeting rooms; continental breakfast buffet included; pets OK.

Qualicum Bay

Bed-and-Breakfast reservation service (250–335–0506); free; year-round.
Qualicum Bay Resort, 5970 West Island Highway (250–757–2003); $50–$65; pets OK.

Qualicum Beach

Shorewater Resort Condos, 3295 West Island Highway (250–752–6901); $89–$130; beachfront studios; pets OK.
Ben Bow Inn, 3350 West Island Highway (250–752–5666); $72–$105; half block to beach; some kitchen suites; patios; pool, whirlpool; no pets.
Qualicum College Inn, 427 College Road (250–752–9262); $79–$109; historic Tudor hotel overlooking ocean; some fireplaces; indoor pool, Jacuzzi; licensed restaurant, pub; pets OK.

Old Dutch Inn, 2690 West Island Highway (250–752-6914); $80–$100; across highway from beach; licensed dining, lounge; indoor pool, sauna; gift shop; pets OK.

Sand Pebbles Inn, 2767 West Island Highway (250–752–6974); $70–$110; on beach; some kitchens; restaurant; small pets OK.

Bowser

Seacroft Resort, 85 Coburn Road (250–757–8474); $65–$85; cottages and lodge rooms on oceanfront; fireplaces; deck; lounge; boat launch, fishing tackle, boat rentals and charters; no pets.

Shady Shores Beach Resort, 6695 West Island Highway (250–757–8595); $59–$79; beachfront; rooms, cottages; playground; no pets.

Courtenay

Kingfisher Oceanside Inn, 4330 South Island Highway (250–338–1323); $65–$110; oceanview rooms with balconies, kitchenettes; pool, whirlpool; restaurant, lounge; launch ramp; small pets OK; share some facilities with twenty-site RV park.

Coast Westerly Hotel, 1590 Cliffe Avenue (250–338–7741); $95–$155; downtown; some rooms overlook Courtenay River; saunas, exercise room, indoor pool, restaurant, pub; beer and wine store; no pets.

Collingwood Inn, 1675 Cliffe Avenue (250–338–1464); $64–$97; forty-five units; downtown; some kitchens; licensed restaurant and lounge; pets OK.

Comox

Port Augusta Motel, 1950 Comox Avenue (250–339–2277); $55–$95; near Comox Harbour; pool; restaurant, lounge.

Kye Bay Guest Lodge & Cottages, 590 Winslow Road (250–339–6112); $550–$700 weekly; waterfront views of Georgia Strait; beach; cottages; BBQ; play area; no pets; April 5–October 15 only.

Jasper's Seaside Resort, 5730 Coral Road (250–334–4141); $60–$65; beachfront condos; ten minutes to airport; no pets.

Alders Beach Resort, 179 Williams Road (250–337–5322); $570–$900 weekly; oceanfront cottages; beach; volleyball; no pets.

Saratoga Beach

Pacific Playgrounds, 9082 Clarkson Drive (250–337–5600); $80; near water; pool; boat launch; tennis; play area.

Oyster River Resort, 9022 Clarkson Drive (250–337–5170); $450–$775 weekly; oceanfront cottages; beach; playground; no pets.

Saratoga Beach Resort, 8958 Clarkson Drive (250–337–5511); $65–$90; seven beachfront cottages; playground; boat launch; no pets; thirty-two RV sites also.
McLeod's Cottage Resort, 8946 Clarkson Drive (250–337–5547); $350–$590 weekly; beachfront cottages and condos; boat rentals; pets OK.
Passages Resort, 8914 Clarkson Drive (250–337–5459); $445–$560 weekly; beachfront cottages; massage, manicure; bonfires; pets OK.

Campbell River

In selecting where to stay, note that on Island Highway, even numbers are across the highway from the ocean, while odd numbers are on the water.

Painter's Lodge & Fishing Resort, 1625 MacDonald Road (250–286–1102); $144–$325; on oceanfront; pool, hot tubs; lounge, pub, gourmet seafood dining with sea view; two tennis courts, fitness center; boats; airport shuttle; no pets; April–October.
Salmon Point Resort, 2176 Salmon Point Road (250–923–6605); $75–$125; oceanside cottages; playground; pub, restaurant; boat launch, fishing charters.
Coast Discovery Inn, 975 Shoppers Row (250–287–7155); $85–$138; ninety units; near marina and mall; Jacuzzis, sauna; pub, restaurant; beer and wine store; health club; meeting rooms; packages; pets OK.
Austrian Chalet Village, 462 South Island Highway (250–923–4231); $74–$104; ocean views, lofts; indoor pool, sauna; pub, restaurant; putting green, Ping-Pong; pets OK.
Bachmair's Apartment Hotel, 492 South Island Highway (250–923–2848); $69–$120; sixteen units; balconies overlook water; kitchens, Bavarian furnishings; fishing charters; pets OK.
Campbell River Lodge and Fishing Resort, 1760 Island Highway (250–287–7446); $70–$80; parklike setting on Campbell River; whirlpool; dining room, pub; fishing and adventure packages; pets OK.
Anchor Inn, 261 Island Highway (250–286–1131); $89–$119; oceanfront; balconies, some kitchens; licensed dining room; lounge with entertainment, dancing; patio; sushi bar; meeting rooms; fishing charters; pets OK.
Haida Inn, 1342 Island Highway (250–287–7402); $54–$74; downtown; ocean views; breakfast included; coffee shop, lounge, pub; live entertainment; beer and wine store; fishing charters; no pets.

Port McNeill

Haida-Way, 1817 Campbell Way (250–956–3373); $56–$75; near downtown; coffee shop, licensed dining, pub; fishing and whale-watching charters; no pets.

McNeill Inn, 1597 Beach Drive (250–956–3466); six units; overlooks harbor; licensed restaurant; deck; fishing and whale-watching charters; no pets.

Dalewood Inn, 1703 Broughton Boulevard (250–956–3304); near wharf; licensed dining; fishing charters; pets OK.

Port Hardy

Almost every home in Port Hardy has become a bed-and-breakfast, but we give you a few of the better inns:

Thunderbird Inn, 7050 Rupert Street (250–949–7767); $75–$86; center of town; coffee shop, dining, pub; entertainment; beer and wine store; fishing charters; no pets.

Airport Inn, 4030 Byng Road (250–949–9434); $65–$95; near airport; coffee shop, licensed dining and lounge; beer and wine store; fishing and hunting packages; small pets OK.

Pioneer Inn, 4965 Byng Road (250–949–7271); $62–$102; near Quatse River; coffee shop, licensed dining room; pets OK; twenty RV sites also.

Glen Lyon Inn, 6435 Hardy Bay Road (250–949–7115); $59–$88; harbor view; near marina; licensed restaurant, lounge; boat launch, moorage, fishing charters; pets OK.

NANAIMO TO TOFINO

While the trip from Nanaimo over the mountains to Ucluelet and Tofino takes about four hours, it is one of unequaled beauty. Wind through ancient trees along Sproat and Kennedy Lakes, explore French Beach and the Pacific Rim National Park's rain forests, and learn about native cultures and environmental activities in Tofino, Clayoquot Sound, and Ucluelet. Newly built and older resorts and restaurants offer once-in-a-lifetime taste experiences, maximizing the use of local seafood, sometimes caught within sight of the dining room. Enjoy!

This trip west from Nanaimo to Tofino includes stops at Port Alberni, Ucluelet, and Pacific Rim National Park, and a possible final stop in Bamfield. Start by taking Highway 19 toward Parksville. Five kilometers north of the Petro Canada station on Highway 19 is a left turn to Highway 4A, which takes you to Highway 4 (Pacific Rim Highway).

Alert: You need to know the following: The trip from Nanaimo to Tofino will take about four hours, give or take a few stops. Leave Nanaimo in the morning to avoid afternoon sun in your eyes (and then return in the afternoon so the sun is behind you in the west). Be sure to get gasoline in Nanaimo if you plan to drive straight through to Tofino. Except for campgrounds, there are really no accommodations between Parksville and Port Alberni, a distance of 31 miles. Some of the roadway between Port Alberni and Pacific Rim National Park is narrow, straight down-or-up slopes, winding, and occasionally partly washed out. *Do not* drive this part of Highway 4 for the first time at night.

Highway 4 is a two-laner and the only way to get to Tofino. Highway crews have been working on the interchange for a few years, so drive cautiously due to surprise curves, mud, and narrow lanes.

The Road House Inn, 8 kilometers from the interchange, is a potential beer or snack stop. Five kilometers from the Road House Inn, you are in COOMBS, an old-fashioned farming community with latter-day country crafts boutiques.

As you approach town from the east, after the Homestead Restaurant, a driving range and petting farm, a tattoo studio, and more, you finally come to the famous OLD COUNTRY MARKET, with goats on the roof.

Old Country Market produces breads and pastas that strikingly resemble those at the Old Farm Market south of Duncan. There's a good cafeteria/cafe here with sandwiches you order ingredient by ingredient, fish and chips, oyster sandwiches, daily specials, and espresso. An outdoor window vends ice cream and frozen yogurt cones to die for, and sometimes you almost do on a hot day. The produce is inexpensive and fresh; much is even organic and locally grown. There's also an intriguing gift-for-yourself emporium with teapots, marmalades, imported clothes, and baskets.

Several small local craft shops wander up the driveway. Check them out.

In another few kilometers you pass the Coombs Rodeo Grounds and Island Butterfly World at Winchester Road. Two kilometers on the right is Hillier's Sausage Company (worth a stop for excellent German and Polish sausages) and Hillier's Water Garden. Another 2 kilometers (1.2 miles) brings you to a local hangout, the Midway Cafe & Gas—a good pit stop on the left, followed by a fruit stand and Seafood Cafe.

Now you start to enter heaven, just fifteen minutes (sans stops) from Parksville. LITTLE QUALICUM FALLS PROVINCIAL PARK is a great site for family camping, picnicking, and inhaling, with waterfalls crashing in the Little Qualicum River gorge. You can swim in natural pools or at nearby Cameron Lake, where there is also boating, waterskiing, and fishing. From the highway you can see Cameron's gorgeous setting in the straight-up mountains. Along the road here, rock cliffs actually hang out over the roadway, at times. Don't look and drive. If you have a picnic along, try the Beaufort Picnic Site on the lake.

Just west, you must stop at world-renowned Cathedral Grove in MACMILLAN PROVINCIAL PARK. Donated by H. L. MacMillan of the giant lumber company MacMillan-Bloedel, Cathedral Grove is one of the few remaining primeval uncut stands of timber accessible to the public. Thousand-year-old growth includes Douglas fir, western hemlock, grand fir, and western red cedar. Signs warn: 300,000 VISIT HERE ANNUALLY AND EVERY TOUCH HURTS. IF WIND BLOWS, DO NOT GO ON PATH SINCE OLD GROWTH TREES CAN FALL WITHOUT WARNING.

In another 10 kilometers you reach the 1,272-foot summit of the roadway and railway of the Beaufort Range. Almost in a blink are Mount Arrowsmith Ski Area to the left and Mount Arrowsmith Park, alpine terrain with T-bars and rope tows for skiers of all levels. A little hard to get to, there is a day lodge, cafeteria, and rental shop. Summer hiking and views are fantastic, with visibility to Van Isle's east coast and even across the Strait of Georgia to the mainland.

Port Alberni

PORT ALBERNI, with a population of 20,000, is 31 miles west of Parksville. Even though it appears on maps to be inland, it is actually at the head of the Alberni Inlet from the Pacific Ocean. Its primary industries are lumber and fishing and all the businesses that support workers in both.

You know you're arriving when you see the Port Alberni City Museum and Information Centre on the left, slightly uphill from the rest of town.

This is a great place to buy fishing and other outdoor equipment and camping supplies you may have forgotten. Local stores and even Kmart fill those needs. Try the Sports Fishing & Outdoor Centre or Northport Plaza. The Clambucket Seafood Restaurant serves fresh local seafood (surprise), and check out Curious Coho Books. Don't miss the Port Alberni Salmon Festival on Labor Day weekend, with a $25,000 first prize.

If you prefer to continue your trip to Tofino and Bamfield by boat, Port Alberni is where you can get the MV *Lady Rose* and the MV *Frances Barkley* to those destinations, as well as to Bamfield, Ucluelet, and the Broken Group Islands. Barkley Sound Service is at 5425 Argyle Street (250–723–8313).

You might want to explore the wharves and marina, where there are lots of artists' studios and small boutiques in a beautiful setting along Alberni Harbour Quay, Port Alberni's park and marketplace on the harbor, at 5440 Argyle Street (250–723–2181). Marinas where you can dock your boat include Clutesi Haven Marina (250–724–6837), China Creek Marina (250–723–9812), and Fish Harbour (250–723–2533).

When the highway comes to a T at the end of the inlet, you head right toward Tofino and cross the inlet on a small bridge. The Rainforest Tree House will be on the right. Try the Clintas Indian Crafts store at Tses-Haht Reserve for convenience foods, hot coffee, and any other emergencies and gasoline. *Local tip:* This is your last chance for fuel before the rugged drive to Ucluelet or Tofino.

After you pass the Arrowvale Campground, aviation fans might want to stop at the Home of the Mars Water Bombers, the largest water bombing plane fleet in the world, headquartered at gorgeous, warm (in summer) Sproat Lake. To your left, Sproat Lake, which is 17 miles long and 1 mile wide, has forty campsites and 146 picnic tables with terrific swimming, boating, and fishing for cutthroat and rainbow trout from April to November, not to mention the pristine air year-round. You can also walk on trails to see prehistoric petroglyphs at Sproat Lake Provincial Park at the north end of the lake near Port Alberni. Both are named for Malcolm Sproat, founder of Port Alberni sawmills and later B.C. agent general in London and Indian land agent until 1880.

Where to Stay in Port Alberni

Barclay Hotel, 4277 Stamp Avenue (250–724–7171); $63–$81; the only true hotel in town; 10 blocks to harbor marina; dining; pool, sauna, tennis; boat launch, fishing charters; no pets.

Coast Hospitality Inn, 2835 Redford Street (250–723–8111); $108–$120; restaurant, pub; beer and wine store; fishing charters; pets OK.

Tyee Village Motel, 4151 Redford Street (250–723–8133); $60–$82; some suites with sitting rooms; restaurant; pool; meeting rooms; fishing charters; pets OK.

Bluebird Motel, 3755 Third Avenue (250–723–1153); $46–$69; fourteen units; closest to harbor; *Lady Rose* tour boat; Alberni Forest Information Centre; no pets.

Timberlodge, Highway 4 (250–723–9415); $75–$95; twenty-two units; dining (except November–March), lounge; sauna, indoor pool; also twenty-four RV sites.

Somass Motel, 5279 River Road/Highway 4 (250–724–3236); $55–$65; fourteen units; across from Somass River; pool; boat parking, 1 block to boat launch; pets OK; also six RV sites.

Where to Stay at Sproat Lake

Maples Resort Motel, 9624 Lakeshore Road (250–723–7533); $60–$85; beach; moorage, boat rentals; waterskiing; no pets.

Westbay Hotel, 10695 Lakeshore Road (250–723–2811); $40–$65; lakeside licensed dining, beer and wine store; moorage, boat rentals; no pets.

We find the trip from Sproat Lake to Tofino to be one of the most beautiful and exhilarating drives in the world. It is well worth overcoming fears, if possible, just to experience these natural wonders. You can also take Pacific Coast Line (PCL) tour buses from Victoria's downtown bus station or Nanaimo if you prefer not to drive. If you're driving, pray that a bus or semi-truck doesn't sit on your tail going down the hill.

Taylor Arm Provincial Park, along the north shore of Sproat Lake, has group camping sites by reservation only and an undeveloped beach. The Taylor River offers good cutthroat trout fishing in spring. The devastation of a 1964 forest fire left gray tree ghosts that are finally mingled with some new growth. Near a turnoff to a rest area on the right, stop at a wide curve and look back at the tall, thin pink wildflowers in the foreground and the sad burnt tree stumps in the distance. Remember this.

You can also see snow on some peaks to the west, even in summer, and begin to feel ocean winds from the west. Soon the Kennedy River will run along the road for 18 miles with you. There is a pull-off here to allow others to pass. Please use it if you're holding up traffic.

You may lose radio reception along here. Notice the signs marking which forest stands were cut, burned, and/or replanted and when. There's another pull-off, and 2 kilometers later the road becomes four lanes at the bottom of a grade, but don't get excited—it's only for a brief spell.

The road, now called the Pacific Rim Highway, was blasted out of rock above Kennedy Lake, Vancouver Island's largest at 24 square miles. There's good trout fishing wherever creeks flow into the lake. Four kilometers later is a beach with boat launching, and another for swimming and picnics down a short road.

Pacific Rim National Park

Soon the highway turns north, at PACIFIC RIM NATIONAL PARK. Turn right 21 miles (34 kilometers) to Tofino and left 5 miles (8 kilometers) to Ucluelet. The Park Information Centre is 1.5 miles (2 kilometers) to the right of this junction, with informative staff offering advice, maps, and brochures on the park.

UCLUELET and TOFINO, two former fishing villages, are now major tourist destinations since they are on the ocean and are excellent for camping, fishing, surfing, whale watching, kayaking, and walking on the beach. Between the two towns lies Long Beach, one of the finest beaches on the island, with a provincially maintained rain forest and access to the beach for wheelchairs, as well as easy parking near the beach. Both towns are launching points for boat tours, charters, and various explorations; have good dining, scenic vistas, and interesting shops; and in Tofino the best exhibit of modern native art.

Fine point: Official Guide to Pacific Rim Park Reserve, an outstanding collection of local history and information on beaches, intertidal zones, tide pools, rain forest, recreation, and trails, is an excellent book for lovers of nature, beaches, wildlife, and rain forests. Written by J. M. Mac- Farlane, H. J. Quan, K. K. Uyeda, and K. D. Wong, and published by Blackbird Naturegraphics, Calgary, Alberta, it's available in bookstores on Vancouver Island.

You are driving through the Long Beach Unit of Pacific Rim National Park, extending from Ucluelet on Barkeley Sound on the south to Tofino on Clayoquot Sound on the north. Long Beach itself

RAIN FOREST OF PACIFIC RIM NATIONAL PARK

rolls on through the broad curve of Wickaninnish Bay for 10 kilometers (6 miles). It was hard to get to until the paved highway was completed in 1970, but Long Beach now receives more than 450,000 tourists annually, 80 percent between May and October. Sea lions, starfish, and respectful people mingle delicately along this romantic stretch.

Ten kilometers (6 miles) north of the junction going toward Tofino you reach WICKANINNISH BEACH, a part of sandy Long Beach named for one of the Clayoquot chiefs at the time Europeans arrived in the 1770s. Surfing and sailboarding (wet suits required—for your sake) and strolling or wheeling are popular activities here. Long Beach is completely wheelchair accessible, has good rest rooms and outdoor shower, public telephones, $2.00 parking for one hour, and $5.00 day pass usable at all Pacific Rim beaches. There's also a reminder: PLEASE REFRAIN FROM COLLECTING ANYTHING WHILE IN A NATIONAL PARK; and a caution about Long Beach's severe riptide:

NOVICE SURFERS/BODY BOARDERS SHOULD STAY 200 METERS FROM SMALL ROCK.

Within another 4 kilometers (2.4 miles) you can enter the rain forest, an experience that will send you rhapsodic. Combers Beach, 1 kilometer (.6 mile) north of here, is actually a continuation of Long Beach. Green Point Campground in 2 kilometers (1.2 miles) is the only major campground within the park. Teeming tide pools form here from seawater flowing into cracks of bedrock. Schooner Cove is a bay with a long white-sand beach to which you have to hike from the parking lot between Portland Point and Box Island, where harbor seals hang out on the rocks occasionally. Hikers can get here at low tide.

Long Beach Golf Course is on the right.

Radar Hill was used by the Royal Canadian Air Force during World War II, and you can see why: spectacular views of the edge of the world—including Meares Island, Tofino Inlet, and the Gowlland rocks.

After you officially leave the park you will come to Pacific Rim Ranch, with trail rides available at Pacific Rim Resort, and Pacific Sands Beach Resort on the left (oceanside), Orca Lodge on the right, and then Wickaninnish Inn.

The **WICKANINNISH INN** is an elegant and environmentally sensitive restaurant and inn that opened in August 1996 to immediate rave reviews. It's right on the edge of the world, 3 miles south of Tofino at Chesterman Beach, the longest beach on the west coast of Vancouver Island outside Pacific Rim National Park. Recycled old-growth lumber removed from St. Anne's Academy in Victoria gives its interior a heavy, cedar-beamed, warm, solid wood appearance. Giant windows in every room overlook the Pacific Ocean all the way to Japan, with waves crashing under the dining room during storm season. Try the Ancient Cedar Spa for a very special, romantic, full spa experience.

CRAB CHOWDER
Jacques Forgues of the West Coast Crab Bar, Tofino

Ingredients

28 oz. clam nectar

28 oz. milk

5 large potatoes

½ cup flour

¼ tsp. garlic powder

¼ tsp. paprika

1 tsp. lemon pepper

1 ½ tbsp. chicken soup base

16 oz. fresh crabmeat

Preparation

Cut potatoes into medium cubes and steam twelve minutes. Mix clam nectar, milk, spices, chicken broth, and flour; stir well. Add potatoes and crabmeat. Simmer for three hours. If too thick, add more milk. Serves six.

WICKANINNISH INN, AT THE END OF CHESTERMAN BEACH

In the On-the-Rocks Lounge you can sample single malt Scotches and then move on to the Pointe Restaurant for breakfast, lunch, or dinner prepared by Chef Jim Garraway.

The restaurant features seafood caught within a stone's throw; chanterelles, boletus, angel wings, and pine mushrooms are brought in from neighboring forests; gooseneck barnacles come off the rocks on the beach; and Indian Candy made from salmon marinated for six days and smoked comes from Tofino.

Wickaninnish Inn, Osprey Lane at Chesterman Beach, Tofino (250–725–3100); Web: www.wickinn.com; E-mail: wick@island.net; $180-$220 winter, $320–$360 summer; ocean views; full-service spa; two-person soaker tubs, Jacuzzis; fireplaces; balconies; fine restaurant; exercise room; pets OK; about 3 miles south of Tofino. Wheelchair accessible. Credit cards: Visa, MasterCard, American Express.

One of the most beautiful and natural fine-resort settings along this coast is the native-run Tin Wis Resort and Conference Centre. If you can't stay there, at least park and walk to the beach. A paved path helps with wheelchairs. Outdoor dining is superb in any weather short of rain. The woodwork alone is worth the trip.

From here on you will see lots of motels and lodges. It is imperative to make reservations during the summer.

Tofino

Tofino, or "Tough City," is small, and it's easy to get around here. Highway 4 becomes Campbell Street in Tofino, which is basically 5 blocks long and 3 blocks wide. The Spanish named the town for Don Vincent Tofino, a famous Spanish hydrographer with a reputation for native fights and wild living. But don't let the nickname scare you. Much of that has been cleaned up with aggressive social and self-help programs.

Several restaurants serve good food, including the WEST COAST CRAB BAR (601 Campbell, 250–725–3733), where you order your half or whole crab hot or cold. Try the crab chowder, Caesar salads, and garlic toast, and enjoy the decent house wines and cheerful, upbeat atmosphere. A happening place where many locals stop. Book reservations.

Locals also frequent the SCHOONER RESTAURANT AND MOTEL (331 Campbell, 250–725–3444) for its great basic food with a flair at reasonable prices in an amusing shipwreck atmosphere. At breakfast, Eggs a Paire is $4.95 with perfect potatoes and toast; the Kitchen Sink includes almost all of it, from spicy sausage to mushrooms, in an omelet at $7.50; and Kathleen's favorite, the Eye Opener, contains fresh oysters, mushrooms, and green onions.

Lunch and dinner are memorable, and the house ghost is included. Sole Clayoquot in a delicate lemon caper sauce is excellent at $16.95, or you might try the seafood hot pot of curried yummies at $17.95. Local oysters are a must. The Schooner has historical maps and paintings, a public phone outside, and is a member of Cuisine Canada and the Canadian Culinary Alliance.

Across the street, THE LOFT (346 Campbell, 250–725–4241) serves a local seafood clubhouse sandwich with smoked salmon and shrimp for $8.50, corned beef hash and poached eggs at $6.95, or the required half crab at lunch for $9.95 and $13.95 at dinner, slightly more than at the Crab Bar.

If you stay out too late and don't want to walk home, call Tofino Taxi, (250) 725–3333.

Tofino has several galleries with local arts and crafts, and you can find them easily on your own. If you only have time for one, stop in at Roy Vickers's EAGLE AERIE GALLERY at 350 Campbell (250–725–3235). As the only native artist with his own gallery, Vickers and his work inspire and dominate. He also shows work of other First Peoples artists, such as that of his brother Art Vickers as well as Ed Hill. Each picture has a legend with it, so you can learn just by reading. All woodwork within the gallery was carved by native artists, including the rails, canoes, and eagles.

Roy Vickers is a recovering drug and alcohol addict and is proud of it. A percentage of sales of certain works is given to First Peoples recovery programs. The entire gallery feels like a life-revering chapel.

A block north and down the hill are some stops well worth the short walk along Main Street, which is just above the Wharf and Meares Landing.

Teensy and excellent Tough City Fish Store has a sign on the door begging you to JUST SAY NO TO DRUGS—DON'T EAT FARM FISH. Next door, Tough City Boutique looks like a day-care center because the charming owner's children spend their days here with Mum, who sells one of the best selections of informal, feminine, and sexy imported clothes from Asia and Central America. Be sure to visit the Village Gallery and Bed & Breakfast.

One door up, Wildside Booksellers carries the best selection of regional travel and adventure books we have seen, and it also sells excellent coffee, runs the B&B next door, and books kayaking lessons and trips.

The Rainforest Interpretive Centre is a place adults and kids absolutely must experience. Friendly staff and educational exhibits mix in one room with clusters of local children drawing, weaving, listening, learning about nature, and telling stories. You can enjoy a panoramic view of Tofino and Clayoquot Sound

ROY VICKERS'S EAGLE AERIE GALLERY, TOFINO

from the back deck. Pacific Rim Whale Festival (250–726–4447) goes on from mid-March to early April. There's a Sea Fest Labour Day Weekend, and the twenty-five-year-old Pacific Rim Arts Society Festival for two weeks in mid-July. *Fine points:* You'll find pay phones at First and Main Streets.

At MEARES WHARF you can get boats to see Clayoquot Sound—both its beauty and its devastation due to clear-cutting. Loads of fishing charters are available, and almost anyone in town can set you up and make a booking for you. Chinook Charters, at 450 Campbell Street (800–665–3646 or 250–725–3431), will take you fishing, whale watching, or on a tour of Clayoquot Sound. Reservations recommended.

As you travel back down Pacific Rim Highway, stop again at the rain forest and Long Beach just to inhale the beauty, sea air, and majestic nature we often forget to preserve.

It is mandatory to make reservations ahead to stay in Tofino.

Where to Stay on the Beach

Wickaninnish Inn, Osprey Lane at Chesterman Beach (250–725–3100); $120–$300; over the ocean; soaker tubs, fireplaces; exercise room, excellent restaurant; pets OK; 3 miles south of Tofino.

Best Western Tin Wis Resort, 1119 Pacific Rim Highway (250–725–4445); $85–$175; on the beach; licensed patio restaurant, lounge; no pets; 2 miles south of Tofino.

Pacific Sands Beach Resort, 1421 Pacific Rim Highway (250–725–3322); $140–$190; condos and cabins on 1-mile-long beach; decks or patios; no pets; 4 miles south of Tofino.

Orca Lodge, Pacific Rim Highway (250–725–2323); $79–$98; dining, licensed lounge; continental breakfast; pets OK; 2–3 miles south of Tofino.

Crystal Cove Beach Resort, MacKenzie Beach (250–725–4213); $94–$180; oceanfront log cottages with kitchens, fireplaces, hot tubs; 130 RV sites; 2 miles south of Tofino.

Ocean Village Beach Resort, 555 Helleson Drive (250–725–3755); $94–$130; cottages on beach; kitchens; indoor pool, whirlpool; no pets; 2 miles south of Tofino.

Middle Beach Lodge, Pacific Rim Highway (250–725–2900); $72–$195; cottages and lodge suites; private beach; fireplaces; oceanfront lounge; dining, BBQ; surfing, kayaking; no pets; 2 miles south of Tofino.

Where to Stay in Downtown Tofino

Weigh West Marine Resort, 634 Campbell Street (250–725–3277); $85–$135; harbor views; some decks and fireplaces; marine pub, restaurant; moorage, fishing charters; no pets.

Cable Cove Inn, 201 Main Street (250–725–4236); $95–$175; adults; waterfront; decks, fireplaces, hot tubs, Jacuzzis, four posters; continental breakfast; no smoking, no pets.

Schooner Motel, 311 Campbell Street (250–725–3478); $69–$135; sixteen units; town center, overlooks harbor; kitchens; no pets.

Duffin Cove Resort Motel, 215 Campbell Street (250–725–3448); $100–$175; thirteen units; town center; views; some cabins; balconies, patios; BBQ; no pets.

Maquinna Lodge, 120 First Street (250–725–3261); $60–$80; dining with harbor view, pub; beer and wine store; free airport pickup; no pets.

Ucluelet

From Long Beach, instead of turning left to go back toward Port Alberni and Nanaimo, continue straight toward Ucluelet, self-proclaimed "Whale Watching

KAYAK LESSON BEFORE TAKEOFF INTO
CLAYOQUOT SOUND, TOFINO

Capital" of the world. Ucluelet, an old fishing port first settled in prehistoric times, is somewhat protected from Pacific storms and close to the channels where migrating salmon feed. The name comes from *yu-clutl-ahts,* which means "the people with a good landing place for canoes."

In 1959 Ucluelet became connected by road with Port Alberni, ending a century of reliance on boat transportation. Unofficial motto: "On the Edge."

An obvious fun place to drink and dine in Ucluelet is the Canadian Princess Hotel, a docked ship you can't miss on the left (water side) coming in to town on Peninsula Road, the main street in town. The food is generous and good. Several motels present themselves.

Try Crow's Nest Books, which also has public telephones, and the Chamber of Commerce on Main Street for more information. Main runs down to Government Wharf. Blueberries Bakery Cafe & Cappuccino Bar on Peninsula Drive is a must-stop for locals. We like it, too. On the way down to the water you'll find the Tourist Information Centre and Roman's Galley Restaurant, an obviously locally popular restaurant with bar and Italian food.

A final culinary note: Smiley's Family Restaurant is the local people's hangout for good breakfasts, burgers, fish and chips, and bottomless coffee cups.

The gas station at the north side of Ucluelet is the last chance for fuel, water, rest rooms, and telephones before the climb over the summit back to Port Alberni. Visit Bamfield, if you wish, or head back to Nanaimo and Victoria.

Where to Stay in Ucluelet

Canadian Princess Resort, Peninsula Road (250–726–7771); $49–$129; a permanently moored historic coast steamship with seventy-six staterooms; continental breakfast included; fishing excursions, nature cruises; fully licensed restaurant; no pets; not wheelchair accessible.

West Coast Motel, 247 Hemlock Street (250–726–7732); $69–$125; most rooms overlook harbor; indoor pool, sauna, exercise room, squash; dining in season; no pets.

Island West Fishing Resort, 160 Hemlock Street (250–726–4624); $65–$89; overlooking harbor; private marina; pub, dining; guided fishing and whale watching; pets OK; thirty-six RV sites adjacent.

Thornton Motel, 1861 Peninsula Road (250–726–7725); $70–$80; some suites sleep six; near marina; no pets.

Bamfield

Bamfield is a 300-person fishing village and sea rescue station that is the northern terminus of the West Coast Trail from Port Renfrew, and that was the departure point for the Pacific cable to Australia from 1902 to 1959. Bamfield was named for retired ships carpenter William Eddy Banfield, the first settler in 1849, but when the post office was established the name was misspelled as "Bamfield," and it stuck.

An oddity: Bamfield is reputed to have the highest per capita education of any town in Canada. The reason is that most of the populace are marine biologists and highly educated scientists in the field.

Bamfield can be reached by turning left onto Third Avenue off Highway 4 in Port Alberni, and continuing for 62 miles. Or you can take the trip by ferry (Barkley Sound Service, 5425 Argyle at Port Alberni marina). It has become a popular destination for hikers, whale watchers, anglers, and tourists.

Where to Stay in Bamfield

Bamfield Trails Motel, Frigape Road (250–728–3231); $59–$79; overlooks inlet; some kitchens, pub, boat and plane tours; pets OK.

Bamfield Inn, Customs House Lane (250–728–3354); $80–$120; historic lodge overlooking harbor; dining, lounge; hot tub, fishing charters; no pets.

Seabeam Fishing Resort & Campground (250–728–3286); overlooking Grappler Inlet; boat rentals and charters; also eight-unit lodge with shared baths, use own bedding ($15–$40).

CHAPTER 6

THE OTHER ISLANDS

*A*long the eastern shore of Vancouver Island in the Strait of Georgia lie the Gulf Islands: Salt Spring, Pender, Saturna, Mayne, Galiano, Thetis, Valdes, Gabriola, Lasqueti, Denman, and Hornby. Farther north, in the narrow passage between the Lower Mainland and Vancouver Island, are the Discovery Islands, which include Quadra, Cortes, and Sonora. Cormorant and Malcolm Islands dot the northern exit from the Johnstone Strait in the open sea. All offer excellent fishing, whale watching, native arts, and dining. Enjoy with respect.*

GULF ISLANDS

Salt Spring Island

Salt Spring lies along the east coast of Vancouver Island from just north of Swartz Bay to a point opposite Chemainus.

Take your choice of three B.C. Ferry routes: from Swartz Bay landing at Fulford Harbour; from Crofton to Vesuvius Bay; or from Vancouver (Tsawwassen) to Long Harbour. All take about thirty-five minutes. Seaplanes also bring passengers from both Vancouver and Victoria.

Your best bet is to take an automobile on the ferry, giving you the freedom to explore Salt Spring, from its rambling roads to several very swimmable lakes, and to get a spectacular view of the channel from Mount Maxwell's peak. If you land at Fulford, drive over the hill from Fulford to the principal community of **Ganges**.

Salt Spring's substantial artists' colony has more than thirty-five galleries and studios, plus bookstores and shops. Enjoy a variety of restaurants and pubs close to Fulford Harbour and Ganges.

Fulford village is charming and low-key, with an outdoor flea market, pub,

TARTE AUX POMMES AU FROMAGE BLANC
Susan and Julia Grace, Moonstruck Organic Cheese, Inc.,
Salt Spring Island

Ingredients
large pastry round (crust)
4 large apples, sliced
butter
cinnamon, nutmeg, and brown sugar for tossing and sprinkling
Moonstruck Fromage Blanc (brie or camembert)

Preparation
Preheat oven to 400°F. Make a larger than usual round of pastry and lay in pie plate so that the edges fold over the sides. Fill with sliced apples and dot with butter. If you wish, you may toss the apples in cinnamon, nutmeg, and a little brown sugar. Fold over the pastry, leaving about a 6-inch round in the center. Spread the exposed apples liberally with Moonstruck Fromage Blanc and then coat the cheese with brown sugar. Bake for ten minutes at 400°, then reduce the temperature to 350°. The pie is done when the pastry is lightly browned and you can hear the apples bubbling (about another thirty minutes). This tart never lasts a meal, so if you want leftovers, make two.

collectibles shops, and excellent coffee. There's also the Vesuvius Inn, a historic church, and a friendly atmosphere. For camping try St. Mary Lake inland, or shore facilities at Ruckle Provincial Park and Mouat Provincial Park.

During Artcraft, which starts the last weekend in May and continues until September, 250 Gulf Island artists and artisans hold exhibits at Mahon Hall in Ganges, 10:00 A.M.–5:00 P.M. daily. The Salt Spring Festival of the Arts peps up Ganges for four weeks starting the first full weekend in July. Catch the irreverent performances of the Hysterical Society (250–537–4167).

Other events include Sea Capers in mid-June, ArtSpring Home Tour in mid-July, Fulford Day in mid-August, and the Fall Fair the third weekend in September.

Food lovers absolutely must make a trip to MOONSTRUCK ORGANIC CHEESE-MAKERS OF FINE ORGANIC CHEESES. To get there from Fulford Harbour, where the ferry brings you, follow Rulford-Ganges Road north to Cusheon Lake Road and turn right. When Cusheon Lake Road ends at Beddis Road, turn right on Beddis. Moonstruck is less than a mile on the left.

Julia and Susan Grace offer farm and cheese-making tours on Thursday from 1:30 to 3:00 P.M. and are open for farm sales June 1–September 30 or by appointment in winter.

Julia converted from raising veggies for sale and cooking for fans to making cheese after Susan yearned to have a cow and finally bought one. Now Susan manages the "herd" of sixteen super-clean jerseys, and Julia makes highly unusual and divine cheese. Kathleen is totally addicted to Blossom's Blue and Blue Moon.

❧ *Moonstruck Organic Cheese-Makers of Fine Organic Cheeses, 1306 Beddis Road, Salt Spring Island V8K 2C9; E-mail:grace@saltspring.com.*

Where to Stay

For information on vacancies and reasonable accommodations on the island, call Salt Spring Island Visitor Information Centre, (250) 537–5252. See also "Where to Stay."

Hastings House, 160 Upper Ganges Road, Ganges (250–537–2362); $365–$495; dining; wheelchair accessible.

Salty Springs Seaside Resort, 1460 North Beach Road (250–537–4111); $159–$189; kitchens, decks; no phones; no pets.

Cusheon Lake Resort, 171 Natalie Lane (250–537–9629); $98–$148; log and A-frame chalets; beach, fishing, boats; no pets.

Harbour House Hotel, 121 Ganges Road (250–537–5571); $74–$89; overlooks harbor; restaurant, pub; beer and wine store; no pets.

Fulford Inn, 2661 Fulford-Ganges Road (250–653–4432; 800–652–4432); $60–$70; overlooks harbor; restaurant, pub; no pets.

Pender Islands

Just east of Salt Spring Island in the Strait of Georgia are the two Pender Islands (North and South), linked by a short bridge. You will find balmy summer weather, coves, and well-kept beaches for boating and swimming, arts and crafts studios, a nine-hole golf course, and great scenic hikes. The big event of the year is the Pender Island Summer Solstice Festival in June.

Take B.C. Ferries from Swartz Bay on Vancouver Island and Tsawwassen on the mainland. Schedule is varied. Hanna's Air flies in to the Penders from Salt Spring Island.

Where to Stay

Cliffside Inn on-the-Sea, Armdale Road, North Pender Island (250–629–6691); $115–$195; beach; seaside hot tub; dining; honeymoon suites; fireplaces, decks.

ASPARAGUS CRÈME BRÛLÉE
Marilyn Chilvers of Oceanwood Country Inn,
Mayne Island

Ingredients

1½ tbsp. unsalted butter	6 egg yolks
3 tbsp. chopped shallots	1½ cups whipping cream
1 cup asparagus, cut into ¼-inch pieces	salt and pepper
1 tsp. finely chopped garlic	Pinch nutmeg
⅛ cup white wine	

Preparation

Preheat oven to 325°F. Sauté the shallots in the butter for thirty seconds on medium-high heat. Add asparagus and garlic, cook for another two to three minutes, add wine, and continue cooking until liquid is gone. Remove to a plate to cool, then divide among six ramekins. Mix egg yolks, cream, salt, pepper, and nutmeg. Pour into ramekins and place them in a hot-water bath. Water should come two-thirds of the way up the sides of the dishes. Cover pan and bake for twenty to thirty minutes or until just cooked. Cool. These may be made ahead and served at room temperature. Serve with any type of plain crackers.

Pender Lodge, 1329 MacKinnon Road (250–629–3221); $90–$150; four cottages; decks, pool, tennis, croquet, some fireplaces; no pets; March–October.
Inn on Pender Island, 4709 Canal Road, North Pender Island (250–629–3353); $59–$79; licensed restaurant; small pets OK.

Saturna Island

Saturna Island (31 square km.) lies just east of the Penders and south of Mayne. The Community Center at Lyall Harbour, where the ferry docks, is where things happen. Still fairly primitive, Saturna is ideal for hiking, boating, and not disturbing wildlife.

Reach Saturna by B.C. Ferries from Swartz Bay on Vancouver Island and Tsawwassen on the mainland, as well as by flight on Harbour Air (604–278–3478) or Sea Air (604–273–8900). Boaters dock at Winter Cove Marine Park.

An added benefit to traveling to Saturna Island is the newish SATURNA ISLAND VINEYARDS, which recently released its first wines from the 1998 harvest. No wonder—Saturna Island has lassoed one of B.C.'s finest winemakers,

Eric Von Krosigk, a graduate of the Beverage Engineering program at the University of Geisenheim in Germany. Eric is already making fine chardonnay, riesling brut, pinot noir, and merlot, all less than $20.

To get to the winery from the ferry, follow East Point Road to the General Store, turn right onto Harris Road (next to the recycling center), and follow Harris all the way up and over the mountain. When you reach the bottom (of the mountain and road), turn left, and you are at the winery. The signs help.

And, most conveniently, you might want to book reservations at the winery-related Saturna Lodge and Restaurant, whose fine chef, Hubertus Surm, creates meals that will tantalize your senses. to go directly to the lodge from the ferry, take the first right onto Boot Cove Road. At the stop sign, turn right on Payne Road, go to the next stop sign, and the lodge is the first driveway on the right.

❧ *Saturna Island Vineyards, 130 Payne Road, Saturna Island V0N 2Y0; (250) 539–2254 or (800) 539–8800; Web: www.saturnavineyards.com; E-mail: wine@saturnavineyards.com. Winery hours: 11:30 A.M.–4:30 P.M. Wednesday–Sunday May–September, 11:30 A.M.–2:30 P.M. March 1–May 1. Wheelchair accessible. Credit Cards: Visa, MasterCard.*

Where to Stay

Saturna Lodge and Restaurant, 130 Payne Road (250–539–2254); $80–$130; licensed lounge, elegant prix fixe dinner, B. C. wine list; overlooks water; nature, marine and vineyard tours.

East Point Resort, East Point Road (250–539–2975); $77–$94; beach, launch, boat rentals.

Breezy Bay B&B, 131 Payne Road (250–539–2937); $55–$65; 1890s heritage house; beach, views, kayaking; no pets.

Mayne Island

Although smallest of the Gulf Islands, Mayne Island has a long history as an active community, dating back to the 1860s when it was a stopping point for miners crossing the Georgia Strait to and from the Fraser gold fields on the mainland. Lying just north of Pender and east of Salt Spring, Mayne is the first island on your left when taking the ferry from Tsawwassen to Swartz Bay.

Mayne is well covered by forest and a network of roads to several sheltered bays, including Village Bay, Miners Bay, and Horton Bay, all with docking facilities. Reach Mayne by B.C. Ferries from Swartz Bay on Vancouver Island and Tsawwassen on the mainland. Mayne has art galleries and studios, buildings dating from the nineteenth century, a museum (once a jail), and lovely resorts and beaches.

OCEANWOOD COUNTRY INN enjoys international fame for its lodging with water views from all rooms and for its cuisine. Jonathan and Marilyn Chilvers's English country home features crackling fireplaces, full bookshelves, and a wonderful kitchen overlooking Navy Channel. Ride bikes, listen to Mozart, walk, kayak, play tennis or chess, or drink champagne in the bathtub in front of the fire. Breakfast and tea included. Rates range from $130 to $220, with two nights required if Saturday is included. Oceanwood's restaurant overlooks the water, with the four-course prix fixe dinner available to the public at $35. Thanks to Marilyn Chilvers for her recipe.

Oceanwood Country Inn, 630 Dinner Bay Road, Mayne Island (250–539–5074). E-mail: oceanwood@gulfislands.com. Hours: dinner from 6:00 P.M. Dining room wheelchair accessible with help; rest room is not. Credit cards: Visa, MasterCard.

Where to Stay

Blue Vista Resort, 563 Arbutus Drive (250–539–2463); $50–$100; decks; beach; no pets during tourist season.
Mayne Inn Hotel, 494 Arbutus Drive (250–539–3122); $50–$75; water views; licensed dining room, lounge; no pets.
Fernhill Lodge, 610 Fernhill Road (250–539–2544); $74–$139; sauna; licensed, dinner by reservation; no pets.

Galiano Island

Long, narrow Galiano Island stretches from its southern tip just across a narrow passage from Mayne Island northerly to a point east of Ladysmith on the 49th parallel.

Take B.C. Ferries from Swartz Bay on Vancouver Island or from Tsawwassen to Sturdies Bay, or fly in via Hanna's Air or Harbour Air. Boaters dock at Montague Harbour.

Geared to natural recreation, Galiano (named for a Spanish explorer) features hiking, camping, and bird-watching in three scenic provincial parks; fishing; and boating. Accommodations, eateries, and stores are concentrated in four settlements: Sturdies Bay, Georgeson Bay, Montague Harbour, and Spotlight Cove. Resourceful Hummingbird Pub runs its own bus from the Montague Park Marina to the pub mid-May–October. For a dining treat try La Berengerie (250–539–5392) at Montague Harbour, where ex-Parisian Huguette Benger prepares fabulous meals from vegetarian to venison, praised by *Northwest Best Places.*

Annual events include the North Galiano Jamboree on Canada Day, July 1; Lion's Club Fiesta the first Saturday in August; and Galiano Island Wine Festival in the middle of August.

Call Galiano's visitor information line: (250) 539–2233.

Where to Stay

La Berengerie, Montague Harbour Road (250–539–5392); $50–$75; hot tub; licensed restaurant; complimentary ferry pickup; no pets.

Woodstone Country Inn, Georgeson Bay Road (250–539–5544); $90–$145; licensed dining; no smoking, no pets.

Driftwood Village Resort, 205 Bluff Road East (250–539–5457); $85–$140; pets OK.

Madrona Lodge, 18715 Porlier Pass Road (250–539–2926); $75–$100; in forest near water; launch, moorage; pets OK.

Cliff Pagoda B&B, 2851 Montague Harbour Road (250–539–2260); $50–$70; Japanese-style country inn; harbor views; complimentary ferry pickup; canoes and mountain bikes; no pets.

Little tourism activity exists on Thatis and Valdes Islands, so we move on to Gabriola Island via ferry from downtown Nanaimo.

Gabriola Island

Gabriola (gay-bree-OH-la) Island is an underdiscovered paradise only twenty minutes from Nanaimo by B.C. Ferries that run seventeen times daily. Don't miss the petroglyphs near Degnen Bay, historical farm and community buildings, the huge caves in the sandstone cliffs called the Malaspina Galleries, and First Nations burial grounds.

ARBUTUS TREE ON
GABRIOLA ISLAND

Kayak, play tennis, ride horses, sail, hike, and beachcomb, all within walking distance of everything. Enjoy the environment and wildlife, including otters, seals, eagles, and deer (whose ancestors swam from Vancouver Island) at three waterfront provincial parks: Twin Beaches, Brumburg, and Sandwell. Moor your boat at Silva and Degnen Bays. Call (250) 247–8807 for Silver Blue Charters for fishing and sight-seeing.

Artisans' and artists' galleries and studios are open to the public. Golfers get their fix at the Gabriola Island Golf and Country Club.

This is pub country, where you can meet locals at Silva Bay Pub, White Hart Pub, Windecker's Restaurant, Latitudes at the Sterling Resort, and the Sunset Lounge at the Surf Lodge with a splendid view of the strait.

For more information call the Gabriola Chamber of Commerce, (250) 247–8455 (telephone and fax).

Where to Stay

Sterling Resort & Marina, 3415 South Road (250–247–8662); pub, restaurant; pool, tennis court, marina facility on Silva Bay.
Surf Lodge, 885 Berry Point Road (250–247–9231); $85–$150 for three-bedroom cabin (in season); restaurant, lounge, pub; seven minutes from ferry.

Newcastle Island

For a quick nature outing from Nanaimo, take the ferry to Newcastle Island Provincial Marine Park for camping, historic sites, and trails. No vehicles. Pets must be on leash.

Lasqueti Island

For a real getaway you can take a people-only water taxi from French Creek (north of Parksville on Highway 19) for a forty-five-minute trip to Lasqueti Island. Hike from the village of Lasqueti to Spring Bay to observe eagle nests and explore caves. Call the only hotel for transportation information:
Lasqueti Island Hotel & Resort, Weldon Road (250–333–8846); $90; licensed restaurant; no pets; no TV, no phones.

Denman Island

Opposite Fanny Bay lie Denman Island, a mile away, and Hornby Island, two of the most popular beach vacation sites in British Columbia.

Catch the B.C. Ferry at Buckley Bay, 75 kilometers (46 miles) north of Nanaimo on the Island Highway, for a 1.5-kilometer (1-mile) ride to Denman Village on the island. Be sure to visit artisans' and artists' studios. Camp at Fillongley Provincial Park and hike or bike over trails around the island, the flattest of the Gulf Islands. Rent a canoe or kayak and paddle over to nearby Sandy Island Provincial Marine Park.

Where to Stay

Fillongley Provincial Park (250–954–4600); April–October; on east side of island; 3 kilometers from ferry.
Hawthorne B&B, 3375 Kirk Road (250–335–0905); $55–$65; renovated 1904 house; water view; wheelchair accessible; no smoking.

Hornby Island

Cross Denman Island on Denman Road (fifteen minutes) and catch the Hornby ferry at Gravely Bay, for another 1.5-kilometer trip to Hornby.

Hornby Island may be the best spot in British Columbia to camp, hike, bike, and loll on the beach if you feel like just taking it easy. For a change of pace, bird-watch at Helliwell Bay Provincial Park on St. John's Point. We also recommend camping and lying on Tribune Beach to relieve any tensions.

Where to Stay

Sea Breeze Lodge, Fowler Road (250–335–2321); $610–$800 weekly; twelve oceanside cottages; hot tub; fishing, boat rentals; American plan meals during summer; petroglyphs; no pets. Featured in *Northwest Best Places.*
Ford's Cove Marina, Ford's Cove (250–235–2169); $440–$465 per week; on water; fishing supplies and boat fuel; no pets.
Tribune Bay Campsite, Saltspray Road (250–335–2359); 120 sites; large sandy beach; toilets, showers; April–October; $17 minimum.

DISCOVERY ISLANDS

Quadra Island

Just 3 kilometers (2 miles) east of Campbell River lies Quadra Island, which is ideal for sportfishing and finding First People pottery and other art. It also has two internationally praised lodges.

Take a ten-minute B.C. Ferry ride from downtown Campbell River. Attractions include Kwakiutl Museum at Cape Mudge Village, with its displays of costumes and masks from potlatches and other ceremonies. Nearby are the petroglyphs at We-Wai-Kai Beach and the native-built Tsa-Kwa-Luten Lodge, which includes a big house and First People cultural activities. Hiking, fishing, boating, and scuba diving (oh, so cold) round out the possibilities, not to mention eating and loafing.

Quadra Island is the home of April Point Lodge & Fishing Resort, now part of the Oak Bay Marina restaurant and resort group. *Condé Nast Traveler* magazine's January 1997 issue chose this full-service resort as "one of the Best Places to Stay in the World" (See "Where to Stay"). April Point has also been featured in *Gourmet* magazine and *Northwest Best Places*.

Where to Stay

April Point Lodge & Fishing Resort, April Point Road (250–285–2222); $99–$199; suites and seafront guest houses; hot tubs, fireplaces; licensed dining, lounge; fishing; helipad, seaplane connections.

Tsa-Kwa-Luten Lodge, Lighthouse Road (250–285–2042); $80–$125; West Coast native theme featuring elegant woods and design; ocean views; beach; dining; sauna; guided fishing; no pets; April 15–October 15.

Quadra Resort, 680 Raydon Road (250–285–3279); $73; waterfront; moorage, canoes; fishing guides; no pets; May–September.

Cortes Island

Reached by Quadra Island B.C. ferry from Campbell Bay, little Cortes offers miles of white sandy beaches, an old whaling station at Whaletown, a historic church, and trails that span this most beautiful of the Discovery Islands and its lakes.

Where to Stay

Sutil Adventures, Quartz Bay (250–287–2020); $100–$160; sundecks; beach access; boats at ferry dock; bring own food; pets OK.

Cortes Island Motel, Manson's Landing (250–935–6363); $40–$70; eight units; some kitchens; family suites; near beach; pets OK; 9 miles from ferry.

Gorge Harbour Marina Resort, Hunt Road (250–935–6433); May–September; 25 kilometers south of ferry terminal.

Smelt Bay Provincial Park (250–954–4600); June–September; 25 kilometers south of ferry terminal.

Sonora Island

Just north of Quadra Island is sprawling Sonora Island, which can only be reached by private boat or plane. It is home to upscale fishing resort SONORA RESORT AND CONFERENCE CENTRE (250–287–2869), which starts at more than $2,000 for a minimum of two days as part of a flying package from Vancouver and guided fishing trip. Amenities include tennis, lap pool, hot tub, billiard room, gourmet dining, and licensed lounge. By boat it is 48 kilometers (30 miles) from Campbell River.

Cormorant and Malcolm Islands

Far to the north in the open water of Labouchere Passage (also called the Queen Charlotte Strait) and east of the town of Port McNeill lie Cormorant and Malcolm Islands. You can reach both by auto ferry from Port McNeill. The trip is twenty-five minutes to Malcolm and forty-five minutes to Cormorant.

CORMORANT ISLAND. Little Cormorant Island is a cornucopia of native artifacts. These include the potlatch collection at U'Mista Cultural Center, the second tallest totem pole in the world (constructed in 1973 by carver Jimmy Dick and skilled aides), and traditional native dances at the Big House. Members of the Kwakiutl Nation, famed for their art, own half the island.

Alert Bay, the only town, has a long history as a trading post, fishing and cannery center, and stopover for Klondike gold rushers. The town has the ferry terminal; information center; Nimpkish Burial Ground, studded with totem poles; and the Alert Bay Museum. Slightly inland is Gator Gardens, a cedar forest ideal for bird sighting.

Two taxi companies transport visitors and locals. For whale watching or fishing, try Seasmoke Tours (250–974–5225) in downtown Alert Bay or Cannery Row Lodge (250–974–5213).

Where to Stay

Orca Inn, 291 Fir Street (250–974–5322); $39–$65; overlooks strait; licensed restaurant; no pets.
Ocean View Cabins, 390 Poplar Street (250–974–5457); $50–$65; 1 mile from ferry; overlooks bay; pets OK.

MALCOLM ISLAND. Malcolm Island was the site of a turn-of-the-twentieth-century Finnish utopian farming colony, *Sointula,* which means "harmony" in Finnish. The original cooperative general store and a museum provide a taste of the founding community. Recently upgraded Bere Point Regional Park offers sportfishing and whale watching.

Take a ferry from Port McNeill or from nearby Cormorant Island.

Where to Stay

Malcolm Island Inn, 210 First Street (250–973–6366); $44–$51; beachfront; licensed restaurant; store, bank; fishing and whale watching tours; pets OK.

There are also three small B&Bs: *Ocean Bliss* (250–973–6121), *Sea 4 Miles* (250–973–6486), and *Rogue Retreat* (250–973–6222).

CHAPTER 7

OUTDOOR THINGS TO DO

This is our outdoor chapter. Not everyone wants to spend all their time shopping. In fact, some people come to Vancouver Island to experience unusually fine natural wonders. Or a combination of urban and wild. This covers most of what you can do to get closer to nature and to your spirit while exercising your body.

BIKING

Vancouver Island is ideal for casual or organized biking. Most highways have bike lanes. The trip over the mountains to Tofino and Ucluelet on Highway 4 can be harrowing because the road is narrow in places to start with, and in a few places the shoulder and pavement edge have washed out. Check with bike shops for latest information. (See Getting Here and Getting Around for a list of bike shops.)

BICYCLE TOURS OF VICTORIA by Greenday Bicycle Tours & Adventures (250–380–6033) offers excellent tours, including a one-day tour of town (six hours) that includes lunch (at Blethering Place Tea Room), snacks, bicycle, helmet, water bottle, guide, transportation of purchases or excess gear, shopping with discounts in Oak Bay, admission fees to Craigdarroch Castle, Fisherman's Wharf, Beacon Hill Park, Government House, and University of Victoria. The three-day weekend tour of Galloping Goose Trail and Victoria covers 125 kilometers and includes two nights at a B&B, all meals, snacks, guide, transportation of luggage, shopping discounts in Oak Bay, admission to Craigdarroch Castle, and a T-shirt. Tour costs: one-day $69; three-day $399.

DIVING

Cousteau Society and National Geographic leaders agree that "the emerald sea" along British Columbia's shorelines offers some of the best diving in the world. Vancouver Island's bays and inlets, along with currents from the Pacific and between islands, attract abundant and varied marine plant and animal communities, almost as diverse as the divers who come to visit them.

The water is colder than what you may encounter off Monterey, California, for example (brr), but warmer than many inland lakes. The temperatures require use of 6 millimeter (.75-inch) wet suits or dry suits. With these heavier suits, be sure to pay attention to buoyancy control.

Because of Vancouver Island's moderate climate, you can dive year-round. Visibility is best in winter, often exceeding 20 meters (66 feet). In summer, seasonal plankton bloom and can go down 10–20 meters (30–60 feet), below which visibility is good.

You can find some good diving from shore, but the best is to be had off boats. Contact professional dive shops for daylong or several-day charters and excursions. Charter operators do not allow hunting or collection of specimens under a "look but don't take" policy. There is a strong commitment to conservation and preservation in B.C. waters.

SOUTHERN VANCOUVER ISLAND. Currents coming from different directions support a very exciting and diverse marine life here. Good shore diving is found at Ogden Point (Dallas Road) breakwater overlooking the Juan de Fuca Strait and Washington's Olympic Mountains or at Ten Mile Point.

At Race Rocks, which is accessible only by boat, swift currents support multihued invertebrates such as giant barnacles, basket stars, brooding anemones, and pink hydrocoral. In the fall, hundreds of California and Steller's sea lions hover on these same rocks, often performing for their diving audience.

Near Sidney there's a special attraction for trained wreck divers: the HMCS *MacKenzie*, a project of the Artificial Reef Society of British Columbia. The society has made the 100-meter (366-foot) destroyer safe for exploration by properly trained divers.

NANAIMO AND NORTH. Halfway between Qualicum Beach and Courtenay you can take a ferry to Denman and Hornby Islands. In the summer, if you're lucky, you might see the rare six-gill sharks that can grow to more than 6 meters (20 feet). Look for them around Flora Islets, which are part of Helliwell Provincial Park off the southeastern corner of Hornby Island.

Using professional charters is highly recommended.

Blue Meridian Dive Center and Coastal Explorer Dive Excursions, 1956 Zorkin Road, Nanaimo V9S 5T9 (250–753–2055; Fax: 250–753–2004).

Extra-Sea Charters Ltd., 6209 Scollos Place, Nanaimo V9V 1K9 (250–756–0544; Fax: 250–758–4897).

Giant Stride Diving, 60 Kenneth Street, Duncan V9L 1N2 (250–748–8864; Fax: 250–748–8962).

Hornby Island Diving, Ford Cove, Hornby Island V0R I2O (250–335–2807).

Pacific North Outdoor Adventures, 240 Dogwood Street, Parksville V9P 2H5 (250–248–9681).

Seafun Divers Ltd., 300 Terminal Avenue, Nanaimo V9R 5C8 (250–754–4813; Fax: 250–754–5383).

Sundown Diving, 22 Esplanade Street, Nanaimo V9R 4Y7 (250–753–1880; Fax: 250–753–6445).

High Test Dive Charters, S-27 C-30, Gabriola Island V0R 1X0 (250–977–7823 or 250–247–9753).

CAMPBELL RIVER. Campbell River is a town about halfway up Vancouver Island that overlooks Discovery Pass, which is a sort of bottleneck at the northern end of Georgia Strait. The swirling waters create eddies and currents that sustain profuse marine life. At "Row and Be Damned" on Quadra Island, you might see strawberry anemones on the rocky bottom, kel greenlings, ling cod, octopus, rockfish, sulpins, and occasionally meter-long feather-duster worms, sponges, and wolfeels.

Beaver Aquatics Ltd., 760 Island Highway, Campbell River V9W 2C3 (250–287–7652; Fax: 250–287–8652).

Pacific NW Diving Adventures, P.O. Box 58, Cortes Island V0P 1K0 (250–935–6711, phone and fax).

PORT HARDY AND QUEEN CHARLOTTE STRAIT. Sighting killer whales here on the water's surface is fairly commonplace, but seeing one underwater is not. You might, though, spot schools of dolphins and porpoises, or—more likely—the Pacific white-sided dolphins will spot and circle you.

The coast of northern Vancouver Island is diver heaven. You can see dense gatherings of pink soft coral, sponges, giant barnacles and anemones, basket star, rockfish, ling cod, wolfeels, warbonnets, and sculpins.

Caution: Some of the swiftest tidal minglings in the world occur here, occasionally resulting in tidal currents that are more than twenty knots.

The plus side of these exchanges is the radiant collection of marine life you can see at slack tide, including gooseneck barnacles and brooding anemones. Live-aboard dive vessels are recommended.

North Island Diving & Watersports, 8295 Hastings Street, Box 1674, Port Hardy V0N 2P0 (250–949–2664; Fax: 250–949–2600).
Stubbs Island Charters, 24 Boardwalk, Box 7, Telegraph Cove V0N 3J0 (250–928–3185, 205–928–3117, or 800–665–3066; Fax: 250–928–3102).
Sun Fun Divers, 1630 McNeill Road, Port McNeill V0N 2R0 (250–956– 2243).

WEST COAST OF VANCOUVER ISLAND. Barkley Sound, on which Ucluelet is the principal metropolis, is the main dive interest in the area to the south of Pacific Rim National Park.

Among the broken group of islands scattered through the sound you will encounter shallow reefs and profuse marine life, such as wolfeels, octopus, rockfish (including china and vermilion rockfish), ling cod, purple-ringed top snails, tube worms, finger sponges, large fish-eating anemones, and nudibranchs. Barkley Sound is also known as Vancouver Island's other place to spot six-gill sharks.

Foggy weather has contributed to more than a hundred ships wrecking in the area over the centuries, resulting in unusual collections of marine life living within dead boat shells.

From here you can also take charters to Clayoquot Sound, Nootka Sound, Kyuquot, and Cape Scott and watch gray whales migrate south almost anywhere along the west coast of Van Isle.

Pacific Spirit Charters, 4924 Argyle Street, Port Alberni, V9Y 1V6 (250–723–1291 or 800–547–1291; Fax: 250–723–6817).
Subtidal Adventures, P.O. Box 78, 1950 Peninsula Road, Ucluelet V0R 3A0 (250–726–7336, phone and fax).

FISHING

It seems as if there are almost as many fishing guides and charters as there are people needing guidance in fishing waters. All the fishing professionals here treat novices as well as old-timers, the latter of whom probably don't need much help.

Fishing resorts and fishing tours for freshwater and ocean are great experiences of Van Isle. In both cases, you usually don't need to bring your own equipment unless you want to. You can arrive in Victoria, see a brochure and decide this looks like fun, make a call and a reservation, and off you go to heaven, hoping never to have to return home.

Freshwater lakes, rivers, and streams have wild rainbow and cutthroat trout, Dolly Varden char, kokanee salmon, and hatchery-grown introduced species such as brown trout and smallmouth bass. There are more than one hundred steelhead rivers and creeks on Vancouver Island, most accessible by car. Most lucrative fishing rivers include the Cowichan and Campbell/Quinmsam Rivers on the island's east coast, and the Stam/Somass and Gold Rivers on the west coast. Cowichan Lake is known as the "Fly Fishing Capital of Canada."

Freshwater Fishing

For official sportfishing information, call (250) 666–2828.

Nimmo Bay Resort Ltd., Box 696, Port McNeill V0N 2R0 (250–956–4000 or 250–949–2549; Fax: 250–956–2000); Craig Murray.

Hidden Cove Lodge, Box 258, Port NcNeill V0N 2R0 (250–956–3916; Fax: 250–956–3213); Dan and Sandra Kirby.

Salmon Run in Goldstream Provincial Park, November; call (250) 387–4363 for timing.

Yohetta Wilderness Ltd., Box 69, Duncan V9L 3X1 (250–748–4878; Radio: H43–5407; Fax: 250–748–7881); Goetz Schuerholz.

For local lake fishing, try Elk Lake and Beaver Lake (they run together) off Patricia Bay Highway (17).

Ocean Sportfishing

Ocean sportfishing is extremely popular all over Vancouver Island. Almost every outdoors shop, hotel, motel, B&B, or cafe server in Victoria or anywhere else on the island can set you up with a fishing charter, guide, tour, or equipment.

Since listing the larger companies would mean the smaller ones never get larger, we suggest you make your accommodations reservation for where you want to be or go and book fishing through your hosts. Most charters supply all equipment.

Adams Fishing Charters, 19 Lotus Street, Victoria V9A 1P3 (250–370–2326 or 250–727–5575); salmon fishing year-round from Victoria's Inner Harbour from Sooke to Sidney.

Oak Bay Beach Hotel Pride of Victoria Cruises, 1175 Beach Drive, Victoria V8S 2N2 (250–592–3474 or 250–598–4556); trolling or drift fishing, including box breakfast or lunch; $118.

Oak Bay Charters Ltd., 1327 Beach Drive, Victoria V8S 2V2 (250–598–3369 or 250–598–1061); year-round salmon fishing, sight-seeing, cruises; at Oak Bay Marina.

Reel Action Fishing Charters, 961 Haslam Avenue, Victoria V9B 4T1 (250–478–1977 or 250–644–6536); salmon, halibut, and bottom fish around Victoria and Sooke.

Weigh West Marine Resort, 634 Campbell Street, Tofino (250–725–3277); five boats for charter fishing with guides. Rates: charter, $75 per hour per boat (four people plus guide); moorage, 30 cents per foot per day.

Canadian Princess Resort, 1948 Peninsula Road, Ucluelet (250–726–7771); seven-hour trip for chinook, sockeye, coho, and pink salmon (leaves 6:00 A.M.) or four-hour trip bottom fishing for halibut, ling cod, red snapper (leaves 2:30 P.M.); also whale watching and nature cruises; 43- and 52-foot deep-sea cruisers.

GOLF

Golf is only a minor obsession with Vancouver Islanders, which they come by naturally given their Scottish-British heritage. Nearly every town and many neighborhoods have golf courses. Greater Victoria alone has fifteen and is Canada's number one golf city, attracting major golf aficionados from around the world.

Victorians believe that you can play golf 365 days a year here (except, of course, for that one snowy week in early 1997). As is true in most of the Pacific Northwest, golf devotees play with umbrellas, slickers, covered carts, and rain hats year-round.

Golf Courses in Greater Victoria

Victoria Golf Club, 1110 Beach Drive, Oak Bay (250–598–4322); eighteen holes, 6,015 yards, par 70; along the water.

Cedar Hills Municipal Golf Course, 1400 Derby Road, Victoria (250–595–3103); eighteen holes; men: 5,008 yards, par 67; women: 4,975 yards, par 68.

Mount Douglas Golf Course, 4225 Blenkinsop Road, Victoria (250–477–8314); nine holes, 1,500 yards, par 30.

Uplands Golf Club, 3300 Cadboro Bay Road, Victoria (250–592–1818); eighteen holes, 6,315 yards, par 70.

Gorge Vale Golf Club, 1005 Craigflower Road, Victoria (250–386–3401); eighteen holes, 6,382 yards, par 72; book one day in advance, or Thursday for weekends.

Ardmore Golf Course, 930 Ardmore Drive, North Saanich (250–656–4621); nine holes, 2,821 yards, par 34.

Blenkinsop Valley Golf Centre, 4237 Blenkinsop, Victoria (250–721–2001).
Cordova Bay Golf Course, 5333 Cordova Bay Road, Saanich (250–658–4444); eighteen holes, 6,500 yards, par 72.
Glen Meadows Golf and Country Club, 1050 McTavish Road, North Saanich (250–656–3921); eighteen holes, 6,850 yards, par 72.
Prospect Lake Golf Course, 4633 Prospect Lake Road, Saanich (250–479–2688); nine holes, 2,121 yards, par 32 (with tricky sixth hole water).
Royal Oak Golf Course, 40 Marsett Place, Saanich (250–478–9591); nine holes, 2,031 yards, par 32.

Outside Victoria

Arbutus Ridge Golf Club, 3515 Telegraph Road, Cobble Hill (250–743–5000).
Broome Hill Golf & Country Club, Sooke (250–624–6344).
Comox Golf Club, 1718 Balmoral Avenue, Comox (250–399–4444).
Cowichan Golf & Country Club, P.O. Box 38, Duncan (250–746–5333).
Crown Isle, Clubhouse Drive, Courtenay (250–338–6811).
Duncan Lakes, 6507 North Road, Duncan (250–746–6789).
Eaglecrest Golf Club, 2035 Island Highway West, Qualicum Beach (250–752–6311).
Fairwinds Golf Course Ltd., 3730 Fairwinds Drive, Nanoose Bay (250–468–7666).
Fiddler's Green Golf Centre Inc., 1601 Thatcher Road, Nanaimo (250–754–1325).
Galiano Golf & Country Club, 24 St. Andrews Street, Galiano Island (250–539–5533).
Glengarry Golf Links, 1025 Qualicum Road, Qualicum Beach (250–752–8786).
Gold River Golf & Country Club, Box 819, Gold River (250–283–7335).
Ladysmith Golf Club, 380 Davis, Ladysmith (250–245–7313).
Long Beach Golf Course, Tofino (250–725–3332).
Longlands Par 3 Golf Course, Comox (250–339–6363).
March Meadows Golf & Country Club, 10298 South Shore Road, Honeymoon Bay (250–749–6241).
Morningstar International Golfcourse, 525 Lowrys Road, Parksville (250–754–8232).
Mount Brenton Golf Club, 2816 Henry Road, Chemainus (250–246–9322).
Mulligans Executive Par 3, 4985 Cotton Road, Courtenay (250–338–2440).
Nanaimo Golf & Country Club, 2800 Highland Boulevard, Nanaimo (250–758–5221).

Pacific Playground Golf Course, Saratoga Beach, Campbell River
(250–337–8212).
Pender Island Golf & Country Club, 2305 Otter Bay Road, Pender Island
(250–629–6659).
Pleasant Valley Golf Course, Highway 4, Port Alberni (250–724–5333).
Port Alberni Golf Club, 6449 Cherry Creek Road, Port Alberni
(250–723–5422).
Port Alice Golf & Country Club, Box 460, Port Alice (250–284–3213).
Pryde Vista Golf Course, 155 Pryde Avenue, Nanaimo (250–753–6188).
Qualicum Beach Memorial Golf Club, 115 Crescent Road, Qualicum Beach
(250–752–6312).
Salt Spring Island Golf & Country Club, Ganges (250–537–2121).
Sequoia Springs Golf Club, 700 Petersen Road, Campbell River
(250–287–4970).
Seven Hills Golf Course, Port Alice Highway, Port Hardy (250–949–9818).
Storey Creek Golf Club, McGimpsey Road, Campbell River (250–923–3673).
Sunnydale Golf Society, 5291 Island Highway, Courtenay (250–334–3342).

Courses offering golf vacation packages include Crown Isle Golf Club
(praised by *Golf Digest,* near Courtenay, 250–338–6811); Fairwinds Golf &
Country Club (Nanoose Bay, twenty-five minutes north of Nanaimo, 250–
468–7666); Glengarry Golf Links (near Qualicum Beach, 250–752–8786);
Eagle Crest Golf Club (Qualicum Beach, 250–752–6311); and Morningstar
International (between Parksville and Qualicum Beach, 250–754–8232).

HIKING

Vancouver Island offers extremely satisfying novice or expert hiking, either
on well-cared-for paths or on land few people have experienced.
We mention hiking along trails throughout our itineraries, but here are a
few highlights:
Pacific Rim National Park on the island's west coast is a newer park with
excellent trails and abundant wildlife and rain forests, six hours from Victoria.
Western Wilderness Excursions (250–727–2356) gives rain forest tours, which
we guarantee will hook you.
Goldstream Provincial Park offers day hiking and a few tent campsites
with grand forests, rushing water, and amazing wildlife, all just forty minutes
from Victoria. Freedom Adventure Tours (250–592–2487) leads hikes in the
Sooke area.

West Coast Trail, which you reach from Port Renfrew, is a six-day hike for experienced hikers. Either drive there or take West Coast Trail Express shuttle, (250) 280–0580.

Making Tracks Hiking Tours for Adults 50+ (250–727–0243) offers van transport to rain forests and guided hikes of the Juan de Fuca Marine Trail, Carnanah, and the West Coast Trail day hike from Bamfield. Leader Liz Wood also takes hiking tours to other countries. (Mailing address: P.O. Box 36003, Esquimalt PO, Victoria.)

KAYAKING AND CANOEING

Kayaking and canoeing in Canada are often lumped together as "paddling," in the sense of propelling oneself through water in a skinny boat with a paddle or oar. Every hotel, motel, B&B manager, and jitney driver knows someone who can arrange kayaking or canoeing for you. Most outdoors outfitter stores sell or rent kayaks and either give lessons or connect you to someone who does.

It is important that you do all the safety things and wear all the safety stuff they tell you to. We highly recommend lessons, particularly if you've never paddled this seriously before.

On Vancouver Island you can paddle out from Victoria's Inner Harbour, where the water can be pleasantly calm or pleasantly rough and challenging. Paddling within the Inner Harbour and the Gorge on calm days is like paddling on a still, glassy lake.

More experienced paddlers might try waters between Oak Bay and Gonzales Bay, McNeill Bay, Cattle Point, the Trial Islands ecological reserve, or the Discovery Islands and their marine recreation area and campgrounds. On Van Isle's west coast try Albert Head to Witty's Lagoon, Weir's Beach by William Head to Pedder Bay, and (for experienced kayakers) from Pedder Bay through Eemdyk Pass to Becher Bay, and then an even tougher route from Becher or Pedder to Race Rocks. Even more risky but doable is the East Sooke Park shoreline toward Whiffin Spit near Sooke Harbour. What a way to arrive at Sooke Harbour House!

For more information consult May Ann Snowden's *Island Paddling: A Paddler's Guide to the Gulf Islands and Barkley Sound*.

We also recommend you try one of the great outdoors shops in Victoria. OCEAN RIVER SPORTS (1437 Store Street, 250–381–4233) has everything you need, rents kayaks and canoes (with paddles), and gives lessons and tours for kids and adults. It also has a great mailing list, so you can plan trips around its tours. The personnel gladly dispense enthusiasm and confidence for free.

Here are some others to try:

Jeune Brothers & Peetz Great Outdoors Store Ltd., 570 Johnson Street, Victoria (250–386–8778).

Whale House, 532 Broughton Street, Victoria (250–383–6722).

Mayne Island Kayak & Canoe Rentals, 359 Maple, Mayne Island (250–539–2667).

Ocean Wind Board Sailing, 5411 Hamsterly, Victoria (250–658–8171).

Salt Spring Kayaking Ltd., 2935 Fulford, Ganges, Salt Spring Island (250–653–4222).

Sea Otter Kayaking, 1186 North End, Salt Spring Island (250–537–5678).

Sports Rent, 611 Discovery, Victoria (250–385–7368).

Victoria Canoe & Kayak Club, 355 Gorge West, Victoria (250–361–4238).

KID STUFF

Beacon Hill Park, off Douglas Street and Dallas Road (250–381–3253), is an ideal place for kids and adults to work off energy and relax. There's a full, climbable playground; washrooms and telephone right next door; lots of walking and beautiful flowers; music on Sunday afternoons; a wading pool at the Douglas Street entrance, and the fabulous Children's Zoo. No food is sold here, but just outside the Douglas Street entrance is Beacon Drive-In, home of Victoria's best soft ice-cream cones and greasy foods. Watch for Kids Fest in early September.

Greater Victoria Public Library, Broughton Street between Douglas and Blanshard, has a kid-friendly kids and teens department just to the right of the door as you go in. Washrooms are right next to this area.

Other fun places for kids, discussed elsewhere in this book, include Victoria Bug Zoo (1107 Wharf Street, 250–384–BUGS); Victoria Butterfly Gardens (West Saanich and Keating Cross Roads near Butchart Gardens, 250–652–3822); Miniature World (649 Humboldt Street, 250–385–9731); Crystal Garden (713 Douglas Street, 250–381–1213); All Fun Waterslide Recreation Park (2207 Millstream Road, 250–474–4546); Royal London Wax Museum (470 Belleville Street, 250–388–4461; some kids might get scared); and Royal British Columbia Museum (675 Belleville Street, 250–387–5822 or 250–387–3014).

And watch for Children's Day at Sooke Regional Museum in August. Call (250) 642–6351 for timing.

SKIING

Despite its fabulously varied terrain, Vancouver Island really has only two ski areas: Mount Washington Ski Resort and Forbidden Plateau.

MOUNT WASHINGTON SKI RESORT is the island's largest ski area and B.C.'s third largest, with twenty groomed runs, four chair lifts, and a beginners' tow and bunny hill. Nineteen miles of trails can take you to Strathcona Provincial Park. Be sure to stay on trails. Rent equipment at resort; book ahead for resort accommodations. Mailing address: P.O. Box 3069, Courtenay (250–338–1386; 250–338–1515 for snow report). Full-day rates about $30 for adults.

To get there, you can take Gray Line of Victoria's Mount Washington Ski Express (600 Douglas Street, 250–388–5248), or you can drive (about five hours). Take Douglas Street north, follow Highway 1 (Trans-Canada Highway) past Nanaimo, and then go north on Highway 19 toward Courtenay. Follow signs to Mount Washington.

FORBIDDEN PLATEAU is an ideal ski area for beginners, families, timid skiers, and less-than-perfect skiers. That's a lot of us. The vertical drop is 1,150 feet, and with twelve groomed runs there is one chair lift, three T-bars, and a rope tow. Heavenly uncrowded bunny hills with little hotshotting going on. At 2050 Cliffe Avenue, Courtenay (250–338–2919); about $25 for adults. Rent equipment there.

SWIMMING

CRYSTAL POOL AND FITNESS CENTRE is Victoria's primary swimming place. Indoors it has a 50-meter racing and swimming pool, diving pool, and children's pool. It also has other health facilities, including whirlpool, steam, weight, and aerobics rooms.

✤ *Crystal Pool and Fitness Centre, 2275 Quadra Street, (250) 380–7946. Hours: 7:00 A.M.–11:30 P.M. Admission: adults $4.00, children six to twelve $2.00, family (must have someone older than sixteen within arm's reach in pools) $8.00. Wheelchair accessible. Buses 23, 26.*

Elk Lake and Beaver Lake, 8 miles north of Victoria on Highway 17 (Patricia Bay Highway on Saanich Peninsula), are good spots for swimming. The lakes have lifeguards and pleasant picnic areas, plus sailboarding, boating, kayaking, and canoeing.

Other places include Recreation Oak Bay (1975 Bee Street, Oak Bay; 250–595–7946), for swimming and indoor court sports; and Saanich

Commonwealth Place (4636 Elk Lake Road, 250–727–5300), a state-of-the-art family swim center with Olympic-size pools, diving, slides, and ozonated water.

WALKING (AND OTHER) TOURS

Tours of all sorts are available almost anywhere from almost anyone and are a most convenient way to get oriented in a new place, see exactly what you want to see, or find out what you might want to see more of. Since this chapter focuses on the outdoors, that's what we emphasize here. (See "Getting Here and Getting Around" for more tours.)

Victoria is a walker's best friend. Many locals (including us) walk through Beacon Hill Park and along Dallas Road daily, often stopping for refreshments at the Beacon Drive In on Douglas Street or the Ogden Pointe Cafe & Dive Centre.

Architectural Walking Tours (203–245 Bastion Square, Victoria; 800–667–0753) of the Inner Harbour and Old Town are conducted by the Vancouver Island Chapter of the Architectural Institute of British Columbia. July–Labor Day. Tours leave at 1:30 P.M. Admission: free.

Craigdarroch Castle Society (250–592–5323) makes tours of the historic neighborhoods of James Bay, Rockland, and western Victoria.

Grand Circle Tour offers a wide-ranging one-day tour by train, boat, and double-decker bus from Victoria through the Malahat Pass to Duncan and the Cowichan Native Village. It includes a sail on a 50-foot ketch from Cowichan Bay, a picnic lunch, and a tour of Butchart Gardens. Leaves from Johnson Street Bridge (blue) at 8:00 A.M. and returns to Victoria at 6:00 P.M. Tour cost: $98. Contact Great Northwestern Adventure Company Ltd., P.O. Box 57, Cowichan Bay (250–480–7245 or 800–665–7374).

Hallmark Society (250–382–4755) organizes walking tours of James Bay, Chinatown, and downtown.

Islands Art Tours (250–389–2073) gives tours of Cobble Hill wineries and ciderworks, Salt Spring Island Artists Haven, and local galleries of Pender Island, Port Washington, and Hope Bay.

Lantern Tours in the Old Burying Ground (250–598–8870). The Old Cemeteries Society of Victoria hosts nightly tours of Victoria history through its cemeteries.

Murder, Ghosts and Mayhem (250–385–2035) leaves from the Bastion Square Arch on Government Street at 8:00 P.M., rain or shine, June 24–September 1. Fees: $7.00 per person, children twelve and younger free.

North Island Forest Tours (250–956–3844) leave from Beaver Cove, Port McNeill, Port Alice, Port Hardy, Cleagh Creek, Holberg, and Woss for five-hour tours and nature walks through working forest heritage.

Old Town Tours (Cafe Bistingo), Market Square at 560 Johnson Street, (250) 389–0733.

Royal Blue Line picks up at the Black Ball Ferry terminal on Belleville and runs city tours and bus trips to the Butchart Gardens.

Charlayne Thornton-Joe (250–380–0432) runs tours of Chinatown, including places normally not available to visitors.

Timber Tours (800–661–7177) runs a variety of tours, including Lake Cowichan TimberTour, the Oyster River TimberTour at Campbell River, and the Williams Lake TimberTour. Call for extensive details.

Judy Van Loon (250–383–9210) gives historical tours of Old Town starting at Bastion Square.

WHALE WATCHING

Vancouver Island affords high-percentage whale watching because three pods of orca killer whales live here and have favorite feeding spots along its coasts. Just like fisher guides, every manager of an inn, hotel, motel, B&B, or jitney driver knows someone who takes people whale watching. Local tip: Gray whales feed in Tofino from March through October. Try to go with legitimate, established tour guides:

Spring Tide Charters, 950 Wharf Street (250–658–6016 or 800–470–3474).

Great Pacific Adventures, 950 Wharf Street (250–386–2277 or 250–727–3336). Tours not recommended for pregnant women or persons with neck or back problems.

Ocean Explorations, Inner Harbour Dock in front of The Empress hotel (250–383–6722).

Whale House, 532 Broughton Street (250–383–6722).

Oak Bay Beach Hotel Pride of Victoria Cruises, 1175 Beach Drive (250–592–3474 or 250–598–4556); full meal and beverages available.

Whaling Canoe Adventures, Blackfish Wilderness Adventures (250–721–1882 or 250–216–2389); very extensive.

SeaQuest Adventures, 591 Braemar Avenue, R.R. 2, Sidney (250–656–7599); from Port Sidney Marina.

Chinook Charters, 450 Campbell Street, Tofino (250–725–3431 or 800–665–3646); cruises through Clayoquot Sound.

Cypre Prince Whale Tours & Fishing Charters, 430 Campbell Street, Tofino (250–725–2202 or 800–787–2202).

Jamie's Whale Station, 606 Campbell Street, Tofino (250–725–3919 or 800–667–9913); B&B accommodations available.

Sea Trek Tours & Expeditions Ltd., 441B Campbell Street, Tofino (250–725–4412 or 800–811–9155); to Meares Island rain forest, Meares Island.

Subtidal Adventures, 1950 Peninsula Road, Ucluelet (250–726–7336); Ucluelet's oldest charter boat company for gray whale adventures.

CHAPTER 8

HISTORY OF VICTORIA AND VANCOUVER ISLAND

ancouver Island was one of the last places in the world Europeans discovered. The Spanish were in California, the American Colonies declared their independence from Great Britain, and Quebec city and Montreal were well established before Caucasians found the island.

First Peoples reached Vancouver Island more than 7,000 years ago. When the Europeans arrived, they found three related language groups: The Kwakiutl had the northeast corner, the Coast Salish occupied the territory from Victoria past Nanaimo, and the so-called Nootka lived on the west coast.

The natives were and are among the most artistic in the Western Hemisphere, with particular skills in carving. Unlike most people of the new world, they valued acquisition and display of private property, including slaves taken in raids upon their neighbors. Their social structure was in three layers: nobles, common people, and slaves, whose lives existed at the whim of their owners. One charming practice was to bury a slave alive in the hole before a new totem pole was inserted.

The natives lived primarily on a fish-oriented economy, starting with herring in the late winter caught in nets or scooped in with giant rakes, followed later by halibut and then salmon. The Nootkas went whale harpooning in packs of a half dozen canoes. Berries, roots, and meat from otters, seals, deer, and bears supplemented their diet.

Giant cedar trunks were carved into sleek and speedy 60-foot canoes. Cedar also provided bark, which could be shredded into a sort of thread to weave blankets, clothing, and baskets. Natives lived in long houses, structures with permanent wooden frames that were divided into family cubicles. In late spring the wood siding was carried to the coast to build a temporary village for the season.

The desire to display wealth led to the potlatch (from *patshatl,* which meant "giving"), a celebration for almost any cause in which visiting tribes were given lavish gifts and were expected to reciprocate. Often, valuable possessions were broken or canoes burned to show that the owner was too rich to care. As the ultimate conspicuous consumption, occasionally a valuable slave would be ceremoniously clubbed to death during such a festive event.

It was a male-dominated society in which marriages were arranged by uncles and chiefs and women had little to say—except for the women who were shamans. They were respected and thought to possess mystical powers.

In A.D. 499 five Chinese Buddhist monks, led by Hui Shen, sailed to Vancouver Island (they called it Fusang) and returned to China. Their story triggered Russian interest in North America 1,200 years later.

The Spanish made forays north in 1774. On August 8 of that year, in bad weather, Capt. Juan Perez Hernandez anchored the *Santiago* off the shore of the island but did not land.

On July 12, 1776, Capt. James Cook again set out for the Pacific Ocean, armed with the highly accurate chronometer invented by John Harrison, England's preeminent clock innovator. It made east to west navigation possible no matter how rough the sea or erratic the humidity. Unlike the Spanish explorers, who did not have a similar device, Cook would know exactly where he was and be able to return to a given place. His two ships were the 420-foot old tub *Resolution* and the smaller but more maneuverable *Discovery.* On board was nineteen-year-old junior officer George Vancouver, who had sailed with Cook since he was fifteen.

COOK DISCOVERS NOOTKA SOUND

After crossing the Pacific and discovering the Hawaiian Islands, Cook reached the Oregon coast in March 1778 before being forced offshore by a storm. He sailed northward, desperate to find a safe landing to repair a mast and take on fresh water.

On the morning of March 28, the weather front lifted enough to reveal the mountains of Vancouver Island, and by afternoon the search for an anchorage was rewarded with the view of an inlet that promised shelter—amazingly, the same spot where Spanish captain Perez had anchored briefly four years earlier. Leading the way into the inlet was the *Resolution,* with Capt. William Bligh at the helm—the same Captain Bligh who would gain infamy as the tyrannical master of the mutinous *Bounty.*

They were soon surrounded by more than thirty canoes filled with natives led by the tall Maquinna, chief of one of two dozen tribes on the island's west coast. For a month Cook's ships berthed at what is now Bligh Island, while they cut a tree for a new mast, caulked the ship, and began trading for furs, particularly otter, which native nobles liked to wear as cloaks and hats.

The Europeans had a poor ear for local names and worse for definitions. Thus, Cook mistook the local words *nu-tka* (noot-tick-ka), which meant "go around," for the name of the place or its people. However, the natives in the inlet called themselves the Mowachaht, and their villages were Tahsis, Kopti, and Yuquot. Today, scholars refer to the language group of the twenty-four west coast tribes as the Nootka people. The anchorage soon became universally called Nootka Sound.

Captain Cook met his death in Hawaii during a fight with natives over a stolen boat. His ships continued on to China, where the men sold otter pelts, causing a fashion sensation.

When Cook's ships made it back to England, the publication of his journals stimulated British interest in the west coast of the island, still thought to be part of the mainland. First on the scene was the *Harmon,* skippered by James Hanna, who reached Nootka Sound in August 1785. However, as a joke Hanna's crew exploded gunpowder under Maquinna's chair, causing a fight in which twenty natives were killed.

The East India Company sent four ships to Nootka Sound in 1785 and 1786 but lost interest in the long haul and expense. However, they left behind a young physician, John Mackay, who was too ill to travel.

Charles William Barkley steered his *Imperial Eagle* into Nootka Sound in June 1787. With him was his seventeen-year-old red-haired bride, Frances, the first white woman to set foot on Vancouver Island, who wrote literate journals for her husband. Dr. Mackay informed Barkley that this land was probably an island. Barkley headed south of Nootka and found Clayoquot Sound and then the broad entryway to Alberni Inlet, which he modestly named Barkley Sound.

Swinging around the southern cape of the island, he was startled to find his ship in a wide strait. He exclaimed, "This is Juan de Fuca's Strait," and the name remains. Almost 200 years earlier, a Greek captain, Apostolos Valerianos, had been employed by the Spanish to explore the west coast. The Greek gave himself the Spanish name Juan de Fuca.

Other explorers doubted de Fuca because he often embellished his reports with fantastic discoveries in order to justify his employment. Among his claims was that in 1592 on the North American coast he had sailed into a wide strait and beyond that a broader sea at latitude 47 and 48 degrees (but no longitude), identifiable by a high rock pillar on the southern shore of the entrance. Such a formation exists near Cape Flattery and is called Fuca's Pillar.

Capt. John Meares survived after being caught in ice in Alaska and made it to Nootka Sound in 1788 with two ships of his own. Meares brought materials to build a schooner for trading up and down the coast and bought a parcel of land from Maquinna to establish a permanent settlement.

The first American ships to arrive were the *Lady Washington* and the *Columbia,* the latter captained by Robert Gray and the first U.S. ship to sail around the world. In 1792 Gray returned to the northwest and discovered the Columbia River, which he named for his sturdy ship.

Two Spanish ships landed at Nootka in March 1789, commanded by Estaban Jose Martinez, who completed a fort on an island. Martinez seized four ships sent by Meares, sending two to Mexico and holding their commander. British sailors were packed off to China on an American ship that happened to show up.

THE BRINK OF WAR

Meares sailed from China to England and presented to the government an exaggerated demand for British action against Spain for his claimed losses and mistreatment of his crews. He stormed against the "insult to the British flag" while hiding the fact that his ships carried Portuguese papers. Prime Minister William Pitt put fourteen naval ships on readiness for action and obtained promises of support and warships from Holland and Prussia. The "Nootka incident" had brought the two greatest sea powers to the brink of war.

The French Revolution had made Spain's alliance with France worthless, and the Spanish had to deal. A negotiated settlement called the Nootka Sound Convention was reached on October 28, in which Spain lost ground for the first time since 1493, when the Pope—no great cartographer—divided the new world at a longitudinal line between Spain and Portugal. Meares got a hefty financial settlement, his buildings and possessions were restored, and, more significantly, it was agreed that Spain's dominion was limited to lands in its actual possession or approved by treaties.

Meanwhile, the Spaniards sent a bark to reconnoiter the coast of present-day Sooke and Royal Roads. At each landing its captain, Manuel Quimper, formally "took possession" of the land for Spain.

In 1792 the Spanish commander at Nootka, Francisco Eliza, sailed up the east coast of the island beyond Nanaimo, proving conclusively that this land mass was an island. A thorough exploration was conducted along the east coast of the island by Alejandro Malaspina, an Italian sailing for Spain. After he completed his trip around the globe, Malaspina found that his sponsoring admiral had been sacked. Malaspina was clapped in jail and eventually banned from Spain, leaving his charts moldering in storage.

VANCOUVER EXPLORES THE COAST

The British government sent out the sloop *Discovery* and the armed tender *Chatham,* both under the command of George Vancouver, Captain Cook's one-time midshipman. From the Spanish he was to receive ships and goods seized from Meares and then make a thorough survey of the northwest coast. Vancouver was equipped with several chronometers for accurate mapmaking and navigating, and a naval surgeon, Archibald Menzies, to collect botanical specimens.

Starting April 29, 1792, Vancouver and the master of the *Chatham,* William Broughton, began a meticulous survey of the shorelines of the Strait of Juan de Fuca, which Vancouver claimed for King George. Proceeding up the east coast of the island, they encountered two Spanish ships. Together the English and Spanish explored the coastlines for three weeks until Vancouver and Broughton left on their own to thread the passage to the northern cape of the island and then south to Nootka to settle matters with the Spanish.

Waiting for Vancouver was the Spanish naval commander for the west coast, Juan Francisco de la Bodega y Quadra. The two men struck up an instant friendship but were unable to reach a settlement on anything more than returning Meares's property. After agreeing to refer the issues to their governments, as a final gesture of friendship Vancouver proposed that the island be named Quadra and Vancouver Island. This name lasted until the 1840s, but Quadra died in 1793.

Vancouver mapped the mainland coast, left for England, and died in 1798, never returning to North America.

Into the western picture slogged Alexander Mackenzie, a partner in the North West Company, a fur-trapping outfit that had established a trading post on Lake Athabasca in the northeast corner of what is now Alberta Province. On May 9, 1793, accompanied by an assistant, six husky *voyageurs,* and two Indians, he headed toward the Rocky Mountains in a 25-foot canoe. Battling turbulent currents and managing a portage up steep cliffs, they crossed the Continental Divide in five weeks and found a tributary to the Fraser River.

After 400 miles down the treacherous Fraser, Mackenzie struck out overland toward the ocean. Mackenzie reached Elcho Harbor near Bella Coola, the first man ever to cross the continent. On a large rock he painted the words: ALEXANDER MACKENZIE FROM CANADA BY LAND 22 JULY 1793. It would be another dozen years before Americans Meriwether Lewis and William Clark reached the Pacific and even longer before there were further overland explorations by the British.

SPAIN BACKS OFF

British and Spanish officials met at Nootka on March 23, 1795, raised the British flag, and began the dismantling of the Spanish fort. Spain was through in the northwest, never again to venture north of San Francisco Bay. The race for the fur business and settlement of the land was now between the British and the Americans.

The North West Fur Company sent Simon Fraser over the Great Divide in 1808, and on the west side he canoed down the Fraser River into what he called New Caledonia—a poetic name for Scotland. In 1811 the source of the Columbia was found by another North West explorer, David Thompson.

The fate of the British-American rivalry in the northwest was going to be settled a continent away. On June 19, 1812, the United States declared war on Great Britain on the complaint that the British warships were impressing American merchant seamen and trying to restrict American trade. For many of the war hawks, the real American aim was to annex part of eastern Canada. In the spring of 1813, the British dispatched two warships to back up the claims of the North West Company against those of American John Jacob Astor's company at Astoria. Before the British arrived on the Pacific Coast, the isolated Astorians sold their outpost to the Northwesters at a distress price.

BRITISH-U.S. STALEMATE

The War of 1812 ended in a draw. In 1818 the United States and Great Britain agreed that they would table for ten years the issue of authority over what was called Oregon Country by the Americans and the Columbia Department by the British—today's British Columbia, Oregon, Washington, Idaho, and a corner of Montana. Meanwhile, settlement and commercial use by citizens of both countries would be permitted. In 1827 the United States and Britain decided on ten more years of joint occupation.

In 1821 the Hudson's Bay Company and the North West Company merged under the name Hudson's Bay Company, saving money and gaining a total monopoly of the fur trade in Canada. In 1825 HBC factor (a title for the com-

THE *BEAVER* IN THE INNER HARBOUR IN 1874

pany's frontier bosses) Dr. John McLoughlin established Fort Vancouver on the north shore of the Columbia as the western headquarters for the HBC.

In 1835 "Napoleon" George Simpson, HBC's chief in Canada, ordered the *Beaver,* the first steamship to appear on the west coast of the new world, to explore the coast and rivers, supply company outposts, and pick up furs in order to make remote permanent posts unnecessary.

Simpson had met James Douglas in 1828, at age twenty-five the second-in-command at Fort Vancouver. Douglas was born in Guiana, the illegitimate son of a Scotch merchant and his Creole mistress from Barbados. He was educated in Scotland, where he had to gain respect with his fists, and joined the North West Company as a clerk when he was sixteen. At twenty-two he was named assistant to factor William Connolly at Fort St. James in the northern area of New Caledonia. Three years later he married Connolly's sixteen-year-old daughter Amelia, who was half Cree Indian, "by the custom of the country" (an Indian ceremony), often repudiated or ignored by traders when they wished to desert their native wives. Amelia insisted that—unlike her mother—she would not be abandoned, and in 1837 the Douglases were married by the HBC chaplain at Fort Vancouver.

Skipper William H. McNeill of the *Beaver* explored Vancouver Island's coast in 1837 and reported favorably on the harbor at its southern tip known as

THE FORT VICTORIA BASTION

INSIDE THE STOCKADE AT FORT VICTORIA

"Camosun" or "Camosack" (mispronunciations of "Cammossung," which was native language for the gorge). Although HBC factor McLoughlin did not want to move his center of operations, Simpson ordered him to send Douglas to sail up on the *Cadboro* in 1842 for a final evaluation of the site as a new western headquarters for HBC.

FOUNDING FORT VICTORIA

Douglas's report was enthusiastic, stating that "the place itself appears a perfect 'Eden' in the midst of the dreary wilderness of the north west coast" and adding that "there is no other seaport north of the Columbia where so many advantages will be found combined." He also reported that the inlets at Sooke and Esquimalt had potential, but their rocky entrances required substantial improvements to be safe for shipping.

On March 13, 1843, Douglas returned on the *Beaver* to select the exact site for the post. He and fifteen of his men embarked the next morning at Clover Point, walked to Beacon Hill, and then turned back to the inner harbor where Douglas decided to build the fort. The HBC ruling council had intended to name its newest outpost Fort Adelaide for the Queen's baby girl, or Fort Albert for the Queen's husband. However, the council diplomatically changed its collective mind and sent word that the name would be Fort Victoria, to honor the mother rather than the child or consort.

Several thousand Coast Salish natives lived in the area's numerous villages, each occupied by a particular clan or subgroup. These included the Songhees (a corruption of the name Stsanges), made up of six different groups living around what is now Victoria. One group was the Is-Whoy-malth, which has come down to us as Esquimalt (pronounced ess-kwy-malt). Two tribes, both apparently called Saanich, lived on the peninsula of that name. There were also the Sooke, who inhabited the area from Sooke to Point-No-Point, and beyond them, two tribes of Clallams who had migrated across the strait from the Olympics. At Cadboro Bay there was a substantial village of the so-called Songhees. This settlement had existed for at least 2,500 years, with a fort to protect them against coastal raiders like the Haida. Northerly up the east coast of the island and inland was a large band, the Cowichan.

The Songhees across the gorge agreed to supply pickets for a fence for the fort at the rate of forty pickets for one blanket. Leaving a melancholy Charles Ross in charge, with twenty-five-year-old Roderick Finlayson as Ross's assistant, Douglas went to the mainland to inspect other HBC trading posts.

Sited above the natural wharf of steep shoreline, the HBC crew of workmen built an 18-foot stockade fence, 330 feet by 300 feet. Using only axes, handsaws, and chisels, they constructed a three-story bastion armed with a nine-pound cannon and pocked with portholes from which to fire at enemies.

By the time Douglas returned in October, there were two finished log dwellings, and a main hall and quarters for the "officers" of the HBC were under way. A Christmas party with a rocket display from the *Cadboro* was held in the main building. The *Beaver* brought horses, cattle, equipment, and wheat seed, which was planted in December. The dyspeptic Ross died of an intestinal ailment in June 1844, having been ill most of the year, and Finlayson was put in day-to-day charge of Victoria.

Trouble arose when some of the imported oxen were killed and roasted by the Songhees. Finlayson demanded payment, and the chief of the village became very angry. Soon Cowichan reinforcements appeared on the scene, and the fort was peppered with rifle shots from the growing crowd of war-whooping natives. The fifty HBC men in the fort were outnumbered at least fifty to one.

Finlayson ordered the cannon fired at an empty Songhee lodge, and with one shot it was blasted into a pile of boards and splinters. He told the native leaders that he would do the same to the rest of the village just north of the fort. The power of the cannon convinced them to pay for the oxen. Finlayson then demanded that the Songhees remove their village, which they refused to do. As a face-saving settlement he offered to have his men perform the labor of dismantling the lodges and transporting the village across the gorge.

DRAWING THE BORDER

During the next round of British-U.S. negotiations on the future of "Oregon," which took place in Washington, D.C., the British offered to make the dividing line the 49th parallel from the Rocky Mountains to the Columbia River and then down that river to the coast (thus retaining the western two-thirds of present-day Washington state for the English), with Victoria and any other port below the 49th to be "free" to the United States. The offer was rejected in one day.

President James K. Polk countered with a proposal that Oregon be divided at the 49th parallel—including across Vancouver Island—with no British navigation rights on the Columbia below the border, but offered to make an American Victoria a free port for the English. This proposal was promptly dismissed by the British.

In his State of the Union message of December 2, 1845, Polk claimed that all of Oregon should belong to the United States. The British made a new compromise offer: The border would be the 49th parallel, except that the southern portion of Vancouver Island would remain British, and they would have certain trade rights south of the border. Polk said no.

American sentiment for taking the entire Oregon territory grew rapidly, with the slogan "Fifty-four-forty or fight" trumpeted in the press. That demand would have stretched U.S. territory clear to Russian Alaska, cut off the Pacific Ocean coastline from any British use, and incorporated large areas in which there were almost no Americans.

On May 13, 1846, the United States declared war on Mexico, aimed at acquiring California, Arizona, New Mexico, and the rest of Mexican territory north of the Rio Grande. Eight days later, on May 21, President Polk gave notice to Great Britain that the joint occupation agreement would be terminated in one year. The British navy began preparing for a sea war with the United States, basically over who would get the southern tip of Vancouver Island. Even a limited war with England, or British naval interference, would jeopardize the entire Mexican enterprise, so the Senate approved the British compromise offer.

Three days later, on June 15, 1846, British negotiator Richard Packenham and U.S. Secretary of State James Buchanan signed the convention: All of Vancouver Island would be British, while the 49th parallel would divide the rest of what was then called Oregon. Left undecided was the fate of the islands between Vancouver Island and the Washington coast; joint authority over them would continue until resolved by arbitration.

DOUGLAS TAKES OVER

Western HBC supervisor McLoughlin retired on January 1, 1846 (and remained in Oregon), and James Douglas was named in his place.

Farming began to provide sustenance (particularly potatoes) for the fifty men in the fort and for British sailors on ships sent into the Esquimalt harbor during the threat of war with the United States. A sawmill was built on a stream flowing to Esquimalt, but after 1848 its principal customers were San Franciscans who needed lumber to build houses and commercial establishments for the influx from the California gold rush.

British navy ships *Fisgard, Pandora,* and *Constance* surveyed the harbors at Victoria, Esquimalt, and Sooke in 1846 and produced a detailed map in 1849.

The HBC began hiring people in England to fulfill particular job descriptions and sent them to the new colony. Among the first were the Reverend John Staines and his wife, Emma, to serve as chaplain and jointly as schoolteachers to the children of the HBC employees. Staines was instantly annoyed that neither schoolhouse nor church had been provided, so he had to operate out of log cabins. Emma—the only totally white woman in Victoria—did not hide her attitude of superiority toward the half-breed wives of the HBC men.

A bankrupt former army officer, Capt. Walter Grant, was sent to be chief surveyor and to start colonizing by bringing eight men to plant farms. There were two problems with Grant: He knew nothing about surveying, and he knew nothing about farming. He brought his cricket bats and balls, a library, and two small ornamental brass cannons, but no transit or level.

After several slow and inaccurate surveys, the charming, hard-drinking Grant resigned as surveyor in early March 1850. He did succeed in building a small lumber mill in Sooke that year, but its output was meager. Before leaving in 1853 to rejoin the army, Grant sold his property in Sooke to John Muir, his stalwart wife, Annie, and other members of the Muir family.

The Muirs were a tough breed of Scots who had come in 1849 as coal miners for HBC's Fort Rupert diggings at the northern tip of the island. Their first two years were disasters. Meat on board the HBC ship went bad, and the coal

GOVERNOR JAMES DOUGLAS

at Fort Rupert was of poor quality. The HBC man in charge jailed two of the Muirs for sedition after they complained about conditions. The Muirs chose to quit mining and buy Grant's land at Sooke and soon had the lumber mill producing. Also getting into the lumber business in Metchosin, between Victoria and Sooke, was an HBC ship captain, James Cooper, financed by partner Thomas Blinkhorn. Soon they had a lumber ship running from Victoria to San Francisco on a regular basis.

The worst impediments to settlement in Victoria were the policies of the HBC. The company had reserved a 20-mile radius from Victoria for its own officers to purchase. The price was set at a pound (more than $5.00) an acre for a minimum plot of one hundred acres, a fairly steep charge intended to attract only gentlemen farmers. Below the border, the American government was virtually giving away land.

The HBC had formed the Puget Sound Agricultural Company, which needed to sell its land south of the border in order to transfer the operation to Vancouver Island, where four large farms were laid out. The theory was that the farms would be operated by squires who brought in families of farmworkers from the British isles. But what the colony needed was hands-on settlers, like HBC retiree John Work, who planted a farm he called Hillside.

THE COLONY OF VANCOUVER ISLAND

With the border question settled, the British government decided to make Vancouver Island a crown colony and leave the mainland under the Colonial Office. Recognizing the control of the island by the Hudson's Bay Company, the government leased the entire island to the HBC at the nominal rate of seven shillings a year (less than $25) for five years with the proviso that the company had to successfully encourage colonization or lose its lease. Constituting the island a British colony also marked the dropping of the name Quadra from its dual label.

Secretary of State for Colonies Earl Grey did not want James Douglas as governor. Officially Grey expressed concern that Douglas was too much the company man, and he would have a conflict of interest as official leader as well as chief factor for the HBC. Unofficially there was also the matter of class prejudice because Douglas was not upper crust—not even close—but a bastard, partially black, Scottish not English, married to a half-breed. A thirty-one-year-old barrister with social connections named Richard Blanshard wanted an appointment that would launch his governmental career. Thus, young Blanshard was appointed the first governor of Vancouver Island Colony on July 9, 1849, and started the long trip around the Horn in September.

Governor Blanshard stepped off the ship *Driver* on March 9, 1850, to read to a handful of sailors and HBC officials the proclamation of formation of the crown colony and his own appointment. The ground underfoot was deep mud, and a light snow flecked his soft mutton-chop whiskers.

Poor Blanshard. By experience and temperament he was ill-suited to the frontier, and much of the time he suffered from the aftereffects of malaria. The real power lay with Douglas since almost everyone worked for the company, and the island was leased by the HBC. After six months as a figurehead, Blanshard sent in his resignation on November 18, 1850, but it took ten months for his request and its acceptance to travel to London and back.

In August 1851, Blanshard appointed a legislative council made up of Douglas as chairman; John Tod, a frontier-tough HBC veteran turned farmer (whose farmhouse in Oak Bay is the oldest building in western Canada still standing); and Captain Cooper. Finally in September 1851, the acceptance of Blanshard's resignation came, and with it the appointment of James Douglas as governor of the Colony of Vancouver Island. The Colonial Office made Blanshard pay his own way home.

Gradually new settlers arrived, some under the misapprehension that this was a land where hard work was not necessary, others as servants, workmen, miners, disappointed California gold rushers, navy men, and those sent by the HBC. A small colony of Hawaiians (called Kanakas), recruited as laborers and household servants, were housed in cabins outside the fort.

Of the four large farms laid out by the Puget Sound Agricultural Society, only two were successful: Constance Cove on the southwest bank of the gorge operated by Thomas Skinner, and the Craigflower sheep-raising station at the head of the gorge set up by PSAS director Kenneth McKenzie. Viewfield Farm, at the western side of the entrance to the inner harbor, was a flop.

Capt. Edward Langford, an ex-officer in charge of the farm at Colwood, built a small mansion on the way to Sooke and was a charming host, especially to naval officers interested in Langford's five pretty daughters, who could play the colony's only piano. Even Douglas sent his daughter Agnes to study at a Langford daughter's academy for young ladies. But as a farmer he never got his hands dirty. Langford is credited with giving Victoria its first flavor of English manners, and he displayed upper-class habits by running up huge bills (seventy gallons of liquor in one year) on credit with the HBC before departing for England in 1861.

More prosperous were the Cadboro Bay Farm (Uplands), run directly by the HBC; the Beckley Farm, cleared south of James Bay; the Ross Farm, east of Beacon Hill Park and developed by the son of the late Charles Ross; and the spreads of Work and Tod.

The James Bay area got its kick start as the neighborhood for homes of the socially prominent when in 1851 Governor Douglas built a two-story house, the first with plastered interior walls, located just behind where the provincial archives building now stands.

Douglas as Governor/Dictator

Governor Douglas was a virtual dictator who expected the legislative council to rubber stamp his decisions. He faced several challenges besides stimulating immigration. He wanted to build up trade in lumber, coal, and farm products to replace furs as a long-term basis for the island's economy. Vancouver Island needed roads, harbor improvements, and schools for the increasing number of children.

Douglas was unhappy with John Staines, both as God's representative and as an educator, and the antipathy was mutual. Mrs. Douglas was a particular target of the superior airs of the Staines and a handful of other English snobs. Never mind that Amelia Douglas was attractive, a strict mother, and performed many quiet charities, including serving as midwife to young women, like Mrs. Yates, wife of an HBC ship's carpenter. Mrs. Douglas was also tough, having talked a Carrier Indian band into freeing her husband when she was still in her teens.

Young Dr. John Sebastian Helmcken was not one of the snobs. Two days after Christmas in 1852, he married pretty seventeen-year-old Cecilia Douglas. Governor Douglas gave them an acre for a house next door to his own property. The Helmcken house still stands by the Royal British Columbia Museum.

James Yates, the former HBC carpenter who owned a popular tavern, objected to paying an annual license fee of 120 pounds. One night his friend Captain Cooper left Yates's place shouting against "taxation without representation" before tumbling face down in the muddy street. Newcomers shared the sentiment, resenting the assumed power of the HBC to raise revenue, sell property at an inflated price, and rule their lives. Particularly objectionable to entrepreneurs like Cooper was the iron-clad rule against trading with the natives on the mainland.

On February 4, 1854, a public meeting stirred up by Staines, Cooper, Yates, Langford, and Skinner voted to send the Reverend Staines to the Colonial Office in London with a laundry list of grievances, including Douglas's alleged "gross partiality, acrimony, malice, and indecorum." Staines

Amelia Douglas

did not get far. The ship *Duchess of San Lorenzo,* on which he sailed, was battered by a storm off Cape Flattery, turned on its side, and foundered. Staines was found a few days later clinging to the wreckage, dead of exposure. The anti-Douglas movement also foundered.

FIRST PEOPLES IN A NEW WHITE WORLD

Douglas managed to keep relations with the natives on a relatively even keel by a mixture of diplomacy, force, justice, and trade and by using friendly native leaders as go-betweens.

In 1850 and 1852 Douglas negotiated treaties with Indian bands to obtain title to much of the land from Sooke to Fort Victoria and beyond. In 1851 he began "buying" land from the First Nations, starting with Saanich, northeast of the fort.

Ownership of specific plots of land was a foreign concept to most Indians, but they eventually were willing to sell the right to "use" much of the land so long as the agreement guaranteed that the existing tribal villages would be exempted and that open land would be available to them for hunting and fishing. In return the tribes received money, blankets, and tools. These were easy terms for the HBC because they were vague and in the long run not strictly honored, since white settlers were allowed to overrun much of the open land.

The basic problem for the First Nations was the breakdown of native society. The rhythm of the seasonal taking of fish, gathering, hunting, and preserving, as well as the making of baskets and carvings, had been interrupted forever. Social classes had been muddled, the role of chiefs and women, for better or worse, confused, and the ancient litanies and ceremonies corrupted. The lure of money offered by sex-starved male settlers and sailors sometimes led the men of a family to force wives, daughters, sisters, and slaves into prostitution. Money, unknown two generations earlier, replaced barter and work.

And there was the disease of hard liquor, unknown on the island until the white man's arrival. Although the official policy of the HBC prohibited sales of liquor to the Indians, it was poorly enforced. Whiskey became the symbol and reality of loss of dignity and self-respect. In this they followed the example of many of the settlers, who all too often had become drunkards. Faced with the end of civilization as they had known it, some natives simply gave up. Nevertheless there survived a strong vein of pride, respect for talent, and eventually revival of First Nations's culture.

One of the first acts of Douglas as governor was to have streets laid out in

Victoria in 1851 by thirty-year-old Joseph Despard Pemberton, a trained engineer from Dublin sent by the HBC to replace Grant as chief surveyor. However, the streets were dusty lanes in summer and muddy messes in winter. Within two years there was a total of seventy-nine homes in and around the fort. The non-native population of the Victoria area was 300 men, women, and children. Another 150 settlers lived elsewhere on the island, including a handful in Sooke and Fort Rupert, and 125 at the new community of Nanaimo (Joseph Pemberton's corruption of the native word *Syn-ny-mo,* which meant "the great and mighty people").

CHIEF COAL'S REWARD

The coal at Fort Rupert was scant and of poor quality. HBC officials let it be known that there would be rewards to anyone, white or Indian, who found new veins. An Indian named Che-wech-i-kan had seen imported coal used in the forge in Victoria, but it took him a year to return to a vein of coal he knew about, load up his canoe, and paddle down to Victoria. HBC trader Joseph McKay was sent back with the intrepid native, who took him to Nanaimo Bay, and what became known as the Douglas vein, near the present-day Malaspina Hotel. It was so rich in quality coal that it was mined for twenty-eight years. For his efforts the Indian received a bottle of whiskey, and McKay gave him the official title of *Tyee Coal* (Chief Coal) for life.

Douglas promptly bought 6,000 acres at Nanaimo for the HBC and rehired John Muir to start up the mine with full authority over its operation. Muir brought his relatives up and within six days sent 4,380 barrels of coal by ship to Fort Victoria. He erected a house, a company store, several other buildings, and the bastion armed with two cannons. Nanaimo produced coal for almost a century, and the sturdy bastion still can be visited. Douglas hoped the coal sales would provide needed revenue, but the market had been overestimated, and nine years later, in 1862, the HBC sold its mining claim to a British corporation, the Vancouver Mining and Land Company.

Three schools, including the still surviving Craigflower School, were built by 1855; they required a nominal fee of $5.00 or so per year. There were soon other schools, private and parochial (Catholic and Anglican), but the first free schools were built in the 1860s and 1870s. Construction of a road between Victoria and Sooke began in 1854. In 1856 colonization was encouraged when the HBC Board in London adopted a plan of installment purchases of land on the island.

Increasingly, warships put in at Esquimalt, and in 1865 it became the Pacific headquarters of the Royal Navy, replacing leased facilities in Valparaiso, Chile.

The young naval officers and sailors became a popular addition to the social life of the colony, giving it a distinct English flavor.

The event that changed Victoria forever was the report of the discovery of gold on the mainland along the Thompson and Fraser Rivers. White settlers in the interior had observed Indians scooping gold from the creek beds, and by 1857 the possibility of wealth from gold was an open "secret" in Victoria.

THE GOLD MINERS' INVASION

On April 25, 1858, the first shipload of 450 American gold seekers clambered down from the *Commodore,* paid $5.00 for a mining "license," loaded up with supplies, and then were ferried to the mainland. Within four months 16,000 hopeful miners poured through Victoria. In response to this American invasion, Douglas decreed, entirely without legal authority, that no American boat could enter the Fraser River carrying liquor or arms without a license issued by the HBC. Then he sent a British gunboat to enforce this ban.

Compared to California's bonanza, the Fraser River gold rush never amounted to much in actual metal taken from the ground, but the influx of people changed the near wilderness to a land of opportunity. Among the immigrants to Victoria in 1858 was a Nova Scotian who had been a California '49er, whose birth name was William Smith. Smith had petitioned the California legislature to change his name to Amor DeCosmos ("lover of the world").

DeCosmos founded a newspaper, the *British Colonist.* The first 150-copy issue was printed in December 1858 and sold for 25 cents. In 1860 the *Colonist* became a daily, making it the oldest daily newspaper on the west coast of North and South America.

Victoria leaped in population from 500 to 5,000 and then slipped back to 1,500 permanent residents by the end of 1859. Stores, the Victoria Hotel (the first hostelry of brick, still standing at 901 Government Street), cafes, and the first theater (1857) had been built. Douglas released lands reserved by the HBC and urged his friends and associates to buy the prime acreage, advice that made several men wealthy.

British Colonial Secretary Bulwer Lytton proposed that the HBC give up its lease of Vancouver Island, which would remain a colony, and a new Crown colony would be formed on the mainland called New Caledonia. Queen Victoria rejected New Caledonia as a name and suggested British Columbia instead to make it clear it was British and to avoid confusion with the French island of New Caledonia in the South Pacific.

Lytton agreed to retain Douglas as governor of Vancouver Island and also appoint him governor of British Columbia on condition that Douglas terminate all of his connections with the HBC, including stock, position, and salary.

Thus on August 2, 1858, the bill creating British Columbia was approved; Douglas received his commission as its governor on November 19, 1858. In December he became Sir James Douglas when the Queen conferred on him the Order of the Bath. Replacing Douglas as HBC chief for the west was his son-in-law Alexander Dallas.

A small army of bureaucrats was dispatched by the Colonial Office, including alcoholic George H. Cary as attorney general for Vancouver Island, who would go insane and then die within a half dozen years, and Douglas's implacable political enemy, Capt. James Cooper, as harbor master.

LAW, ORDER, AND JUDGE BEGBIE

With increased population came rowdiness and crime. In 1858 Douglas named farmer August Pemberton, the uncle of surveyor Joseph Pemberton, commissioner of police and magistrate of the police court, to catch and then try drunks, thieves, and hoodlums. At the same time the British government sent Royal Irish Constabulary veteran Chartres Brew to handle law enforcement on the mainland. Pemberton would later marry Brew's sister.

The legislative council adopted what may have been the first gun control ordinance in the new world, a ban on "belt guns," which the Victoria police enforced against the Americans who arrived with revolvers on their hips. When a band of San Francisco criminals known as "the forty thieves" landed, police commissioner Pemberton and his handful of constables rounded them up and threw them onto the first ship back to California.

Douglas began his dual administration by appointing magistrates of his new domain to handle lesser civil cases and criminal matters. In those areas that were primarily native territory, Douglas named natives to these positions, an unusual show of faith in the First Nations. However, a judicial system designed and administered by someone with legal knowledge was a necessity.

The most notable appointment from England was Matthew Baillie Begbie, as chief judge for the new colony of British Columbia, who was instructed to bring law and order to the mining country. A thirty-nine-year-old civil lawyer who had never seen the inside of a criminal courtroom, Begbie was a strongly built 6 feet, 4 inch man with a well-kept beard and piercing eyes. Although considered inconsistent by legal purists, Judge Begbie brought respect for the law and fear to those

JUDGE MATTHEW BEGBIE,
1859

ALFRED WADDINGTON,
CRUSADER

who did not show respect. For several years he rode circuit, often accompanied by police inspector Brew, holding court wherever the crime was charged.

Begbie could be a terror in the courtroom. When a jury voted to bring in a verdict of manslaughter instead of murder against an American shooter, Judge Begbie called the jurors a pack of horse thieves who deserved to hang. To a prisoner acquitted after being charged with killing a man in a barroom brawl: "Go, and sandbag some of the jurymen! They deserve it!" Once a drunken miner tried to pick a fight with the judge in a frontier tavern. Begbie knocked him cold with one punch.

Judge Begbie stayed on the bench until 1894, becoming chief justice of the combined colonies of British Columbia and Vancouver Island and of the province when the colony became part of Canada. During the thirteen years he personally conducted trials he sent twenty-seven men to the gallows, twenty-two of whom were Indians. Nine of the hangings were performed publicly in front of the Victoria police station.

In 1875 he was knighted, and in 1877 he built a large house in the Fairfield area with three tennis courts, a sport he vigorously promoted and played. He never married. He was a founder of both the Victoria Philharmonic Society (1859) and the Union Club (1879). His funeral in 1894 was one of the largest in Victoria's history. The law school at University of Victoria is named for him.

Peter O'Reilly, a tall former official of the Irish Revenue Police, showed up in Victoria in 1859 with nothing but a letter of recommendation from the British secretary of state. Douglas promptly sent young O'Reilly deep into the mainland as a magistrate and assistant gold commissioner. Upon his arrival in

Kootenay Valley, magistrate O'Reilly announced to the assembled populace, "Now, boys, there must be no shooting, for if there is shooting there will surely be hanging."

Young John Carmichael Haynes, a former constable for Brew, was appointed justice of the peace. He promptly made his reputation by riding into a mining town and single-handedly stopping a 1,000-man lynch mob bent on hanging a man who turned out to be innocent. Henry Crease served more than a decade as attorney general for the colony, and in 1870 joined Begbie on the Supreme Court. In both positions he was tough on miscreants.

"Never in the pacification and settlement of any section of America have there been so few disturbances, so few crimes against law and order," wrote H. H. Bancroft, the great on-the-scene western historian, about Victoria and British Columbia during their frontier days.

English civil engineer Joseph Trutch and his American wife, Julia, landed in Victoria in May 1859. Douglas gave Trutch lucrative contracts as surveyor of the lower Fraser River, for construction of the Cariboo Road and a bridge over the Fraser with part-payment being the right to collect tolls for seven years.

Benjamin Pearse purchased 300 acres northeast of the fort before he turned thirty and in 1860 built the first mansion outside of the James Bay neighborhood, which he called Fernwood, at the corner of Fort and Fernwood. Beacon Hill Park was set aside for public recreation, and soon there were a cricket field, a horse racetrack, and a seven-hole golf course on its grounds.

THE BIRDCAGES, THE PIG WAR, AND PREJUDICE

To house the government of Victoria Island, five buildings were erected on the south side of the Inner Harbour in 1859, using the colonial design commonly employed in the Orient. Painted in deep red with white trim and ornamented with filigree and pagoda-like roofs, they were promptly nicknamed "the Birdcages." A bridge across the east end of James Bay was constructed the same year to extend Government Street between downtown and the new buildings.

In June 1859, an American settler on San Juan Island shot an HBC-owned pig. The HBC demanded that the American be fined and forced to pay for the pig, but the shooter claimed that there was no fine under American law. At stake was whether English or American law governed, and the two squads of soldiers—British camped at one end of the island and U.S. at the other—were ready to enforce the law as they saw it. American reinforcements were sent from Oregon, and their captain declared this was "United States territory." The British countered with two navy steamers anchored off San Juan. What became known as the Pig War was settled before it escalated further when Gen. Winfield Scott, chief of staff of the U.S. Army, arrived in November to negotiate with Governor Douglas. The joint authority over the San Juans continued.

The American Fugitive Slave Act and the Dred Scott decision of the Supreme Court placed blacks in free states in constant jeopardy. This prompted a letter to Governor Douglas from a group of blacks in San Francisco asking if they would be welcome. The answer was yes. Thus thirty-five black Americans booked passage to Victoria on the first ship of gold seekers from California. In thanks for this hospitality, at the time of the Pig War forty-three of them created the Victoria Pioneer Rifle Company, commonly called the African Rifles. They trained in natty uniforms from England.

Many of the black immigrants became pillars of the community. Peter Lester and Mifflin Gibbs established Lester & Gibbs, which quickly matched the HBC store as a retail market in the city. Wellington Moses and his wife hosted a boardinghouse on Fort Street that catered to English women who demanded quality. Escaped slave Sam Ringo owned Ringo's, a popular restaurant on Yates Street.

Gibbs was elected three times to the city council. Like many of the other Americans, a majority of the black community returned to the United States by

THE BIRDCAGES (OLD PARLIAMENT BUILDINGS)

WHARF STREET FROM FORT STREET, 1860S

the end of the decade, including Gibbs. Within three years of his return he was elected the first black judge in the United States. Unlike the Hawaiians who lived in cabins along Humboldt Street and the Chinese community centered on Fisgard Street, the blacks lived wherever they wanted, including a group that settled on Salt Spring Island.

Despite the fact that many of the Chinese merchants were very successful and Chinese servants were managing Caucasian households, the Chinese were subjects of discrimination. Later the city of Victoria adopted a policy that no Chinese could be hired by the city, and a provincial $50 head tax on each Chinese immigrant was imposed in 1885; it eventually escalated to $500.

A smallpox epidemic in 1862 killed a third of the Indian population of the island. It started at their annual summer gathering at the Songhee settlement on the west side of the Gorge and spread to native villages in the north. Europeans and Americans who contracted smallpox usually recovered with damaged complexions, but it was often fatal for natives.

That same year, two bride ships sponsored by the Anglican Church arrived, carrying women from England and Australia via San Francisco, most of whom were seeking husbands among the successful miners, and some of whom came to ply an ancient profession. Both groups were generally successful.

VICTORIA IN TRANSITION

San Francisco businesses flooded in, including Wells Fargo stagecoaches and the Union Iron Works. Brick buildings on Wharf Street replaced the wooden structures that had been used in the 1850s. The hastily raised tents of 1858 and 1859 were no more. City streets were improved, but oil and gravel would await the turn of the twentieth century. A bridge spanning the Gorge for a road to Sooke and beyond was built at Point Ellice.

The city of Victoria was incorporated and the first municipal election held on August 16, 1862. By a show of hands a gathering of some 400 voters elected as mayor Thomas Harris, a sports-loving butcher who weighed 300 pounds. At the first council meeting, when Harris sat down his chair collapsed under his weight. Despite this inauspicious start, the city council attacked a series of problems, such as pollution. The location of privies and the hours for transportation of what was euphemistically called night soil were limited, slaughterhouses and tanneries were outlawed within city limits, and downtown buildings were restricted to one story.

Natural gas from the Victoria Gas Company lit its first store in September 1862, and a short time later it began installing street lights. In 1863 the Albion Iron Works was founded. The Spring Ridge Water Company prepared plans in 1864 to deliver water into the city from a nearby spring through pipes made of hollowed logs. That same year, telegraph lines from the east reached the west coast, delivering messages and news in minutes instead of months. A connecting Atlantic cable followed in 1866.

On the mainland, the gold in the Fraser River and Cariboo area had pretty much played out by 1864, and the miners headed back to the U.S., causing an economic depression in Victoria. There was a brief flurry of gold fever when an exploration party found some of the metal west of Sooke that same year. This Leechtown strike petered out in a single season.

Adding to the town's economic woes was the collapse of Macdonald's Bank and a loss of $100,000 to its depositors. Originally an HBC employee, the charming and young Alexander Macdonald had founded the bank and built a mansion on Michigan Street. While he was conveniently on the mainland, a burglary of the bank was apparently staged by Macdonald in collusion with an employee to cover up the bank's insolvency. Macdonald soon skipped town in the middle of the night on a departing ship.

On the positive economic side were discoveries of additional rich veins of coal near Nanaimo and the construction of a lumber mill at Alberni Inlet. Starting in 1859, Governor Douglas issued several proclamations that made land available to settlers at reasonable prices. Potential farmers colonized the Saanich

GOVERNMENT STREET FROM THE CORNER OF FORT STREET,
1866

peninsula as early as 1858, and by 1862 they began settling the Cowichan Valley over the hills from Victoria, the Comox Valley north of Nanaimo, and Salt Spring and Gabriola islands. Coal mines attracted men to Courtenay and other small communities that sprang up along the east coast of the island.

March 1864 marked the end of an era as Sir James Douglas's terms as governor of the two colonies expired. He retired with almost universal praise and a gala civic banquet. To replace Douglas, the British Colonial Office chose two career colonial officials: courtly Arthur Kennedy for Vancouver Island and bumptious Frederick Seymour for British Columbia. Kennedy shepherded the Common School Act for free education through the Vancouver Island Assembly. The British Parliament adopted an act merging the two colonies as British Columbia, officially proclaimed on November 19, 1866. London promptly chose Seymour as the governor of the unified colony.

VICTORIA WINS OUT

Seymour had the power to declare New Westminster the colony's capital, but he tossed the ball to the combined legislative council, with the recommendation that New Westminster be chosen. For Victoria it was do or die. To avoid the economic dustbin, the city needed the spending that government offices would bring and the prestige as the chief city of the colony.

Dr. Helmcken introduced a resolution in the council proposing Victoria as the capital, and after a daylong debate, Victoria won by a vote of thirteen to eight. Governor Seymour maneuvered a new vote of the council, which advocates of New Westminster had been lobbying. William Franklyn from Nanaimo was to give a prepared speech favoring New Westminster, calling Victoria "Nanaimo's cruel stepmother." This break in the ranks of Vancouver Islanders could sway two more uncertain votes and spell disaster for Victoria. Dr. Helmcken made sure Franklyn had a few drinks, and his seatmate, William Cox, first shuffled the pages of Franklyn's speech and then picked up Franklyn's eyeglasses and surreptitiously removed the lenses. Half-drunk and unable to read, he stumbled to a halt after a few sentences. A bemused council again voted for Victoria.

The same week Victoria became the provincial capital, the British Parliament passed the British North American Act, creating the Dominion of Canada of Lower Canada (Quebec), Upper Canada (Ontario), New Brunswick, and Nova Scotia, effective July 1, 1867. The same day the North American Act was adopted, American Secretary of State William Seward signed a treaty with Russia for the purchase of Alaska, which put British Columbia in a pincers between American territories.

Governor Seymour sank into chronic alcoholism. He fell ill of dysentery, died on June 10, 1869, and was buried at the naval base in Esquimalt. He was promptly replaced by Anthony Musgrave, governor of Newfoundland, who was instructed to promote the entry of British Columbia into Canada.

DR. JOHN SEBASTIAN
HELMCKEN

AMOR DECOSMOS

In Victoria, Amor DeCosmos was an outspoken proponent of joining the Dominion—at first in his *Colonist* (which he had sold) and later in the pages of his new paper, the *Standard;* as a member of the legislative council; and as an organizer of the Confederation League. On the other side, forty-four Americans petitioned President Ulysses S. Grant to propose the annexation of British Columbia by the United States. In the meantime, with the admission of Manitoba as a province, the western border of Canada moved closer.

Governor Musgrave sent a message to the legislative council at the Birdcages on February 16, 1870, asking for union with Canada provided the national government assumed the colony's debt, guaranteed some internal improvements, and "if a railway could be promised." After three days of debate the opponents were satisfied, and on March 12 the proposal passed unanimously.

During the debate Dr. Helmcken predicted that "the United States will probably ultimately absorb both this Colony and the Dominion of Canada." Nevertheless, Musgrave appointed Helmcken, together with B.C. lands and works commissioner Joseph Trutch and Dr. Robert Carrall from the Cariboo, to negotiate with the Canadian government about conditions of joinder. Helmcken became more enthusiastic about a Canadian rail line as they rode the train across the American prairie.

They fared much better than anticipated. If British Columbia would join Canada, the colony's debt would be paid, Esquimalt would be the naval base with a new dry dock, the B.C. legislative council would become a more popularly elected body, and the province's population for subsidies and parliamentary representation would be initially counted almost double (60,000 instead of 36,000) by including Indians and Chinese. And best of all, the government agreed to finance a railroad to the west to begin in two years and be completed in ten. The railroad promise was made even though there were no surveys of potential routes, no known usable passes over the Rockies, no organization to design or build the rail line, and no decision as to the location of the western terminal.

BRITISH COLUMBIA JOINS CANADA

The Canadian Act incorporating British Columbia into Canada passed in March 1871 was confirmed in May by the Queen, with July 20, 1871, set as the incorporation day. At midnight of July 19 in Victoria bells were rung, Roman candles and other fireworks shot off, and crowds cheered themselves hoarse. The *Colonist* called it "the Birth of Liberty." One side effect of confederation was that the national government took over administration of Indian affairs and promptly prohibited the natives from commercial fishing.

Joseph Trutch was appointed lieutenant governor for British Columbia (under the governor general for Canada), the Crown's representative on the scene. Voting franchise was granted to all males, and an election of twenty-five members of the legislative assembly was conducted. However, the right of native Indians and Chinese to vote was canceled by legislation in 1874. After immigration began from Japan and India, the vote was denied to those of Japanese ancestry (1895) and to East Indians (1907).

Canada's first prime minister, John A. Macdonald, and Trutch both wanted Helmcken as premier of the new province, but the doctor, a widower with three children to raise, declined. Instead Trutch chose lawyer John Foster McCreight, who proved ill-suited due to his bad temper and meager knowledge of politics. For thirty years there were no political parties in British Columbia, and on national issues the voters leaned toward whatever helped the province.

The Reverend Edward Cridge was sent from London in 1854 to replace the unfortunate Staines as minister for the Church of England. By 1856 he had built the mother church for both colonies. Dean Cridge was never one to avoid controversy in support of what he believed. He welcomed the American blacks who arrived in 1858 and resisted the efforts of some of his flock who wanted them seated in segregated pews. Later he stormed out of a new church built for his congregation when he disagreed with the liturgical philosophy of the minister sent by the bishop to give the inaugural sermon. The result was an unseemly dispute with Anglican bishop George Hills, who had Cridge locked out. In 1876 Cridge founded the Reformed Episcopal Anglican Church, built on property donated by Douglas.

The Catholics, first on the scene in 1843, built a church in Esquimalt in 1847, followed by a small church in Victoria (a shack plastered by the priest himself) in 1853. That year, Father Modeste Demers became bishop for Vancouver Island and arrived by canoe from the American shore of Puget Sound. Demers erected the first St. Andrew's in 1858. Father Augustin Brabant lived with the Nootka people for many years, and Father Peter Rondeault canoed to Cowichan Bay, where he constructed a stone church with the help of Indian laborers in 1864. The United Church of Canada, the Presbyterians, the Baptists, and the Methodists were all established in Victoria by 1863.

In 1862 the Jewish community, which had grown through immigration from San Francisco, built Temple Emanuel. Today it is the oldest synagogue in continuous service in North America and the second oldest congregation in the west (San Francisco's Temple Emanu-el is the oldest). Most of the residents of Victoria attended the cornerstone-laying ceremony in a show of ecumenical goodwill.

Husky Methodist missionary Thomas Crosby, with the voice of a prophet, toured the island tirelessly in a crusade against alcohol and the whiskey dealers who sold to the Indians. His other targets were the continued practice of slavery by some Indian tribes and the sale of their teenage daughters to the lonely miners, millworkers, and farmers—often at an age that would make it a crime in most societies.

While often this form of concubinage would end with the unfortunate girl abandoned when the weather turned warm or the "husband" wanted to move on, in some cases the relationships blossomed and became permanent marriages—how many, no one knows. As the old Northwesters had learned, Indian women more often than not were hardworking, agreeable companions.

FARMING, LUMBERING, MINING

Settlers, some of them squatters on unoccupied land, began various forms of agriculture. Dairies, cattle and sheep ranches, vegetable gardens, and potato and hay fields sprinkled the countryside from Victoria, through the Saanich Peninsula, Cowichan Valley, Chemainus, Nanaimo, and north to Comox Valley. Roads were actually just trails over hills and through forests, so farm products usually came to Victoria by boat.

Serious lumbering began to take hold, starting with clearing the forests for farms and communities, building sawmills and then selling lumber to builders in Victoria and the towns, and finally shipping wood products for foreign purchase.

The first large mill was constructed at Alberni (now Port Alberni) at the head of Alberni Inlet, with seventy workers under the direction of manager Gilbert Malcolm Sproat (for whom Sproat Lake is named). It was ideal because ships could sail all the way into the heart of the forest up the inlet from the west coast. However, within a few years the hills around the mill had been denuded of timber, and without transportation further into the woods there were no more trees for the mill, and it closed down.

That became the pattern for the early lumber business. A site by the coast or a convenient harbor would become a lumber bonanza and then be clear-cut before being abandoned for a new available forest. There seemed to be an unlimited supply of cedar, Douglas fir (named for botanist David Douglas, who explored the island around 1830), pine, oak, and other valuable timber. More than a half dozen towns flourished until the timber was gone, and then the lumber company would move on to a new forest, leaving a rotting ghost town in its wake. Chemainus proved to be an exception, where a mill operated from 1862 to 1983.

The biggest industry was coal mining, reaching a million tons a year before the end of the nineteenth century. And the biggest man in coal was Robert

Dunsmuir. Promising his wife a castle if she would accompany him, Dunsmuir came from Scotland in 1851 as an HBC mine manager at Fort Rupert. He stayed on to supervise operations for the British company that bought the HBC mines in Nanaimo. In 1869 he discovered the Wellington coal field, established an instant coal empire, and became a robber baron in the mold of Americans like John D. Rockefeller and Andrew Carnegie. Dunsmuir built company towns, got elected to the provincial legislature against a candidate backed by his employees, hired cheap Chinese labor, and was more concerned with profit than mining safety.

Explosions, cave-ins, and accidents occurred in the mines with depressing regularity, but promised improvements were not forthcoming. A strike of miners in 1877 for a 20 percent raise in wages was put down with the help of government troops who evicted miners from their homes. When they returned to work, their pay was slashed. On May 3, 1887, 150 out of 157 men on the afternoon shift were killed in an explosion at Number One mine at Nanaimo. The flag on the Nanaimo bastion is still flown at half-mast every May 3. The Japanese government sent a consul to investigate the conditions at the mines of R. Dunsmuir & Sons in 1891 and recommended that the 500 young Japanese miners leave. Some 373 men were killed in the mines between 1884 and 1912.

Waddy's Dream

All of British Columbia wanted the promised transcontinental railroad, but Victorians felt passionately that the western terminal had to be at Victoria in order to retain its status as Canada's western port. The dream of a western terminus in Victoria—or more accurately, across the gorge at Esquimalt—had sprung full-blown from the mind of Alfred Waddington, an inveterate crusader, who came north from San Francisco after making a small fortune in the gold rush. "Waddy" was a character, second only to DeCosmos, who fought for government reform with a flood of pamphlets. Once the province was unified he was elected to the Assembly.

In 1864 he struck on the novel idea of a railroad hopping across the islands from Bute Inlet on the mainland to a point on Vancouver Island near Campbell River and then south to Esquimalt. Obsessed with his scheme, over the next eight years he spent much of his fortune on his own survey crews and cutting a path just east of his chosen inlet, combined with trips to Ottawa and London to sell his idea. No matter that his cuts collapsed and nineteen of his survey crew were massacred in revenge for raping several Indian women.

Within days after Prime Minister Macdonald promised to start building a transcontinental railroad in two years, the national government authorized twenty-one survey parties to search out a right-of-way west from Winnipeg and a practical pass over the Rocky Mountains. Over the next few years the leaders of the various surveying teams argued for their favorite routes. There were tales of heroism and endurance high in the mountains, but no decision. Remarkably, the most suitable and southerly opening in the mountains—Kicking Horse Pass—had been discovered by geologist Dr. James Hector as early as 1857, but it was ignored because Dr. Hector had been badly hurt by a landslide at the site (he was so seriously injured that Indian workers started to bury him), and it was an English and not Canadian expedition.

Never mind the details or the hazards, Victoria had fallen in love with Waddington's plan as an alternative to terminating the railroad on the mainland.

Prime Minister Macdonald was challenged in the next election by the Liberal Party led by a Scottish-born stonemason, Alexander Mackenzie (no relation to the explorer), in 1872, and he needed the support of Victoria parliamentary seats—which he got. In a cynical payoff, exactly two years after admission of British Columbia, Macdonald's government again declared that Esquimalt would be the terminus and arranged for an official celebration there of the "first turn of sod" for the terminal, delighting Victorians. The dignitaries then went home and waited.

Macdonald was voted out, and Mackenzie, who said the railroad promise to British Columbia was "insanity," was chosen prime minister in January 1874. The result was that only segments of the railroad would be built in the east. Victorians and British Columbians in general felt betrayed. Emotions ran high, particularly since the nation was suffering from an economic depression. Waddington died of smallpox in 1872, but his scheme lived on.

That same year, German kaiser Wilhelm, acting as independent arbiter, ruled that the border between the state of Washington and British Columbia (the decision of which had been put on hold since 1846) would run through the channel just 10 miles south of Saanich, instead of the midpoint in the Strait of Juan de Fuca, thereby awarding the San Juan Islands to the United States. The Americans had won the Pig War at the arbitration table.

RAILROAD POLITICS

Amor DeCosmos, his beard and hair tinted with black dye, replaced the testy John Foster McCreight—who had punched out a legislator—as B.C. premier in December 1872. When Mackenzie and the Liberals took power,

DeCosmos decided to become pragmatic for once in his career. Figuring the railroad to British Columbia would be delayed for the foreseeable future, he negotiated a tentative deal with the national government: If it would build a dry dock at Esquimalt to increase naval business, then DeCosmos would relent on holding the national government to the "terms of union" and waive the guarantee of a ten-year completion date for the railroad.

The "Lover of the World" had badly miscalculated hometown sentiment. When he presented his proposal to the Assembly on February 7, 1874, 800 Victorians gathered downtown to denounce it. Led by Dr. Helmcken and Senator William MacDonald from Victoria, the mob poured across the James Bay Bridge and invaded the Birdcages. The Assembly Speaker and DeCosmos fled to the Speaker's office, where they were locked in. Taking over the Assembly, the protesters formed the Terms of Union Preservation League on the spot. DeCosmos promptly resigned. His successor as premier, George A. Walkem, although from the mainland, backed the Esquimalt terminus and called DeCosmos a man who had "all the eccentricities of a comet without any of its brilliance."

Governor General Lord Frederick Dufferin decided an official tour by the Queen's representative might be helpful, and he and his wife arrived at the Esquimalt harbor on August 16, 1876. Socially their visit was a success, with ten days of parties, Indian canoe races, a tour of the island, and driving the first piling for the promised dry dock. But politically Lord Dufferin found the hearts of Victoria hardened.

The week after Lord Dufferin left, the B.C. legislature voted nineteen to nine in favor of a resolution to secede from Canada. When the resolution reached

THE INNER HARBOUR, 1870S

London, it was shelved. Annexation to the United States was openly discussed. Nevertheless, on July 22, 1878, Prime Minister Mackenzie chose the mainland Burrard Inlet (near present-day Vancouver) as terminus for the railroad.

Waddington's scheme was a dead duck.

While the hope of a city died, so did its founder, on August 3, 1877. Sir James Douglas was laid to rest after a funeral at Dean Cridge's new church, with hundreds lining the route of the procession. The *Colonist* editorialized: "Today a whole province is in tears."

Victoria built a new city hall in 1878 when Roderick Finlayson was mayor. Six years later the city almost lost the building to a man owed $25,000 by the municipal government. Victoria officials had carelessly allowed the creditor to obtain a default judgment from the court, and in December 1884 a public sheriff's sale of the building was held. As the bidding opened, Joseph Spratt, head of Albion Iron Works, jumped up and announced that he would pay the judgment provided that no one else bid up the price. Spratt, representing a group of thirteen citizens, stared around, daring anyone to challenge his offer. No one did, and the city hall was saved.

VICTORIA COMES OF AGE

The 1880s became a decade of modernization for Victoria. The city acquired Beacon Hill Park from the province and began a century of planting, lake creation, and laying paths to augment the existing greenery and playing fields. A telephone system with one hundred subscribers opened (1880), water from dammed-up Elk Lake reached Victoria (1881), electricity to businesses became available (1882), electric streetlighting began replacing gas lights (1883), a new wooden bridge for wagon traffic was built across the Gorge at Point Ellice (1885), firemen began to be paid (1886), a provincial museum was set up in the Birdcages (1886), the first public lavatory was built—men only—at Bastion Square (1888), home mail delivery was initiated (1888), construction commenced on the Jubilee Hospital (1889), and installation of a city sewer system was begun to replace privies and septic tanks (1890). A second newspaper, the *Daily Times,* appeared in 1884.

Victoria's first renowned artist was Phoebe Pemberton (daughter of surveyor general Joe Pemberton), who studied in London and was the first woman to be awarded a gold medal in Paris. Some of her classic works can be viewed at the Art Gallery of Greater Victoria. In the last half of the nineteenth century, Victoria's leading photographer was a woman, Hannah Maynard, who specialized in portraits, street scenes, Indians, and news events.

The First Nations's traditional potlatch was declared illegal by the Canadian national government in 1884, on the grounds that these celebrations led to wastefulness and wanton revelry. Provincial Chief Justice Begbie ruled against strict enforcement of the ban, but the Canadian parliament passed an amended statute to thwart his judicial interference.

Canadian Pacific Railroad workmen (including more than 6,000 Chinese), directed by American engineer Andrew Onderdonk, scraped, dug, and blasted their way through the British Columbia mountains and down the Fraser River Canyon to complete the linkup with the national railroad, which had crept across the plains from Winnipeg. The last spike was driven on November 7, 1885, and the first train from Montreal pulled into Fort Moody, a few miles east of the water's edge, on July 4, 1886.

DUNSMUIR BUILDS AN EMPIRE

Construction of the promised Esquimalt and Nanaimo Railway was held up by lack of federal will, lack of financing, and inability to find a company willing to tackle the job. Finally, in 1884, coal king Robert Dunsmuir put together a syndicate, including San Franciscan Charles Crocker, and haggled his way with the national government into a contract with a $750,000 subsidy *and* two

GOVERNMENT STREET AT FORT STREET, 1890s

million acres of Vancouver Island land. Farms, mills, mines and formerly isolated communities were now connected with Victoria. The coming of the E & N spawned the town of Duncan in the Cowichan Valley.

Joan Dunsmuir got the castle promised by her husband, for in 1887 he ordered the construction of a baronial monument to his success on a commanding hill in the Rockland neighborhood, which he called Craigdarroch Castle. Dunsmuir died in 1889 just before the castle's completion, leaving behind a nasty legal fight between Joan and son James over ownership. Their other son, Alexander, was in California representing company interests, founding the town of Dunsmuir, building a mansion in Oakland, and drinking himself to death.

In addition to King Coal, Vancouver Island's economy received a boost by the growth of the fish-canning industry in the 1880s, using Indian women and Chinese at starvation wages. The industry produced more than a million cans a year at its peak. By 1920 it became evident that the salmon catch was dropping due to overfishing in spawning rivers like the Fraser. Large stands of timber were opened up to lumber-company blades by the building of new roads, the development of coastal ports like Port Renfrew, and the installation of shortline railroads from the forest to the coast beginning in Chemainus in 1900, followed by a railway to Port Alberni.

SNUGGLING AND SMUGGLING

There were other businesses operating in Victoria. Prostitution had first begun in the Victoria area with Indian female slaves. Soon there was an infusion of women from California, several of whom became madams operating houses and strings of girls. A third wave consisted of Chinese women, the virtual slaves of Chinese men who had country girls shipped in. White slave rings of kidnapped or misled women from Europe added to the mix.

The legislature decided to license the houses as dance halls rather than shut them down. A report by the Victoria chief of police to the city council in 1886 listed fourteen known brothels on Broad, Broughton, and Wharf Streets with at least fifty-two prostitutes. Reputedly a tunnel ran from the exclusive Union Club to one of the houses. In addition, there were more than one hundred Chinese courtesans on Fisgard, some Indians, and freelancers. Bawdy houses operated openly in Port Alberni and Nanaimo.

Polite society chose to turn a blind eye. Many of the women managed to marry their way out of the profession and take a proper place in the community, so no one wished to look closely into personal histories. Eventually the prostitutes were forced into a red-light district rivaling San Francisco's Barbary Coast—with one-dollar girls on Chatham Street and three-dollar girls on Herald Street. In 1907 a fire swept the area, only temporarily shutting down business. In 1910 there was an official abatement of the district, which scattered rather than stopped prostitution.

Some things never change. In February 1998 the Victoria police reported in the *Times-Colonist* that its principal concerns in regard to prostitution were protecting streetwalkers from assault and making sure that runaways of the ages "twelve, thirteen, and fourteen" were not involved in the "sex trade."

Avoidance of American import duties led to smuggling of everything from lumber to liquor from coves around Victoria to Washington state. After the United States adopted Asian exclusion policies, Chinese men wishing to get into the U.S. were carried across the Sound in fishing boats but might be tossed overboard if an American cutter approached. These smugglers were a rough bunch who did not hesitate to beat or kill anyone crossing them. Author Jack London patterned the title character of *The Sea Wolf* after Capt. Alex McLean, one of the most vicious.

Opium was a major smuggled commodity, since it could be produced legally in Victoria in fourteen factories (some in Fan Tan Alley) and sent to the United States, where the drug was illegal. Women's bustles were a favorite place to transport the opium, since hardly anyone would search a woman. In 1908 opium production was outlawed in Canada, and the open factories closed.

In 1890 the first electric streetcar lines were laid up Government and Douglas Streets from Fort Street to Hillside, and out to the new Jubilee Hospital at Richmond and Cadboro Bay Roads as well as to the Willows Hotel, fairground, sports fields, and exhibition hall nearby. Within a year the rails were extended beyond the hills to Oak Bay, and over the bridge across the Gorge at Point Ellice to Esquimalt. During the following dozen years a web of streetcar lines linked all of Victoria. The easy transportation stimulated the growth of posh developments along Rockland Avenue and in Oak Bay. Victoria's official population swelled to 21,735 by 1891. Victoria's streets became macadamized in stages beginning in the late 1890s.

The Victoria and Sidney railroad up the Saanich Peninsula was inaugurated in 1896, but it closed down when an electric interurban line opened in 1913. It lasted only a decade, but a Canadian National Railways line ran between Victoria and Sidney from 1917 to 1935. They were both victims of the popularity of the automobile and improved roads. However, they made movement to these suburbs practical and popular.

The Victoria Theatre (later the Royal) opened in 1885; 1893 saw the founding of the Victoria Yacht Club and the Victoria Golf Club. The first primitive movie theater, the Searchlight, opened its doors in 1897. At the turn of the twentieth century Klondike gold instant millionaire Alex Pantages started the Pantages, the first of his famous chain of vaudeville houses and theaters across the United States and Canada.

A four-day celebration of Queen Victoria's birthday was winding up on May 26, 1896, with a regatta and mock battle staged on the far side of the Gorge. Streetcar Number 16, crowded with 140 sightseers—double its seating capacity—made its swaying way to the Point Ellice Bridge. Conductor George Farr joked, "If we get over the bridge, we'll be lucky." A few seconds later the center span of the bridge collapsed, catapulting Number 16 into the water. Fifty-five passengers (including Farr) died in the wreck, despite heroic efforts of holiday boaters. The Point Ellice disaster holds the dubious distinction of being the worst streetcar accident in the history of North America.

In 1906 some 243 property owners in the Oak Bay area petitioned the city of Victoria to be annexed, but they were turned down. Thus Oak Bay incorporated as a city in July of that year, made up of the Uplands farm (which was developed into 523 lots with paved roads, underground utilities, and strict landscaping requirements) and lands of families of pioneers Tod, Pemberton,

POINT ELLICE STREETCAR DISASTER, MAY 26, 1896

McNeill, and Ross. Edwardian-style homes were built there for several decades, starting in the 1880s.

Saanich was also incorporated as a city that same year, and Esquimalt followed in 1912.

THE GARDEN CITY

Twenty-five-year-old architect Francis Mawson Rattenbury stepped ashore at Victoria with a satchel full of drawings from his uncle's London firm and a head full of dreams of big designs. A month later the provincial government announced a competition for the design of a large Parliament building to replace the Birdcages. Remarkably, Rattenbury won the competition over fifty-eight entries from other architects, all of them older and more experienced, with a design that made it obvious that he had a clear understanding of what made a building monumental.

He soon became a favorite of the Canadian Pacific Railroad, which employed his talents for thirty years. He also designed major additions to Parliament between 1911 and 1916.

Victoria made a conscious decision at the turn of the twentieth century to play to its strength: tourism. Herbert Cuthbert founded the Tourist Development Association in 1901, which he ran for fifteen years with the support of city businesses.

Victorians lived up to their self-created legend. In April 1903, the Tally Ho horse-drawn tourist carriages clopped around the city streets for the first time. The cluster streetlights made their appearance in 1911. In 1937 the city council began providing and funding the hanging flower baskets. English-style double-decker buses, rickshaws, and boats for water tours became part of the Victoria scene.

The Canadian Pacific expanded into all phases of travel, beginning with the purchase of coastal passenger ships with *Princess* names as well as three sleek liners to cross the Pacific. In 1891 the CPR's *Empress of India* landed at Victoria to great fanfare after crossing the Pacific from Yokohama, Japan, in just ten days. The CPR also purchased the E & N Railroad in 1905 and began planning a hotel with more than 500 rooms on James Bay, to be named The Empress.

Buying the marshland east of the bridge, the CPR filled it in, drove wooden pilings down to bedrock, and then convinced the city to build a causeway to replace the bridge, thus completing the site for the hotel. Francis Rattenbury was the obvious choice as the architect. The Empress immediately became a symbol of the city's English elegance ("high tea at The Empress"). Since it opened in 1908 it has played hostess to King George VI, Queen Elizabeth, Winston Churchill, Franklin D. Roosevelt, Princess Margaret, the King of Siam, and thousands of other notables.

FRANCIS RATTENBURY

Jenny Butchart wanted to beautify the land-scarring pit left from the limestone quarry that her husband Robert—a cement baron—had pioneered on their large estate overlooking Tod Inlet. When the excavation was exhausted in 1904, the Butcharts began carting in soil and planting flowers, trees, shrubs, and lawns until the Butchart Gardens became a forty-acre expanse of floral beauty open to the public.

Nature did not always cooperate with Victoria. There were major fires in the city in 1883, 1904, and 1907, mostly destroying old wooden structures. During the night of October 26–27, 1910, several square blocks of downtown along Government and Broad Streets between Trounce Alley and Fort Street burned down. The snowstorm of the century that fell in February 1916 clogged the streets, knocked streetcars off their tracks, and paralyzed the city. In the winter of 1996–97, another fluke snowstorm stopped almost everything in Victoria for several days because its snowplows had been sold in 1990.

"The Graveyard of the Pacific" is an apt name for the seas north and south of the entrance of the Strait of Juan de Fuca, because at least 130 ships were sunk or shipwrecked along the Vancouver Island coast and the Strait. The worst sinking was the *Pacific,* an American side-wheeler, which went down in a collision in 1870 with a loss of 275 lives and only two survivors.

In 1906 the *Valencia,* a steamship from San Francisco, missed the Strait and crashed onto the rocks at Shelter Bight on the western shore of the island. It took two days for the ship to break up and sink, with no help from the uninhabited 60-foot cliffs above. Since there were no means to reach them in time, 136 passengers drowned. The shock of this tragedy prompted the province to carve out the 47-mile-long West Coast Trail from Port Renfrew in the south to the fishing hamlet of Bamfield at Alberni Inlet. Although a rugged hiking trail, it was passable to bring help and for wreck victims to find shelter beneath the towering cliffs.

RICHES, RESOURCES, AND DISCONTENT

West coast Canada's first successful pulp mill for paper manufacture opened at Swanson Bay on Vancouver Island in 1909. Provincial chief forester H. L. MacMillan set up a B.C. lumber marketing program in 1912. After World War I, he left the government to join with American J. H. Bloedel in developing a vertically integrated lumber company that owned forestlands, mills, and ships, eventually becoming the giant MacMillan Bloedel Company.

The provincial government gladly encouraged such developments by granting twenty-one-year leases of timberlands to companies willing to build and operate a mill. A branch line of the railroad reached Port Alberni to rejuvenate lumbering there. The fur business was a shadow of the HBC days, but seals were still killed for their skins until the Canadian government outlawed sealing on the west coast in 1911.

Victoria acquired a site for industrial development in 1911 when it paid the surviving Songhees $434,000 for their Indian reserve on the west side of the Gorge and relocated them in Esquimalt.

The commencement of construction of the Panama Canal, which would make travel and trade from Europe and the east coast much shorter and safer, set off a euphoric escalation of public optimism and real estate values in Victoria. Between 1908 and 1912 lot prices multiplied as much as eight times. Fortunes were made, particularly by many of the more than one hundred real estate firms, while Victorians dreamed of spectacular growth. In 1913 the real estate bubble burst, causing a general recession, losses of fortunes, and a tidal wave of bankruptcies. The Bank of Montreal foreclosed on the new owner of Dunsmuir's castle and sold it to the city for $35,000. Only wartime ship construction and other military manufacturers restored the economy.

In Cumberland, near Nanaimo, coal miners went on strike in 1913 for better working conditions and safety, and a May Day sympathy general strike across the island followed. The premier called out troops, supposedly to protect property from strikers' vandalism and restore order, but in reality to help the owner, James Dunsmuir, bring in strikebreakers. The army occupied the Nanaimo–Cumberland–Ladysmith area until the start of the world war a year later.

POLITICS, PATRIOTISM, AND PROHIBITION

Provincial government was conducted without political parties for its first thirty years. This meant that, to be elected, each premier had to put together a personal coalition, without long-term responsibility for developing and

THE ARMY COMES TO NANAIMO TO PUT DOWN STRIKE, 1913

maintaining a specific program. Thus, there were fourteen premiers between 1871 and 1903, usually lasting only for a year or two. The system changed when thirty-two-year-old Richard McBride took office in June 1903 as a Conservative who required his supporters in the Assembly to follow policies of the party.

McBride's most audacious act as premier occurred the week England went to war with Germany in August 1914. Rumors of an impending attack on Esquimalt Naval Station by German cruisers were rife, and with no British ships on hand, Victoria and Vancouver were virtually defenseless. Over in Seattle lay two new submarines built for the navy of Chile, but the Chilean government had defaulted on payment. So McBride secretly sent a provincial check of $1,150,000 to the shipbuilding company, and the next morning the subs sailed into Esquimalt Naval Base, where nervous gunners almost fired on them.

The fear of naval attack turned to rage in May 1915, when a German submarine in the Atlantic sank the passenger ship *Lusitania,* in which more than a dozen Victorians died, including Lieut. James Dunsmuir Jr. In Victoria a well-liquored mob of about 500 (cheered on by a thousand more) trashed a German beer garden, the German Club, the Kaiserhof Hotel, a brewery with a German name (which was British-owned), and began looting stores. When the crowd marched on the mansion of Lieutenant Governor Frank Barnard to ridicule his wife, who was of German heritage, Premier McBride sent out the militia to put a stop to the rioting. However, he succumbed to public demand by interning German aliens in camps until the end of the war.

Victoria's special contribution to the war effort was Arthur Currie. A real estate broker who was on the brink of bankruptcy after the 1913 real estate collapse, Currie was colonel of a reserve unit with no military experience. When he was asked to command a new Victoria battalion headed for France, Currie was so poor he could barely afford a new uniform.

Promoted to commander of the First Canadian Division, he was outspoken in rejecting the bullheaded British and French strategy of sending waves of troops into the face of enemy fire. He demanded precision, planning, careful reconnaissance of the battleground, and use of a variety of tactics. After leading Canadian troops to victory at the Battle of Vilmy, where the Germans were stopped cold, Major General Currie replaced an English general as commander of the entire Canadian Corps in 1917. His leadership made his troops effective and proud to be Canadians and not just cannon fodder. After the war he did not return to Victoria but became head of McGill University.

An anti-alcohol campaign had gone hand in hand with the women's drive for the vote. On October 1, 1917, as a wartime measure British Columbia adopted a prohibition against liquor production and sales. Within a few months, eighty saloons and hotels that had relied on pub business closed their doors in greater Victoria. Smuggling liquor from the United States and running illegal stills became profitable industries. In 1919 the United States adopted the prohibition amendment to its constitution, and in 1921, British Columbia repealed its prohibition act, so the flow of smuggled liquor was reversed to run south from B.C. into the U.S.

The provincial repeal of prohibition gave each municipality the right of local option to choose prohibition for its jurisdiction. To the surprise of many, in a referendum the people of Victoria voted not to allow sales of liquor by the glass. If anyone in Victoria wanted a drink, he had to have it at home or drive out of town for it. Restaurants, tourist hotels, and private clubs might find a way to provide a drink—Winston Churchill was served whiskey in a silver goblet at The Empress—but alcoholic drinks could not be sold legally within the city limits.

Remarkably, for a city relying on tourist trade, the ban was continued by public vote in 1931. Finally it was lifted in 1954, with the first cocktail lounge opening in the Strathcona Hotel.

A BIT OF ENGLAND AND EMILY CARR

Architect Francis Rattenbury and his wife, Florrie, were no longer speaking to each other when he began his affair in 1923 with the enticingly beautiful twenty-six-year-old Alma Pakenham. He and his partner, Percy James, were designing his last two great projects: the Canadian Pacific Steamship Terminal on the Inner Harbour (now the Royal London Wax Museum) with its stately precast concrete columns, and the Crystal Gardens, originally an ambitious multiuse amusement center.

Francis and Alma harassed Florrie unmercifully until she granted Rattenbury a divorce in 1925. Appalled by his conduct, Victoria society ostracized Rattenbury and his young bride, while his clients cut him off. In 1930 the couple moved to England, where Rattenbury took up serious drinking. In a few years Alma took up with their eighteen-year-old chauffeur. Under Alma's influence, her young lover beat the famed architect to death on March 24, 1935. When the youthful killer was sentenced to hang, Alma stabbed herself several times in a messy suicide. Her lover's death sentence was commuted.

EMILY CARR

In 1927, Victoria's chief of publicity, George Warren, a former San Franciscan who had never been to England, coined a new slogan for the city: "a little bit of old England." (It replaced his earlier invention, "follow the birds to Victoria.") While this sobriquet referred to a style of conduct—polite, genteel, restrained—it was also reflected in the private as well as public gardens, and the Tudor-style homes (more than fifty designed by Samuel Maclure) built in the Rockland section and Oak Bay during the first quarter of the twentieth century.

Victoria was not quite ready for Emily Carr. Growing up in the James Bay cluster, Emily was forever in rebellion against the memory of her English-born father, who had ruled the family with an "unbendable iron will" (her words) until his death in 1888 when she was sixteen. She studied art beginning at age seventeen, first in San Francisco and later in London and Paris; drew native women at Ucluelet; cartooned for a left-wing newspaper; lived in the woods to get a feel for the forests; and ran a boardinghouse, which she called the "House of All Sorts," for anyone who needed shelter. But most of all she painted Vancouver Island in a rich, impressionistic style, catching the mood of the countryside. Although praised by the leading Canadian artists of the east, her art was sneered at by westerners, who expected graphic representations and who, as Emily put it, "couldn't see the forest for the trees."

Lauren Harris, the director of the Canadian National Gallery of Art, began a campaign to introduce Emily to the greater world of art in Ottawa and New York. Suddenly in 1927 she became a national celebrity. Victoria and Vancouver reluctantly embraced Emily Carr.

Her unconventional way of life was barely tolerated by Victoria's society, and rumors that she was a lesbian were whispered about. She left the mystery unresolved in her *Growing Pains: An Autobiography* when she said, "I gave my love where it was not wanted; almost simultaneously an immense love was offered to me which I could neither accept nor return." Some event, or somebody, deeply wounded this passionate woman, who had been a Victorian prude unwilling to paint nudes.

By her late sixties, arthritis curbed her painting and teaching, but the reading of one of her old manuscripts on CBC radio was immensely popular. There followed publication of *Klee Wyck* ("the smiling one"), which won the Governor's Prize. In the half dozen years left to her, she wrote five more books, which were all instant best-sellers, including *The Book of Small* and *The Heart of a Peacock.*

THE MALAHAT ROAD IN THE EARLY 1920S
(Courtesy of Canadian National Railways)

DEPRESSION, WAR, AND CULTURAL REVIVAL

Faced with the Great Depression, Dr. Simon Fraser Tolmie, a veterinarian, and his Conservative administration (1928–33) were paralyzed. In greater Victoria 12,000 people were out of work, and in Saanich 380 families went on relief. In Victoria, many homes purchased for inflated prices in the twenties were lost to foreclosure for failure to pay taxes or mortgages. The Victoria city government hired the unemployed for a great cleanup campaign, which allowed it to claim it was "the cleanest city in North America."

Canada followed Great Britain into World War II in 1939. Once again, military expenditures stimulated the economy and revived the shipyards. On June 20, 1942, a Japanese submarine lobbed a volley of shells at the Point Estevan lighthouse on the west coast north of Nootka Sound, the first attack on Canadian soil since the War of 1812.

When the Japanese bombed Pearl Harbor on December 7, 1941, and overran Hong Kong and much of the South Pacific, panic gripped the island. Japanese immigration to Vancouver Island dated back to the 1870s, and a majority were Canadian citizens. There was no evidence of disloyalty or sabotage by any of them. Nevertheless, in early 1942 Canada followed the lead of the United States, and all 10,000 people of Japanese descent on Vancouver Island were transported to internment camps in towns like New Denver in the Kootenays. This left their property, farms, fishing boats, and businesses for sale at dirt-cheap prices. A majority never returned. Years later the government of Canada, embarrassed by this obviously racist and illegal act, paid partial reparations to the survivors.

Voting rights were restored to people of Chinese and East Indian ancestry in 1947, and to native Indians and those of Japanese descent in 1949.

Victoria's streetcar system was dismantled in 1948 to be replaced by fleets of buses. The last streetcar to run was draped in black crepe.

Starting in the 1890s, when Cowichan women began knitting sweaters with ancient native designs, the revival of Indian art grew. Using modern steel knives, young natives with artistic talent found they could carve even better than their ancestors. Totem poles were raised by a new generation of carvers, encouraged by the work of artists like Chief Wilks James, who carved a splendid pole on the Nanaimo waterfront in 1922. Crops of poles rose in the town of Duncan and in Thunderbird Park in Victoria, and more recently at the Cowichan Native Village in Duncan. Native art appeared in galleries from downtown Victoria to Tofino on the west coast. A carving industry developed, both from master carvers and mass-produced copies. Modern artists with roots in the ancient designs added new dimensions to the renaissance in native art.

When the ferries between Vancouver City and Vancouver Island went on strike in 1958, Premier W. A. C. "Wacky" Bennett seized the ferries and kept them for the province, built new terminals, and created the government-run B.C. Ferry Corporation.

The University of Victoria was founded in 1963, with a campus built on the green rolling bluffs above Cadboro Bay northeast of the city. UVic soon took its place as one of the leading Canadian universities and the dominant national collegiate basketball power for both men's and women's teams.

Victoria's newspaper rivals the *Colonist* and the *Daily Times* merged in 1980 into the *Times-Colonist*. Alternative, entertainment, and neighborhood newspapers like *News* and *Monday* (which comes out on Thursday) have sprung up in the years since.

The history of Victoria and Vancouver Island can be summed up in a roll call:

> *The First Peoples lived in harmony with its natural wonders.*
> *Capt. James Cook found it.*
> *George Vancouver explored it.*
> *James Douglas came to find furs and created a colony.*
> *Roderick Finlayson built a fort.*
> *Joseph Pemberton laid out a city.*
> *John Tod and John Work cultivated the land.*
> *John Muir founded two towns, a mill, and a mine.*
> *Amor DeCosmos and Alfred Waddington dreamed its dreams.*
> *John Helmcken and Joseph Trutch gave it stability.*
> *Matthew Baillie Begbie brought law and order.*
> *Robert Dunsmuir and H. R. MacMillan exploited its resources.*
> *The woodsmen, the miners, and the fishermen boosted the economy.*
> *The Chinese and a dozen other nationalities provided their labor.*
> *Francis Rattenbury designed its monumental buildings.*
> *Jenny and Robert Butchart turned a crater into a garden.*
> *Emily Carr painted its beauty and described its life.*
> *The Canadian Pacific brought the visitors.*
> *Its religious leaders gave it moral tone.*
> *Its shops, restaurants, and hostelries provided excitement.*
> *Native carvers, weavers, knitters, and artists revived the culture.*
> *And the people gave it the charm.*

BIG SNOW, FEBRUARY 1916

ANOTHER BIG SNOW,
NEW YEAR'S WEEK,
1996–97
*(Photo courtesy of
Earl Schmidt)*

CHAPTER 9

LIST OF LISTS

Here are lists that you can use to quickly find places to visit and events to attend.

Antiques Shops
Victoria

Note: Listing is according to walking pattern, from downtown and then walking east on Fort Street.

Wendy Russell Antiques, 525 Fort Street; (250) 385–9816.
1800 Shop Antiques, #3, 1113 Langley near Fort (behind Murchies), (250) 384–3215.
Penny Black Antiques, stamps and coins, #1, 1113 Langley Street (behind Murchies), (250) 389–2210.
Liberty Victoria Antiques & Art, 618 Broughton Street, (250) 385–6733.
Ronald W. Ward Antiques, 1008 Broad Street, (250) 475–4408.
A & D Antiques, B-638 Yates Street, (250) 383–3515.
White Ram Antiques, 638 Yates Street, (250) 383–5581.
TJ's Decorative Art, 716 View Street, (250) 480–4930.
JR Antiques, 706 Fort Street; (250) 380–6624.
Pacific Antiques, 805 Fort Street, (250) 388–5311.
Recollections Antique & Collectible Mall, 817A Fort Street, (250) 385–1902.
Classic Silverware, 826 Fort Street, (250) 383–6860.
Fred Newberry Antiques, 835 Fort Street, (250) 388–7732.
Romanoff & Company Antiques, 837 Fort Street, (250) 480–1543.
Old 'n' Gold, 638 1011 Fort Street, (250) 361–1892.
David Robinson Ltd., 1023 Fort Street, (250) 384–6425.
Voss Art & Antiques, 1033 Fort Street, (250) 386–1850.
Antiek Mor & Les, 638 1035 Fort Street, (250) 382–3203.
Faith Grant The Connoisseur Shop Ltd., 1156 Fort Street, (250) 383–0121.
J. & J. Jewellery & Gifts, 1044 Fort Street, (250) 361–4480.
Vanity Fair Antique Mall, 1044 Fort Street, (250) 380–7274.

Charles Baird Antiques, 1044 A Fort Street, (250) 384–8809.
Domus Antica Galleries, 1040 Fort Street, (250) 385–5443.
Old Vogue Shop, 1034 Fort Street, (250) 380–7751.
Applewood Antiques, # 1, 1028 Fort Street, (250) 475–1028.
Fanny Davis Antique & Gently Used Furniture, 1028 Fort Street,
    (250) 360–1889.
Jeffries & Co. Silversmiths Ltd., 1026 Fort Street, (250) 383–8315.
Jean Hutton Custom Framing Prints Old & New, 1016 Fort Street,
    (250) 382–4493.
Britannia & Co., 828 Fort Street, (250) 480–1954.
Den of Antiquity, 826 1509 Rockland Avenue, (250) 384–4014.
Avenue China & Chintz, 2225 Oak Bay Avenue, (250) 475–4408.

South-Central Vancouver Island

Buckingham's Browsorium Ltd., Trans-Canada Highway, 940 Esplanade,
    Ladysmith; (250) 245–8850.
Tin Man Treasures, 720 First Avenue, Ladysmith; (250) 245–4425.
Olde Dairy, 12 and 18 Roberts Street, Ladysmith; (250) 245–3473.
Post Office Mail, 340 Esplanade, Island Highway, Ladysmith;
    (250) 245–7984.
Balmoral House of Antiques, 10758 Chemainus Road, Chemainus;
    (250) 245–7009.
Timeless Antiques & Collectibles, 10445 Chemainus Road, Chemainus;
    (250) 246–3737.
Chemainus Valley Antique Centre, 3088 Henry Road, Trans-Canada
    Highway, Chemainus; (250) 246–2372.
Downstairs Collectibles & Antiques, 466 St. Julian Street, Duncan;
    (250) 748–2270.
Jim Shockey Folkart Interiors Ltd. and Antiques & Collectibles,
    4731 Trans-Canada Highway at Whipple Tree Junction; (250) 746–1988.
Cobble Hill Country Furnishings, Cobble Hill Road, 2.2 kilometers
    (1.3 miles) west of Trans-Canada Highway.
Crafty Old Lady, 1490 Fisher Road, Cobble Hill, 2.2 kilometers
    (1.3 miles) west of Trans-Canada Highway; (250) 743–7613.

Bookstores

We include major downtown Victoria and Sidney bookstores you can get to
easily, as well as secondhand and antiquarian bookstores.

New Books (and some used)

Atman Bookstore, 1308 Government Street, metaphysical, spiritual, meditation tapes; (250) 383–3032.

Bolen Books, 78, 1644 Hillside Avenue in Hillside Shopping Center; a huge multi-interest local, modern bookstore with everything imaginable and excellent service; (250) 595–4232.

Cadboro Bay Book Ca., 3840B Cadboro Bay; a lovely neighborhood bookstore with large selections of children's and gardening books, as well as art and literature; (250) 477–1421.

Chapters, 1212 Douglas Street, the mother of all Canadian chain bookstores; (250) 380–9009.

Coles—The Book People, Mayfair Shopping Center, 3147 Douglas Street; general Canadian chain bookstore with some discounts on interesting remaindered books; (250) 388–3199.

Crown Publications, 521 Fort Street, government publications, travel guides, nautical charts, topographical and mining maps, local interest from history to cooking; (250) 386–4636.

Fairfield Book Shop, 247 Cook Street, large selection of current paperbacks, including science fiction, new and used; (250) 386–9095.

Hawthorne Books, 1027 Cook Street, new and used books, original art by Vancouver Island artists, poetry readings, and publishing books in French and German; (250) 383–3215.

Ivy's Bookshop, 2184 Oak Bay Avenue, Oak Bay Village; general books for adults and children in a cozy atmosphere; (250) 598–2713; also 5118 Cordova Bay, (250) 658–8442.

Munro's Books, 1108 Government Street, full range of new books on every topic, great discount tables, large children's selection, personal care, thought by many to be Canada's finest bookstore; (250) 382–2464.

Russell Books, 734 Fort Street, new and old books, run by fascinating family; (250) 361–4447.

Smithbooks, Eaton Centre mall; general chain bookstore with good travel and Canadiana sections, discounted remainders; (250) 384–3077.

Tanner's Books—A Bookstore and More, 2436 Beacon, Sidney; deep stock of books of all kinds, greeting cards, stationery, maps and nautical charts, international newspapers; (250) 656–2345; Fax: (250) 656–0662.

Triple Spiral Books, 3 Fan Tan Alley; metaphysical supplies and services, excellent book collection, spiritual readings, classes in natural magic, elegant artwork by owner; (250) 380–7212.

Secondhand and Antiquarian Bookstores

Archie's, 145 Menzies, (250) 385–4519.
Beacon Books, 145 2372 Beacon, Sidney, (250) 655–4447.
Fairfield Book Shop, 247 Cook Street, (250) 386–9095.
Haunted Bookstore, 9807 Third Street, Sidney, (250) 656–8805.
Oak Bay Books, 1964 Oak Bay, (250) 592–2933.
Poor Richard's Books Ltd., 968 Balmoral Road, (250) 384–4411.
Renaissance Books, 579 Johnson Street (upstairs), (250) 381–6469.
Snowden's Book Store, 619 Johnson Street, (250) 383–8131.
Tell Me A Story Family Bookshop, 1848 Oak Bay Avenue, (250) 598–8833.
Timeless Books, 676 Granderson Road, (250) 474–3324.
Unheard-of Books, 1848 Oak Bay Avenue, (250) 598–1422.
Vintage Books, 839 Fort Street, (250) 382–4414.
Wells Books, 832 Fort Street, (250) 360–2929.

Galleries

Art Gallery of Greater Victoria, 1040 Moss Street, (250) 384–4101.
Caswell Lawrence Fine Art Gallery, 1014 Broad Street, (250) 388–9500.
Community Arts Council of Greater Victoria, 6G, 1001 Douglas Street,
    (250) 381–2787.
The Drawing Room, #4, 840 Fort Street, (250) 480–7730.
Emily Carr House, 207 Government Street, (250) 383–5843.
Fran Willis Gallery, 200, 1619 Store Street, (250) 381–3422.
Gallery at the Mac, McPherson Playhouse, 633 Pandora Street,
    (250) 361–0800.
Gallery 1248, 1248 Fort Street, (250) 380–1248.
Martin Batchelder Gallery, 712 Comorant Street, (250) 385–7919.
Open Space, 510 Fort Street, (250) 383–8833.
Rogue Art, Fourth Floor, Eaton Center, Government and Fort,
    (250) 384–0184.
West End Gallery, 1203 Broad Street, (250) 388–0009.
Winchester Galleries, 1010 Broad Street, (250) 386–2773; 1545 Fort Street,
    (250) 595–2777.

Laundromats

There are two downtown laundromats, both within walking distance of the
Inner Harbour.

One nameless laundromat hides under the Tourism Victoria Centre at the Inner Harbour, next to Milestone's cafe. There are also showers, rest rooms, and public telephones here.

Another, Prestine Drycleaners & Laundromat, 255 Menzies, is about 4 blocks from Belleville, next to the James Bay Coffee Company, a great place to sip away your laundry time.

Nightlife/Music

Bartholomew's Bar & Grill, 777 Douglas Street, cozy, noisy pub with good local bands almost nightly at 8:30 P.M.; good food, too; (250) 388–5111.

Bengal Lounge, 777 The Empress, 721 Government Street; Friday and Saturday, no cover; (250) 384–8111.

Big Bad John's, Strathcona Hotel, 919 Douglas Street; a dark bar with all the peanuts you can eat; (250) 383–7137.

BJ's Lounge, 642 Johnson; popular gay and lesbian lounge; videos, live and canned music; good food; (250) 388–0505.

Bowman's Sparerib House, 825 Burdett Avenue (Cherry Bank Hotel); sing-along Wednesday through Sunday nights; (250) 385–5380.

Blethering Place, 2250 Oak Bay Avenue; teahouse turns into music place Friday–Sunday evenings; (250) 598–1413.

The Blues House, 1417 Government Street; music almost every night; (250) 386–1717.

Bravo Restaurant and Lounge, 1218 Wharf Street; comedy or music some nights; (250) 479–3374 or 386–2900.

Charles Dickens Pub, 633 Humboldt Street (in Empress hotel); music some weekends, usually no cover; (250) 361–2600.

Crocodile Bar & Grill, 560 Johnson Street, Friday- and Saturday-night music; usually no cover; (250) 386–525.

Cuckoo's Nest, 919 Douglas Street; sports bar and grill in Strathcona Hotel; karaoke or DJ music most nights; (250) 383–7137.

Darcy McGee's, 1127 Wharf Street; new friendly Irish pub on Victoria scene with open mike and Celtic music nights; (250) 380–1322.

Due West, 741 Goldstream Avenue at Highway 1A, Westwind Plaza Hotel; dance to Top 40 Wednesday–Saturday evenings; Friday buffet dinner show; (250) 478–8334.

Diego's, 3386 Douglas Street; live music Friday and Saturday nights; (250) 475–7575.

Esquimalt Inn, 856 Esquimalt Road, Esquimalt; country-western, Tuesday–Saturday nights; country jam, Saturday and Sunday afternoons; (250) 382–7161.

Fat Tuesday's, 123 Gorge Road; live R&B music some nights; (250) 383–7545.

George & Dragon, 1302 Gladstone Avenue; hot live music, improv comedy, acoustic open stage; (250) 388–4458.

Gorge Pointe Pub, 1075 Tillicum Road; sports lounge with pool tables, dartboards, live music on weekends; (250) 386–5500.

Goose and Trestle, 310 Gorge Road; Friday, Saturday, Tuesday karaoke; (250) 382–2485.

Hermann's Jazz Club, 753 View Street; every day the best in live jazz; sometimes a minimum charge; (250) 388–9166.

Hugo's Brew Club, 625 Courtney Street; a new pub with microbeers, good menu; (250) 920–4844.

Icehouse, 1961 Douglas Street; live music Friday and Saturday; (250) 382–2111.

James Bay Inn, 270 Government Street; music Friday and Saturday evenings or afternoons; (250) 384–7151.

Karaoke Club, Paul's Motor Inn, 1900 Douglas Street; karaoke, dance parties, and contests every night; (250) 382–9231.

Legends, 919 Douglas Street; Victoria's largest dance floor, eighties and nineties music, some live, some DJ, some special concerts, every night; (250) 383–7137.

The Limit, 1318 Broad Street; top live rock concerts, most require prepurchase; (250) 592–1275.

McMorran's, 5109 Cordova Bay Road; various live performances; (250) 658–5527.

Millennium Jazz Club, 1605 Store Street (below Swan's); cool jazz; (250) 360–9098.

Moka House, 345 Cook Street; popular coffeehouse has live music, often on weekend nights; no cover; (250) 388–7377.

Monty's Showroom Pub, 1400 Government Street; exotic dancers; (250) 386–3631.

Oak Bay Beach Hotel, 1175 Beach Drive; famed heritage hotel often has live music, sometimes dancing, with fine cuisine; (250) 598–4556.

Pagliacci's, 1011 Broad Street; oh-so-popular restaurant features top local musical groups Sunday through Wednesday evenings; (250) 386–1662.

Pandora Patio Cafe, 755 Pandora Avenue; live music Sunday evening; (250) 383–0076.

Rathskeller Restaurant & Schnitzel House, 1205 Quadra Street; German oompah music Friday and Saturday; (250) 386–9348.

Red Lion Cabaret, 3366 Douglas Street; contemporary rock Wednesday–Saturday; (250) 475–7575.

Rick's Lounge and Piano Bar, Ocean Pointe Resort; piano music Friday and Saturday; (250) 360–5850.

The Limit, 1318 Broad Street; top live rock concerts, most require prepurchase; (250) 592–1275.

Starbucks on Cook, 320 Cook Street; live music on Friday evening; (250) 380–7606.

Steamers Pub, 570 Yates Street; local brews; hip music with special shows by hot new musicians (lots of Celtic); no cover; (250) 381–4340.

Sticky Wicket Pub & Restaurant, 919 Douglas Street (Strathcona Hotel); English atmosphere, excellent brews, rooftop dining in summer; (250) 383–7137.

Swan's, 506 Pandora Street; house-made ales and beers at this popular gathering spot; varied live music Sunday–Thursday; no cover; (250) 361–3310.

Sweetwaters Nite Club, 27 Market Square, 560 Johnson Street; dancing to hits from seventies, eighties, nineties; dress code and cover charge Friday and Saturday; (250) 383–7844.

Tally-Ho Motor Inn, 3020 Douglas Street; comedy Tuesday and Saturday; dancing Wednesday–Saturday; (250) 386–6141.

Uforia Night Club, 1208 Wharf Street; (250) 381–2331.

Wasteland Cabaret, 858 Yates Street; canned hip-hop and rock, dancing; (250) 920–9950.

Yukon Jack's, 1450 Douglas Street; music performers some weekends; (250) 383–4157.

Pharmacies

We list the pharmacies most convenient to downtown Victoria, with the additions of some that are open late.

Eaton's, Eaton Centre, Government and Fort Streets, (250) 382–7141. Hours: Monday–Wednesday, Saturday 9:30 A.M.–5:30 P.M.; Thursday–Friday until 9:00 P.M.; Sunday noon–5:00 P.M.

London Drugs, 201–911 Yates Street, (250) 381–1113. Hours: daily 9:00 A.M.–10:00 P.M., Sunday 10:00 A.M.–8:00 P.M.

McGill & Orme, 649 Fort Street, (250) 384–1195. Hours: daily 9:00 A.M.–6:00 P.M.

Pharmasave, 230 Menzies Street, (250) 383–7196. Hours: daily 9:00 A.M.–
6:00 P.M.

Shoppers Drug Mart, 3575 Douglas Street (Town & Country Shopping
Centre), (250) 475–7572. Hours: daily 9:00 A.M.–midnight.

Popular Bus Destinations

Here are some popular attractions and the Victoria Regional Transit buses to
take to them from downtown. You can catch most buses on the east side of
Douglas Street across from the Eaton Centre and Pacific Coast Savings and at
other stops along the street. Signs over the bus stops list which buses stop at
which corner.

Antique Row, 700–1000 blocks of Fort Street and more; Buses 5, 10, 11, 14.

Art Gallery of Greater Victoria, 1040 Moss Street; Buses 10 Haultain;
11, 14 UVic.

Beacon Hill Park, Douglas Street at Superior (Southgate) through to Dallas
Road; Bus 5.

Butchart Gardens, 800 Benvenuto Avenue, Brentwood Bay; Bus 75.

Canadian Forces Base, Esquimalt; Buses 23, 24, 25, 26.

Canwest Shopping Centre, 2945 Jacklin Road; Buses 50, 51.

Craigdarroch Castle, 1050 Joan Crescent; Buses 11, 14.

Craigflower Manor, 110 Island Highway; Bus 14 Craigflower.

Crystal Pool (swimming), 2275 Quadra Street; Bus 6.

Elk Lake and Beaver Lake Regional Park, Haliburton Road at Sayward Road;
Buses 70, 75.

Emily Carr House, 207 Government Street; Bus 5.

Fisherman's Wharf, St. Lawrence and Erie Streets; Bus 30/31 James Bay.

Fort Rodd Hill National Historic Site, 603 Fort Rodd Hill Road; Bus 50
(plus a scenic walk).

Goldstream Park, Bus 50, then Bus 57 and a short walk.

Gonzales Hill Regional Park, off Denison Road; Bus 2 Gonzales
(and an uphill hike).

Government House, 1401 Rockland Avenue; Bus 1 Richardson.

Gyro Park, off Sinclair Road with beach and playground; Bus 11.

Hillside Shopping Centre, 1644 Hillside Avenue; Buses 4, 10, 27, 28.

Horticulture Centre of the Pacific, 505 Quayle Road; Bus 21 and walk.

Juan de Fuca Recreation Centre, 1767 Island Highway; Buses 50, 51, 52, 61.

Kinsmen Gorge Park, Tillicum Road and Gorge Bridge; Buses 10 Gorge, 26,
or 14 Craigflower and a walk.

Mattick's Farm, 5325 Cordova Bay Road; Bus 30 or 31, then 32.

Mayfair Shopping Centre, 3147 Douglas Street; Buses 30, 31.

Mount Douglas Park, off Ash Road with hiking trails to viewpoint; Bus 28.

Mount Tolmie Park, off Mayfair Drive; Bus 14 UVic (and uphill hike to viewpoint).

Oak Bay Recreation Centre, 1975 Bee Street; Buses 7, 11.

Oak Bay Village, Oak Bay Avenue at Hampshire Road; Bus 1 Willows and Bus 2 Oak Bay.

Panorama Leisure Centre, 1885 Forest Park Drive, Sidney; Bus 70.

Peninsula Trail Rides, 8129 Derrinberg Road; Bus 70.

Point Ellice House, 2616 Pleasant Street off Bay Street; Bus 14 Craigflower.

Royal Roads University (Hatley Castle), Sooke Road; Bus 50, then Bus 61 or Bus 52.

Saanich Centre, Quadra Street at McKenzie Avenue; Buses 6, 26.

Saanich Commonwealth Place, Elk Lake Drive; Buses 6, 30, 31 and a short walk, or 70, 75.

Saanich Historical Artifacts Society, 7321 Lochside Drive; Bus 75 (and a long walk).

Saanich Plaza, Blanshard Street at Ravine Way; Buses 30, 31, 26.

Sandown Harness Raceway, 1810 Glamorgan Road; Buses 70, 72, walk.

Saxe Point Park, off Fraser Street; Buses 24, 25.

Sidney Fisherman's Market, Beacon Avenue at the water, Sidney; Bus 70, 72, 75.

Sidney Museum, 2538 Beacon Avenue, Sidney; Bus 70, 72, 75.

Sooke Pot Holes, Sooke Road at Sooke River Road; Bus 50, then 61.

Sooke Regional Museum, Sooke Road at 2070 Phillips; Bus 50, then 61.

Swan Lake Nature Sanctuary, Swan Lake Road; Buses 70, 75, 26 or 51 and walk.

University of Victoria (UVic), Finnerty Road; Buses 4, 11, 14, 26, 39 UVic, 51.

Uplands Park/Cattle Point, Dorset Road and Beach Drive; Bus 11 or 1 Willows and a short walk.

Victoria Butterfly Gardens, 1461 Benvenuto Avenue; Bus 75.

Waterslides (All Fun Recreation Park), 2207 Millstream Road; Bus 50, then 57 and a walk.

Willows Beach, Beach Drive and Dalhousie Road; Bus 1 Willows.

Witty's Lagoon, 4021 Metchosin Road; Bus 50, then 54 and a long hike (Monday–Saturday only).

Rest Rooms

We all know that often the hardest thing to find in a new place is a clean, usable, functioning washroom or rest room. In addition to those in restaurants and fast-food places, here are a few available without purchase, no questions asked if you conduct yourself properly.

Parliament buildings, Government and Belleville; to left as you go in front door, up or down a half flight. *Not wheelchair accessible.*

Royal British Columbia Museum, Government and Belleville; to the left as you enter main door, down hallway. *Wheelchair accessible.*

Causeway, north end to left of Milestone's deck; also showers and laundromat here. *Not wheelchair accessible.*

Sam's Deli, 805 Government across from Tourism Victoria; to left of front door at back wall. *Wheelchair accessible, barely.*

Eaton Centre Mall, Fort and Government; ground floor about halfway back on north side and fourth floor to the right in the food area. *Wheelchair accessible.*

Murchie's Tea & Coffee Ltd., 1110 Government Street, next to Munro's Books and across from Eaton Centre; downstairs in back. *Wheelchair accessible from Langley Street.*

Greater Victoria Public Library, Broughton and Blanshard above Douglas; turn right inside front door, way over to right wall, down short hallway. *Wheelchair accessible.*

Theaters

Belfry, 1291 Gladstone, (250) 385–6815; prestigious and highly praised theater company produces several plays a year in the intimacy of a converted church.

Herald Street Centre for the Arts, 520 Herald Street, (250) 383–0716.

Kaleidoscope Play House, 556 Herald Street, (250) 383–8124; avant-garde plays, dances, and concerts by local company.

Langham Court Theatre, 805 Langham Court, (250) 384–2142; performances by the Victoria Theatre Guild.

McPherson Playhouse, 3 Centennial Square, Pandora and Government Streets, (250) 386–6121; Victoria's Pacific Opera, September–May; Victoria Symphony, August–May; British comedy in summer; also light opera and musicals by the Victoria Operatic Society; other major entertainers in concert.

Newcombe Theatre, 675 Belleville, (250) 356–0726; Royal British Columbia Museum Theatre; slide shows and documentaries.

Phoenix Theatre, University of Victoria, (250) 721–8000; high-quality student productions.

Royal Theatre, 805 Broughton at Blanshard, (250) 361–0820 or (250) 386–6121; touring plays, concerts, and dance.

In summer there is also the *Fringe Theatre* (250–383–2663), which puts on street comedy and other acts at various locations during the On the Fringe Festival, and the Shakespeare Festival, in which two Shakespearean troupes alternate nightly in a large tent next to the Inner Harbour for several weeks. Advance purchases of tickets (from $10) at the tent are strongly recommended.

CHAPTER 10

ANNUAL EVENTS AND FESTIVALS

Greater Victoria, Sooke, Duncan, Cowichan Valley

January

Polar Bear Swim, January 1, Elk Lake.
Pacific Cup Hockey Tournament, Victoria; a three-day tournament of old-time hockey players, Memorial Arena and other venues; (250) 361–0537.

February

Pacific Northwest Wine Festival, first full weekend, at the Empress, Ocean Pointe; tastings, banquet of wineries of B.C., Washington, Oregon, Idaho; call any local wine shop.
Fine Arts Festival, University of Victoria, Department of Fine Arts; (250) 721–7755.
Flower Count, Victoria's annual weeklong count of displayed flowers, sponsored by Greater Victoria Chamber of Commerce; (250) 383–7191.

March

Victoria French Festival, first half of March, many events; (250) 388–7350.
Be A Tourist In Your Own Hometown, Victoria, second weekend, cheap ticket packages.
Victoria Rock and Gem Show, third full weekend, 195 Bay Street, www.island-net.com/-v/ms.
Victoria Sewing & Crafts Show, third full weekend, Victoria Conference Centre; (250) 479–7316.

April

Terrivic Dixieland Jazz Party, Victoria, five-day international festival, last 5 days of month; (250) 953–2011; www.islandnet.com/-bbs/jazz.html.
Spring Art Show, second weekend through middle of month, Cowichan Native Village, 200 Cowichan Way, off Highway 1, Duncan; (250) 746–1633.

Brentwood Rowing Regatta, Mill Bay, fourth weekend, Brentwood School.

Greater Victoria Performing Arts Festival, first full weekend in April through middle of May, one ticket ($15) covers all shows at twelve venues—dance, music, singing; (250) 386–9223.

May

Cinco De Mayo Celebration, Victoria, three-day Mexican fiesta, weekend closest to May 5, Market Square, sponsored by Victoria Immigrant and Refugee Centre; (250) 361–1909.

National Forestry Week, Duncan; first full week, special displays and programs at B.C. Forest Museum, on Highway 1 just north of Duncan.

Government Street Market, on 1600 block, every Sunday through September.

Shawnigan Rowing Regatta, second weekend, Shawnigan Lake School.

Literary Arts Festival, third Thursday–Sunday, (250) 381–6722; E-mail: literary@write.com.

Heritage Days, Village of Lake Cowichan; third full weekend; (250) 749–6681.

Victoria Day Parade, Victoria; a provincial holiday, Monday before May 24, honoring Queen Victoria's birthday, featuring 142 entries from British Columbia and loads of American high school bands down Douglas Street from Mayfair Mall to the Convention Centre behind The Empress hotel; (250) 382–3111.

Luxton Pro Rodeo, weekend of Victoria Day, Luxton Rodeo Grounds, Sooke and Luxton Roads; (250) 478–4250; E-mail: sandywest@home.com.

Mill Bay Country Music Week, last week, line dancing for three days at Cowichan Community Center, country music for four days, Keey Park Arena.

Esquimalt Lantern Festival, last Saturday evening, Spinnaker's to West Bay Marina; (250) 383–8557.

June

Buccaneer Days Craft Sale, second Saturday and Sunday, Archie Browning Curling Rink, Esquimalt; (250) 384–4889.

Lake Days, Lake Cowichan; second weekend, festival.

Jazzfest International, Victoria; ten days of sixty concerts and workshops featuring cool jazz, blues, and world music, sponsored by Victoria Jazz Society; (250) 388–4423; www.vicjazz.bc.ca.

Victoria Flower and Garden Festival, third weekend, Juan de Fuca Recreation Centre, 1767 Island Highway; (250) 382–3658.

Folk Fest, last week, at the Inner Harbour, which is transformed into a bazaar of ethnic food booths, arts, and crafts, with music, dance, and community theater performances from 11:00 A.M. to 10:00 P.M.; (250) 388–4728.

July

Canada Day, July 1 holiday, fireworks at Inner Harbour, stage shows at bandshell and huge cake and clowns in Beacon Hill Park, (250) 382–2127; Sidney has three-day celebration with parade and other events, including fireworks at Tulista Park, (250) 656–4365; Salt Spring Island, fireworks at Ganges; (250) 537–4223.

Sidney Build a Boat Competition, July 1, bottom of Beach Avenue, near bandstand, build a boat and sail it on prescribed course; (250) 656–1125.

Fifth Regiment Band Concert, Victoria; every Sunday in July, 2:00–4:00 P.M. at Fort Rodd Hill Historical Park, 603 Fort Rodd Hill.

Folkfest, Victoria; first week of July, intercultural folk celebrations, Centennial Square, sponsored by International Cultural Association of Greater Victoria; (250) 388–4728.

All Sooke Day, Sooke; third Saturday, logging sports competition and salmon BBQ, Sooke Community Park; (250) 642–6351.

Moss Street Paint In, Victoria; third Saturday, in the Art Gallery of Greater Victoria block, with more than sixty local artists, sculptors, and illustrators showing and practicing their art; dancing and samples of local beer in the evening; (250) 384–4101.

Latin Music Festival, Victoria; three-day Latino music and folklore celebration, Market Square, sponsored by Victoria Immigrant and Refugee Centre; (250) 361–1909.

Victoria Shakespeare Festival, starts approximately second week of July through first ten days of August, tent in Inner Harbour, professional quality with wide range of plays and events, tickets around $10; (250) 360–0234; www.island-net.com/-tinconnu.

Duncan-Cowichan Summer Festival, third weekend, downtown Duncan.

Vancouver Island Blues Bash, Victoria; fourth weekend, free in the afternoon, fee at night, Market Square; (250) 388–4423.

King's Cup Maritime Festival, Sooke; last weekend, longboat races and boat building, Sooke Harbour; (250) 642–6351.

Islands Folk Festival, Duncan; third full weekend, more than one hundred dancers, workshops, children's activities, constant entertainment; at Providence Farm, Tzouhalem Road near Duncan; (250) 748–3975; www.folkfest.bc.ca.

August

Symphony Splash, Victoria; B.C. day, first Sunday of August, Victoria Symphony plays pop concert from barge in Inner Harbour, huge audience on lawns of Parliament, bring a dinner in basket, folding chair or blanket; (250) 385–9771.

Victoria Western Communities Summer Festival, Colwood; Juan de Fuca Recreation Centre; (250) 474–6003.

Cowichan Bay Sailing Regatta, first full week, at Cowichan Bay.

Victoria International Airshow, two days, Victoria International Airport; (250) 656–3337.

Victoria International Comedy Festival, three days, primarily at Market Square, but also at other sites.

Sunfest, Victoria; weekend of world music, Market Square; (250) 388–4423.

Sooke Fine Arts Show, twelve-day juried art exhibit of artists from greater Victoria, starting first full weekend, light lunch available, at Sooke Arena, 1 block up from corner of Sooke Road and Phillips; (250) 642–6351.

First Peoples' Festival, Victoria, second full weekend, three-day free event at Heritage Court and Thunderbird Park with art and cultural activities of Vancouver Island's three First Nations—Coast Salish, Nuu-chah-nulth, and Kwakwaka'wakw—sponsored by the Victoria Native Friendship Centre (250–384–3211) and Royal British Columbia Museum (250–387–2134).

Dragon Boat Festival, Inner Harbour, Victoria; third weekend, local groups form teams to compete in racing traditional Chinese dragon boats; food, health, educational, and souvenir booths around Inner Harbour; (250) 472–2628.

Fringe Theatre Festival, Victoria, starts next to last Saturday of August and runs for ten days; more than forty different acts, music, and alternative theater presentations at various Victoria locations, many of high quality, some indoors and some on the street; most require a purchased entrance badge; (250) 383–2663.

Vancouver Island Blues Bash, last weekend, free and ticketed concerts and performances featuring blues and R&B indoors and outdoors all over town; (888) 672–2112.

September

Classic Boat Festival, Victoria, first weekend, a great display of boats of all sizes in and around the Inner Harbour on Labor Day weekend, including a schooner race, sponsored by the Victoria Real Estate Board; (250) 385–7766.

Cowichan Exhibition, first full weekend, Duncan Exhibition Grounds; (250) 748–0822.

October

Royal Victoria Marathon, both a marathon and 8-kilometer run start and finish in front of the Parliament buildings; (250) 382–8181.

November

Great Canadian Beer Festival, second weekend, Victoria Conference Centre, 4:00–9:00 P.M., featuring only all-natural beers, samples $1.00 each; (250) 595–7729.

Nanaimo to Port Hardy, Port Alberni, West Coast

January

Sea Lion Festival, Nanaimo; last weekend, celebrating the migrating sea lions; (250) 754–8474.

February

Trumpeter Swan Festival, Courtenay; first weekend.

March

Pacific Rim Whale Festival, Ucluelet/Tofino; middle of March through first week of April, whale watching and varied events; (250) 726–7742.

April

Brant Wildlife Festival, Parksville/Qualicum; second weekend, celebrating Brant geese migration; (250) 752–9171.

Spring Art Show, Cowichan Native Village, 200 Cowichan Way, Duncan; 250 native artists; (250) 746–1633.

Saanich Peninsula Arts & Crafts Society Show & Sale, Saanich Fairgrounds, 1528 Stelly's Crossroad, Brentwood Bay; last weekend; (250) 652–3314.

May

Comox Valley Highland Games, Lewis Park, Courtenay; third Saturday; (250) 897–1822.

June

Great Walk, Gold River to Tahsis; 62.5-kilometer (37.5-mile) marathon walk sponsored by Tahsis Lions Club; (250) 934–6570.

Chemainus Daze, Chemainus; last weekend, pancake breakfast, hamburger bake, parade, family fun, Waterwheel Park and Old Town; (250) 246–4701.

Steam Train Rides, Port Alberni; last weekend in June through August, along the waterfront from Alberni Valley Museum; (250) 723–2181.

Nanaimo's Heritage Days, last ten days of month, various locations in Nanaimo; (250) 753–5868.

Cumberland Miners Memorial, next to last Sunday of month, services and all-day honor to labor martyr "Ginger" Goodwin, evening BBQ, downtown Cumberland; (250) 336–2445.

Comox Valley Annual Pow Wow, Comox; last weekend, recently inaugurated, Comox Valley Exhibition Grounds; (250) 334–9591.

July

Canada Day, July 1, Parksville; pancakes, bazaar, entertainment, fireworks (250–248–3613); Port McNeill, airshow and fireworks at airport (250–956–4708 or 250–956–4130); Port Hardy (250–949–6665); Port Alberni, three days of events at E & N Railway Station (250–723–2181); Ucluelet, family picnic on Village Green (250–736–7744).

Annual Festival of the Arts, Salt Spring Island; four weeks starting first weekend, at Activity Centre, Ganges; (250) 537–4223.

Comox Valley Folk Festival, Comox; second weekend; blues, folk, bluegrass, R&B; Courtenay Fairground, Headquarters Road; (250) 334–2352.

Pacific Rim Summer Festival, Ucluelet and Tofino; last two weeks, chamber music and multicultural concerts, various venues; (250) 726–7572.

Sandcastle Competition, Parksville; second weekend, parade, Masters Invitational, Saturday night dance, Beach Community Park off Highway 19; (250) 954–3999.

Comox International Airshow, Comox; third weekend, air acrobatics, stunt flying; (250) 339–8201.

Marine Festival, Nanaimo; last weekend, street fair, fireworks, laser show, silly boat regatta, Jet ski races; (250) 754–8474.

International Bathtub Races, Nanaimo; final Sunday of Marine Festival, race from Nanaimo across the strait to the mainland.

Ukee Days, Ucluelet; third weekend, salmon bake, Village Green; (250) 726–7742.

August

Vancouver Island Brewery Annual Pacific Rim Retreat, Tofino, first weekend, beach volleyball, clambake, Cox Bay; (250) 721–3280.

Filberg Festival, Comox; long weekend at beginning of month; arts, crafts, entertainment, food; put on by Fore & Aft Foods, Heritage Lodge & Park, 61 Filberg Road; (250) 334–9242; www.filbergfestival.com.

Summer Festival, Campbell River; second weekend, arts and crafts, loggers sports, parade, downtown; (250) 287–2044.

Mill Bay Fishing Derby, second weekend, Mill Bay marina.

Nanaimo Realty Salmon Fishing Derby, second weekend, Qualicum Beach.

Volleybash, Parksville; last weekend, Canadian Beach Volleyball Championships at all levels, including professionals, Saturday BBQ, Sunday finals; (250) 721–3280.

September

Port Alberni Salmon Festival, four days starting first Friday, Clutese Haven Marina; (250) 723–8165.

Dixieland Jazz Festival, Nanaimo; first full weekend, Dixieland jazz and vintage car rally; (250) 754–8474.

Gyro Boat Show, Nanaimo; first three-day weekend, exhibit of boats from throughout Northwest, Cruiseship Dock in downtown; (800) 663–7337.

Islander Days, Gabriola Island; first long weekend, exhibitions and activities at various locations.

Alberni District Fall Fair, four days over second weekend, Alberni Fairgrounds; (250) 723–9313.

Ladysmith Fall Fair, second weekend, Jameson Community Center.

Salt Spring Island Fall Fair, Farmers' Institute, 351 Rainbow Road; third weekend; (250) 537–4755.

INDEX

ABOUT THE
AUTHORS

*K*athleen and Gerald Hill are native Californians who divide their time between Sonoma in the northern California wine country and Vancouver Island, British Columbia. As a team the Hills wrote *Northwest Wine Country: Wine's New Frontier, Sonoma Valley: The Secret Wine Country, Victoria and Vancouver Island: A Personal Tour of an Almost Perfect Eden, Napa Valley: Land of Golden Vines, Monterey & Carmel: Eden By the Sea, Santa Barbara & the Central Coast: California's Riviera; The Real Life Dictionary of the Law, The Real Life Dictionary of American Politics* (soon to be republished as *Facts on File: Dictionary of American Politics*) and an international exposé, *The Aquino Assassination.* Kathleen is the author of *Festivals USA* and *Festivals USA— Western States,* and she has written articles for *The Chicago Tribune, San Francisco Magazine, Cook's Magazine, San Francisco Examiner Magazine, James Beard Newsletter,* and other periodicals, while Gerald was editor and coauthor of *Housing in California.* Gerald also practices law to support their writing habit.

The Hills occasionally co-teach American government and politics at the University of British Columbia, and often comment on American politics on B.C. radio station CKNW.

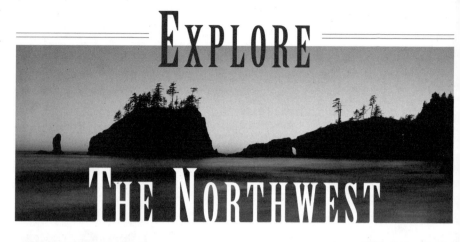